D0225448

Corwin on the
Constitution

Corwin on the Constitution

VOLUME TWO

The Judiciary

Edited with an Introduction
by RICHARD LOSS

Cornell University Press, *Ithaca and London*

Soc
JA
38
C67
1981
V. 2

Copyright © 1987 by Cornell University

All rights reserved. Except for brief quotations in a review, this book, or parts
thereof, must not be reproduced in any form without permission in writing from the
publisher. For information, address Cornell University Press, 124 Robert Place,
Ithaca, New York 14850.

First published 1987 by Cornell University Press.

International Standard Book Number 0-8014-1996-4
Library of Congress Catalog Card Number 80-69823
Printed in the United States of America
Librarians: Library of Congress cataloging information
appears on the last page of the book.

The paper in this book is acid-free and meets the guidelines for
permanence and durability of the Committee on Production Guidelines
for Book Longevity of the Council on Library Resources.

ROBERT MANNING
STROZIER LIBRARY

JUL 27 1987

Tallahassee, Florida

*Constitutional law has for its primary purpose
not the convenience of the state but the
preservation of individual rights.*
EDWARD S. CORWIN

Contents

Corwin on the
Constitution

Introduction

Edward S. Corwin (1878–1963) was born near Plymouth, Michigan. He studied under Andrew C. McLaughlin, the distinguished constitutional historian, before graduating from the University of Michigan in 1900. Corwin received his doctorate in history from the University of Pennsylvania in 1905 after study with the historian John Bach McMaster. Woodrow Wilson, then president of Princeton University, soon invited Corwin to become one of Princeton's original preceptors, and he taught there until 1946. A prolific author, Corwin wrote eighteen books and published numerous essays in legal and professional journals in addition to editing the 1953 annotated *Constitution*. In 1935 he was a constitutional adviser to the Public Works Administration; in 1936 he was first special assistant and then constitutional consultant to the attorney general. A biography of Corwin, which he reviewed before publication, declared that "in politics he is an independent."

Why *Corwin on the Constitution*? One reason is Corwin's eminence among commentators on the Constitution. Elevating Corwin into the front rank of immortals among American constitutional commentators are the quantity, timeliness, profundity, comprehensiveness, and objectivity of his writings as well as their relationship to the law that came before and after. Corwin's essays are a resource for training citizens, as well as judges and lawyers, in the nature of the Union and the purpose of American government.

"The weaknesses of a written Constitution," wrote Thomas Cooley, "are...that it is often construed on technical principles of verbal criticism, rather than in the light of great principles."[1] An exposure to Corwin's essays enables citizens, political scientists, law teachers, and judges to defend more effectively the American way of life and the American idea of freedom. Justices of the United States Supreme Court have appealed to Corwin's writings as authority in

---

1. T. Cooley, *The General Principles of Constitutional Law* 22 (1891).

opinions and dissents. During the period January 1938 through October 1977 the justices cited Corwin's writings a total of seventeen times: eight times in dissents, seven times in opinions, and twice in concurring opinions. With four citations in dissents and two in opinions, *The President: Office and Powers* is Corwin's most often cited writing.[2]

Corwin on the Constitution follows the precedent set by *Presidential Power and the Constitution: Essays by Edward S. Corwin,* which I edited in 1976 for Cornell University Press. The acceptance of the latter work and the importance of Corwin's thought justified the collection of his essays, which were hitherto scattered in sometimes out-of-the-way journals. Now citizens, historians, political scientists, law teachers, and judges may confront Corwin's thought as a whole, because this collection is comprehensive with few exceptions. I will have achieved one of my goals if *Corwin on the Constitution* contributes to a deeper understanding of the character and purpose of the American Constitution.

The essays in this volume have a natural unity in dealing with Article III (the judicial article) of the Constitution. Volume II is thus a sequel to Volume I, which treated Articles I and II of the Constitution, and to *Presidential Power and the Constitution,* which gathered most of Corwin's essays on the presidency. In Corwin's opinion, the essays included in this volume are among his most important works: "I consider that my most creative work has been in digging out the foundational doctrines and assumptions underlying American constitutional law, and especially those doctrines and assumptions which have been in the past enforced by the Supreme Court against legislative power, both state and national. It is these articles ... which have drawn most attention from judges and students of law and political science."[3]

For the sake of convenience, I have grouped the essays under the headings "The Origins of Judicial Review," "The Development of Judicial Supremacy," "The Exercise of Judicial Review," and "Appraisals of Judicial Review." Corwin's essay "The Supreme Court and Unconstitutional Acts of Congress" (1906) asks, "What is the real basis of ... judicial amendment of the Constitution?" He concludes that the "major premise of most of the great decisions of the Supreme Court is a concealed bias of some sort—a highly laudable bias perhaps, yet a bias."[4] The concealed premise was a "certain theory of government, embodied in the Constitution itself," namely, Lockean individual rights. "The real logic upon which the right of a federal Supreme Court to question the validity of acts of Congress rests ... is the logic of a certain way of looking at the relation of the individual to government."

2. Casimir Bartnik kindly collected these citations for me from the legal computer system known as Lexis.

3. Corwin to E. G. Conklin, 15 April 1942, Corwin Papers, Category I, Carton III, Princeton University Library.

4. Corwin, "The Supreme Court and Unconstitutional Acts of Congress," 4 *Mich. L. Rev.* 616, at 625 (1906).

Corwin believed that in "The Establishment of Judicial Review" (1910) he had "amply shown" that judicial review "originally rested upon the basis of common right and reason and natural law" and was later transferred to the written Constitution.[5] Although in America judicial review was established upon the basis of a doctrine of fundamental law known only to judges, the keeping of the Constitution falls in the first instance to parties to lawsuits: "Constitutional law has for its primary purpose not the convenience of the state but the preservation of individual rights."[6] "Marbury v. Madison and the Doctrine of Judicial Review" (1914) holds that the legal basis of judicial review is supplied by a view of the Constitution as law enforceable by courts and by the distinction between the making and the interpretation of law. Judicial review "rests upon certain general principles thought by its framers to have been embodied in the Constitution." In the last analysis judicial review rests on the assumption that judges "alone really *know* the law."

The essays on the development of judicial supremacy examine the reconciliation of legislative supremacy in the written Constitution with adequate supervision of the legislature as well as the relation between due process and the state legislature's police power. In "The Supreme Court and the Fourteenth Amendment" Corwin holds that "fear of popular majorities . . . lies at the very basis of the whole system of judicial review, and indeed of our entire constitutional system." The article traces the Fourteenth Amendment from the piecemeal protection of equal rights of the races to protection of laissez-faire for corporations. Corwin finds that the authors of the Fourteenth Amendment intended to make the first eight amendments binding on the states and the national government. After reviewing Court decisions, he concludes that the "ultimate question" before the Supreme Court was whether the state legislatures or the United States Supreme Court should be the final guardian of individual rights.

In "The Doctrine of Due Process of Law before the Civil War" (1911) Corwin's purpose is to show the development of the due process clause. He states the "leavening principle of American constitutional law, the notion that legislative power, quite independently of the written Constitution, is not absolute, but is constrained both by its own nature and by the principles of republican government, natural law and the social compact." The protection of property rights or vested rights is "generally speaking . . . always the significance of the doctrine of due process of law." "The most conspicuous fact about our constitutional law as it stood on the eve of the Civil War was the practical approximation of the police power of the states to the sovereignty of the state legislatures within their respective constitutions."

The essays on the exercise of judicial review are of more than routine

5. Corwin, "The Establishment of Judicial Review," 9 *Mich. L. Rev.* 283, at 306 (1910).
6. *Id.*, at 316.

interest. "Constitution v. Constitutional Theory" (1925), one of his most important essays, displays Corwin in a skeptical attack against the use of the founders' intention in constitutional interpretation. He summarizes his main argument as follows. "For many practical purposes" the Constitution is the judicial version of the founders' intention—what Corwin calls constitutional law. Earlier he had defined the Constitution so as to include certain important statutes, certain usages of government, and judicial decisions that attempt to define certain terms of the formal Constitution, but his essay is ·concerned primarily with the unwarranted relationship of judicial constitutional law to constitutional theory. Constitutional law or the judicial version of the Constitution "derives in no small part from speculative ideas about what the framers of the Constitution or the generation which adopted it intended it should mean— constitutional theory." The most important ideas of constitutional theory are synonymous with the founders' intention. The source of the maxim that a court must give effect to the will of the lawgiver—that is, the authority of the founders' intention—"comes straight from the law of wills." Ideas of the founders' intention, Corwin concludes, "whatever their historical basis—and that is frequently most precarious—have no application to the main business of constitutional interpretation, which is to keep the Constitution adjusted to the advancing needs of the time."

Corwin's main argument in "Constitution v. Constitutional Theory" is thus a detailed critique of constitutional theory or the resort to the founders' intention in understanding the Constitution. Several observations are pertinent here. First, Corwin concedes that his criticism departs from the attitude of the average Supreme Court justice, who takes constitutional theory or the founders' intention "very seriously." Second, Corwin makes the most extreme criticism possible of the founders' intention, drawing attention not only to the Supreme Court's shaky history but to the inherent poverty of constitutional theory. One might accept Corwin's criticism of the Court's historical scholarship without being compelled totally to reject the founders' intention.

Corwin's alternative to the founders' intention is the popular-will explanation of the Constitution's supremacy and authority. He understands the Constitution as a law deriving "all" of its force "from the people of the United States of this day and hour." The Constitution is a "living statute, to be interpreted in light of living conditions." Thus its merit and authority arise not from the excellence or justice of its principles but from their popular origin and appeal. The main argument of the essay informs us that by 1925 Corwin's jurisprudence had already rejected the higher law, which he was to make famous in 1928 with his essay "The 'Higher Law' Background of American Constitutional Law." Corwin's alternative to both the founders' intention and the higher law explanation of the Constitution's authority was an almost wholly popular, democratic, and majoritarian Constitution.

Thomas Reed Powell tellingly argued against Corwin's thesis with the moderate observation that "I do feel that judges owe some respect to things as they were in the beginning."[7] Powell aptly noted the imbalance between the destructive and constructive parts of Corwin's thesis. Powell remarked of Corwin's criticism of the founders' intention that "if he stills the winds of foolish doctrine," "he must give us in their place some guides to the way of wisdom in making an indefinite series of practical judgments," or he cannot be "the Moses to lead us from the land of the Constitution as our fathers knew it."[8] Corwin failed to replace the founders' intention with anything more substantial than what Powell called "Mr. Corwin's chaotic conception of the scope of national power." Powell detected the primitive nihilism in Corwin's thesis that the sufficient and "proper point of view from which to approach the task of interpreting the Constitution is that of regarding it as a living statute, palpitating with the purpose of the hour, reenacted with every waking breath of the American people, whose primitive right to determine their institutions is its sole claim to validity as a law and as the matrix of laws under our system."[9] "Constitution v. Constitutional Theory" is a turning point in Corwin's jurisprudence because much of his later work tended to elaborate the popular will explanation of the Constitution's supremacy. This remarkable essay deserves to be read together with "The 'Higher Law' Background of American Constitutional Law."

"Judicial Review in Action" (1926) traces judicial review to the American doctrine of separation of powers, but the "entire history of judicial review is that of the progressive relaxation of the restraints which are implied in its doctrinal foundation." The essay defines judicial review as the power of a court to determine the validity of the acts of a legislature in relation to an unwritten "higher law" regarded as binding on both the court and the legislature. The essay examines the nature and limitations of judicial review, judicial freedom in constitutional interpretation, and the purpose and method of constitutional interpretation. In this essay Corwin extends his criticism of the founders' intention—or, as he calls it here, "historical interpretation" (in contrast to "adaptive interpretation")—and stresses the Court's freedom to choose among various constitutional interpretations. Interpretation for Corwin involves lawmaking. He attributes the coherence of American constitutional law to the fact that the "values which are safeguarded by judicial review remain essentially the same as they have always been." Despite his criticism of Marshall's exegesis of the founders' intention, Corwin praises Marshall's opinions in comparison with the opinions of the Taney Court, which "are hardly more than historical curiosities today." This essay is notable for Corwin's movement away from the rationalistic account of judicial review so evident in his early essays. Although Corwin does

---

7. Powell, "Comment on Mr. Corwin's Paper," 19 *APSR* 305, at 306 (May 1925).
8. *Id.*, at 308.
9. Corwin, "Constitution v. Constitutional Theory," 19 *APSR* 290, at 303 (May 1925).

not use this term, he is increasingly preoccupied with the lack of objective authority for judge-made law.

"Reorganization of the Federal Judiciary" (1937), Corwin's testimony on Franklin D. Roosevelt's proposal to pack the Supreme Court, objects to the "undue extension of judicial review" over legislation. The mere addition of justices would not guard against the recurrence of the problem, so Corwin proposes that the Court be both enlarged and divided into sections to handle questions in different legal areas. Corwin is imprecise about whether the justices of most recent appointment would compose the constitutional panel or whether the entire Court would rule on constitutional questions.[10] Corwin reveals that he has reconsidered his early writings on judicial review and that he now regards judicial review as "far more a matter of doubt than I did then."[11] Under questioning Corwin testified that "I want judges who will keep their sickle out of the political field, if possible; and as far as possible stick to concrete principles." Corwin's alternative to the founders' intention, and the one for which Thomas Reed Powell had pressed him years before, is "concrete principles." Corwin's defense of the New Deal concedes that "it is a good point—that a written Constitution was devised with the idea of putting certain limits on the power of the legislature." His testimony fails to reconcile the

10. *Reorganization of the Federal Judiciary,* U.S. Congress, Senate, Committee on the Judiciary, 75th Cong., 1st sess., on S. 1392, pt. 2, at 183, 197, 202.

11. *Id.,* at 184. Corwin's historical inquiries into the founders' intention on judicial review failed to generate further study by Alexander Bickel, a leader among the next generation of commentators on the Constitution. Bickel first argues that "the authority to determine the meaning and application of a written constitution is nowhere defined or even mentioned in the document itself. This is not to say that the power of judicial review cannot be placed in the Constitution; merely that it cannot be found there" (A. Bickel, *The Least Dangerous Branch* 1 [1962]). Turning to the founders' intention, Bickel accepts the historical research of Charles Beard's *Supreme Court and the Constitution* (1912) on the authority of Felix Frankfurter (Bickel, at 15). Yet Edward S. Corwin had found Beard's research unconvincing (Corwin, review of Beard, *The Supreme Court and the Constitution* [1912], in 7 *APSR* 330 [1913]). Bickel concludes that "the Framers of the Constitution specifically, *if tacitly,* expected that the federal courts would assume a power—of whatever exact dimensions—to pass on the constitutionality of actions of the Congress and the President, as well as of the several states" (Bickel, at 15; italics added; see also the reference to "scholarship" at *id.* 104, par. 2, l. 4). Corwin's increasing skepticism on the founders and judicial review is nowhere mentioned as a part of the "scholarship" Bickel purports to discuss. But the founders' intention is really irrelevant for Bickel, for two reasons: first, "nothing but disaster could result for government under a written constitution if it were generally accepted that the specific intent of the framers of a constitutional provision is ascertainable and is forever and specifically binding, subject only to the cumbersome process of amendment" (Bickel, at 106); second, "judicial review is a present instrument of government. It represents a choice that men have made, and *ultimately we must justify it as a choice in our own time*" (Bickel at 16; italics added). Bickel's choice for his time was that "the constitutional function of the Court is to define values and proclaim principles" (Bickel, at 68; see also 69, 30). The difficulties that legal positivism and historicism create are not even faced in Bickel's jurisprudence of principle. Bickel's moral and constitutional horizon is only apparently broader than Corwin's; it is actually a contraction of Corwin's horizon, with presentism preventing the kind of fundamental reflection that would surpass or even equal Corwin's.

majoritarianism of his concrete principles with this salutary limitation of a written Constitution.

The "principal" purpose of "Standpoint in Constitutional Law" (1937) is to show how the constitutional document, understood as a bulwark of rights, has been absorbed in constitutional law and how constitutional law is "derived chiefly" from ideas and theories "outside" of constitutional law. The Supreme Court has exercised a high degree of selectivity over these outside ideas and theories. Corwin's thesis is that if the Supreme Court is to "retain its power of judicial review, it must adapt that power to the underlying popular character of our political institutions, and hence must adopt a sympathetic attitude toward clearly established contemporary needs and opinion." "It is judicial practice, ratified by popular acquiescence, which established judicial review of acts of Congress in the first place." Turning to Marshall, Corwin qualifies his earlier criticism in writing that "the constitutional law of John Marshall gave embodiment . . . to ascertainable intentions of the framers." In this sense Marshall's constitutional law "sprang very immediately from the constitutional document itself." Contrary to what Corwin had implied in "Constitution v. Constitutional Theory" and "Judicial Review in Action," the founders' intention was verifiable after all, at least by those as gifted as John Marshall. Corwin concludes that "laissez-faire-ism has been the most important single influence determining the content of our constitutional law during the last fifty years." "For most of the Court's excursions in the constitutional sphere," the "constitutional document has become hardly more than a formal point of reference." This means that in the constitutional field "the Court is a legislature," and when its interpretations prevail with finality, "it is a super-legislature."

The essays grouped under "Appraisals of Judicial Review" try to answer more particularly whether the Supreme Court's decisions were "good law and good Constitution." In "The Dred Scott Decision in the Light of Contemporary Legal Doctrines" (1911) Corwin finds that the pronouncement that the Missouri Compromise was unconstitutional was not *obiter dictum* according to the definition of the Marshall Court's constitutional cases. The majority did not base their decision on Calhounist premises; and Justice Curtis failed to refute Taney's argument on Dred Scott's claim to citizenship. "Game Protection and the Constitution" (1916) finds the Migratory Bird Act to be constitutionally valid as a deliberate assertion by Congress of the nation's proprietorship of the migratory game of the nation or as a necessary and proper act for the preservation of the country's navigable streams.

According to "The Child Labor Decision" (1922), the Supreme Court's decision in Bailey v. Drexel Furniture, setting aside title XII of the Internal Revenue Act of 1921, which levied a special tax of 10 percent of their profits on certain classes of concerns employing child labor, raises two fundamental questions: "Is the Supreme Court entitled to define the purposes for which

Congress may exercise its taxing powers, and if so, why not all of its powers?'' The logic of the decision in Bailey v. Drexel Furniture overrides previous decisions and makes the Supreme Court "the supervisor of the purposes for which Congress may exercise its constitutional powers." The essay concludes that the Bailey decision "must be written down as a piece of grandmotherly meddling," wrong in principle, even if it does not prove mischievous in practice.

The implied thesis of "Moratorium over Minnesota" (1934) is that the issue between Chief Justice Hughes and Justice Sutherland in the Blaisdell case is one of approach. "Most" constitutional issues are determined by the Court's approach and the Court is "usually a perfectly free agent in choosing its approach." The essay reproves Sutherland for resort to the founders' intention. "The Constitution must mean different things at different times if it is to mean what is sensible, applicable, feasible." "The Schechter Case—Landmark, or What?" (1936) argues that the Schechter decision reveals "notable weaknesses," that the chief justice's opinion is unnecessarily broad, and that his doctrine is "gravely defective." The decision also is ambiguous. The Court, rather than applying realistic concrete principles, is guilty of "dogmatic conceptualism."

In "The Court Sees a New Light" Corwin holds that "American constitutional law has first and last undergone a number of revolutions, but none so radical, so swift, so altogether dramatic as that witnessed by the term of Court just ended." The essay chronicles the 1937 decisions by which the Court transformed itself from an adversary to the coadjutor of the New Deal. The thesis of "Statesmanship on the Supreme Court" (1940) is that the Supreme Court would no longer bolster economic against political power as it did from 1887 to 1937. The Court would therefore be free to support humane values of free thought and free speech. The recent revolution in our constitutional law was superior statesmanship on the part of the Supreme Court. Nevertheless, Corwin's last word on the New Deal is one not of praise but of qualified disapproval in "John Marshall, Revolutionist *Malgré Lui*" (1955). This essay examines in part whether Marshall can be conscripted as a patron of the New Deal. Since liberty, not social equality, was the lodestar of Marshall's political philosophy, his principles defy conscription for the purpose of blessing the New Deal in general or the Darby decision in particular. In the matter of the New Deal, as with most other questions, Corwin was a master of balance who trimmed the sails of the constitutional ship of state in order to avoid extremes.

In this volume we find Corwin traveling full circle from his early rationalistic account of judicial review and complimentary attitude toward the founders' intention through his criticism of constitutional theory and the founders' intention to end up criticizing the moral basis of the New Deal according to John Marshall's political thought. Corwin's rehabilitation of John Marshall is compatible with the judgment that the Supreme Court's lapses from the standards of historical research are no reason to banish the founders' intention from the scholar's tools. Corwin's essays critical of constitutional theory unintentionally demonstrate the difficulty of finding an alternative to the founders' intention as a guide to the "way of wisdom in making an indefinite series of practical judgments."

"Edward S. Corwin stands among the giants of American constitutional commentators—with Kent, Story and Cooley," the editors of his essays wrote in 1964. "More than any other scholar of our time, he justified and illustrated his own incisive observation: 'If judges make law, so do commentators.' "[12] Although Corwin has attained the eminence of Kent, Story, and Cooley, it would be misleading to ignore some differences between Corwin and his predecessors. First, Kent, Story, and Cooley favored the treatise as a literary form, whereas Corwin was primarily an essayist. Second, Kent, Story, and Cooley wrote the original edition of their treatises for the bench and bar, but Corwin's commentary on the Constitution, *The Constitution and What It Means Today*, is a popular work that presupposes no constitutional acumen. Third, Corwin's concern to be contemporary in viewpoint permeates *The Constitution and What It Means Today* with a "presentism" that is absent from the work of Kent, Story, and Cooley. Fourth, Corwin alone among these law writers specialized in constitutional law. Kent's *Commentaries*, for example, is only partly concerned with constitutional law; it deals also with the law of nations and private law. Fifth, Corwin at times answered constitutional law questions with a greater degree of closure then his predecessors; Story, to take only one example, tended to recognize the necessity of leaving certain questions open. Sixth, Corwin cited none of his predecessors as a source of his thought, though he acknowledged his debt to John Marshall: "on the fundamental issue . . . of the nature of the Constitution and its source, I have felt free to adopt throughout the point of view of Chief Justice Marshall."[13]

Seventh, Marshall, Kent, and Story respected the founders' intention as a source of constitutional understanding, whereas Corwin searched for a more contemporary understanding. Marshall, for example, wrote in Cohens v. Virginia, 6 Wheat. 264 (1821), that "great weight has always been attached, and very rightly attached, to contemporaneous exposition." "The opinion of the *Federalist* has always been considered as of great authority. It is a complete commentary on our Constitution." Marshall's other opinions on constitutional law illustrate the uses he made of the founders' intention and his underlying moderation. In Gibbons v. Ogden, 9 Wheat. 186 (1824), he wrote that "as men, whose intentions require no concealment, generally employ the words which most directly and aptly express the ideas they intend to convey, the enlightened patriots who framed our Constitution, and the people who adopted it, must be understood to have employed words in their natural sense, and to

---

12. Alpheus Mason and Gerald Garvey, "Introduction," in Mason and Garvey, eds., *American Constitutional History: Essays, by Edward S. Corwin* ix (1964).

13. E. S. Corwin, *The Constitution and What It Means Today* vii (1920).

have intended what they have said." In his dissent in Ogden v. Saunders, 12 Wheat. 213 (1827), Marshall discloses his principles in construing the Constitution: "To say that the intention of the instrument must prevail; that this intention must be collected from its words; that its words are to be understood in that sense in which they are generally used by those for whom the instrument was intended; that its provisions are neither to be restricted into insignificance, nor extended to objects not comprehended in them, nor contemplated by its framers, is to repeat what has been already said more at large, and that is all that can be necessary." Marshall went so far as to deduce the founders' intention from their education: "When we advert to the course of reading generally pursued by American statesmen in early life, we must suppose that the framers of our Constitution were intimately acquainted with the writings of those wise and learned men whose treatises on the laws of nature and nations have guided public opinion on the subjects of obligations and contract. If we turn to those treatises, we find them to concur in the declaration that contracts possess an original, intrinsic obligation, derived from the acts of free agents, and not given by government. We must suppose that the framers of our Constitution took the same view of the subject, and the language they have used confirms this opinion." The founders' intention did not serve Marshall as a constitutional talisman. Discussing the *Federalist* in McCulloch v. Maryland, 4 Wheat. 316 (1819), Marshall concluded that "the opinions expressed by the authors of that work have been justly supposed to be entitled to great respect in expounding the Constitution . . . but in applying their opinions to the cases which may arise in the progress of our government, a right to judge of their correctness must be retained." Even the founders' intention was subject to the tribunal of reason.

Story conceded the analytical difficulties of invoking the founders' intention: "The *Federalist* denied that the President could remove a public officer without the consent of the Senate. The first Congress affirmed his right by a mere majority. Which is to be followed?"[14] Corwin went beyond this manly candor to reject the founders' intention root and branch in his essays "Constitution v. Constitutional Theory" and "Judicial Review in Action," both of which are included in this volume. Hence Corwin is incorrect in asserting that he continues Marshall's point of view on the nature and source of the Constitution except in a sharply abridged form limited to Marshall's idea that the nation is paramount to the states. Corwin's "adaptive" rules of interpretation in "Judicial Review in Action" deserve comparison with Story's "first and fundamental rule in the interpretation of all instruments": "to construe them according to the sense of the terms and the intention of the parties. Mr. Justice Blackstone has remarked that the intention of a law is to be gathered from the words, the context, the subject matter, the effects and consequence, or the reason and spirit

14. 1 Story, *Comm.* 301 n. 1 (4th ed., ed. T. Cooley, 1873).

of the law.''[15] "Light may be obtained . . . from contemporary facts or expositions, from antecedent mischiefs, from known habits, manners, and institutions, and from sources almost innumerable.''[16] By rejecting the founders'
intention as Marshall and Story understood it, Corwin walls off his readers
from perhaps the most valuable part of their constitutional heritage. What
appears in Corwin's writings to be an immense enlargement of the constitutional horizon is actually a contraction of the horizon of Marshall, Kent, and Story.
In sum: important differences as to the nature and source of the Constitution
separate Corwin from Marshall, Kent, and Story. In one respect, however,
Corwin more resembled Kent and Story than Cooley. Cooley, it is argued,
"expressly repudiated any notions of higher law," but "like Kent, Story tended
to give natural law an historical content, thus shifting the theoretical basis of
positive law from natural law to history.''[17] Corwin also tended to give natural
and higher law a historical content, shifting the theoretical foundation of
positive law from nature to history and tradition.

Volume I of *Corwin on the Constitution* deals with the foundations of
American constitutional and political thought and Articles I (the powers of
Congress) and II (the president's power of removal) of the Constitution. The
essays on constitutional and political thought address fundamental problems of
the Constitution, democracy, and natural and higher law. The essays ascend
from opinion about the Constitution to constitutional theory between 1776 and
1787 to the idea of higher law. In an essay on political science Corwin
appraises the democratic dogma in light of certain conclusions of the social
sciences. After stating the lessons of the Constitutional Convention of 1787 for
a Chinese audience, he examines the relationship of the Constitution and New
Deal democracy. Another essay shows how the idea of evolution replaced the
idea of natural law in American constitutional and political thought. Two
remaining essays analyze the contribution of natural law to American constitutional law and the thought of founder James Madison. In addition to Corwin's
less important essays on the powers of Congress, Volume I contains "The
President's Removal Power under the Constitution," a criticism of the theory in
Myers v. United States that the president may remove at his pleasure executive
officers of the United States government.

The argument of my introduction to Volume I may be stated in brief. First in
time, Corwin objected to constitutional worship, by which he meant popular
veneration of the Constitution's principles and the statesmen's use of the
founders' political science. Corwin believed that Lincoln ended constitutional
worship and made opinion about the Constitution more democratic and realistic

15. *Id.*, at 295.
16. *Id.*, at 296.
17. F. Aumann, *The Changing American Legal System: Some Selected Phases* 205 (1940); see
also E. K. Bauer, *Commentaries on the Constitution, 1790–1860* 329 (1965; 1952); see Aumann, at
129.

than the founders' political science. The problem of higher law was, to a large extent, whether unchangeable standards, superior to the will of human rulers, existed to guide human legislators. Corwin's essay "The 'Higher Law' Background of American Constitutional Law" discouraged belief in higher law by weakly defending it against the analytical school's separation of what is legal from what is just. Corwin also accepted the positive idea of law and the dependence of thought on its historical setting, that is, historicism. In effect, Corwin labored to show that higher law was an illusion because no unchangeable standards existed to guide human legislators. Along with his criticism of constitutional worship and his rejection of higher law, Corwin advocated popular sovereignty and an instrumental Constitution. Corwin deliberately replaced the founders' political science and higher law with the idea of progress, an instrumental Constitution, majority rule, and a dominant presidency. Corwin's late defense of natural law was limited and flawed because he defended natural law against Mr. Justice Holmes and the legal positivists without replying to the more important objections of historicism and egalitarianism.

Although the essays of Volume II stand by themselves, they may be most readily understood in light of the essays in Volume I that discuss higher law. The essays of Volume I that treat the higher law background of American constitutionalism elaborate the concern of certain essays in Volume II with the Supreme Court's idea of "reasonableness," tracing this doctrine back to English and Roman sources on the idea of reason.[18] Discussing the Supreme Court and legislative power, Corwin found that in the "last analysis" an assumption of judicial review was that "judges alone really *know* the law.[19] He related the authority of the Supreme Court to supposed judicial knowledge of a higher law superior to ordinary law. Corwin's prior concern with the Supreme Court's barriers against legislative power led him to elaborate the justification for judicial review with the idea of "reasonableness" associated with higher law. The essays on higher law are a destination reached in Corwin's position. For Corwin judicial review stands or falls with the doctrine of reasonableness and the idea of reason in the higher law tradition.

The question arises whether Corwin always upheld the truth and vitality of higher law as a final account in moral philosophy. Despite appearances to the contrary, this question must be answered in the negative. Corwin observes in effect that the distinctiveness of his approach to judicial review is its emphasis on the role of ideas as opposed to institutions. He "would insist upon the rationalistic background of American constitutional history" as opposed to its institutional background.[20] Corwin saw clearly, but failed to criticize, the historicist ideas that reinforced the institutional approach to judicial review.

18. E. S. Corwin, *Liberty against Government* xii (1948).
19. Corwin, "Marbury v. Madison and the Doctrine of Judicial Review," 12 *Mich. L. Rev.* 538, 572 (1914); italics in original.
20. Corwin, "The Establishment of Judicial Review," 9 *Mich. L. Rev.* 102, 103 (1910).

This historicism interprets ideas as a result of time, place, and circumstances, and it includes many of the same assumptions that later led Corwin to downgrade the founders' intention as a way of understanding the Constitution. The historicists as well as the institutionalists "represent the Constitution as preeminently a deposit of time and event," and this is precisely the argument Corwin adopted in his critique of the founders' intention.[21] One criticism of Corwin is that he fails to make the radical break necessary from the assumptions of historicist writers who stress the institutional account of judicial review. As his essay "The 'Higher Law' Background of American Constitutional Law" makes clear, Corwin's rejection of higher law is a result of his acceptance of the thesis of evolution or progress; the idea of progress enabled Corwin to dismiss higher law as in principle an objectively true and final account. Corwin's position shows the impossibility of accepting both the original understanding of higher law and historicism and the immense danger of historicism for the justification of judicial review according to reason.

The reader first perusing Corwin's essays will find a golden harvest of more than forty years of study and reflection on the American Constitution. These essays are inevitably controversial in that Corwin and other skilled commentators disagree on important matters such as the basis of judicial review. Moreover, Corwin changed his opinion about the basis of judicial review and John Marshall. Readers are therefore compelled to think for themselves. The question that arises at the end of each essay should be: How do you decide the case or issue?

Critical respect is the proper attitude with which to begin a voyage through Corwin's essays. Did Corwin reject more of the Marshall tradition than he preserved? Are the parts of the Marshall tradition that Corwin rejected more valuable and important that the parts he preserved? If so, does not Corwin's position act as a roadblock to the recovery of the founders' comprehensive understanding of good government in the United States? The effort to grapple with Corwin is the highest tribute to him as a master scholar and constitutional guide. The task will be accomplished only by his most attentive pupils, just as Corwin himself strove as a student and scholar to surpass Andrew C. McLaughlin, his teacher and mentor.

I have made minor changes in the essays for consistency and ease of reading. I have attempted to supply information lacking in Corwin's citations, and I have standardized quotations from the *Federalist* according to Jacob Cooke's edition; but semicolons replace dashes in the middle of a sentence, and "Constitution" (for the national Constitution) is always capitalized. My editorial comments in the text and notes have been placed in braces in order to distinguish them from Corwin's brackets. Some footnotes have been renumbered.

21. *Id.*, at 102.

I.

THE ORIGINS OF
JUDICIAL REVIEW

1. The Supreme Court and Unconstitutional Acts of Congress

THE power of the Supreme Court of the United States to supervise congressional legislation has been so generally assumed in the recent discussions, both in and out of Congress, of the proposed Rate Bill, and is indeed so apparently settled today that it becomes of interest to inquire into the intention of the Constitutional Fathers in this matter. Did the Fathers intend that the federal judiciary should have the right to declare an act of Congress of no effect because transgressing constitutional limits? It does not detract from the interest of this question that two recent authorities who attempt to answer it—without, however, going into the subject at any length—express opposing opinions. Thus Mr. Cotton, the editor of the *Constitutional Decisions of John Marshall*,[1] says with reference to Marshall's decision in Marbury v. Madison,[2] decided in 1803: "That opinion is the beginning of the American system of constitutional law. In it Marshall announced the right of the Supreme Court to review the constitutionality of the acts of the national legislature and the executive, the coordinate branches of the government. . . . Common as this conception of our courts now is, it is hard to comprehend the amazing quality of it then. No court in England had such a power, there was no express warrant for it in the words of the Constitution; the existence of it was denied by every other branch of the government and by the dominant majority of the country. Moreover, no such power had been clearly anticipated by the framers of the Constitution, nor was it a necessary implication from the scheme of government they had established." On the other hand, Professor McLaughlin in his *Confederation and the Constitution*,[3] though he concedes that "it is hard to speak with absolute assurance," deduces the power in question with considerable confidence from

From 4 *Michigan Law Review* 616–30 (1906). Reprinted by permission.

1. 1 *The Constitutional Decisions of John Marshall* Intro. xii–xiii (J. P. Cotton, ed., 1905).
2. {1 Cranch 137 (1803).}
3. *The Confederation and the Constitution* (vol. 10 of *American Nation*) 250 (1905).

that clause of the Constitution which extends the judicial power of the United States to all cases "arising under this Constitution." "Certainly," he says, "the Constitution was by this clause recognized and proclaimed as law and we may at least assert that by force of logic, if not because of the conscious purpose of the members of the Convention, this power was bestowed,—the power to declare of no effect an act of Congress contrary to the law of the land."

It is evident that the issue thus presented may be clarified by analysis. Our authors are really at variance at three distinct points: 1. Did the framers of the Constitution bestow in terms the power in question upon the federal judiciary? 2. If they did not, did they yet believe that the judiciary would have the power, simply by virtue of its position in relation to the other departments of government, and particularly in relation to a rigid Constitution? 3. Was there more than one way of conceiving the federal judiciary's position in these relations? Let us consider these questions in the order in which they are propounded.

As mentioned above, Professor McLaughlin ventures the opinion that power to supervise federal legislation and to nullify it when inconsistent with the Constitution was expressly bestowed upon the federal judiciary by the clause, "cases . . . arising under this Constitution," of Art. III, sec. 2, of that instrument. In this connection he cites Brinton Coxe's *Judicial Power and Unconstitutional Legislation,*[4] a work highly polemical in tone and written with the avowed purpose of proving that "the framers of the Constitution actually intended . . . that the United States Supreme Court should be competent in all litigations before it to decide upon the questioned constitutionality of United States laws, and to hold the same void when unconstitutional"; that this power rests, not upon mere "inference or implication," but upon "express texts" of the Constitution. But one "express text" is adduced: viz.; the one quoted by Professor McLaughlin. Coxe's argument in behalf of his contention is as follows: "On August 6th that committee [of five] reported the draft of a Constitution. The beginning of the 2nd section of its 11th Article reads: 'The jurisdiction of the Supreme Court shall extend to all cases arising under laws passed by the legislature of the United States.' On August 27th, when the 11th Article of the draft Constitution was under consideration, and the above text was reached, the following proceedings took place, as reported by Madison: 'Dr. Johnson moved to insert the words "this Constitution and" before the word "laws." Mr. Madison doubted whether this was not going too far, to extend the jurisdiction of the court *generally to cases arising under the Constitution* [Coxe's italics], and whether it ought not to be limited to cases of a judiciary nature. *The right of expounding the Constitution, in cases not of this nature, ought not to be given to that department.* The motion of Dr. Johnson

---

4. "Especially Pt. IV," i.e., pp. 294ff; the work appeared in Philadelphia in 1893.

was agreed *nem. con., it being generally supposed that the jurisdiction given was constructively limited to cases of a judicial nature.'"*

The above argument is open to disparagement at several points. In the first place, the Johnson amendment was carried *nem. con.,* and almost without discussion, a rather suspicious circumstance in connection with a proposition of so great importance, as Mr. Coxe would fain make it. In the second place, it is difficult to see what Mr. Coxe adds to the clause, "cases under the Constitution," by laboriously drawing it from Madison's *Notes,* instead of going directly to the Constitution for it. For, in the third place, the clause itself needs elucidation, and until that need is met, there is a plain step of the flimsiest kind of conjecture between the fact that such a clause was incorporated in the Constitution and the *contention* which Mr. Coxe makes that, the federal judiciary was thereby vested with the right to veto unconstitutional acts of Congress. What then does the phrase, "cases . . . arising under the Constitution" mean?

Fortunately Madison expounded this very phrase in the Virginia Convention.[5] "It may be a misfortune," said he, "that in organizing any government, the explication of its authority should be left to any of its coordinate branches. There is no example in any country where it is otherwise. There is a new policy in submitting it to the judiciary of the United States. That cases of a federal nature will arise, will be obvious to every gentleman, who will recollect that the states are laid under restrictions; and that rights of the Union are secured by these restrictions; they may involve equitable as well as legal controversies. With respect to the laws of the Union, it is so necessary and expedient, that the judicial power should correspond with the legislative, that it has not been objected to. With respect to treaties, there is a peculiar propriety in the judiciary expounding them." A careful inspection of the order in which Madison develops his thought in the above quotation will reveal that his idea of "cases under the Constitution" was that they were "cases of a federal nature," arising because of unwarranted acts not of Congress but of the states. This analysis, moreover, is conclusively confirmed by Hamilton's words in *Federalist* Number 80.[6] "It has been asked," he writes, "what is meant by 'cases arising under the Constitution,' in contradistinction from those 'arising under the laws of the United States'? The difference has already been explained. All restrictions upon the authority of the state legislatures furnish examples of it. They are not, for instance, to emit paper money; but the interdiction results from the Constitution and will have no connection with any law of the United States." In a word, what was effected by the incorporation of the clause in question, in the Constitution, was the bestowal upon the federal government of a veto, to be unobtrusively[7] exercised through its judicial department, upon

5. Madison, 5 *Writings* 217–18 (Hunt, ed., 1900–1910).
6. *The Foederalist* (Henry B. Dawson, ed., New York, 1863).
7. Vd. Madison to Jefferson, October 24, 1787.

certain categories of state legislation. How vastly different this veto of the central government upon the legislation of the local law-making bodies is—even though it is exercised by the judicial organ of the central government—from a veto upon the acts of any legislature, whether central or local, by a merely coordinate judiciary—it is hardly necessary to dwell upon at length. Only imagine the judicial committee of the British Privy Council, which vetoes a number of acts of colonial legislatures every year, interposing its veto upon an act of Parliament! Moreover, the distinction I am pointing must have been present to the minds of the framers of the Constitution, who as colonists had seen many of their legislative projects fall before the veto of the home government, but were only too painfully aware of Parliament's claims to supremacy.

It is significant, with reference to the discussion just closed, that those who expressed themselves in the Constitutional Convention, as of the opinion that the federal courts would have the right to declare unconstitutional acts of Congress null and void, all did so before the Johnson amendment was ever framed. On June 4[8] a proposition was brought forward in the Convention that, the judges of the Supreme Court, acting with the executive, should comprise a council of revision of congressional legislation. In speaking to this proposition, Gerry of Massachusetts, Wilson of Pennsylvania, Mason of Virginia, and Luther Martin of Maryland all asserted at various times and with various qualifications, the power of the Supreme Court to sit in judgment upon the constitutionality of congressional legislation. Gerry, instancing a similar power in state judges with reference to state legislation, saw in this attribute of the courts a "check against encroachments on their own department." Wilson "thought there was weight in this observation." Martin and Mason used the broadest terms. Said the former: "As to the constitutionality of laws, that point will come before the judges in their proper character. In this character they have a negative on the laws." Said the latter: "They [the judges] could declare an unconstitutional law void."

These assertions, however, did not go unchallenged. Bedford of Delaware declared himself "opposed to every check on the legislature, even the council of revision. . . . The representatives of the people were the best judges of what was for their interest, and ought to be under no external control whatever. The two branches would produce a sufficient control within the legislature itself." Equally positive was Mercer of Maryland's declaration August 15, when the matter of a council of revision came up for final consideration: "He disapproved of the doctrine that the judges as expositors of the Constitution should have the authority to declare a law void. He thought laws ought to be well and cautiously made and then be uncontrollable." "Mr. Dickinson [of Delaware]

8. Vd. Madison, 3, 4 *Writings* (Hunt, ed.) (index in vol. 4).

was strongly impressed with the remark of Mr. Mercer as to the power of the judges to set aside the law. He thought no such power ought to exist. He was at the same time at a loss what expedient to substitute." Apparently the exact trend of Dickinson's words is uncertain. On the other hand, Gerry, in the utterance above quoted, limited the supervisory power of the federal judiciary to a self-defensive veto against Congressional encroachment; while the tone of Wilson, in accepting even this restricted suggestion, is that of a man weighing a novel idea.

In a word, the debates of the Convention reveal a diversity of opinion on the question under review. The same is true of the discussions of the Constitution that succeeded the Convention.[9] On the one hand, Wilson—now no longer in doubt—in the Pennsylvania convention. Marshall in the Virginia convention, Ellsworth in the Connecticut convention, and Hamilton in the New York convention, as well as in *Federalist* Number 78, argue at length for the right of the Supreme Court to nullify unconstitutional acts of Congress. On the other hand, they *do argue,* and Hamilton in particular, in the above mentioned number of the *Federalist,* expounds the theory of judicial paramountcy—for such we may fairly designate it—with a degree of elaboration that is at least significant. Moreover, the weighty authority of Madison is, I think, demonstrably on the other side. Thus in the Virginia convention, confronted with the question as to what remedy would be available in case the federal government should make a treaty in excess of constitutional warrant, he responded that the remedy would be the impeachment of those who negotiated the treaty and the retirement of those who ratified it.[10] Likewise, when in *Federalist* Number 45 he discussed the possibility of the federal government's embarking upon "unwarrantable measures," he again suggests a purely political remedy—one which, by the way, is a plain hint of his famous Virginia Resolutions of 1798. "The disquietude of the people," he says, "their repugnance and perhaps refusal to cooperate with the officers of the Union; the frowns of the executive magistracy of the state, the embarrassments created by legislative devices . . . would oppose . . . difficulties not to be despised." Moreover, "ambitious encroachments of the federal government . . . would be signals of general alarm. Every government would espouse the common cause. A correspondence would be opened. Plans of resistance would be concerted." This idea of state "interposition" to oppose unwarrantable acts of the federal government seems, therefore, to have been a favorite notion of Madison's from the outset, and apparently connotes a quite different idea of the judiciary from that which sustains the paramountcy of the courts. Indeed, when, eleven years later, Madison again came forward with the notion of "interposition," the sole answer returned to his suggestion by several of the Northern legislatures[11] was to assert the power

9. Vd. principally vols. 2–4, Elliot's *Debates* {. . . *on the Adoption of the Federal Constitution*}.
10. 5 *Writings* 215 (Hunt, ed.).
11. Vd. particularly the resolutions of Rhode Island's legislature.

of the Supreme Court to overturn unconstitutional acts of Congress. But this is anticipating. To return to the period of the adoption of the Constitution, we have the following piece of evidence from Madison's pen, in October, 1788:[12] "In the state constitutions," he says, in a letter to John Brown of Kentucky, "and indeed in the federal one also, no provision is made for the case of a disagreement in expounding them; and as the courts are generally the last in making the decision it results to them, by refusing or not refusing to execute a law, to stamp it with its final character. This makes the judicial department paramount in fact to the legislature, which was never intended and can never be proper." Whatever weight may be accorded Madison's testimony regarding "the intention" of—presumably—the framers of the state and federal constitutions, the above quoted passage certainly makes plain his own position, as also it does, once more, the lack of unanimity among the framers of the Constitution as to the scope of judicial power in dealing with legislation.

This exhausts all evidence that bears directly upon our second main topic, but it ought to result in a farther illumination of the view entertained in 1787 of the role of the judiciary as such, to attend briefly to Madison's and Gerry's testimony as to the growing disposition of state courts to set themselves up as the chosen guardians of the state constitutions, against legislative encroachments. Already, at the time of the Federal Convention, the courts—and in most cases the Supreme Courts—of five states had set up a claim of right to pass upon the validity of state legislation: that of Virginia in the case of Commonwealth v. Caton et al., 1782; that of New York in Rutgers v. Waddington, in 1784; that of New Jersey in Holmes v. Walton, in 1785; that of Rhode Island in Trevett v. Weeden, in 1786; and that of North Carolina in Bayard v. Singleton, in 1787, shortly after the adjournment of the Constitutional Convention. Only in the last two cases, however, were state laws actually nullified on the ground of their incompatibility with the state constitution; for though a law was overturned by the decision in Rutgers v. Waddington, it was on the ground of its violation of natural reason and natural rights. But though no law was overturned, the entire ground upon which the theory of judicial paramountcy rests, under a rigid constitution, seems to have been canvassed by the court in the very first of these decisions.[13] "If the whole legislature . . . should attempt to overleap the bounds prescribed to them by the people," said Justice Wythe, "I . . . will meet the united powers at my seat in this tribunal and, pointing to the Constitution, will say to them, here is the limit of your authority; and hither shall you go, but no further."

So much for the initial statement of this doctrine and its development at the hands of the state judiciary up to the time of the Federal Convention. It did not go unchallenged in the states any more than it did in the Convention itself.

12. 1 *Letters and Writings* 195 (1865).
13. 4 Call (Va.) 5.

Thus Pendleton, the president of the Virginia court, designated the issue raised by his confrères, "a tremendous question, the decision of which might involve consequences to which gentlemen may not have extended their ideas." The Rhode Island legislature removed the judges for their presumption in Trevett v. Weeden. Iredell's elaborate argument[14] in justification of Bayard v. Singleton were called forth by a general protest that the decision made the state subject, not to the representatives of the people but to three individuals; and among the protestants were not only Iredell's associates on the bench but also Richard Dobbs Spaight, one of North Carolina's delegates to the Constitutional Convention. Finally, each of these decisions was succeeded by a formal repeal of the law that had been visited with the judicial condemnation; and in 1788, the Virginia court, while still holding to its language of six years earlier, contented itself with recommending, in the Case of the Judges,[15] the repeal of the obnoxious statute. It cannot be said that the doctrine of judicial paramountcy was yet established in 1789; a relatively novel doctrine, it was still charged with the burden of proof. On the other hand, it was shouldering the burden with apparent success and was making rapid progress toward general acceptance by at least the juristically minded portion of the American people.

We come now to the third phase of our subject: an examination of the argument framed in justification of allowing the courts to pass upon the validity of the acts of a coordinate legislature. The essence of Hamilton's argument in *Federalist* Number 78, and likewise of Marshall's in Marbury v. Madison, except for the fact that Marshall cites rather incidentally the clause, "cases . . . arising under the Constitution," is as follows: The Court, like the other coordinate departments, is sworn to uphold the Constitution; it is also sworn to enforce the laws made under the authority of that Constitution; but, perchance, that authority has been transcended by the legislature; there is then a discrepancy between the Constitution and the law made to its derogation; but the Constitution is the act of the people and designed by them to be fundamental, the law is merely the act of the legislature, the people's representatives; obviously the latter must yield to the former, if the power to amend the Constitution, which the people have reserved to themselves, is not to be transferred to the legislature, and the Constitution thus put on a level with ordinary enactment.

It would be useless to deny, even if it were desirable to do so, that this is a very convincing piece of legal dialectic. Yet, if we can put ourselves back to a time when the doctrine in defense of which it was formulated had not behind it a long lapse of years and many precedents, it is probable that we shall find that, like most abstract argumentation, it abounds in assumptions and dilemmas, which we either approve or ignore in our present attitude toward it. To begin

14. 2 McRee, *Life and Correspondence of James Iredell* 145ff. and 168ff. (1858).
15. 4 Call (Va.) 135.

with, why should a constitution—more particularly a state constitution—be regarded as more fundamental than a law? Of course, it is answered that the former is the act of the people themselves, the latter of their representatives. But the fact of the matter is, that but two of the thirteen state constitutions in existence in 1789 had ever been referred to the people for their approval. Nor has the practice of allowing constitutional conventions to promulgate the result of their labors without referendum {become?} obsolete today. Why then should the enactment of the people's representatives of say three decades ago have greater validity than the enactment of the people's representatives of today? Why should a constitutional convention, as transient a body as any electoral college, as responsive, without doubt, to the whims of its little day, be so much more authoritative a body than the state legislature, the continual embodiment of the state's residual sovereignty? Or granting the feature of referendum as a necessary item in the establishment of a state constitution, why should a constitution thus established be of greater authority than a law enacted by the legislature and likewise submitted to popular referendum? I am arguing against the rigid constitution, you suggest. That, however, is not the object of my questions. I wish to show that, to instance the fundamental character of a constitution—of a state constitution, particularly—in arguing for judicial paramountcy, is to argue in a circle, since, *prima facie,* the principal mark of the Constitution's fundamental character is its defense by the paramount judiciary.

But turn now more particularly to the relation of the federal judiciary to the federal Constitution. As we saw above, it seems fairly certain that the framers of the Constitution did not expressly confer upon the federal courts the power to question the validity of federal legislation; the power is therefore alleged to flow from the nature of the judicial office itself. But is it a judicial power? If the President's power of veto makes him a branch of the legislature, as is generally admitted—and such indeed is the historical character of the veto—why does not *its* power of veto make the Supreme Court a branch of the legislature too? But, whereas the President's legislative function is expressly bestowed upon him by the Constitution, that of the Supreme Court is derived only by implication—and that, moreover, in the face of the theory of a government of delegated powers and of the other theory of separation of powers. Suppose the President had secured his veto power in the same way that the Supreme Court did its similar power! Suppose the Supreme Court, whose power to nullify unconstitutional acts of Congress rests upon a process of ratiocination, should nullify an act of Congress the alleged unconstitutionality of which also rests entirely upon argumentation! Yet what was the significance of the divided bench in the Dred Scott decision, in Hepburn v. Griswold, in the Income Tax Case?[16]

{16. Dred Scott v. Sanford, 19 How. 393 (1857); Hepburn v. Griswold, 8 Wall. 603 (1870); Pollock v. Farmers' Loan and Trust Co., 157 U.S. 429 (1895); 158 U.S. 601 (1895).}

This brings us finally to what is perhaps the most basic assumption of the argument for judicial paramountcy: the assumption of the impersonality of the courts. "The question may be asked," says a critic[17] of the Supreme Court's decision in the Income Tax Case, "what power is there to prevent Congress from passing an unconstitutional act, if the Supreme Court has a right to prevent it? This question may be answered, Yankee fashion, by asking another. If the Supreme Court should make an unconstitutional decision, what is there to prevent that?" The first of these queries proceeds on the supposition that the Supreme Court knows and speaks the unvarying language of an immutable Constitution; the second insinuates that that tribunal is not quite so aloof from the here and now. In the light of history, the Supreme Court stands forth as nearly immaculate as any similar human institution ever did, and we need not trouble ourselves for a moment with crude considerations of that sort. On the other hand, it is perfectly obvious that the impersonality of the Supreme Court is merely fictional and tautological. It always speaks the language of the Constitution, merely because its opinion of the Constitution *is* the Constitution. But would any one assert that the Constitution has not been extended and amended by the Supreme Court? Such an assertion would deprive that body of one of its chief claims to fame. Yet once grant this, and the question at once arises: what is the real basis of such judicial legislation—or rather judicial amendment of the Constitution? The truth is that the major premise of most of the great decisions of the Supreme Court is a concealed bias of some sort—a highly laudable bias perhaps, yet a bias. For example, the question at issue in McCulloch v. Maryland was the meaning of the phrase "necessary and proper": did it mean "absolutely necessary" or "convenient"? Marshall said it meant "convenient." But why, except because he was a nationalist? Now, however, suppose he had decided that the phrase in question had borne the other meaning. His particularlistic bias would have resulted in the overthrow of the will of the federal legislature. Or to put the whole matter in a sentence: the real question at issue when the validity of an act of Congress is challenged before the Supreme Court is *not* whether the fundamental Constitution shall give way to an act of Congress, but whether Congress' interpretation of the fundamental Constitution shall prevail or whether it shall yield to that of another human, and therefore presumably fallible, institution—a bench of judges. The existence of a rigid Constitution, therefore, does by no means inevitably depend upon its final interpretation by the judiciary. Throughout the period between the formation of the government and the outbreak of the Civil War the discussion of the constitutionality of proposed measures was the predominant characteristic of congressional debates, and in that entire period but two decisions of the Supreme Court determined the constitutional merits of

17. S. Pennoyer, "The Income Tax Decision and the Power of the Supreme Court to Nullify Acts of Congress," 29 *Am. Law Rev.* 550, at 553 (1895).

congressional acts adversely: One, Marbury v. Madison, the decision by which the right of the court to take such a step was determined; the other, the Dred Scott case. Lastly, it should be remembered that the rigid constitutions of France, Belgium, and Switzerland are finally construed by the legislatures of those countries, in the ordinary course of legislation.

But now if most constitutional decisions rest actually upon a concealed premise, and if the right of the Supreme Court to pass upon the validity of congressional legislation must be referred to such a decision, upon what concealed premise does that decision rest? The answer is: a certain theory of government, embodied in the Constitution itself. The Constitutional Fathers and the Federalist party were thoroughgoing individualists of the school of John Locke. They believed that individual rights, and particularly property rights, took their origin in natural law and antedated the formation of government and even of society, and that the sole function of government was to afford protection to those rights. They believed that whenever government, even the "supreme legislature," transcended its trusteeship to the derogation of any of these rights, the right of revolution resulted. On the other hand, indications were not wanting at the moment of the assembling of the Constitutional Convention that notions of popular sovereignty were leavening and democratizing the masses. Accordingly, the Federal Convention presents a very interesting paradox. Brought together for the purpose of creating a government competent to repress popular disorders, the men of 1787 expended no small fraction of their united ingenuity in devising an elaborate system of checks and balances, with the view of holding the government of their creation—particularly the popular organ thereof, the legislature—in permanent leash, against the day when the people should come into their own. The very populace to curb whom new governmental machinery was being erected might some day capture the whole fortress and turn its guns upon its erstwhile defenders. Those guns must be spiked in advance, and the more completely the better. The Constitutional Fathers seized with avidity upon Montesquieu's picture of a constitution,[18] whose well devised checks kept the organs of government most normally in a "state of repose or inaction." The federal government was balanced against the states and these against the government; each portion of a triple-branched legislature was set against the others; the people were made a curb upon their representatives, and they upon the people. It was then but a step farther, and a very rational one, to set the judiciary against the legislature. The courts were at once the authors and interpreters of the common law, the most usual source of individual rights; they had often, in both England and the colonies, intervened in the defense of individual rights against administrative usurpation; they were the ancient defenders of the rule of law against prerogative; and if the common law sometimes fell short of expectations, the courts were occasionally willing

18. *Spirit of the Laws,* bk. 11, chap 6: the British constitution is referred to.

to invoke natural law, as was done in Rutgers v. Waddington, and in other cases.[19] Finally natural rights were rapidly being reduced to writing and introduced into the state constitutions in the form of Bills of Rights. Indeed, this practice, the efficacy of which Madison, consistently enough, was very skeptical of, may be looked upon as a very distinct contribution to the cause of judicial paramountcy; as the addition of the first ten amendments to the federal Constitution in 1791 may be looked upon as a distinct step forward the adoption of that doctrine into the federal government twelve years later. The real logic upon which the right of the federal Supreme Court to question the validity of acts of Congress rests, is the logic of a certain way of looking at the relation of the individual to government.

The extension of the doctrine of judicial paramountcy subsequently to the foundation of the federal government[20] may be traced along two lines: its acceptance by the judiciary, state and federal, and the attitude taken toward it by political leaders. By 1805, the doctrine had been thrice judicially asserted in South Carolina; twice in Pennsylvania; twice in New Jersey; once in Maryland; and twice in North Carolina. The courts of the new states to the west also took up with the notion very promptly. It secured admission in Kentucky in 1801, in Ohio in 1806, in Tennessee in 1807, in Vermont in 1814, in Louisiana in 1813,[21] etc. On the other hand, there was a severe contest over the doctrine in the New Jersey court in 1804, in the case of State v. Parkhurst; and as late as 1825, Justice Gibson of the Supreme Court of Pennsylvania, in deciding Eakin v. Raub,[22] overrode and denounced the doctrine, which he declared was held, "as a professional dogma . . . rather as a matter of faith than of reason." Yet twenty years later, even this last heretic renounced his error, because of his "experience of the necessity of the case."

But of course we are primarily interested in the adoption of the doctrine by the federal Supreme Court. The steps toward this consummation in Marbury v. Madison were very gradual. By the 25th section of the Judiciary Act of 1789, the Supreme Court was vested with the power to review and either to affirm or reverse, any decision of the highest court of a state, denying the validity of a law, treaty, commission, or other authority of the United States. The fact that Ellsworth, a believer, it will be remembered, in the doctrine by judicial paramountcy, was chiefly instrumental in framing this measure, has given color to the notion that its enactment represents the deliberate acceptance by Congress of the same doctrine. The debates in the House of Representatives[23] do not favor such a conjecture.

19. E.g., Bowman v. Middleton, 1 Bay (S.C.) 252.
20. Vd. an excellent article by William M. Meigs, "The Relation of the Judiciary to the Constitution," 19 *Am. Law Rev.* 175–203 (1885).
21. Vd. loc. cit., at 185–88.
22. 1 J. B. Thayer, *Cases on Constitutional Law* 133ff. (1895).
23. 1 Annals of Congress at 826–66.

Gerry alone, of all the speakers, asserted that the Supreme Court would have a veto upon acts of Congress, and even he, as previously, in the Constitutional Convention, limited the applicability of that veto to acts encroaching upon the constitutional rights of the judiciary. That, to his mind, was the meaning of coordinate departments. On the other hand, the other speakers who referred to the 25th section regarded it simply as securing the federal government against the possible bad faith of state judges. Of course, it may be insisted that the Supreme Court is given the power to affirm as well as reverse adverse decisions, but this right may have been confined in the contemplation of the authors of the act to cases involving "commissions," and "authorities,"—presumably of an administrative character.

The first case[24] in which the Supreme Court was called upon to declare an act of Congress void was the Hayburn Case {2 Dallas 409 (1792)} in 1792. No decision was rendered. The second case was that of Hylton v. Ware, in which the constitutionality of an excise on carriages was challenged. The contention was overruled by Justice Chase, in the following language: "As I do not think the tax upon carriages is a direct tax, it is unnecessary for me at this time to determine whether this Court constitutionally possesses the power to declare an act of Congress void, on the ground of its being made contrary to and in violation of the Constitution; but if the Court have such power, I am free to declare that I will never exercise it, but in a very clear case." In Ware v. Hylton et al.,[25] Justice Chase, again delivering the opinion of the Court, made the same declaration with reference to treaties. But four years afterward, in his opinion in Cooper v. Telfair,[26] Chase offers conclusive testimony of the imminent adoption into the federal government of the doctrine of judicial paramountcy: "It is . . . a general opinion, it is expressly admitted by all this bar, and some of the judges have, individually in the circuits decided, that the Supreme Court can declare an act of Congress to be unconstitutional, and, therefore invalid; but there is no adjudication of the Supreme Court itself on the point. I concur, however, in the general sentiment." This was in 1800. Three years later, Marbury v. Madison was decided. As far as the courts and the lawyers were concerned, "that point was settled."

But now what of the attitude of the political branches of the government and of the political leaders? The debate on the Judiciary Act of 1802[27] drew forth a number of very long and elaborate arguments in behalf of judicial paramountcy. Breckenridge of Kentucky alone made explicit protest: "To make the Constitution a practical system," said he, "the power of the courts to annul the laws of

---

24. A summary of these first cases will be found in Judson S. Landon's *Constitutional History of the United States* at 257–59 (1889).

25. 3 Dallas 199–285 (1796).

26. 4 Dallas 19 (1800).

27. 2 Benton, *Abridgment {of the Debates of Congress, from 1789 to 1865}* at 546ff. (1857–61).

Congress cannot possibly exist"; and further, since this is a government of equal departments, if the Courts have such a power, Congress must have the correlative power to annul the decisions of the courts. Breckenridge—the author, by the way, of the Kentucky Resolutions of 1799—spoke the language of the new democracy making war with the old-time Federalism, driven already to its last ditch,—the courts themselves. Jefferson's battle with the federal—and federalist—judiciary, comprising defiances, attempts at impeachment, and, when these failed, efforts to secure an amendment of the Constitution to make judges removable upon the address of both Houses of Congress,[28] is too complicated a matter to decipher in these pages. The great Republican regarded the federal judiciary as "a subtle corps of sappers and miners constantly working to undermine the foundations of our confederated fabric. . . . An opinion is huddled up in conclave, perhaps by a majority of one, delivered as if unanimous, and with the silent acquiescence of lazy and timid associates, by a crafty Chief Justice, who sophisticates the law to his mind by the turn of his own reasoning."

Yet I cannot find that Jefferson ever actually denied the right of the Supreme Court to judge of the validity of acts of Congress. His remarks on Marbury v. Madison are sometimes quoted as if they constitute such a denial, but without reason: they refer rather to the *obiter dictum* portion of that decision. Instead, he seems to have been inclined to make banal concession of the right in question, but by seizing upon the dogma of coordinate departments, which, as we have seen, is one of the main pegs of the argument justifying this very right in the courts, to have ridded the actual exercise of that right either of binding force upon the other departments or of the characteristics of legal precedent.[29] "Each department of the government," he declared, "is truly independent of the others, and has an equal right to decide for itself what is the meaning of the Constitution and the laws submitted to its action." This was likewise Madison's position,[30] and that of Jackson and Lincoln. Thus Madison wrote in 1810:[30] "In a government whose vital principle is responsibility, it never will be allowed that the legislative and executive departments should be completely subjected to the judiciary, in which that characteristic feature is so faintly seen." Jackson's words in his famous Bank veto message are well known: "Each public officer who takes an oath to support the Constitution," he declared, "swears that he will support it as he understands it, and not as it is understood by others. . . . The authority of the Supreme Court must not, therefore, be permitted to control the Congress or the executive when acting in their legislative capacities." And he might have added, "nor the latter in his executive capacity"; since this is the plain inference from his refusal to enforce the Supreme Court's decision in Worcester v. George {6 Pet. 515 (1832)}. Had he gone one step farther and

---

28. Vd. 2 Benton, Abridgement 546ff.
29. Landon, *Constitutional History of the United States* 231.
30. 2 *Letters and Writings* 479.

insisted upon enforcing some law which the Supreme Court had declared unconstitutional, he would have succeeding in pressing the theory of coordinate departments to self-evident absurdity.

The right of the judiciary to pass upon the validity of legislation, tentatively broached in an insignificant commonwealth case, in 1782, by way of pure *obiter dictum,* became the foundation rule of American constitutional law and the characteristic function of American courts, whether state or national, in little more than two decades. This may have been a fortunate development, but it is also inevitable whether or not fortunate that aggressive popular statesmen should never willingly give over to juristic hands the entire keeping of the keys of constitutional truth. Said Lincoln, in his first inaugural, apropos the Dred Scott decision: "If the policy of the government, upon the vital questions affecting the whole people, is to be irrevocably fixed by the decisions of the Supreme Court the moment they are made, as in ordinary cases between parties in personal actions, the people will have ceased to be their own masters, having to that extent resigned their government into the hands of that eminent tribunal." One would like to know whether President Roosevelt, in defining the "sovereign," in his last message, as the government which represents the people as a whole, intended to include more than the political departments within his designation.

2. The Establishment of Judicial Review

I

WHEN Gladstone described the Constitution of the United States as "the most wonderful work ever struck off at a given time by the brain and purpose of man," his amiable intention to flatter was forgotten, while what was considered his gross historical error became at once a theme of adverse criticism. Their contemporaries and immediate posterity regarded the work of the Constitutional Fathers as the inspired product of political genius and essentially as a creation out of hand. Subsequently, due partly to the influence of the disciples of Savigny in the field of legal history, partly to the sway of the doctrine of evolution, and partly to a patriotic desire to claim for the Constitution a conformity to the historic spirit and needs of the American people like to that claimed for the English constitution by English writers, and so inferentially, similar elements of durability, it has become the custom of writers to represent the Constitution as preeminently a deposit of time and event and to accord to the Fathers the substantial but more modest merit of having merely ratified the outcome of habit and usage. This point of view, I am persuaded, has a large admixture of error and the other a correspondingly large element of truth. Because they were not utopists, because they had experienced some disillusionment from their earlier attempts at constitution-making, because they had some conception of the limits set by possibility, all this affords no adequate proof that the Fathers were not of their time and did not participate largely in its way of thinking. "The collected wisdom acquired from a long succession of years is laid open for our use in the establishment of our forms of government," wrote

Part I from 9 *Michigan Law Review* 102–25 (1910); part II from 9 *Michigan Law Review* 283–316 (1911). Reprinted by permission.

*This article is Chapter IV of the writer's work now in preparation, *The Growth of Judicial Review*.

41

Washington in 1783.[1] Here exactly is the attitude of eighteenth century rationalism: its confidence in the reasoned and sifted results of human experience; its belief in the efficacy of ideas for the remedying of institutions, its firm persuasion more particularly of the existence of an available political science and of its mastery of that science,—such was the point of view of the latter quarter of the eighteenth century—the greatest era of reform in government that modern history has seen—such was the point of view of the Constitutional Fathers. They believed that the human reason can often intervene successfully to arrest the current of unreflective event and divert it to provided channels. They drew no fallacious line between the "organic" and the "artificial," for their thinking admitted no such categories. Readers of Plutarch, they were confident of their ability to emulate the achievements of Lycurgus and Solon and leave a nation blessed with a polity moreover which would be superior to all existing polities in that it would be founded upon nature and reason and not upon force or chance.[2] But this being the point of view of the Fathers, it necessarily results that their indebtedness to the past was for ideas rather than for institutions. Whenever therefore they borrow from the past any of the really distinctive features of our constitutional system, for example federalism, checks and balances, judicial review, they will be found to have taken them, not in the form of institutions tested and hammered into shape by practice, but as raw ideas.

The case of judicial review furnishes a particularly good example of the issue between those who, like myself, would insist upon the rationalistic background of American constitutional history and those who would insist upon its institutional background. The exponents of the latter view, pointing out the fact that the colonial legislatures were sometimes in origin merely the directorates of trading companies whose faculties were defined and limited by their charters, attribute to that fact the origin of the American idea of legislative power as limited; and they often adduce in this connection the case of Winthrop v. Lechmere, in which the British Privy Council, in 1728, disallowed a Connecticut enactment on the ground that it transgressed the terms of the colonial charter. The difficulty with this view is, that its advocates feel under no necessity of showing that those who are supposed to have succumbed to the alleged influence knew anything of it. Winthrop v. Lechmere, for instance, —entirely aside from the fact that the Privy Council viewed its action in annulling the Connecticut enactment as legislative rather than judicial,—was

---

1. Still better, see A. Hamilton, *Federalist* No. 9; also J. Adams, *Defense of the Constitutions,* in 4 *Life and Works* 283, 290, 292, 579 (1850–56). Adams is writing of the state constitutions, but his point of view was applicable to the United States Constitution.

2. See 4 Adams 292 footnote; also Melancton Smith in P. L. Ford's *Pamphlets on the Constitution* 109 (1888); also {J?} MacIntosh {Mackintosh?}, *French Revolution* {*Vindiciae Gallicae: Defense of the French Revolution?*} 115 {London 1791}; see also Dickenson on experience and reason, in Madison's Notes of the Convention, August 13.

totally unknown to those who brought about judicial review. And the main proposition rests upon similar ground. It is true that our revolutionary forefathers regarded legislative power as limited; but the legislature they were particularly discussing was Parliament. But, it is urged, that is the very point. The Americans were applying ideas derived from their experience as colonists to the imperial legislature, forgetful or unconscious of the limitation that their source imposed upon the availability of such ideas. There is one circumstance that is fatal to this contention, namely, that the Whig advocates of the American cause in Parliament itself, including in their number the greatest lawyer of the times, Lord Camden, urged the same idea of Parliament's power as limited. Where then did these men get it from? The truth of the matter is, that all the literary evidence goes to establish the idea of legislative power as limited upon a foundation entirely independent of American colonial history, upon the foundation, to-wit, of the idea of *fundamental law.* This idea reaches back far beyond Magna Carta; it furnishes the basis of Parliament's argument against the pretensions of the Stuarts, and Locke's justification of the Glorious Revolution of 1688. It is still strong in England, even at the moment the passage of the Declaratory Act gave expression to the antagonistic but relatively modern idea of Parliament's power as unlimited.[3]

The literary evidence with reference to the basis of judicial review is equally definite. All the law and doctrine upon that topic goes back finally to Coke's famous dictum in Dr. Bonham's case:[4] "and it appears in our books, that in many cases, the common law will control acts of Parliament and sometimes adjudge them to be utterly void; for when an act of Parliament is against common right and reason, . . . the common law will control it, and adjudge such act to be void." Coke proceeds to cite examples and precedents to confirm his utterance, and recent investigation shows that his use of these was well justified.[5] But, it is a more noteworthy fact still that reiterations of the dictum by Coke's successors on the bench, and by commentators, had given to it, by the middle of the eighteenth century, all of the character of established law. Thus Lord Hobart, some years after, wrote as follows:[6] "Even an act of Parliament made against natural equity . . . is void in itself"; and a quarter century later Lord Holt is reported as saying,[7] "What my Lord Coke says in Dr. Bonham's case . . . is far from any extravagancy, for it is a very reasonable

3. For a statement of the view combated in the text, see B. Adams, 54 *Atlantic Monthly* 610 ff. (1884); also Borgrand, *The Rise of Modern Democracy* (1894). On Winthrop v. Lechmere, see 1 J. B. Thayer, *Cases on Constitutional Law* 34–39 (1895); also B. Coxe, *Judicial Power and Unconstitutional Legislation* 211–13, 370–82 (1893). On the subject of fundamental law, see ch. 2 above; also C. H. McIlwain, *The High Court of Parliament and Its Supremacy* ch. 2 and references (1910).

4. 8 Coke 107, 118.

5. McIlwain, ch. 4.

6. Day v. Savage, Hobart 85a.

7. City of London v. Wood, 12 Modern Reports 687.

and true saying, that if an act of Parliament should ordain that the same person should be party and judge . . . it would be a void act of Parliament.'' The law thus laid down finds statement in Bacon's *Abridgement,* first published in 1735; in Viner's *Abridgment,* published 1741–51, from which Otis later quoted; and in Comyn's *Digest,* 1762–67, but written some twenty years earlier.[8]

"Coke Lyttleton" wrote Jefferson many years later with reference to the period preceding the Revolution, "was then the universal law book of students and a sounder Whig never wrote, nor one of profounder learning in the orthodox doctrines of the British constitution or what is called British rights.'' Coke's perceptible influence in the colonies, however, goes back to a much earlier period, and we read that in 1688 "the men of Massachusetts did much quote Lord Coke.'' Earlier still in the case of Giddings v. Brown,[9] Coke's dictum received practical application,—which it never did in England—though the act overturned was merely a town meeting vote. A Massachusetts town had voted its minister a dwelling and with that end in view had imposed a tax, for his refusal to pay which plaintiff had had his goods distrained. Magistrate Symonds based his judgment for plaintiff upon the following grounds: "The fundamental law which God and nature has given to the people cannot be infringed. The right of property is such a right. In this case the goods of one man were given to another without the former's consent. This resolve of the town being against fundamental law, is therefore void, and the taking was not justifiable.'' This decision is interesting not only as the earliest hint of judicial review in America, but also as affording the earliest statement that I at any rate have seen, of the proverb which may be regarded as the "folk-origin,'' so to speak, of American constitutional law, that "the property of A cannot be given to B without A's consent.'' Writing in 1759, Cadwalader Colden[10] makes casual reference to a "judicial power of declaring them [laws] void.'' This does not prove however, I think, that there actually was anything like judicial review in the American colonies; the reference is almost certainly to Coke's dictum.

The opening event in American constitutional history is James Otis' argument in the Writs of Assistance case at Boston in February, 1761. "Then and there,'' wrote John Adams, long afterwards, "the child Independence was born.'' He might well have added, that then and there American constitutional theory was born. The question at issue was whether the British customs officials, one Paxton in particular, should be furnished with general search warrants enabling them to search for smuggled goods. The application was opposed for the Boston merchants by Thacher and Otis. Thacher contented

8. Quincy, Early Massachusetts Reports, Note to Paxton's Case 520 ff.; to be found also in 1 Thayer 48 ff.; see also 1 W. Blackstone, *Commentaries* 91.

9. Reinsch, "Colonial Common law," 1 *Select Essays in Anglo-American Legal History* 376 (1907–9).

10. 2 New York Historical Society Collections 204. See also Chalmers, *Political Annals,* 1 New York Historical Collections 81 (1868). See also Chalmers, *Colonial Opinions* 373–82 (1814).

himself with denying that such a writ as was asked for was warranted by any act of Parliament and, more particularly, that the court to whom the application had been made had authority in the premises. Otis, on the other hand, plunged at once into the most fundamental issues.[11] His argument was essentially this, that whether such writs were warranted by act of Parliament or not, was a matter of indifference, since such act of Parliament would be "against the Constitution" and "against natural equity" and therefore void. "If an act of Parliament should be made in the very words of this petition, it would be void. The executive courts must pass such acts into disuse."[12] The great importance of Otis' argument is that it brought Coke's dictum forward at a moment when it was sure to draw to itself widespread popular attention. In 1765, Governor Hutchinson, referring to the opposition to the Stamp Act, wrote as follows: "The prevailing reason at this time is that the act of Parliament is against Magna Carta, and the natural rights of Englishmen, and therefore, according to Lord Coke, null and void." Otis repeated his argument more than once, as did also his reporter, John Adams. As late as 1776, at the outbreak of war, Justice Cushing charged a Massachusetts jury to ignore certain acts of Parliament as void and inoperative and was congratulated by Adams for so doing.[13]

Meantime, the doctrine of Otis' argument had spread abroad and had been extended to other issues. I have in mind particularly George Mason's argument in the case of Robin v. Hardaway,[14] which arose in Virginia in 1772 and was reported by Thomas Jefferson. The plaintiffs in this action, Mason's clients, were descendants of Indian women who had been brought into Virginia at various times by traders and sold as slaves under an act of assembly passed in 1682. Mason developed his argument under four headings, the first of which comprised the thesis that the act "was originally void itself, because it was contrary to natural right." "If natural right, independence, defective representation, and disavowal of protection, are not sufficient to keep them from the coercion of our laws, on what other principles," Mason inquired, "can we justify our opposition to some late acts of power exercised over us by the British legislature? Yet they only pretended to impose on us a paltry tax in money; we on our free neighbors, the yoke of perpetual slavery. Now all acts of the legislature apparently contrary to natural right and justice are, in our laws, and must be, in the nature of things, considered as void. The laws of nature are the laws of God; whose authority can be superseded by no power on earth. . . . All human constitutions which contradict their law, we are in con-

---

11. 2 Adams *Life and Works* 521–25.
12. Note the term "executive courts." In connection with the doctrine that the courts might declare an act of Parliament void, it is important to recall that the royal dispensing power, while acknowledged to extend to statutes, stopped short at the common law. The old distinction between *mala in se* and *mala prohibita* is also important in the same connection. McIlwain, at 310 ff.
13. See note 7, above.
14. Jeff. 109 (Va.).

science bound to disobey. Such have been adjudications of our courts of justice." Mason concludes by citing Coke and Hobart. The court adjudged the act of 1682 repealed.

But Coke's dictum supplies only the original basis of the doctrine of judicial review; its later basis is supplied by the written constitution.[15] The argument for judicial review within the written constitution as stated by Hamilton in the *Federalist* No. 78, less satisfactorily by Marshall in Marbury v. Madison,[16] and by the Virginia judges at great length in Kamper v. Hawkins[17] rests upon the following propositions: first, that the Constitution emanates from the people and is fundamental; secondly, that a legislative enactment emanates from mere agents of the people; thirdly, that the Constitution is a law and as such is enforceable by the courts. The historical evaluation of such an argument is a matter of difficulty, since it compels an endeavor to draw with precision the line between the contemporary meaning of the terms used and their meaning as used in the argument. This difficulty inheres, of course, in any attempt to give an historical account of institutions. For, as Bagehot puts it, "Language is the tradition of nations; each generation describes what it sees but it uses words transmitted from the past." But in a case like that before us the difficulty is even greater, for it is this very capacity of words to take on new meanings without alteration of form that constitutes the appeal of the argument we are called upon to deal with.

It is undoubtedly true that from the outset the Constitution was regarded as fundamental, and also as emanating in some sort from the sovereign people, but the two ideas did not then stand in the same relation of effect and cause that they do today. The Constitution was regarded as fundamental, but like the British constitution, on account of its content rather than its source. Also it was regarded as emanating from the people, but from the sovereign people in extraordinary and revolutionary assemblage, casting off all existing political ties and creating society anew. But that society once set agoing, where then were the sovereign people, save on election days, if not in the legislature, which in these early state constitutions *was practically omnipotent?* Nor did this assumption involve the notion necessarily that the legislature could change the constitution. As the Massachusetts Circular Letter[18] had asserted with reference to Parliament under the British constitution, it was indeed sovereign but only upon the basis of the constitution that made it so, wherefor it could not alter

15. See Morey, 9 {Annals} *Am. Academy of Social and Political Science* 398 ff.; also Davis, *J. H. Univ. Studies*, 32d series, at 473 ff.; 7 F. N. Thorpe, *American Charters, Constitutions and Organic Laws*, especially the first Virginia Bill of Rights and ensuing constitution, 3812ff. (1909).

16. 1 Cranch 137 (1803).

17. 1 Va. Cas. 20.

18. W. MacDonald, *Documentary Source Book* 148 (1908). The indebtedness of the phraseology of this document to Vattel is evident: see above, ch. 2. {The chapter reference seems to be to Corwin's work in preparation, *The Growth of Judicial Review*.}

that constitution "without destroying the basis of its own existence." Of course, it would have been quite logical, on the basis of Coke's dictum, for judicial review to have been retained as one way of keeping legislative power within the now written constitution, but the evidence is that it was for the time being dropped, the point of view of the revolutionary state constitutions being exactly that the legislative power, with its direct accountability to the people, was the securest possible defense of the constitution and of the rights secured therein. And should a breach of the constitution occur, there were still the ballot-box, the right of petition, a council of Censors perhaps, and ultimately that very ancient right, going back to Magna Carta itself, the right of revolution.

But it was also urged, that the legislature comprises only the representatives of the people and that their acts are therefore only the acts of the agents of the people, while the Constitution is the act of the sovereign people themselves. To this statement two observations are pertinent. In the first place, as we have seen, the original sovereign people had passed out of existence, save as a highly artificial concept, little able to hold its own alongside the palpable substantiality of the legislature; and although the constitutional convention was gradually coming into use as a part of constitutional machinery to lend this artificial concept reality once more, it was, previous to the establishment of judicial review, itself only in the process of establishment and therefore hardly a fact to base an argument upon very securely.[19] But in the second place, if the legislature was only representative of the people and not the people themselves, legally speaking, how of the courts? Hamilton's argument upon this point is as follows: "If it be said that the legislative body are themselves the constitutional judges of their own powers, and that the construction they put upon them is conclusive upon the other departments, it may be answered, that this cannot be the natural presumption where it is not to be collected from any particular provisions in the Constitution. . . . It is far more rational to suppose that the courts were designed to be an intermediate body between the people and the legislature in order, among other things, to keep the latter within the limits assigned to their authority." But *was* it more rational in 1787 to suppose this? It is hardly necessary to say that this was not the point of view embodied in the early state constitutions, whether considered as to their "particular provisions" or in their entirety.

But the advocate of judicial review went on to contend, that the interpretation of the law was the exclusive function of the court and that the Constitution was

---

19. As to the novelty of the Constitutional Convention in 1789 {*sic;* 1787?}, see Ellsworth's testimony in Madison's Notes, July 23. One this and allied topics, see an excellent article by W. F. Dodd, {"The First State Constitutional Conventions,"} 2 *Am. Pol. Sci. Rev.* 545–61 (1908). As to the early identification of the Constitution with a social compact, emanating from a society which had been dissolved by revolution into its constituent elements, see particularly the opinions of the judges in Kamper v. Hawkins, above.

law. But again he assumed the existence of unwonted distinctions and attributed to words a definiteness of meaning that had not hitherto belonged to them. One of the principal objections raised against the early state constitutions from 1780 on was that, contrary to Montesquieu's maxim, all the powers of government were available to the legislature.[20] But that being the case, suppose it granted that the judiciary might on occasion interpret the Constitution, yet that fact would not have operated to withdraw the final interpretation from the legislature, which repeatedly set aside judicial interpretations of the ordinary statutes. But furthermore, *was* direct interpretation of the Constitution a judicial function at all? It is upon this point that most of the argument between the advocate and opponent of judicial review occurred. The advocate argued, that it was, because the Constitution was the law, that is, law in the strict sense of a body or source of rules enforceable by the courts. The argument turns out, upon inspection, to be a mere begging of the question, a proposition identical with the one to be established.[21] For if it was an item of judicial power to interpret the Constitution without legislative intervention, then the Constitution was a body of rules directly enforceable by the courts; and if the Constitution was such a body of rules, then to interpret them, whether finally or not, was a judicial function. The fact of the matter is, that the establishment of judicial review gave the Constitution the character of law, though there was still long discussion as to what portions of it the courts could take cognizance of ere the legislature had acted upon them and put them into operation; and the fact also is that the establishment of judicial review marked a step in the establishment of the distinction between the people, organized in constitutional convention, as the supreme legislative power, and the ordinary legislature as a popular agency merely and therefore subordinate; and finally it marked a similar step with reference to legislative power and judicial power; but none of these subsequent developments, it is evident, was fairly available as a premise of the argument from which, in point of historical fact, they are all deductions. On the other hand, I would not have the fact that unhistorical assumptions underlay the argument for judicial review within the written constitution misinterpreted; for exactly the same thing was true of the counter-argument. The truth is that, when the issue over judicial review was first joined, there were a number of notions on hand which were comparatively undefined and which consequently each side was more or less free to define to suit itself. It was for time alone to determine which side's definitions were to survive to become incorporated in institutions.

The first authenticated case, and indeed the only one anterior to the Constitutional Convention in 1787, in which a court ventured to refuse enforcement to a legislative enactment on the ground that it conflicted with the

20. See particularly Jefferson, *Notes on Virginia: 2 Writings* 160–78 (Memorial ed. 1903).
21. Article VI of the Constitution, to which Hamilton makes slanting reference, makes the Constitution supreme law only for the state judges. See below.

provisions of the written constitution is that of Holmes v. Walton,[22] which was argued before the Supreme Court of New Jersey, November, 1779. The New Jersey legislature had the year previous passed a statute, with the purpose of preventing trade with the enemy, which authorized the seizure of all goods in transit to or from the British lines and provided that all actions resulting from such seizures should be tried before a jury of six men. Section 22 however of the Constitution of 1776 stipulated ". . . that the inestimable right of trial by jury shall remain confirmed as part of the law of this colony without repeal forever." It is interesting to note as evidence that the idea of judicial review had not occurred to those who drafted the New Jersey constitution three years before, the fact that they relied for the preservation of this,—as they evidently esteemed it—most fundamental provision of the constitution upon the good faith of the legislature, it being required by the final section of the constitution that every member of that body should take an oath not to assent to any law, vote, or proceeding, to repeal or annul "that part of the twenty-second section respecting the trial by jury." But now, *had* the legislature repealed this section by providing a jury of six in lieu of the old common law jury of twelve; and if it had, was the court authorized to refuse to enforce the objectionable statute? These were the questions before the court, questions which it took ten months—two terms—to ponder over before answering. Ultimately though, on September 7, 1780, the court ordered judgment for the plaintiff. Unfortunately the opinions rendered by the judges have been lost, but all things considered, it seems highly probable that a petition presented a few weeks later to the House of Assembly from "sixty inhabitants of the county of Monmouth," and complaining that the justices of the supreme court have set aside some of the laws as unconstitutional and made void the proceedings of the magistrates, though strictly agreeable to the said laws, to the encouragement of the disaffected and great loss to the loyal citizens of the state, and praying redress," stated the grounds of the decision accurately. Moreover that the judges would nullify the statute seems to have been prevised some months before the court ventured to make its decision public. For on the very day following the argument of the case, November 12, 1779, a member of the council "obtained leave to bring in a bill amending the " 'Seizure Act.' " To this attempt at amendment the assembly at first offered strong opposition, but ultimately a compromise measure was passed, not requiring, but only empowering, the court of first instance to grant a jury of twelve men. From the standpoint of

22. See article by Austin Scott in *Am. Hist.* (1 *Rev.*: vol. 4, pp. 456169 {*sic*}). See also article by Professor Trent in the same review, vol. 1, at 444 ff., with reference to the case of Josiah Phillips. Professor Trent's attempt to establish the importance of this case fails. Compare 3 Elliot's *Debates* 66–67, 140; 298–99. Slavery was in effect abolished in Massachusetts by judicial decisions in assault and battery actions and the like in the course of the years 1781 to 1793. These decisions, however, were based upon the assumption that the laws authorizing the servile detentions had been repealed by the Constitution of 1780. See G. H. Moore, *Notes on the History of Slavery in Massachusetts* 200–223 (1866).

the necessities of the case, the judges must be deemed to have acted with a good deal of pedantry in Holmes v. Walton, and from the standpoint of present-day constitutional law the assembly, rather than they, was right in its construction of the constitution. The case is none the less an historical landmark, though how far its contemporary fame spread is very uncertain. Five years later Gouverneur Morris, in an address to the Pennsylvania legislature, the aim of which was to dissuade that body from repealing the charter of the National Bank, wrote thus, with palpable reference to this case.[23] "A law was once passed in New Jersey which the judges pronounced unconstitutional and therefore void. Surely no good citizen can wish to see this point decided in the tribunals of Pennsylvania. Such power in judges is dangerous; but unless it somewhere exists, the time employed in framing a bill of rights or form of government is merely thrown away." On the other hand we have certain evidence that Holmes v. Walton was unknown in Rhode Island, as late as 1786.[24]

Between the years 1780 and 1786 the idea of judicial review within the written constitution was broached before a judicial tribunal only once, namely, in the case of Commonwealth v. Caton,[25] which was decided by the Virginia Court of Appeals in November, 1782. The act in question was the so-called Treason Act of 1776. Randolph, attorney general, argued for the commonwealth that whether "the act of assembly pursued the spirit of the constitution" or not, "the court was not authorized to declare it void." The act was upheld but the judges were generally of the opinion that if they had found it to be in conflict with the constitution they would have had power to pronounce it void. "If the whole legislature," declared the learned Wythe, with characteristic vehemence, "if the whole legislature, an event to be deprecated, should attempt to overleap the bounds prescribed to them by the people, I, in administering the public justice of the country, will meet the united powers at my seat at this tribunal, and pointing to the constitution, will say to them, here is the limit of your authority, and hither shall you go, but no further." Pendleton was not so sure: "It has been very properly said," he observed, "...that this act declaring the rights of the citizens and forming their government...must be considered as a rule obligatory upon every department, not to be departed from on any occasion. But how far the court, in whom the judiciary power may in some sort be said to be concentrated, shall have power to declare the nullity of a law passed in its form by the legislative power, *without exercising the power of that branch contrary to the plain terms of the constitution*, is indeed a deep, important, and I will add, a tremendous question,

23. 3 Sparks, *Gouverneur Morris* 438 (1832).
24. See Trevett v. Weeden, below. Varnum in his argument in that case did not mention Holmes v. Walton. It is a case where the argument from silence is conclusive.
25. 4 Call 5 (Va. 1782).

the decision of which might involve consequences to which gentlemen may not have extended their ideas."[26]

The thing that effectively forced general attention to the suggestion of judicial review, as a retarding agency in our constitutional system, was the financial legislation put forth by some of the states in the years 1785 and 1786, considered in connection with which therefore the case of Trevett v. Weeden[27] becomes perhaps, though no statute was overturned by it, of greater actual importance in the history of judicial review than Holmes v. Walton, above. The case arose in Rhode Island in 1786, under an act of the legislature denouncing a penalty of £100 against any one who should refuse paper money at its face value in exchange for commodities, and creating a special court of three judges for the trial of complaints against recalcitrant creditors. Weeden, a butcher, fell under the condemnation of the act by having refused a tender of currency by plaintiff for some meat. The latter at once proceeded to action under the statute, but the case, through some inadvertence, was brought, not before the special court of three judges, but before the supreme court. Weeden's counsel Varnum proceeded therefore to base his client's case in part upon the contention that the court did not have jurisdiction, but his main argument, which he elaborated at great length, was that the statute was unconstitutional and void. Trial by jury, he argued, had been secured to every Englishman by Magna Carta and had been established in Rhode Island by the provisions of the charter according the inhabitants all the "liberties . . . of free and natural subjects . . . as if they . . . were born within the realm of England." Of course Rhode Island was now independent, but that did not affect the matter since the colonial charter had become the constitution of the state, which the legislature could not alter "without destroying the basis of their existence." But who in the particular instance was to decide whether the legislature had altered the constitution or not? "Have the judges a power to repeal, to amend, to alter laws, or to make new law?" "God forbid! In that case they would become legislators." "But the judiciary have the sole power of judging of laws . . . and cannot admit any act of the legislature as law which is against the constitution," the judges, though strongly sympathizing with Varnum's argument upon the constitutional point, dismissed the action upon the point of jurisdiction. They did not however by their caution escape censure, for they were promptly cited before the assembly to assign the reasons for their judgment, the tendency of which, it was declared, was "to abolish the legislative authority." The judges pleaded their innocence in the particular case,

---

26. The italics are my own.

27. On Trevett v. Weeden, see J. M. Varnum's pamphlet *Case, Travett against Weeden* (Providence, 1787); 1 Thayer 73–78; Coxe, at 234–48; 1 J. B. McMaster, *History of the People of the United States* 337–39 (1883). McMaster shows that in contemporary opinion, Trevett v. Weeden was regarded as a genuine case of judicial review. For a reference to Trevett v. Weeden in the Convention of 1787, see Madison's Notes, July 17.

though some of them were candid enough to reveal their true sentiments, in consequence of which three of them failed of reappointment the following year. Trevett v. Weeden was often alluded to in the Constitutional Convention and the illustration it afforded of the feebleness of the state judiciaries in the face of legislative hostility furnished the strongest argument for the provision eventually made for appeal in constitutional cases from state courts to the United States Supreme Court.

But Trevett v. Weeden is important in another connection also: it is a transitional case. Ostensibly Varnum bases his argument upon the Rhode Island charter, which he pretends to treat as the written constitution of the state, but actually, in order to bring the document to bear upon the matter he is arguing, he goes far afield into the history of "British liberties," resorting to both Coke and Locke, to supply it the desired content. In form, his argument is, in main, an argument for judicial review under the written constitution, but in effect, it is an argument for judicial review upon the basis of such portion of the *fundamental law* as the court may deem to have found recognition in the written constitution. And indeed Coke's dictum was still very much alive. In the Symsbury Case,[28] which arose in 1784, in Connecticut,—which interestingly enough also still retained its colonial charter with slight modification,—we have a genuine case of judicial review of the earlier type, a later grant of land by the legislature being set aside in the interest of an earlier similar grant of the same parcel, upon the ground that "the act of the general assembly . . . could not legally operate to curtail the land before granted." An interesting side light is thrown upon this decision by a remark of Ellsworth in the Constitutional Convention. "Mr. Ellsworth," Madison records, "contended that there was no lawyer, no civilian, who would not say, that ex post facto laws were of themselves void. It cannot, then be necessary to prohibit them."[29] Since Ellsworth hailed from Connecticut, we may well believe that he had the decision in the Symsbury case in mind.

Furthermore, Coke's dictum found reinforcement about this time from a new source. America was now an independent state or a group of independent states, the responsibility of which under the law of nations must be ascertained and maintained. The law of nations however, at this epoch, rested largely upon the law of nature. The study of the law of nations therefore conduced not only to fortify earlier researches into the law of nature but conversely to call attention to the law of nations, the legally binding character of which was admitted by courts of the eighteenth century quite universally, as itself a possible limitation upon legislative enactments. On the other hand, however, a counter influence was also coming into play at the same time. Blackstone, with his theory of legislative sovereignty, was gradually superseding Coke as the

28. Kirby 444–47 (Conn.).
29. Madison's Notes, August 22.

universal textbook, with the result that the former's description of Parliament was coming to be applied to the state legislatures. The first clash between the new and the old ideas occurs in Rutgers v. Waddington,[30] the date of which is 1783.

The case was an action of trespass brought by plaintiff under the so-called Trespass Act against defendant, for his occupancy of plaintiff's premises during the late British possession of New York City. The act provided that no defendant in such action should be admitted "to plead in justification any military order or command whatever of the enemy for such occupancy," etc. Defendant's counsel, Alexander Hamilton, and others, adducing the old rule of international law vesting in the conqueror (that is, in this case, the British commander in New York City), the disposal of the rents and profits of the enemy's real property, denied the right of any particular state or nation so to alter or annul any portion of the law of nations as to deprive a foreigner from appealing to it in the courts of that country. The court in its opinion in favor of plaintiff asserts the supremacy of the legislature in the strongest terms but at the same time manages to evade the operation of the statute in this particular case. "The supremacy of the legislature," runs the court's opinion, "need not be called into question; if they think *positively* to enact a law, there is no power which can control them. When the main object of such a law is clearly expressed and the intention manifest, the judges are not at liberty, although it appears to them *unreasonable,* to reject it; for this were to set the *judicial* above the *legislative* which would be subversive of all government"—all of which, of course, is straight from Blackstone. "But," the court continues, "when a law is expressed in *general words* and some *collateral matter* which happens to arise from those general words is *unreasonable,* then the judges are in decency to conclude that the consequences were not foreseen by the legislature, and therefore they are at liberty to expound the statute by *equity* and only *quoad hoc* to disregard it." As may be surmised, this rather disingenious {disingenuous?} performance called forth protests. Among other things, it was pointed out that the law of nations was the same when the statute was passed as at the time of the action, and that therefore the contention that the legislature did not intend the consequences of its act was scarcely sustainable by candid reasoning. The main emphasis of the protestants however was upon the very issue which the court had endeavored to avoid raising: "That there should be a power vested in courts of judicature whereby they might control the supreme legislative power we think is absurd in itself. Such power in courts would be destructive of liberty and remove all security of property. The design of courts of justice, in our government, from the very nature of their institution, is to *declare* laws, not to *alter* them. Whenever they depart from this design of their institution they confound legislative and judicial powers." Practically too, the decision in

---

30. *Rutgers v. Waddington,* pamphlet (H. B. Dawson ed. 1866); see also 1 Thayer 63–72; and Coxe, 223–33.

Rutgers v. Waddington proved abortive. "Accordingly," says Hamilton, "many suits were brought and many judgments given . . . and many compromises were made, and large sums paid, under the despair of a successful defense."[31]

In one way however, owing to the fact that it had been partly argued upon the basis of the Treaty of 1783, Rutgers v. Waddington was of immense importance. On February 23, 1787, Jefferson wrote John Adams from Paris criticizing the latter for speaking of Congress as a "diplomatic assembly" merely. "Separating into parts," Jefferson argues,[32] "the whole sovereignty of our States, some of these parts are yielded to Congress. Upon these I should think then (Congress) both legislative and executive, and that they would have been judiciary also, had not the Confederation required them for certain purposes to appoint a judiciary. It has accordingly been the decision of our courts that the Confederation is a part of the law of the land, and superior to the ordinary laws, because it cannot be altered by the legislature of any one state. I doubt whether they are at all a diplomatic assembly." Jefferson's reference is to Rutgers v. Waddington, as is made plain by Hamilton's remark just quoted as to the efficacy of that decision, which was meant to disabuse Jefferson of his erroneous impressions as to the purport of that decision. Others, also, however, held the same impression apparently,—whether from Jefferson or not. At any rate, on March 21st, 1787, Congress voted resolutions in which they declared: first, that the legislatures of the several states could not of right pass any acts for construing, limiting, or impeding the operations of, the national treaties which "become in virtue of the confederation, part of the law of the land and are not only independent of the will and power of such legislation but also binding and obligatory on them''; secondly, that all such acts repugnant to any such treaty ought to be forthwith repealed; and thirdly, that such repeal should be in general terms, in order that "the courts of law and equity" in all causes wherein such acts were by their terms operative might decide according to the true meaning and intent of the treaty, said act or acts "to the contrary thereof in anywise notwithstanding." Some three weeks later (April 13th, 1787), Congress embodied these resolutions in a circular letter to the various states, in which the following words occur: "Our national Constitution having committed to us the management of the national concerns with foreign states and powers, it is our duty to take care that all the rights which they ought to enjoy within our jurisdiction by the laws of nations and the faith of treaties remain inviolable . . . when therefore a treaty is constitutionally made, ratified, and published by us, it becomes binding on the whole nation, and superadded to the laws of the land without the intervention of the state legislatures . . ."[33] The importance of the circular letter we shall discover in a moment.[34]

31. 5 Hamilton, *Works* 116, 7 *Works* 198 (Lodge's ed. 1904)
32. 6 *Writings* 98 (Mem. ed. 1903).
33. 12 Journals of Congress (ed. of 1801), under dates mentioned.
34. In this connection, see also 2 Bancroft, *History of the Constitution* 472 (1882); and 7 *Harv.*

In connection with the Constitutional Convention four questions arise: first, did that body in terms confer upon the federal judiciary the power to pass upon the constitutionality of acts of Congress? secondly, if not, did it yet conceive that that power would belong to the judiciary as an item of judicial power? thirdly, with what intention was article 6, paragraph 2, inserted in the Constitution? fourthly, was it the intention of the framers of the Constitution that appeals should lie from the state courts to the United States Supreme Court?

The answer to the first question is an unqualified negative. The only clause of the Constitution ever adduced directly or indirectly as conferring such a power is the phrase, "cases arising under this Constitution" is article 3, section 2, and this is construed by both Hamilton and Madison in the *Federalist* and by Madison in the Virginia Convention, to signify cases arising under state laws alleged to infringe the Constitution.[35] Any categorical answer to the second question is on the other hand quite impossible. Such discussion on the floor of the convention as touched upon the possibility of the federal judiciary's having the power to review acts of Congress under the Constitution arose in connection with the proposition embodied in the eighth resolution of Randolph's plan, to associate the executive and "a convenient number of the national judiciary to compose a council of revision" of acts of Congress. Gerry opposed this proposition: he thought the judiciary would derive a sufficient check against encroachment from their power of deciding upon the constitutionality of laws and he urged the impropriety of giving the judges a hand in making laws upon the constitutionality of which they should have subsequently perhaps to pass in their judicial capacity,—an argument which was reiterated or applauded at various times by King, Martin, Strong, Charles Pinckney, and Rutledge. On the other hand, of those who championed the idea of a council of revision, Madison, Wilson, and Mason accepted explicitly the idea of judicial review but were disposed to minimize the force of Gerry's objection. "There was weight" in it, Wilson thought, "but this power of the judges did not go far enough. Laws might be unjust . . . destructive, and yet may not be so unconstitutional as to justify the judges in refusing to give them effect"; an argument to which Gerry responded to the effect that the "representatives of the people rather than the judges" should be the "guardians of their rights and interests."[36] There can be no doubt therefore that the idea of judicial review, within narrow limits, and particularly as a weapon of self defense on the part of the courts against

---

L. Rev. 415 ff. (1894). It seems evident that Jefferson's correspondent was in error. Madison apparently was uncertain whether the Articles of Confederation, resting as they did upon the ratification of the state legislatures merely, could be given paramountcy within the states, to the derogation of conflicting state laws. See 1 Elliot 400; also 5 *id.*, 99 and 171. I owe these citations to Coxe.

35. *Federalist*, Nos. 44 and 80 (Lodge ed.); 5 Madison *Writings* 217–18 (Hunt ed. 1900–1910).

36. Follow the discussion in Madison's Notes, under the dates June 4–6 and July 21; see also Madison's speech, June 23.

legislative encroachment, had made considerable headway among the membership of the Constitutional Convention. Further than this, moreover, Pinckney
and Rutledge of South Carolina foresaw that the federal judiciary would be the
"umpire between the United States and the individual states," an idea which is
voiced by Madison in the *Federalist,* and in the state conventions, interestingly
enough by two future chief justices of the United States Supreme Court and one
associate justice, Ellsworth of Connecticut, Marshall of Virginia, and Wilson of
Pennsylvania.[37]

But this is only one side of the question. The debate over the proposed
council of revision also brought out strong expressions of disapprobation of the
idea of judicial review. Bedford of Delaware, a strong state's rights man, but
also,—and quite logically—a strong believer in legislative power, expressed
himself at an early date as "opposed to every check on the legislature, even the
council of revision . . . he thought it would be sufficient to mark out in the
Constitution its boundaries to the legislative authority, which would give all the
requisite security to the rights of the other departments. The representatives of
the people were the best judges of what was for their interest and ought to be
under no external control whatever."[38] Mercer of Maryland was of the same
persuasion: "He disapproved of the doctrine that the judges as expositors of the
Constitution should have authority to declare a law void," a remark which
impressed Dickinson of Delaware strongly. He too "thought no such power
ought to exist. He was at the same time at a loss what expedient to
substitute . . . Mr. Gouverneur Morris suggested the expedient of an absolute
veto in the executive."[39] As the clause "cases under this Constitution" was
inserted in the Constitution less than a fortnight later by unanimous vote of the
Convention, it seems plain that it was not intended or understood to confer
upon the federal judiciary a branch of power which certain members of the
Convention were so loath to admit as adhering to the judicial office.[40]

But there is further evidence, either of disbelief or of only vacillating belief
in judicial review, on the part of members of the Convention. While the
Convention was in session the supreme court of North Carolina, after more
than a year's hesitation, pronounced unconstitutional, in the case of Bayard v.
Singleton,[41] an act of confiscation dating from the Revolution. The counsel for
plaintiff in this action upon whose argument the statute was pronounced void

37. Rutledge, in Madison's Notes, August 27; Pinckney, August 10; Madison, in *Federalist*
No. 39; Wilson, in 2 Elliot's *Debates* 489; Ellsworth, *id.,* 196–97; Marshall, 3 *id.* 553; see also 3
Elliot 205, 324–25.
38. Madison's Notes, June 4.
39. *Id.,* August 15.
40. *Id.,* August 27. See below.
41. 1 Martin 42 (47) (N.C.). The decision is further interesting as resting in part upon a
recognition by the court of the Articles of Confederation as a "part of the law of the land,
unrepealable by any act of the general assembly." This, however, was not the main point upon
which the constitutional question turned. See Chapter VI below. {The chapter reference seems to be
to Corwin's work in preparation, *The Growth of Judicial Review.*}

was James Iredell. His argument had, at the time of its first transpiration, created a furor of criticism from the party, composed both of laymen and layers—and very strong in North Carolina at this time, as we learn—which had come to adopt the theory of legislative sovereignty. Now that Iredell had won his cause, Richard Dobbs Spaight, a North Carolina member of the Federal Convention, took up the cudgels for the defeated cause. Spaight's letter to Iredell, which is dated Philadelphia, August 12, 1787, runs in part as follows: "The late determination of the judges at Newbern must in my opinion produce the most serious reflections in the breast of every thinking man, and of every well wisher to his country . . . I do not pretend to vindicate the law which has been the subject of controversy; it is immaterial what law they have declared void; it is their usurpation of the authority to do it that I complain of, as I do most positively deny that they have any such power; nor can they find anything in the Constitution, either directly or impliedly, that will support that, or give them any color of right to exercise that authority. Besides it would be absurd and contrary to the practice of all the world, had the convention vested such powers in them . . . and the state, instead of being governed by the representatives in general assembly, . . . subject to the will of three individuals, who united in their own persons the legislative and judiciary powers, which no monarch in Europe enjoys. . . . If they possess the power, what check or control would there be to their proceedings, or who would take the same liberty with them that they have taken with the legislature, and declare their opinion to be erroneous?" Iredell's answer of a fortnight later states no new argument for judicial review, but it puts in a single sentence the real reason for it in the minds of its advocates: "In a republican government (as I conceive) *individual liberty* is a matter of the utmost moment, as, if there be no check upon the public passions, it is in the greatest danger."[42]

The great importance of the Constitutional Convention, however, in connection with the development of judicial review, arises from its action in utilizing the idea in solving the problem of federal control over state legislation.[43] Randolph's sixth resolution, taking a page from colonial history, when the mother-country had exercised a similar power over colonial legislation, gave to the national legislature the power "to negative all laws passed by the several states contravening" in its opinion the articles of union, and on May 31, the Convention, sitting in committee of the whole, agreed to this proposition without debate. On June 8, Charles Pinckney went a step farther, moving "that the national legislature should have authority to negative all laws which they should judge to be improper." Madison, instancing "the constant tendency in the states" "to oppress the weaker party within their respective jurisdictions" and urging the necessity in the general government of a prerogative to "control

42. 2 McRee, *Life and Correspondence of James Iredell* 169–76 (1857–58); see also *id.*, 145–49.

43. Follow the discussion in Madison's Notes, under the dates furnished in the text.

the centrifugal tendency of the states," seconded the motion. Wilson too championed the idea: of course the states would object to such control, "federal liberty being to them what civil liberty is to private individuals; and as the savage is unwilling to purchase civil liberty by the surrender of his personal sovereignty in a state of nature, so would the states be unwilling to yield their political sovereignty"; but an effectual control in the whole over its parts had become a necessity. Dickinson of Delaware also was favorable, and possibly the notion would have gone farther had not Dickinson's colleague Bedford begun to point out some objections to its practicability which caused even Madison's enthusiasm to wane. A vote being taken, only Massachusetts, Virginia, and Pennsylvania were affirmative. On June 15, Patterson introduced the "small state plan," the sixth resolution of which, obviously traceable to the circular letter of Congress of the previous April, provided that "all acts of the United States in Congress made by virtue of and in pursuance of the powers hereby . . . vested in them and all treaties made or ratified under the authority of the United States shall be the supreme law of the respective states or their citizens; and that the judiciary of the several states shall be bound thereby in their decisions, anything in the respective laws of the individual states to the contrary notwithstanding." Three days later Hamilton offered his plan, article 10 of which provided that all state laws contrary either to national laws or to the national Constitution should be utterly void, and vested the state governors, who were to be appointed by the general government, with the veto power over state laws.

The question of the national veto came up again July 17th, in connection with the report of the committee of the whole. Morris opposed this power, even within the limits set to it in that report, "as likely to be terrible to the states." It was Sherman however who made the greatest contribution to the discussion. Such a power he thought unnecessary: "The courts of the states would not consider valid any law contravening the authority of the union." Madison was not easily convinced: "Confidence," he said, "cannot be put in the state tribunals as guardians of the national authority and interest. In all the states there are more or less dependent on the legislatures. In Rhode Island the judges who refused to execute an unconstitutional law were displaced and others substituted by the legislature, who would be the willing instruments of the wicked and arbitrary plans of their masters." Sherman reiterated his point: "such a power [of veto] involves a wrong principle, to wit, that a law of a state contrary to the Articles of Union would, if not negatived, be valid and operative." The veto was thereupon voted down three to seven. The proposition embodied in the Paterson plan was then moved by Luther Martin and adopted without a dissenting vote. On August 23rd, on motion of Rutledge of South Carolina, who had opposed the federal veto throughout, the Paterson proposition was given essentially its final form by the insertion of the term "this Constitution," meaning the Constitution of the United States, and the term, "the constitution," meaning {t}he constitution of any state.

But the advocates of a national veto were still dissatisfied; and immediately following the adoption of Rutledge's motion, Pinckney again offered the rejected proposition in a somewhat mitigated form. The usual arguments were forthcoming against the idea; but Wilson urged convincingly that "the firmness of the judges," meaning the state judges, "is not of itself sufficient, something further is requisite." On the motion for commitment the vote stood five to six. Pinckney then withdrew his motion but evidently the sentiment for "something further" was growing. Finally on August 27th, Dr. Johnson of Connecticut, "moved to insert the words 'this Constitution and' before the word 'laws'," in the judiciary article of the report of the committee of detail. The motion "was agreed to *nem. con.*, it being generally supposed that the jurisdiction given was constructively limited to cases of a judiciary nature." Already on the 22nd the Convention had begun the task of formulating specific limitations upon state legislation.[44]

It is at this point that my last question becomes pertinent, namely, was it the intention of the framers that appeals should lie from the highest state courts to the United States Supreme Court, or more precisely, that they should lie from the highest state court to the United States Supreme Court in cases "arising under this Constitution"? Subsequently it was denied that this could have been the case, on the ground, essentially, that such appeals derogated from the sovereignty of the states and from that equality within their sphere which, by the theory of the federal system, they enjoy with the national government. For by this theory, it was argued, Congress must treat the courts of the states as those of coordinate sovereignties and not attempt to vest the national courts with coercive powers over them. The theoretical strength of this argument we shall be able to estimate a little farther on, but historically it had no ground to stand upon. On June 4th, the Convention had taken up the first clause of Randolph's ninth resolution, providing for a national judiciary "to consist of one or more supreme tribunals and of inferior tribunals" and the clause had been adopted unanimously. Next day however Rutledge had moved reconsideration on the ground that the "State tribunals might and ought to be left in all cases to decide in the first instance, the right of appeal to the national tribunal being sufficient to secure national rights and uniformity of judgment." Sherman had seconded the motion while Madison had objected to it, because of his fears of the "biased directions of a dependent judge or local prejudice of an undirected jury." Dickinson and Wilson had been with Madison. Nevertheless Rutledge's motion had carried six to four, a plain triumph for the states rights party. Wilson and Madison had then moved, conformably with an idea dropped by

44. Brinton Coxe arrives at the conclusion, inadmissible as I have shown, that the Constitution confers the power of review of acts of Congress upon the national judiciary. See Coxe 336–42.

Dickinson, that "the national legislature be empowered to institute inferior tribunals" and this motion, leaving the matter to the discretion of Congress, had been carried by a vote of eight to two, only South Carolina and Connecticut voting in the negative. Finally on July 18th, the Convention had adopted this recommendation from the committee of the whole unanimously, Sherman of Connecticut remarking that he "was willing to give the power to the legislature but wished them to make use of the state tribunals whenever it could be done with safety to the general interests."[45]

Nothing could be plainer than the purport of this discussion and of these votes, namely that jurisdiction in the first instance of causes of this kind specified in the Constitution of the United States, with subsequent appeal to the United States Supreme Court, was the maximum concession that was demanded in the Convention by the pro-state party. The evidence of the discussion attending upon the ratification of the Constitution is to the same effect. A principal argument against the Constitution was that the national judiciary would swallow up the state judiciaries and the clause of the Constitution investing the judicial power of the United States "in one Supreme Court and such inferior courts as the Congress shall from time to time ordain and establish" was construed in support of this argument to signify "that the supreme and subordinate courts of the Union should alone have the power of deciding those causes to which their authority is to extend." In *Federalist* 82 Hamilton attacks this construction as affecting an "alienation of the state power by implication" and offers the alternative construction, denoting simply, "that the organs of the national judiciary shall be one supreme court and as many subordinate courts as Congress shall think fit to establish." Thus the state courts are left "their primitive jurisdiction" unimpaired, save that they exercise a portion of it concurrently with the federal judiciary, but, Hamilton proceeds, the necessary consequence of participation by the state courts in the national jurisdiction is that appeals shall lie from those courts to the United States Supreme Court." "The Constitution in direct terms," he contends, "gives an appellate jurisdiction to the Supreme Court in all the enumerated cases of federal cognizance in which it is not to have an original one, without a single expression to confine this operation to the inferior federal courts. The objects of appeal, not the tribunals from which it is to be made, are alone contemplated." Furthermore to deny such appeal would subvert the most serious purposes of the national judicial power.

The judicial power of the United States was set in operation by the Judiciary Act of 1789.[46] By the logic of the act, as by that of Art. III of the Constitution, this power falls into two great classes of cases: those over which jurisdiction is conferred on the United States because of the nature of the questions involved, for example "cases arising under the Constitution"; and those over which

45. For a somewhat fuller discussion of this topic, see Coxe 342–48.
46. 1 Stat. at Large of the United States 73ff. (1789).

jurisdiction is conferred because of the character of the parties interested, for example cases between citizens of different states. Cases of the first class were left by the act to originate in the state tribunals, while by the 25th section appeal was provided to the United States Supreme Court on three occasions: namely, first, where "is drawn in question the validity of a treaty or statute of, or an authority exercised under, the United States, and the decision is against their validity"; secondly, "where is drawn in question the validity of a statute of, or an authority exercised under, any State on the ground of their being repugnant to the Constitution, treaties, or laws of the United States, and the decision is in favor of their validity"; and "thirdly, where is drawn in question the construction of any clause in the Constitution or of a treaty or statute of, or commission held under, the United States, and the decision is against the title, right, privilege, or exemption specially set up or claimed by either party, under such clause of the said Constitution, treaty, statute or commission." In such cases it was provided that the decision of the highest state court might be "reexamined and reversed or affirmed in the Supreme Court of the United States upon a writ of error, the citation being signed by the Chief Justice or judge or chancellor of the court rendering . . . the decree complained of, or by a justice of the Supreme Court of the United States." As is obvious, it is the second class of cases over which jurisdiction was conferred upon the United States in the interest of providing an impartial tribunal. By the Act of 1789 accordingly original jurisdiction in this class of cases, where the matter in dispute should be above $500, was vested in the federal circuit courts concurrently with the state courts, while by the 11th section of the act provision was made for the removal of such causes from the state to the national courts upon petition of defendant. In the debate pending its passage the act was criticized by the pro-state party almost exclusively for its provision of an inferior federal judicature. Except a few admiralty and prize courts, this party urged, the purposes of the Constitution would be amply met by leaving the national jurisdiction to the state courts in the first instance, with an appeal in each case to the United States Supreme Court; and one spokesman of this party, Jackson of Georgia, pointed explicitly to the 11th and 25th sections of the act as harmonizing with this notion.[47] Yet it was this very 25th section which the states rights party was, some twenty-five years later, to attack as particularly reprehensible from a constitutional point of view.

II

In tracing the establishment of judicial review subsequently to the inauguration of the national government it will be important to bear in mind that there are two distinct kinds of judicial review, namely, federal judicial review, or the

47. For the debate in the House, which alone is reported outside McClay's *Journal*, see 1 Annals of Congress 826–66 (Gales & Seaton eds. 1789). For Jackson's speech, see *id*. 845–46.

power of the federal courts to review acts of the state legislatures under the
United States Constitution, and judicial review proper, or the power of the
courts to pass upon the constitutionality of acts of the coordinate legislatures.

That the Judiciary Act of 1789 contemplated, in the mind of its author,
Ellsworth, the exercise of the power of review by the national courts of acts of
Congress can be scarcely doubted, but how far others accepted this view of the
matter it is impossible even to conjecture, so entirely silent upon this point are
the brief records of the debate.[48] Perhaps the first congressional reference to
such a power occurs in the House debate of February 21st, 1791, upon the bill
to establish a national bank. Jackson of Georgia offered the argument that
Congress ought not to adopt a measure which ran the risk of being "defeated
by the judiciary of the United States, who might adjudge it to be contrary to the
Constitution and therefore void," an objection which however Boudinot of
New Jersey and Smith of South Carolina were prompt to convert into an
argument for the measure. Said the former, far from controverting this right in
the judiciary "it was his boast and his confidence. It led him to greater decision
on all subjects of a constitutional nature, when he reflected that if, from
inattention, want of precision or any other defect, he should do wrong, that
there was a power in the government which could constitutionally prevent the
operation of such a measure from affecting his constituents."[49] There can be, I
think, not the least doubt that a steadily developing feeling of unworthiness on
the part of legislatures and a growing disposition to abdicate all final responsibility to the judiciary has been at once a cause and a consequence of the
advancing power of the court among us. It is therefore rather suggestive to
come upon this point of view at so early a date.

But would the courts accept such responsibility? If we are to judge from the
slow and tentative steps by which the Supreme Court of the United States
advanced to occupy the region of power to which legislative emissaries were
inviting it, they were reluctant to do so. On the other hand, the cause of judicial
review was appreciably advanced at this time by a confusion that these same
tentative steps show to have been existing, probably from the outset, but never
so manifestly as now, in the minds of the judges between their official capacity
as judges and their capacity as individuals. In March 1792 Congress passed a
statute for the settlement of certain pension claims against the United States,
which directed the United States courts to pass upon such claims, subject to
review by the secretary of war and by Congress. But immediately the most
serious objections were raised to this statute by the judges themselves. The act
in question, it was urged, either enlarged the power of the circuit courts beyond
constitutional limits by conferring upon them non-judicial powers, or it diminished them unconstitutionally by providing appeals from their determinations to

---

48. {1} Annals of Congress (Gales & Seaton eds. 1789). See index. For the Senate debate,
see Maclay's *Journal, passim* (1890).
    49. See 3 Annals 325–29 (1792).

one of the political branches of the government. As a statement of fact, there is of course no controverting this criticism, but was the fact stated one of which the judges had power to take cognizance? The judges had sworn to support the Constitution, it is true, but then *what* was the Constitution? *where* was it to be found? *whose* reading of it was to prevail? Congress also had sworn to support the Constitution; must it not therefore be deemed alone responsible for its acts? The judges as individuals felt with good reason that Congress had, either intentionally or unintentionally, transcended its powers; but did they know this as judges? It is with such questions as these that, without much conjecture, we can see the circuit judges plying themselves on this "painful occasion"; it is such questions as these that "excited feelings" which they hoped "never to experience again." The course finally taken varied somewhat in the different circuits. In the New York circuit the judges, headed by Chief Justice Jay, decided to execute the law, acting as commissioners. In the North Carolina circuit Iredell and his associates doubted their power to take this course but were not called upon to decide the point. In the Pennsylvania circuit Wilson and his associates flatly declined to proceed under the act in any capacity. Eventually the constitutional question reached the Supreme Court upon the petition of one Hayburn for a writ of mandamus to compel the circuit court of Pennsylvania to enroll the petitioner as a pensioner. Randolph, the attorney general, admitted the power of the court "to refuse to execute, but the unfitness of this occasion," thus suggesting a power in the court to weigh expediency against unconstitutionality. "The court observed," records the reporter, "that they would hold the matter under advisement until next term; but no decision was ever pronounced as the legislature, at an interim session, provided in another way for the relief of the pensioners."[50]

In the years following the Hayburn case, the Supreme Court seems to have been pretty well agreed as to its duty to refuse enforcement to an unconstitutional act of Congress, and indeed as to its power to pronounce such an act void. Yet one skeptic there still remained, Justice Samuel Chase, who became associate justice in 1796. That same year the Court was asked to pronounce a congressional tax upon carriages a direct tax, and since it was not apportioned in accordance with the constitutional rule for direct taxes, unconstitutional and void. In his opinion, which was at one with the rest of the Court upon the immediate issue, Chase touched upon the larger constitutional question thus: "As I do not think the tax on carriages is a direct tax, it is unnecessary at this time for me to determine whether this court *constitutionally* possesses the power to declare an act of congress *void* on the ground of its being contrary to . . . the Constitution, but if the court have such power, I am free to declare, that I will never exercise it but in a *very clear case*."[51] A short time afterward

50. 2 Dall. 409 (1792). For the circuit court's disposition of the matter see the note to the case in the L. Ed. of the Reports, Bk. I, 436, note 2.
51. Hylton v. United States, 3 Dall. 171 (1796).

Chase reiterates the same sentiment with reference to a treaty of the United States,[52] and two years later is evidently still of the same view. Finally in 1800 in his opinion in Cooper v. Telfair[53] he reluctantly capitulates "to the general sentiment" of bench and bar. His statement is notable particularly as attributing the power to review acts of Congress not to the federal judiciary generally, but only to the Supreme Court. Three years later, in Marbury v. Madison,[54] the Supreme Court for the first time pronounced a congressional enactment unconstitutional and void. The Court had at last given authoritative form to its pretensions. So far as lay within its power it had established its right to pass upon the constitutionality of acts of Congress—by assuming that right. The question was now, would Congress acquiesce in its pretensions?

The election of 1800 gave the Jeffersonian Republicans possession of the political branches of the general government, but the judiciary with its life tenure remained Federalist. And what was still more exasperating, one of the last acts of the late administration had been to put through a law which, while it reduced the number of judges of the Supreme Court to the existing number of Federalist incumbents, enlarged the number of national district courts from seven to twenty-three, grouped into six circuits, which courts were of course promptly filled up with Federalists also.[55] How distasteful this measure was to the incoming administration is easily conceivable. "They have retired into the judiciary as a stronghold," wrote Jefferson to Dickinson, in December, 1801. "There the remains of federalism are to be preserved and fed from the Treasury, and from that battery all the works of republicanism are to be beaten down and destroyed."[56] In his message of the same month, Jefferson conveyed the hint for the repeal of the obnoxious measure, and a month later Breckenridge of Kentucky introduced the necessary resolution in the Senate.[57] The debate following, which consumed a month's time in each House, underwent an interesting evolution. At the outset the necessity of the new courts furnished the principal topic of discussion; more and more, however, the constitutional question came to the fore, until at the close the assertion of certain constitutional principles furnished, in certain quarters at least, a leading purpose of the repeal finally voted.[58]

The Constitution provides that "the judicial power of the United States *shall* be vested in one supreme court and in such inferior courts as the congress may from time to time ordain and establish"; it authorizes Congress "to constitute tribunals inferior to the Supreme Court;" it provides that "the judges both of

52. Ware v. Hylton, 3 Dall. 199 (1796); Calder v. Bull, 3 Dall. 386 (1798).
53. 4 Dall. 14 (1800).
54. {1} Cranch 137 (1803).
55. 1 H. Adams, *History of the United States* 274 (1889–91).
56. *Id.,* 257.
57. {11} Annals 15–16, 23 (1802).
58. *Id.,* 25–185, 510–985.

the supreme and inferior courts, shall hold their offices during good behavior."[59] From these clauses of the Constitution it is that the debate on the constitutional question set out. On the one hand, the Federalists contended that, since Congress cannot remove a judge save by the process of impeachment, it could not take his office away from him, since to do so was to effect by indirection what cannot be done directly. The Republicans admitted the premises of this argument, but they denied the conclusion. Undoubtedly, they said, a judge is irremovable so long as his office continues, but when the office is abolished the judge ceases being judge by that fact. Can Congress then abolish the inferior federal courts? No, said the Federalists, for once an inferior court is created, it is established by the Constitution and is brought under the aegis of the Constitution as truly as the Supreme Court itself; becomes, in other words, part and parcel of the judicial department in which the judicial power of the United States "*shall* be vested." This argument the Republicans contradicted flatly: the inferior courts are established by acts of Congress and Congress may repeal an act establishing inferior courts as freely as it may repeal any other act, for example, an act establishing an executive bureau. The trend of the discussion soon became evident. What you are asking for, said the Republicans to their opponents, is a degree of independence for the judiciary such as is not to be found even in the British constitution, upon which our Constitution is at this point modelled. The Federalists admitted the charge. The judiciary, they asserted, is in no way subject or subordinate to the legislative department save such subordination, as for example, in the matter of appeals to the Supreme Court, be explicitly stipulated in the Constitution. The spirit of the Constitution is totally contrary to such subordination, and for this reason: the Constitution contemplates the existence in the Federal judiciary of the power to keep Congress within its constitutional limits, for the exercise of which power, there must be predicated of the judicial department the completest equality in all its branches with Congress.[60]

The gauntlet was down: would the Republicans take it up? Breckenridge soon showed that they would. "I did not expect," he began,

> to find the doctrine of the power of the courts to annul the laws of Congress as unconstitutional so seriously insisted on. I presume I shall not be out of order in replying to it. It is said that the different departments of government are to be checks on each other and that the courts are to check the legislature. If this be true, I would ask where they got that power and who checks the courts when they violate the Constitution? Would they not by this doctrine have the absolute direction of the government? . . . I deny the power which is so pretended. If it is derived from the Constitution, I ask gentlemen to point out the clause which

59. Art. III, sec. 1; Art. I, sec. 8, par. 9.

60. The principal exponents of the Republican point of view were Breckenridge of Virginia and Baldwin of Georgia in the Senate and Giles and Randolph of Virginia in the House. The leading Federalist debaters were Ross of Pennsylvania in the Senate and Bayard of Delaware in the House.

grants it. . . . Is it not truly astonishing that the Constitution, in its abundant care to define the powers of each department should have omitted so important a power as that of the courts to nullify all acts of Congress which, in their opinion, were contrary to the Constitution. . . . To make the Constitution a practical system this pretended power . . . cannot possibly exist. My idea . . . is that the Constitution intended a separation of the powers vested in the three departments, giving to each exclusive authority on the subjects committed to it; that these departments are coordinate and revolve each within the sphere of its own orbit, without being responsible for its own motion, and are not to direct or control the course of others; that those who make the laws are presumed to have an equal attachment to, and interest in, the Constitution, and are equally bound by oath to support it; and have an equal right to give a construction to it; that the construction of one department of the powers vested in it, is of higher authority than the construction of any other department; and that, in fact, it is competent to that department to which powers are confided exclusively to decide upon the proper exercise of those powers; that therefore the legislature have the exclusive right to interpret the Constitution in what regards the law making power, and the judges are bound to execute the laws they make. . . . Although therefore the courts may take upon them to give decisions which impeach the constitutionality of a law and thereby, for a time, obstruct its operation, yet I contend that such a law is not the less obligatory because the organ through which it is to be executed has refused its aid. A pertinacious adherence of both departments to their opinions would soon bring the question to issue, in whom the sovereign power of legislation resided, and whose constructions of the law-making power should prevail. . . . I ask, . . . if gentlemen are prepared to admit, and in case the courts were to declare your revenue, impost, and appropriation laws unconstitutional, that they would thereby be blotted out of your statute book and the operations of government be arrested? It is making, in my mind, a mockery of the high powers of legislation. I feel humbled by the doctrine and enter my protest against it.[61]

No sooner had Breckenridge finished than Gouverneur Morris was on his feet. "I arise to congratulate this house and all America," he exclaimed melodramatically,

that we have at length got our adversaries upon the ground where we can fairly meet. They have now, though late, reached the point to which their arguments tended from the beginning. Here I knew they must arrive, and now I ask, if gentlemen are prepared to establish one consolidated government over this country? Sir, if the doctrine they advance prevail, if it be that of the Union. . . . The honorable member tells us the legislature have the supreme and exclusive right to interpret the Constitution so far as regards the making of laws, which being made, the judges are bound to execute. And he asks where the judges got their pretended power of deciding on the constitutionality of laws? . . . I answer, they derived power from authority higher than the Constitution. They derive it from the constitution of man, from the nature of things, from the necessary progress of human affairs. When you have enacted a law, when process thereon has been issued, and suit brought, it becomes eventually necessary that the judges decide on the case before them, and declare what the law is. . . . This, sir, is the principle and the source of the right for which we contend. But it is denied; and the supremacy of the legislature insisted upon. Mark then, I pray, the results. The

61. {11} Annals 178–80 (1802).

Constitution says, no bill of attainder or ex post facto law shall be passed.... Suppose that, notwithstanding these prohibitions, a majority of the two Houses should, with the President, pass such laws.... The courts dependent on the will and pleasure of the legislature, are compelled to enforce (them).... Examine then the state to which we are brought. If this doctrine be sustained ... what possible mode is there to avoid the conclusion that the moment the legislature of the Union declare themselves supreme, they become so? The analogies so often assumed to the British Parliament will then be complete. The sovereignty of America will no longer reside in the people, but in Congress. And the Constitution is whatever they choose to make it.

And with what result?

While I was far distant from my country, I felt pain at some things which looked like a wish to wind up the general government beyond its natural tone; for I knew, *that if America should be brought under one consolidated government, it could not continue to be a republic.* I am attached to republican government, because it appears to me favorable to dignity of sentiment and character.... But if a consolidated government be established, it cannot long be republican. We have not the materials to construct even a mild monarchy. If therefore the states be destroyed, we must become the subjects of despotism.[62]

In the debate that followed upon this rather paradoxical colloquy, between a states-rights Republican urging the sovereignty of the national legislature and a Federalist advocating the the necessity of judicial review in the interest of states rights, a certain few facts stand forth prominently. In the first place, it is evident that even among Republicans, the power of the Supreme Court was regarded very often as an established fact, while Federalists characterized the opposing doctrine as "monstrous and unheard of." Also it is evident that the necessity of judicial review was by no means an exclusively Federalist persuasion. The French Revolution was still of too recent memory not to make it seem possible even to those whose political creed was trust in the people that the time might come, when to have the judges in a position to "save society from itself" would be rather desirable.[63] Finally, to many of both parties, the doctrine of a legislature sovereign within the Constitution was a sealed book. This was revealed particularly by the treatment that Randolph's argument on the constitutionality of the resolution received. With rare candor, Randolph admitted that if the object of the repeal was to get rid of the judges rather than the courts, it was unconstitutional; that the whole question was, with what intention was the repeal being made,—an argument which was received by his opponents with scorn and by his friends with coldness.[64] In short, the idea of a sovereign legislature setting limits to its own action in accordance with the moral duty of its members was too abstruse. Much easier, much more obvious,

62. *Id.* 180–82.
63. *Id.* 529, Henderson of North Carolina speaking: Baldwin of Georgia and Bacon of Massachusetts are good examples of Republicans who accepted judicial review: see latter's remarks at 982.
64. *Id.* at 658.

was the idea of somebody standing outside the legislature with power to censure its acts. The final outcome of the debate was twofold. On the one hand, the act of repeal was passed by the full Republican majority and the dependence of the courts, in the last analysis, upon congressional opinion was proved beyond contradiction. On the other hand, congressional opinion was shown to be, substantially, even overwhelmingly, on the side of the notion of judicial review, and it was morally assured that any overt attack upon the judiciary would find some of the staunchest supporters of the administration in opposition.

Nevertheless, the judiciary was not yet out of peril. Indeed all the outward signs of victory lay with the enemy. Nor was that enemy sated, nor even satisfied, with his triumph. Sixteen circuit courts had been swept away, but the very citadel of judicial pretensions, the Supreme Court, still remained essentially intact. In command of this citadel, moreover, was John Marshall, the eternal enemy of Thomas Jefferson, and within its walls was to be found, who could doubt, the exact quintessence of that poisonous Federalism to supply the antidote of which to a suffering people was the mission of the Republican party.[65] How then was the Supreme Court to be dealt with? The easiest course obviously would have been to deal with it as the inferior courts had been dealt with, but that was out of the question, since it was admitted on all hands that the Supreme Court was the creation of the Constitution itself. Still the size of the Supreme Court is not specified by the Constitution and so is always subject to congressional determination, with the one exception that an incumbent shall not be displaced. Thus the Court had been established originally with six justices, but by the act of 1801, with a vacancy existing, had been cut down to a membership of five. Why might it not therefore at this time be indefinitely enlarged and its Federalist membership swamped? The proposition seems a simple one but two obstacles stood in the way of its adoption. The more serious one I have already indicated, in the sentiment entertained by many Republicans regarding the place and power of the judiciary in our constitutional system; and the second obstacle supported the first: for if economy did indeed require the curtailing of the inferior judiciary, did not the same consideration oppose any undue enlargement of the supreme tribunal? By the act of 1802, the Supreme Court was increased to seven members but the increase was for sufficient reason and was in no wise dictated by partisan considerations. But one method of attack then remained available, namely, impeachment, and even here difficulties were not lacking. The Constitution provides that civil officers of the United States may be impeached for "high crimes and misdemeanors."[66] But what are "high crimes and misdemeanors?" Are indictable offenses alone

65. See a letter from Jefferson to Dickinson, December 19, 1801, 4 *Works* 424 (Washington), cited in 1 Adams 257; see also W. E. Dodd, "Chief Justice Marshall and Virginia," 12 *Am. Hist. Rev.* 756 ff.

66. Art. II, sec. 4.

comprised within this description? Or do acts to the political distaste of the impeaching body, the House of Representatives in this case, fall within the category? Persuasive of the first view is the legal significance of the terms themselves, but fortifying the second view there is, in the first place, the history of impeachment as it comes from England, and in the second place, the fact that by the Constitution the judicial tenure is during "good behaviour," which would seem to require of judges a somewhat higher degree of propriety of conduct than abstention merely from acts of crime. Furthermore as it happened, the advocates of the broad view of impeachment were able, on the very threshold of the struggle for which they were girding themselves, to create what formally at least was a precedent. Pickering of the federal district of New Hampshire was insane, but by our system, the only way to dismiss him was by impeachment, which was carried through successfully early in 1803.[67] But if an insane man, incapable of defending himself, could thus be disposed of, if offence in other words was determined by the public exigency, rather than private delinquency, to what further use might not impeachment be put? The question was soon to be answered.

Marshall handed down the decision in Marbury v. Madison, (above), February 24, 1803. Marbury had been nominated for justice of the peace of the District of Columbia by the president, his nomination had been ratified by the Senate and his commission had been made out, signed, countersigned, and sealed, all in the closing hours of Adams' administration. One thing only there had not remained time to do, namely, to hand over the commission to the appointee, and this the new president now ordered should not be done, Marbury thereupon instituted mandamus proceedings against Secretary of State Madison in the Supreme Court. The question of jurisdiction having been raised, it was incumbent on the Court to dispose of that first; since, however, Marshall foresaw that he would have to decide against his jurisdiction, he determined to pass first upon the merits of the case. The delivery of the commission was, he held, a purely ministerial act plainly required by the law, wherefore mandamus could issue against the secretary of state to compel it. The suit, however, ought to have been instituted in a lower court, since by the Constitution the original jurisdiction of the Supreme Court is confined to controversies to which ambassadors and states are parties. True, the suit had been brought in accordance with an act of Congress, but that act, being in palpable contradiction of the Constitution, was void. The case must accordingly be dismissed for want of jurisdiction. Regarded merely as a judicial decision, the decision of Marbury v. Madison must be considered as most extraordinary, but regarded as a political pamphlet designed to irritate an enemy to the very limit of endurance, it must be considered a huge success. Nor was Jefferson's justifiable anger diminished

---

67. 2 Adams 143, 153–58.

by his recognition of the fact that the circumspection of his antagonist had withheld from him all pretext for an open declaration of war.[68]

The peace, however, was not long to be kept. Little more than two months after Marshall's fling at the president, his associate, Chase, addressed a grand jury at Baltimore with a violent tirade against Republicanism. Animadverting particularly to the recent judiciary act, Chase declared the independence of the national judiciary to be already "shaken to its foundations," and the Constitution about to "sink into a mobocracy," all of which "mighty mischief" was due, he asserted, "to the modern doctrines by our late reformers, that all men in a state of society are entitled to enjoy equal liberty and equal rights." The date of Chase's outburst was May 2nd. Eleven days later Jefferson wrote Nicholson, member of Congress from Maryland, suggesting that "this seditious and official attack upon the principles of our Constitution . . ." ought not to go unpunished. Meantime Pickering's impeachment was dragging, not to be finally disposed of till March 12th, 1804. The same day the House of Representatives, without debate, voted by a solid party vote, 73 to 32, that Chase should be impeached. But again there was a delay of nearly a year. Finally, however, on February 9th, 1805, the trial began. From the first things went badly with the project; but what was particularly calamitous, was the hopeless muddle its promoters were in as to their theory of impeachment: was it an inquest of office or an indictment of crime? Randolph took the one view, Nicholson the other. On March 1st the Senate was ready to vote. The impeachers were beaten horse and foot: on one article the verdict of "not guilty" was unanimous, on others nearly so; even on the most promising article, the one touching the Baltimore charge, the northern Republicans and Gaillard of South Carolina held with the Federalists,—thus demonstrating once more, that on the judiciary question, the Virginia school represented only a section of the party. It can hardly be said that Chase's acquittal established any theory of impeachment in our constitutional law, but "it proved impeachment to be an impracticable thing for partisan purposes," a "mere scare-crow" in fact; it proved that "Chief Justice Marshall was at length safe," that "he might henceforward at his leisure fix the principles of constitutional law;" it proved finally that the Supreme Court might pass upon the constitutionality of acts of Congress, not merely with impunity, but indeed with the acquiescence and applause of Congress itself.[69] The moment of Chase's acquittal Randolph, "hurrying from the Senate Chamber to the House," offered a resolution for submitting a constitutional amendment, making all national judges removable by the president upon the joint address of both Houses. It was referred to the committee of the whole, reintroduced next year, received some discussion, and was finally voted down. Between the years 1809 and 1812 nine resolutions of

68. *Id*. 147.
69. *Id*. ch. 10.

similar purport, though of varying terms, met similar fates; as did another in 1816, and another in 1822.[70]

Thus was judicial review established in the general government because of the acquiescence of the department to be restrained in what it considered to be the constitutional order of things. But meantime it was seen that judicial review is a two-edged sword: it restrains national power but it also sanctions it. Accordingly the question now arose of the position of the Supreme Court in the federal system. The source of the difficulty in this connection is fortunately easily uncovered: it lay in the elusive idea of state sovereignty. In the convention, in the state conventions, and in the *Federalist,* the states are spoken of as remaining sovereign under the new system, though it is recognized that they have parted with essential portions of their sovereignty to the national government.[71] The question that now presented itself therefore was, what practically was signified by the term "sovereign" as thus applied to the states. In the case of Chisholm v. Georgia[72] the question at issue was whether the United States Supreme Court could take jurisdiction of a suit instituted by a citizen of South Carolina against the state of Georgia. The language of the Constitution was perfectly explicit in favor of the jurisdiction,[73] but the attorneys of the defendant state contended that this language must be construed in the light of the principle that a sovereign can be sued only in its own courts and at its own consent,—a line of argument in support of which they were able to quote Hamilton in the *Federalist* and Marshall in the Virginia Convention.[74] In other words state sovereignty was set up as a sort of interpretative principle limiting the operation of the Constitution. Not only did the Court overrule the plea by a vote of four to one, but in the opinions of Chief Justice Jay and of Justice Wilson the applicability of the term "sovereign" to the governments of the states was flatly denied. Only to the people of the United States, who ordained the Constitution, was the term "sovereign," Wilson argued, to be fittingly applied; at least "as to the purposes of the Union" the states are not sovereign. Justice Iredell laid down contrary doctrine: "The United States are sovereign as to all the powers of government actually surrendered. Each State in the Union is sovereign as to all the powers reserved." In other words, sovereignty in the federal system is divided or dual.

The decision in Chisholm v. Georgia (above), was shortly followed by the adoption of the Eleventh Amendment, but this fact, far from impairing the

70. H. V. Ames, *Amendments to the Constitution* 149–51 and App. 366, 371, 380–83, 385, 389, 398, 402, 405, 456, 508a (2 *Am. Hist. Ass. Ann. Report* 1896).

71. For references to the sovereignty of the states in the Convention, see Madison's Notes, under dates of June 9, 11, 16, 18, 19 (particularly King's speech), 21, 25, 27, 30, and July 2. For the same in *Federalist,* see Nos. 39, 62, 81. For same in state conventions, see particularly 4 Elliot *Debates* 125.

72. 2 Dallas 435 (1793).

73. Art. III, sec. 2, the fifth cl.

74. *Federalist* 81; 3 Elliot 551 ff.

logic of that decision, seems rather to confirm it. Likewise it did not obtrude at the time any difficulties to the steady extension of federal control over state legislation. Thus in the years immediately following the Eleventh Amendment the Supreme Court not only passed on the validity of state laws under the national Constitution, laws and treaties, without having its right to do so challenged,[75] but also in 1795, in Van Horne's Lessee v. Dorrance,[76] the federal courts began to claim for themselves, in cases falling to their jurisdiction because of diverse citizenship, the right to pass as well upon the constitutionality of state laws under the constitution of the enacting state. This is done upon the principle that in such cases the national judiciary stands in place of the state judiciary. In Calder v. Bull, Justice Chase is disposed to deny the existence of this power, his argument being that the Constitution delegates no "constructive powers" to the United States. Two years later, however, in Cooper v. Telfair Justice Cushing announces the doctrine explicitly, "that this Court has the same power that a court of the State of Georgia would possess, to declare the law in question void." The power thus claimed and since exercised has played, as we shall see in a later chapter, a most important part in the development of constitutional law.

Meantime, however, the conflict between the notion of state sovereignty and the pretensions of the national judiciary had developed a new phase. In the *Federalist,* as I have already mentioned, Madison had accepted the notion that the decision in controversies respecting the boundary line between state and national power would devolve upon the Supreme Court, whose power he described as *ultimate,* and that, moreover, in a paragraph in which he speaks of the states as possesssing "a residuary and inviolable sovereignty."[77] The same twelve-month, however, in which Madison wrote the passage above referred to, he had begun to see new light upon the subject of judicial review; and largely, probably, in consequence of the rather overdone jealousy recently manifested by the Virginia court of appeals for what it pretended to consider its constitutional position,[78] he wrote in October 1788 as follows, to a correspondent in Kentucky: "In the State constitutions, as indeed in the federal one also, no provision is made for the case of a disagreement in expounding them; and as the courts are generally the last in making the decision, it results to them, by refusing or not refusing to execute a law, to stamp it with its final character. This makes the judicial department paramount in fact to the legislature, which was never intended and can never be proper."[79] Throughout the ensuing decade Madison came more and more under the influence both of Jefferson's democracy and of his state sovereignty ideas, with the result that in 1798 he was ready

75. Ware v. Hylton, above; Calder v. Bull, above; see note 52.
76. 2 Dallas 304 (1795).
77. *Federalist* No. 39.
78. See the Case of the Judges, 4 Call (Va.) 135.
79. 1 Madison, *Letters and Other Writings* 105 (1865).

to pen the famous protest of that year against the alien and sedition laws which are known as the Virginia Resolutions.[80] The essential doctrine of these resolutions is to be found in the third one, which reads as follows: "Resolved . . . that this assembly doth explicitly and peremptorily declare that it views the powers of the federal government as resulting from the compact to which the states are parties . . . that in case of a deliberate, palpable, and dangerous exercise of other powers not granted by the said compact, the states who are parties thereto, have the right and are in duty bound to interpose for arresting the progress of the evil and for maintaining within their respective limits the authorities, rights, and liberties appertaining to them." Years later Madison was at great pains to insist that the purport of this language was ambiguous,[81] but the word "respectively" taken with the context, indicates, if language means anything, that the original intention was to assert a constitutional prerogative on the part of the individual states to judge for themselves of the scope of the national powers. And indeed it was so understood at the time. Being communicated to the sister states, the resolutions, together with resolutions of an even more radical stamp from Kentucky,[82] the work largely of Jefferson, drew forth from the northern legislatures responses which were always condemnatory in tone and which usually asserted the position of the national judiciary as the final interpreter of the national Constitution in the most confident terms.[83] On the other hand, it is true that as early as 1800 Madison and his following had begun to reconsider the extreme position taken in the resolutions of 1798 and to seek retreat from it. In his Report to the Virginia legislature in 1800,[84] Madison begins by reiterating the view set forth in the resolutions: the states are sovereign, any decision of the federal judiciary, therefore, while possibly ultimate in relation to the authorities of the other departments of the federal government, can not possibly be so "in relation to the rights of the parties to the constitutional compact, from which the judicial as well as the other departments hold their delegated trusts." Fifty pages farther along, however, Madison's audacity has oozed entirely away. "It has been said," he writes, restating the issue, "that it belongs to the judiciary of the United States, and not the state legislatures, to declare the meaning of the Federal Constitution. But," he urges, in a far different tone to {*sic;* from?} the one with which he set out, "a declaration that proceedings of the Federal Government are not warranted by the Constitution is a novelty neither among the citizens nor among the legislatures of the states . . . nor can the declarations of either, whether affirming or denying the constitutionality of measures of the

---

80. For the Virginia and Kentucky Resolutions, see W. MacDonald, *Select Documents Illustrative of the History of the United States, 1776–1861* 148–60 (1901); or 4 Elliot 528–32, 540–45.

81. 9 *Writings* 444–47, 489–92, 495–98 (Hunt ed. 1900–1910).

82. See note 80, above.

83. H. V. Ames, *State Documents on Federal Relations* Nos. 7–15 (1911); 4 Elliot 532–39.

84. 6 *Writings* 341–406 (Hunt ed.).

Federal Government, . . . be deemed, in any point of view, an assumption of the office of the judge. The declarations in such cases are expressions of opinion, unaccompanied with any other effect than what they may produce on opinion by exciting reflection. The expositions of the judiciary, on the other hand, are carried into immediate effect by force.'' There can therefore have been no impropriety in the conduct of the Virginia legislature, particularly since it was foreseen at the time of the adoption of the Constitution that the state legisla- tures, constituents as they were to be of one branch of the federal government, would often ''descry the first symptoms of usurpation'' and ''sound the alarm to the public.'' Madison's reference is plainly to his own contributions to the *Federalist*,[85] where he sets forth the sheer matter of fact that the state legislatures would frequently be able, by virtue of their normal powers, to obstruct or even indirectly to transform federal policy, but with not the slightest hint in the world that among such powers would be that of intervening between the federal government and the people, its getting rid of the necessity for which, in fact, he repeatedly asserts, was the leading merit of the new system.

In the years following 1800 therefore, the Virginia school dismisses the notion that ''interposition'' had any peculiarly authoritative quality attaching to it because the organ of it was the state legislature. Furthermore, it was quite necessary that they should do so if they were to cleave to the notion of dual sovereignty in the federal system, a notion which also finds implicit but inconsistent reiteration in both the resolutions of 1798 and the Report. I say ''inconsistent'' for this reason: dual sovereignty means dual autonomy,—the right of each of the sovereignties to judge of its own powers, and to control, within the limits which it thus sets itself, the allegiance and obedience of its own citizenship. But if this be admitted, on what possible basis can one of the sovereignties, the state, presume to insert the shield of its sovereignty between the other sovereignty, the federal government, and a portion of the citizenship of the latter, even though the citizenship in question belong also, in another aspect of the case, to the intermeddling state? Nor do these reflections appear to have failed the Virginia statesmen, although when we first find them giving utterance to them, it is in a quite different connection and with a quite different purpose. In 1809, the United States Supreme Court decided the case of the United States v. Peters,[86] wherein, under the tenth section of the Judiciary Act of 1789, it reviewed, and traversed an earlier decision of the same issues by the Supreme Court of Pennsylvania. The Pennsylvania legislature immediately uttered vehement protest against this decision, upon the general ground that, since Pennsylvania was an independent sovereignty, the decisions of its courts, in the matters coming before them, were final. In short, it applied the doctrine of dual sovereignty to the denial essentially of the constitutionality of the whole system of removals and appeals from state to federal courts established by the

85. See *Federalist* 44.
86. 5 Cranch 136 (1809).

Act of 1789. Madison was now president, but casting consistency to the winds, he warned the governor of Pennsylvania in the most solemn way possible, of the deplorable consequences that must ensue from any attempt on Pennsylvania's part to resist a decision of the federal Supreme Court. The Virginia legislature also was strenuously on the side of the national jurisdiction,[87] in fact using stronger language than that of any of the northern legislatures ten years before. But Virginia's vacillations were not yet over: five years later she had once more changed position; and in Hunter v. Martin,[88] the Virginia court of appeals pronounced the 25th section of the Judiciary Act unconstitutional, on the basis of an argument in which the most rigorous and precise application is made of the notion of a dual sovereignty in the federal system. What we see in the federal system, says Judge Cabell in his opinion in this case, is "two governments . . . possessing each its portion of the divided sovereignty, . . . embracing the same territory and operating on the same persons, and frequently on the same subjects," but "nevertheless separate from and independent of each other. From this position . . . it necessarily results that each government must act by its own organs: from no other can it expect, command or enforce obedience, even as to objects coming within the range of its powers." Accordingly, while the judicial power of the general government indubitably extends to cases arising under the Constitution, the acts of Congress and national treaties, that government must provide its own courts to exercise such power. Nor is it to be denied that by "cases arising under" the Constitution of the United States, its laws and treaties, is meant simply cases in which these are drawn in question, and that consequently cases arising under state enactments may from another point of view be such cases. What, then, is the course of procedure in a contingency of this sort: in which court is the action to be brought, that of the state or that of the general government? The question is readily answered: where the action is brought will depend entirely upon the election of the parties. If however the action is once brought into a state court, if the parties elect the state jurisdiction in the matter is final. Nor does Article VI of the Constitution obtrude any difficulties to this view. For while the judges of the state courts are by that article bound to give the Constitution, and laws and treaties of the United States, precedence over conflicting state constitutions and laws, "what that constitution is, what those laws and treaties are, must, in cases coming before the state courts, be decided by the state judges according to their own judgments and upon their own responsibility. To the opinions of the federal courts they will always pay the respect which is due to the opinions of other learned and upright judges . . . but it is respect only and not the acknowledgment of conclusive authority."

As regards logical self-consistency, this argument is of undeniable force, but its merit upon this score simply serves to bring into sharper outline the

87. Ames, No. 24.
88. 4 Munf. (Va.) 1.

historical falsity of its conclusions. For in point of historical fact, as we know, the Constitutional Fathers intended that appeals should lie from state courts to the United States Supreme Court, and accordingly their vague description of the states as "sovereign" must give place to that fact.[89] True, for the time being, owing to Madison's steady refusal to publish his notes,[90] the direct testimony of the Constitutional Fathers, save such as was embodied in the *Federalist,* was inaccessible, while on the other hand the Virginia and Kentucky Resolutions still bore their spurious reputation as a contemporary exposition of the Constitution. Nevertheless, as Story soon demonstrated in his powerful opinion in Martin v. Hunter's Lessee,[91] the historical argument was by no means entirely unavailable to the defenders of the national jurisdiction. The controlling reason for the appellate power of the United States Supreme Court over state decisions, Story points out, is furnished by

> the necessity of uniformity of decisions throughout the whole United States upon all subjects within the purview of the Constitution. Judges of equal learning and integrity, in different states, might differently interpret a statute or a treaty of the United States, or even the Constitution itself. If there were no revising authority to control these jarring and discordant judgments, and to harmonize them into uniformity, the laws, the treaties, and the Constitution of the United States would be different in different states, and might perhaps never have precisely the same construction, obligation, or efficacy in any two states. The public mischiefs which would attend such a state of things would be truly deplorable; and it cannot be believed that they could have escaped the enlightened convention which formed the Constitution.

Thus Story turns his argument from consequences to historical account. It was all very well for the Virginia judges to exclaim, "Let justice be done though heaven fall," but was it conceivable that the Constitutional Fathers had taken so light an attitude toward the very evils which they were met together to remedy? Moreover, the opponents of national appeal, in order to avoid too egregious results from their system, had at the end to abandon their own darling logic. For instead of attacking as Pennsylvania had done, those portions of the Judiciary Act which provide for removals in certain cases from the state to national courts, they urged that Congress would have power to utilize that method in conferring exclusive jurisdiction upon the national courts in the kinds of cases in which, by the 25th section, appeal was resorted to. But, said Story,

> this power of removal is not to be found in express terms in any part of the Constitution; if it be given it is only given by implication, as a power necessary and proper to carry into effect some express power. . . . It presupposes an exercise of original jurisdiction to have attached elsewhere . . . If then the right of removal be included in the appellate jurisdiction, it is only because it is one mode of

89. See above, pp. 59–61.
90. 7 J. C. Hamilton, *History of the Republic of the United States* 286 (1857–65); cf. 6 *id.* 383, showing Madison's inconsistent opinions as to the standard of interpretation for the Constitution.
91. 1 Wheat. 304 (1816).

exercising that power, and as Congress is not limited by the Constitution to any particular mode or time of exercising it, it may authorize a removal either before or after judgment . . . and if the appellate power by the Constitution does not include cases pending in State courts, the right of removal . . . cannot be applied to them.

In short, if the right of removal from state to federal courts, as is conceded, is allowable by the Constitution, by the same token the right of appeal from state courts to the federal courts is similarly allowable; and each moreover, trenches "equally upon the jurisdiction and independence of the State tribunals."

Story's argument, backed up as it was by the great authority of the *Federalist*, should have disposed at once and forever of the issue it dealt with, and probably it would have, had it had the backing also of Madison's notes. Those however were not published till 1840, with the result that Martin v. Hunter's Lessee, (above), turned out to be but the preliminary round of a conflict that was to endure till the very end of Marshall's chief justiceship. In Cohens v. Virginia,[92] in which plaintiff in error had been indicted, tried and penalized for selling tickets for a lottery established by Congress in the District of Columbia, owing to the circumstance that a state itself was a party to the record, the defenders of state immunity pressed their contentions with confidence and vigor. Admitting, they said, that this was a case arising "under the Constitution," and admitting too for the nonce, though this was subsequently denied in the course of the argument, that the United States Supreme Court has appellate jurisdiction from state courts in such cases, yet an exception must be made of controversies to which a state is a party, such an exception being contemplated by the original Constitution and particularly by the Eleventh Amendment, which was claimed to be declaratory of an intention pervading the entire Constitution, and therefore formulative of a binding rule of construction. Ultimately Marshall dismissed the writ of error on the ground that the charter of the lottery company was not intended by Congress to run outside the District of Columbia and that therefore no law of the United States had been violated by the judgment of the Virginia court; but before he did this, improving upon his method in Marbury v. Madison, he examined and refuted with principles as sweeping as their own every argument that had been advanced by counsel for Virginia upon the constitutional question. In particular does Marshall oppose to the doctrine of state sovereignty, the principle of the paramountcy of the national power, on the basis of Article VI of the Constitution, which he treats as inculcating a rule of construction not only for the state judges but necessarily also for federal judges. Quoting that article, he then proceeds: "This is the authoritative language of the American people, and if gentlemen please, of the American States, it marks with lines too strong to be mistaken, the characteristic distinction between the government of the union and those of the States. The

92. 6 Wheat. 264 (1821).

general government, though limited as to its objects, is supreme with respect to those objects. This principle is a part of the Constitution; and if there be any who deny its necessity, none can deny its authority." Nor, he continues, has the Eleventh Amendment altered the Constitution in this fundamental respect. The motive of that amendment "was not to maintain the sovereignty of a State from the degradation supposed to attend a compulsory appearance before the tribunal of the Nation. . . . It does not comprehend controversies between two or more States or between a State and a foreign state. The jurisdiction of the court still extends to those cases, and in those a State may still be sued. We must ascribe the amendment, then, to some other cause than the dignity of the State." Nor is there any difficulty in finding the cause. "Those who were inhibited from commencing a suit against a State, or from prosecuting one which might be commenced before the adoption of the amendment, were persons who might probably be its creditors." Furthermore, the suit in progress was not a *suit against the state of Virginia, but a prosecution by the state* to which a defence was set up on the basis of an act of Congress. The writ of error in the case therefore merely removed "the record into the supervising tribunal" in accordance with the provision made in the Judiciary Act. Marshall concludes his opinion upon the constitutional question with these words: "A constitution is framed for ages to come and is designed to approach immortality as nearly as human institutions can approach it. . . . The people made the Constitution and the people can unmake it . . . but the supreme and irresistible power to make or unmake resides only in the whole body of the people, not in any subdivision of it. The attempt of any of the parts to exercise it is usurpation and ought to be repelled by those to whom the people have delegated the power of repelling it." The pertinency of this passage is supplied by the fact, which Marshall had had the insight to detect from the beginning, that, in the doctrine of state immunity from the national jurisdiction, we have the doctrine of state interposition or, to use the term of the Kentucky resolutions, of "nullification" over again, rid indeed of its self contradiction, but all the more destructive on that account of the fabric of national power.

"Our opinion in the bank case," Marshall wrote Story from Virginia March 24th, 1819, with reference to McCulloch v. Maryland, "has roused the sleeping spirit of Virginia, if indeed it ever sleeps."[93] But if this was the effect of that decision, it can be well imagined what the effect of Cohens v. Virginia, (above), was two years later. Madison indeed was inclined to abide by his original viewpoint, to which, as we have seen, he had returned in 1809. "The Gordian knot of the Constitution," he wrote Judge Roane, "seems to lie in the probability of collision between the federal and state powers, especially as eventually exercised by their respective tribunals." If that knot could not be "untied by the text of the Constitution," he wanted no "political Alexander"

93. Quoted by J. B. Thayer, *John Marshall* 86 (Riverside Biographical Series 1901).

to attempt it. At the same time he had "always thought . . . that on the abstract question whether federal or state decisions ought to prevail, the sounder policy would yield to the claims of the former."[94] Jefferson on the other hand, with increasing old age, was developing more of a monomania than ever in his antipathy for the federal judiciary, which he described in his usual salacious vein as a "subtle corps of sappers and miners, constantly working underground to undermine the foundations of our confederated fabric," or again compared to "gravity, ever acting with noiseless step, and unalarming advance, gaining ground step by step and holding what it gains." But Cohens v. Virginia, (above), he regarded as marking the very climax of John Marshall's usurpations; and now gave free vent to prophecies of some sort of resistance to the pretension of the Supreme Court, should three or four great states receive at its hands the inconsiderate treatment that had been meted out to Virginia.[95] The prophecy was fulfilled to the letter.

In Osborn v. the Bank,[96] which was decided in 1824 and in which the Eleventh Amendment was again brought forward, Marshall laid down the rule that a suit against a state officer claiming to act as such under an unconstitutional law, was not a suit against a state but against the officer himself, who was responsible individually; from which it followed that the Supreme Court might in determining the question of its jurisdiction pass upon the constitutionality of any law the authority of which was pleaded by such officer. The controversy of which this decision was an incident had already, two years earlier, added Ohio to the list of enemies of the federal judiciary, while in the course of the years 1821 to 1823, Kentucky became similarly aligned, owing to the Supreme Court's adherence to its decision in Green v. Biddle, which was originally pronounced by three of the four judges sitting in the case, that is, by less than a majority of the Court.[97] Finally in 1830, Chief Justice Marshall by his action in Tassell's case, brought the Supreme Court into controversy with Georgia.[98] The special protagonists of state sovereignty in these controversies were of course the legislatures of the several states affected, but as early as 1821 the quarrel had been carried to Congress as well. On December 12th of that year Richard M. Johnson, senator from Kentucky, introduced a proposition of amendment to the Constitution of the United States, the essential purport of which was to substitute the Senate of the United States for the Supreme Court in all constitutional cases.[99] The proposition was read twice, considered in committee of the whole a number of times and finally tabled. Nine years later a bill to repeal the 25th

94. 9 *Writings* 65–66; see also *id.* 55–63.
95. 15 *Writings* 297–98 and 326; see also at 389, 421, and 444–52 (Mem. ed. 1903).
96. 9 Wheat 738 (1824).
97. Ames, *Documents* Nos. 45 and 48–51.
98. *Id.* Nos. 58–60.
99. Ames, *Amendments* 161–63.

section of the Act of 1789 was offered from the House Judiciary Committee. It was supported by a majority of the committee and sustained by an elaborate but highly disingenuous report. An equally elaborate report was presented by James Buchanan for the minority. The reports present no new arguments for the positions that they respectively sustained, but confronting each other they throw into sharp contrast the points of view from which the two parties to this question regarded it. The opponents of the Supreme Court, jealous of local liberties, insist upon envisaging constitutional cases as controversies between the United States and the states, in their corporate capacities: the defenders of the Supreme Court on the other hand regard its power in the light of a defence of individual rights.[100] "And in the first place," the minority report proceeds, "it ought to be the chief object of all governments to protect individual rights. In almost every case, involving a question before a state court under this section of the Judiciary Act, the Constitution, laws, or treaties of the United States are interposed for the protection of individuals. . . . If this section were repealed, all these important individual rights would be forfeited." After a brief debate, the bill to repeal was rejected by a vote of 138 to 51. Of this 51, fifteen came from Virginia, eight from Kentucky, seven from South Carolina, and five from Georgia, while the remainder were about equally distributed between North and South. Of the same fifty-one, a majority were born in Virginia, and bred Democrats, upon the states rights doctrines of Thomas Jefferson.[101] In 1832, Marshall rendered his decision in Worcester v. Georgia, reasserting the principles of Cohens v. Virginia, though the inexcusable attitude of Jackson made it mere *brutum fulmen*.[102] Four years later Taney became chief justice. He was a states rights Democrat who subscribed to the whole creed of the dual sovereignty of the states and the United States, but who managed to reconcile with this creed the most thoroughgoing adherence to the precedents established by Marshall in respect to the constitutional position of the federal judiciary. In Prigg v. Pennsylvania,[103] though the various members of the Court diverged considerably in their reasoning with reference to some of the issues raised, the Court was unanimous in following the precedent of Cohens v. Virginia, (above), in dealing with the state statute involved, which was held to be unconstitutional. In Ableman v. Booth,[104] Taney turned the doctrine of dual sovereignty against the doctrine of state sovereignty and asserted the jurisdiction of the United States Supreme Court under the 25th section of the Act of 1789 with vigor and success. In the Dred Scott Case,[105] he declared a congressional statute unconstitutional. By all these decisions moreover he

100. 7 Cong. Deb. App. I xxxiii (1831).
101. I gather these facts from Poore's *Political Register* (1878).
102. W. G. Sumner, *Andrew Jackson* 226–27 (Am. Statesmen Series) (1882).
103. 16 Pet. 539 (1842).
104. 21 How. 506 (1859).
105. 19 How. 393 (1857).

commended the national judicial power to that section of the country from which most of the opposition to it had hitherto come, as by the last one he rendered it temporarily odious to the other section.

We turn back finally to the subject of judicial review within the states themselves. We discover at once, however, that in the interval between the Constitutional Convention and the election of 1800, the question of the power of the courts to review the acts of the coordinate legislatures under the state constitutions, has come to involve another question of even greater importance, namely, the question of the legitimate scope of that power.

I have already indicated the view originally held of the written Constitution. It was regarded as a species of social compact, the act of a society in a state of revolution or state of nature. It derived accordingly its admittedly fundamental character not from its source but rather from its content. Like Cromwell's instrument of government, it contained "somewhat fundamental": and particularly fundamental was any enumeration of individual rights, which gained nothing in the quality of authoritativeness by being so enumerated, though something, it was hoped, of security. Rights, in other words, were not fundamental because they found mention in the Bill of Rights, but they found mention in such Bill of Rights because they were of their own nature fundamental. But now suppose such enumeration were but partial and incomplete, as must indeed be the case almost inevitably, was that fact to derogate from such rights as were not enumerated? Amendment IX to the United States Constitution indicates the contemporary view as to such a contingency. But now observe what character this view imparts to the written constitution: it contains "somewhat fundamental," true; but not all that is fundamental. In other words, a constitution is a nucleus, a core, so to say, of a much wider region of scattered rights, which though lacking definite formulation rest nevertheless, like all rights, upon the law of nature.[106] Suppose now one of these unformulated rights be violated by the state, the purpose of which is to preserve rights: must not the remedy be the same as if a formulated right had been violated? The answer seems obvious, and would have been, but for the entrance at this point of another consideration, namely, the doctrine of legislative sovereignty. Judicial review originally rested upon the basis of common right and reason and natural law—that I have amply shown. The greatest obstacle to the establishment of judicial review, however, was this same doctrine of legislative sovereignty, the basis of which is the assumption that the legislature not merely *represents* but *is* the people. Yet the persuasion grew that judicial review must be retained: how then was it to be reconciled with legislative sovereignty? The riddle was solved by locating "the people" in the constitution-making body, with the result, on the one hand, of giving to the

106. Examine in this connection Justice Paterson's opinion in Van Horne's Lessee v. Dorrance, cited above.

Constitution the quality of positive enactment the authoritative character of which ensues no longer from its content but from its source, and, on the other hand, by reducing the ordinary legislature to a position of subordination to the constitution-making body. Judicial review is thus transferred from its original foundation upon the law of nature to the basis of the written constitution, and so is transformed from an obstacle to the realization of popular sovereignty, to the one indispensable instrument for that realization. But was this transference and transformation complete? This is the question before us.

One of the earliest cases of judicial review following the adoption of the national Constitution was that of Bowman v. Middleton,[107] in which the Supreme Court of South Carolina overturned a colonial enactment of 1712, transferring a freehold from the heir at law to another, on the ground that it was "against common right as well as against Magna Carta to take the freehold of one man and vest it in another . . . without any compensation, or even a trial by jury of the county to determine the right in question." The enactment "was therefore *ispo facto* void and no length of time could give it validity, being originally founded on erroneous principles." Commenting upon this decision in his *Cases on Constitutional Law,* Professor Thayer has endeavored to bring it into harmony with the professed theory of modern constitutional law, by interpreting it as a recognition on the part of the court of the paramount authority, while South Carolina was still a royal province, of Parliament and so of "the statute of Magna Carta."[108] But, I submit, this is not at all the point of view revealed in the language just quoted, which is that of deference not to the source of Magna Carta and "common right," but to its content. The fact of the matter is that Professor Thayer is here illustrating what Professor Maitland has called the "professional fallacy of the law," namely, "the antedating of the emergence of modern ideas." When a court today ventures to assert too overtly principles of "common right," "natural justice," etc. as a possible basis for judicial decision in constitutional cases it exposes itself at once to the criticism of exceeding its constitutional function. But such criticism is from the standpoint of a recognition of the principle of legislative sovereignty. It is quite possible however that in the year 1792, the notion of legislative sovereignty was not very sharply before the judges who decided Bowman v. Middleton, (above), but that, on the contrary, their juristic horizon comprised so to speak the older notion of fundamental law. Consequently the South Carolina court probably felt, not that it was acting extraordinarily at all in basing a decision upon "common rights," but rather that it was acting very modestly, a point of view which at that date it would by no means have been alone in holding.[109]

---

107. 1 Bay (S.C.) 282.
108. 1 Thayer 53n.
109. See 2 McRee, *Iredell* 172, where Iredell evidently regards judicial review on the Cokian basis as less extraordinary than on the basis of the written constitution; see also 1 *Works of James Wilson* 415 (J. D. Andrew ed. 1896).

The old and new views of a constitution, together with the attendant views of the basis and scope of judicial review were first confronted in 1798, in Calder v. Bull,[110] in which a Connecticut statute setting aside a decree of a probate court and granting a right of appeal in a particular case where none had existed by the general law, had been challenged on the ground that it violated the prohibition in the United States Constitution of ex post facto laws. The Court upheld the statute upon the basis of a definition of the prohibition in question that confined its operation to penal legislation. In the course of his opinion however, Justice Chase took occasion to declare that he could not "subscribe to the omnipotence of a State legislature, or that it is absolute and without control, although its authority should not be expressly restrained by the constitution or a fundamental law of the state." He then proceeded to specify some acts that no legislature could pass without exceeding its authority: an act punishing a citizen for conduct "in violation of no existing law"; an act destroying or impairing "the lawful private contracts of citizens"; an act making a man a judge in his own cause; an act taking property from A and giving it to B, without A's consent. Such acts would be violative of the "vital principles" of republican government and "the social compact"; and the power to pass them "cannot be presumed" to have been given to the legislature: "the nature and ends of legislative power will limit the exercise of it." This view Chase's associate Iredell, though he had earlier stigmatized similarly the opposite view, pronounced that of "speculative jurists"; and he laid down the rule, upon the basis of Blackstone's description of the scope of Parliament's power, that "if a government, comprised of the legislative, executive, and judicial departments, were established by a constitution which imposed no limits on the legislative power, the consequence would inevitably be that whatever the legislative power chose to enact would be lawfully enacted, and the judicial power could never interpose to pronounce it void."

The issue between Chase and Iredell comes down to this point: what is the nature and purpose of a state constitution? By Chase's view obviously, a state constitution is a grant of powers, otherwise non-existent, to the limitation of rights, otherwise unlimited, from which it follows that "legislative power" is a particular kind of power, to be used in a particular way and to particular ends and no others. By Iredell's view, on the other hand, it is the purpose of a state constitution to organize and limit power otherwise omnipotent, from which it follows that "legislative power" is but another phrase for "sovereign power." For the moment, on the supreme bench at least, Iredell's view seems to have carried the day. In Cooper v. Telfair,[111] which came up from the circuit court and in which therefore the United States Supreme Court was acting in lieu of the state judiciary, the question at issue was the validity under the state

110. See n. 52, above.
111. See n. 53, above.

constitution of an act passed by the state of Georgia in 1782, declaring certain persons, including plaintiff in error, guilty of treason and confiscating his estates. The clauses of the state constitution principally relied upon by plaintiff were Article I, which declared that "the legislative, executive, and judiciary departments shall be separate and distinct, so that neither exercise the powers belonging to the other," and Article VI, which declared trial by jury "inviolable forever." Notwithstanding these provisions the act in question was upheld upon the ground that the constitution of Georgia did "not expressly interdict the passing of an act of attainder and confiscation by the authority of the legislature." With this judgment Justice Chase concurred, adding moreover that "the general principles in the constitution were not to be regarded as rules to fetter and control, but as matter merely declaratory and directory." "For," he proceeds, "even in the constitution itself we may trace repeated departures from the theoretical doctrine, that the legislative, executive, and judicial powers should be kept separate and distinct." At the same time Chase also adduces the fact, that the act under review was passed during the Revolution, and urges that some allowance must be made on that score. "Few of the Revolutionary acts," he declares, "would stand the rigorous tests now applied." This statement is significant, for it amounts to an admission that the Court was not in this case applying the most rigorous standards that it regarded as possibly available to it.

But now what effect did the "Revolution of 1800" and the ideas upon which it was founded have upon judicial review in the states? Of course the diverse situations presented by the different states were almost, if not quite, as numerous as the states themselves. Some states succumbed to the democratic movement much more easily and completely than others: especially was this true of the frontier and agricultural states, as compared with the seaboard and mercantile states. In some states established precedents existed to fortify judicial review, and in some this was not the case when the democratic movement arose. In some states the judiciary was much more securely placed than in others; in some, conspicuously Connecticut and Rhode Island, the legislature itself was in 1800 and for long thereafter the highest court, so that judicial review would usually have been, as long as this condition obtained, sheer futility. In some states finally the constitutions contained bills of rights which gave both the doctrine of the separation of powers and the doctrine of natural rights the form of popular mandate, while in others the constitutions did neither. In the fact of such variety, obviously, one has to be rather specific.

Perhaps the first note of reaction against judicial review was sounded in Connecticut by Swift in his admirable work, entitled *The System of Laws of Connecticut,* which was published in 1795.[112] Swift rejected absolutely the doctrine of natural rights, though he retained some of its phraseology for, as he

---

112. Z. Swift, *The System {of the Laws of Connecticut}* (1795–96); the passages quoted above are at 16–17, 34–35, 52–53.

admitted, convenience's sake. "The position that when men enter into the social state," he writes, "they give up some portion of natural right to acquire security for the remainder, is manifestly erroneous. . . . To contrast the social state to the natural state, as though the former were artificial and the latter natural, is contrary to truth. No principle of human conduct is more perfectly natural than that which prompts mankind to associate together for mutual benefit." Thus Aristotle is set to refuting Locke. Next follow Hobbes and Bentham, his allies. There are, strictly speaking, Swift continues, no such things as natural rights: there are only civil rights. "For in the civil state, which is deemed the same as the social state, by the administration of the government, the members do acquire certain positive rights, which they can enjoy only in a civil state and which are therefore to be considered as the gift and the offspring of civil institutions. It is in virtue of his being a member of the society that a man is a proprietor and has a right to draw on the capital and not in virtue of any natural state." From this doctrine flows inevitably Swift's notion of representative government, which implies, he insists,

> that the representatives stand in the place of the people and are vested with all their power within the constitution. In the legislature, therefore, consisting of the representatives, is concentrated the majority of the people and the supremacy of the government. They are neither bound to obey the instructions nor consult the will of the people, but being in their place and vested with all their power, they have a right to adopt and pursue such measures as in their judgment are best calculated to promote the happiness and welfare of the community, in the same manner as the people themselves would act if it were possible for them to assemble and deliberate on their common concerns.

But it is evident, is it not, what upon this basis, becomes of judicial review? "Previously to their passing any act," Swift proceeds to argue,

> they (the legislature) must consider and determine whether it be compatible with the constitution. Being the supreme power, and bound to judge with respect to the question in the first instance, their decision must be final and conclusive. It involves the most manifest absurdity and is degrading to the legislature, to admit the idea that the judiciary may rejudge the same question which they have decided; and if they are of a different opinion, reverse the law and pronounce it to be a nullity. It is an elevation of the judiciary over the heads of the legislature; it vests them with supreme power and enables them to repeal all the laws and defeat all the measures of the government. . . . The legislature will lose all regard and veneration in the eyes of the people, when the lowest tribunals of judicature are permitted to exercise the power of questioning the validity and deciding on the constitutionality of acts. A principle so dangerous to the rights of the people and so derogatory to the dignity of the legislature cannot be founded in truth and reason.

Fortunately or unfortunately, Swift's warnings went unheeded even in Connecticut. In 1818 a new constitution was established in which the differentiation of legislative and judicial functions was far more pronounced than in the old colonial charter. In consequence, from that date forward, the Connecticut courts asserted without contradiction the right of judicial review, for which furthermore they steadily invoked not only the written constitution but the doctrine of natural rights, though, it must be admitted, they made very restricted use of this doctrine. Quite in contrast with Connecticut, its compeer of colonial days, Rhode Island retained her colonial charter until 1842, so that not till considerably more than half a century after Trevett v. Weeden was anything heard again of judicial review in that state.[113]

States with normal constitutions that underwent a reaction with respect to judicial review were New Jersey, Virginia, and Pennsylvania. In 1804 in State v. Parkhurst,[114] a New Jersey case, the attorneys at the bar, presumably scions of Blackstone, urged with some insistence that the power of judicial review could not possibly exist within the state constitution. The court appears however to have reiterated its pretensions, as certainly it did numerous times in the years following, having recourse indeed on occasion to the doctrine of natural rights. In 1809, in Emerick v. Harris,[115] the Pennsylvania Supreme Court was confronted with a similar argument, which Chief Justice Tilghman took some pains to meet upon the basis of Iredell's precept of legislative sovereignty within the written constitution. In subsequent cases however, notably that of Eakin v. Raub,[116] in 1825, Tilghman took broader ground, with the result that Justice Gibson in a famous dissent to the chief justice's decision, denied the doctrine of judicial review within the state constitution *in toto*. "In this country," Gibson argued, "the powers of the judiciary are divisible into those that are political and those that are purely civil." The political powers however are "extraordinary and adventitious," being derived for the most part from Article VI of the United States Constitution. Within the state constitution therefore the powers of the state judiciary are in great part civil and are to be reckoned as a branch of the executive power, while the "legislature is to be viewed as the depository of the whole sovereignty of the state." This being the case, upon what possible foundation can the pretended right of judicial review rest? There is certainly no specific grant of such power in the constitution of Pennsylvania. Of course it is said, that it is the business of the judiciary "to ascertain and pronounce what the law is; and that this necessarily involves a consideration of the constitution": granted, but how far? "If the judiciary will inquire into anything besides the form of enactment, where shall it stop?" Furthermore, the advocates of judicial review themselves say that the power is "to be restricted to cases that are free from doubt or difficulty." But to say this "is to betray a doubt of the propriety of exercising it at all. Were the same caution used in judging of the existence of the power that is inculcated as to the

---

113. For Connecticut, see Goshen v. Honington, 4 Conn. 224; and Welch v. Wadsworth, 30 Conn. 149; for Rhode Island, run through the reports anterior to 1842.

114. 4 Halstead (N.J.) 427.

115. 1 Binney (Pa.) 416.

116. 12 S. & R. 330.

exercise of it, the profession would perhaps arrive at a different conclusion.'' But again it is urged, that the judiciary is established by the constitution and is sworn to support it. But what difference does that make? ''It cannot be said that the judiciary is coordinate merely because it is established by the constitution. If that were sufficient, sheriffs, registers of wills, and recorders of deeds, would be so too. Within the pale of their authority, the acts of these officers will have the power of the people for their support; but no one will pretend they are of equal dignity with the acts of the legislature. Inequality of rank arises not from the manner in which the organ has been constituted, but from its essence and the nature of its functions; and the legislative is superior to every other, inasmuch as the power to will and command is essentially superior to the power to act and obey.'' Then as to the oath, it was either designed ''to secure the powers of each of the different branches from being usurped by any of the rest'' and so ''furnishes an argument equally plausible against the right of the judiciary,'' or it is a general oath of ''allegiance to a particular form of government,'' which any citizen might take, but which would not hamper such citizen in agitating a total change in the constitution, or it is simply an official oath ''relating only to the official conduct of the officer'' and conferring no right or duty upon him ''to stray from the path of his ordinary business to search for violations of duty in the business of others,'' who are individually responsible for their own delinquencies. But finally what constitutional power has the judiciary to make its pretended right good? ''For instance, let it be supposed that the power to declare a law unconstitutional has been exercised. What is to be done? The legislature must acquiesce, although it may think the construction of the judiciary wrong. But why must it acquiesce? Only because it is bound to pay that respect to every other department of government which it has a right to exact from each in turn. This is the argument.'' But by the same token, the legislature which has ''at least an equal right with the judiciary to put a construction on the constitution,'' has an equal right to have the judiciary acquiesce in its construction, which however would mean the end of judicial review. Judicial review within the state constitution is therefore, Justice Gibson opines, but a ''professional dogma,'' a ''matter of faith'' rather ''than of reason.'' Subsequently as chief justice, he changed his opinion ''from experience of the necessity of the case,''[117] but to the end he defined the scope of judicial review, generally speaking, from the standpoint of the theory of legislative sovereignty, and held moreover that the function of review was only for the highest state courts and not to be attempted by inferior tribunals.[118] In Virginia the reaction was still more notable, doubtless on account of the logical connection between the notion of state sovereignty within the federal system, and legislative sovereignty within the state. From 1793, the date of Kamper v.

117. Norris v. Clymer, 2 Barr. 277.
118. Menges v. Wertman, 1 Pa. St. 218.

Hawkins, (above), to the outbreak of the Civil War, the Virginia court of appeals, while canvassing the constitutionality of legislative enactments in more than a score of cases, pronounced but one such enactment to have been unconstitutional and that one had been repealed some years previous to the decision.[119] In Maryland and South Carolina on the other hand, the doctrine of state sovereignty did not operate nearly so promptly to check judicial review, but to a comparatively late date the courts of both these states defined their constitutional functions from the standpoint of the theory of natural rights.[120]

Turning now to some of the younger communities, as the country stood at the time of the adoption of the Constitution, we find judicial review delayed in Vermont till 1814,[121] and in Georgia till 1815 and even then producing a remonstrance from the legislature.[122] In the new states to the West on the other hand, judicial review usually followed soon after the setting up of the state constitution, a phenomenon which is to be accounted for by the fact that these were in no sense "original states," but that their sages brought with them the stock of political and legal ideas which they had acquired in the states of their nativity to the East. Thus judicial review was in force in Kentucky as early as 1801,[123] in Tennessee in 1807,[124] and in Ohio either in 1806 or 1807. The most interesting of these cases is the Ohio one. The legislature had in 1805 passed an act defining the duties of justices of the peace. The judge of the third Ohio circuit pronounced portions of this act unconstitutional under both the state constitution and the United States Constitution, his reference to the latter being certain provisions of the first eight amendments, which at that time seem to have been widely regarded as binding upon the states as well as upon the United States. The decision being sustained by the Supreme Court, the House of Representatives, in the session of 1808–09, voted resolutions of impeachment against two of the judges concerned, who however were eventually acquitted.[125] More than a decade later a similar contest, and the last one of the sort, occurred in Kentucky. This was the period when the Kentucky legislature was up in arms against the United States Supreme Court on account of its decision in Green v. Biddle, (above). From denouncing the federal court, it was both natural and logical for the legislature to turn its attention to the similar pretensions of the coordinate judiciary. Accordingly, after formally pronouncing certain statues that the state court of appeals had recently overturned to be "constitutional and valid acts," it next endeavored to vote an address to the governor asking for the

---

119. Attorney General v. Broadus, 6 Munf. 116; see also Turpin v. Locket, 6 Call 113.
120. See Regents v. Williams, 6 Gill and J. (Md.) 365; also Mayor of Baltimore v. State St., 15 Md. 376; also St. v. Hayward, 3 Rich. (S.C.) 389.
121. Chipman's (Vt.) Reports, Introduction, an instructive document.
122. S. Baldwin, *The American Judiciary* 112 (1905).
123. See Kentucky Decisions, 64.
124. See 1 Overton (Tenn.) 243.
125. Cooley, *Constitutional Limitations* 160 n. 3 (1868).

removal of the judges, and when the resolution failed to secure the required two-thirds vote, proceeded first to abolish the office and then to recreate it with four new judges. Two political parties now sprang into existence, one the "old court party" and the other the "new court party." Eventually in 1826, the former triumphed and things were put back essentially upon their original footing.[126]

From the standpoint however of the history of American constitutional law, the history of judicial review in the states, before the Civil War, is, speaking broadly, the history of judicial review in four states alone, New Hampshire, Massachusetts, New York, and North Carolina, and especially in the last three. The contribution of New Hampshire's court consists in its dogmatic insistence upon the doctrine of the separation of powers, New Hampshire's constitution of 1783 being one of those in which that doctrine finds formal statement.[127] Massachusetts' brand of constitutional law in turn receives its peculiar stamp from the judicial emphasis put upon the words of chapter I, article 4 of the state constitution, which reads in part as follows: "And further full power and authority are hereby given and granted to the said general court, from time to time, to make, ordain, and establish, all manner of wholesome and reasonable orders, laws, statutes, and ordinances . . . either with penalties or without; so as the same be not repugnant or contrary to this constitution, as they shall judge to be for the good and welfare of this commonwealth." The important word in this passage is the word "reasonable," a term which the Massachusetts supreme court has always felt itself more or less free to construe as a limitation upon the legislative power.[128] In New York judicial review was established by Kent upon the broadest possible basis. Immediately following Kent's retirement from the bench however, the doctrine of legislative sovereignty within the written constitution began making rapid headway in New York. How was the tide to be stemmed? The New York courts met the situation temporarily by professing to reject the doctrine of natural rights while at the same time retaining the doctrine of limitations inherent to legislative power, which left them the right to construe the phrase "legislative power."[129] But the most notable contribution of all came from North Carolina, where also the doctrine of legislative sovereignty early presented the courts with a difficult problem. The story of the North Carolina doctrine however is the story of the first

126. Baldwin, at 112–15.

127. See particularly the important case of Merrill v. Sherburne, 1 N.H. 204; also the Opinions of the Judges, 4 N.H. 572.

128. See particularly James v. Holden, 2 Mass. 397; Foster v. Essex Bank, 16 Mass. 245; Baker v. Boston, 12 Pick. (Mass.) 184; Austin v. Murray, 16 Pick 126.

129. See Dash v. Van Kleeck, 7 Johns. (N.Y.) 498, comparing Kent's opinion with that of Spencer; compare J. Nelson in People v. Morris, 13 Wend. (N.Y.) 331, and Senator Verplanck in Cochran v. Van Surley, 20 Wend. 381–83; see also Benson v. Mayor of Albany, 24 Barb. 252 ff.; also Wynehamen {sic; Wynehamer} v. People, 13 N.Y. 391ff., *passim;* also Sill v. Corning, 15 N.Y. 303; also People v. Draper, 15 N.Y. 547.

beginnings of our present day constitutional law, and is obviously a theme for another chapter.[130]

To conclude: judicial review arose upon the basis of the doctrine of *fundamental law* and, as we shall appreciate better in the sequel, it has always continued to rest upon that basis when it has proved really effective as a check upon legislative power. Till the opening of the seventeenth century powers of government were regarded in England as legally limited. They were moreover *fused* powers, comprising, as in the Roman Republic, a fund of power which was, in a general way, available to all the principal organs of state, Parliament, the judges, the royal ministers; at least, the functions of government were but very imperfectly differentiated and very incompletely assigned to what today we regard as their proper organs. It is only since that date that this differentiation has been in process of self-conscious effectuation. It has proceeded however, among the two chief branches of the English-speaking race, along two quite different lines. In Great Britain it has taken place under the direction of the principle of legislative sovereignty and has been carried out therefore by Parliament, with the consequence that constitutional law in Great Britain is statutory or rests upon a statutory foundation, and is entirely within the keeping of the state itself. In America, on the other hand, through the establishment of judicial review upon the basis of the doctrine of a fundamental law known only to the judges, the differentiation of the functions of government has fallen to the courts, wherefore the keeping of the Constitution in the United States falls in the first instance to private persons, the parties to "lawsuits," and constitutional law has for its primary purpose not the convenience of the state but the preservation of individual rights.

130. See Univ. of North Carolina v. Foy, 2 Hayw. (N.C.) 310; also Hoke v. Henderson, 4 Dev. 1.

Note.—Since writing Part I of this study, I have come to the conclusion that the decision in Trevett v. Weeden (R.I. 1786) was based, not upon the matter of jurisdiction, but upon the alleged self-contradictory character of the language of the statute involved. The importance of this fact, which is considerable, I shall demonstrate elsewhere. See Coxe, 243–44.

3. Marbury v. Madison and the Doctrine of Judicial Review

WHAT is the *exact legal basis* of the power of the Supreme Court to pass upon the constitutionality of acts of Congress? Recent literature on the subject reveals a considerable variety of opinion. There are radicals who hold that the power owes its existence to an act of sheer usurpation by the Supreme Court itself, in the decision of Marbury v. Madison.[1] There are conservatives who point to clauses of the Constitution which, they assure us, specifically confer the power.[2] There are legists who refuse to go back of Marbury v. Madison, content in the ratification which, they assert, subsequent events have given the doctrine of that decision.[3] There are historians who show that a considerable portion of the membership of the body that framed the Constitution are on record as having personally favored judicial review at one time or another, either before, during, or after the Convention.[4] Finally, there are legal historians who represent judicial review as the natural outgrowth of ideas that were common property in the period when the Constitution was established.[5] In

From 12 *Michigan Law Review* 538–72 (1914). Reprinted by permission.

1. See, for instance, H. L. Boudin, "Government by Judiciary," 26 *Pol. Sci. Q.* 238 (1911).

2. J. H. Dougherty in his recent volume {*Power of Federal Judiciary Over Legislation* (1912)} follows Brinton Coxe in taking this position.

3. This is the position taken by J. P. Hall in his *Constitutional Law,* and by J. P. Cotton in his "Introduction" to his *Constitutional Decisions of John Marshall* (1905).

4. C. A. Beard, *The Supreme Court and the Constitution* (1912). I have also seen an able article by Mr. Frank E. Melvin, Harrison Fellow at the University of Pennsylvania, continuing Professor Beard's investigations. The article is about to be published, I believe, in the *Am. Pol. Sci. Rev.* {Melvin, "The Judicial Bulwark of the Constitution," 8 *Am. Pol. Sci. Rev.* 167 (1914)}.

5. A. C. McLaughlin, *The Courts, the Constitution, and Parties* (1912); C. G. Haines, *The American Doctrine of Judicial Supremacy* (1914). Before, however, any of the above-mentioned works had appeared, the present writer had considered both the theoretical and historical grounds of judicial review at length and had arrived substantially at the conclusions which are emphasized in the following article. See Corwin, "The Establishment of Judicial Review," 9 *Mich. L. Rev.* 102–25, 284–316 (1910) {ch. 2 in this volume}.

the following article I accept this last view as in a general way the correct one. In doing this, however, I discover that I have only raised some further questions. For before ideas contemporary with the framing of the Constitution can be regarded as furnishing the *legal* basis of judicial review, it must be shown that they were, by contemporary understanding, incorporated in the Constitution, that they were regarded by the framers of the Constitution as furnishing judicial review, and that they were logically sufficient to do so. To investigate these questions is the purpose of the study to follow.

I

The position of those who are content to rest the power of the Supreme Court over acts of Congress upon Marbury v. Madison[6] is plainly illogical. For either that decision was based upon the Constitution or it was not. In the former case, however, it is the Constitution that is the real basis of the power, while in the latter the decision was erroneous by the Court's own premises. Still it is urged that whatever the defects of the original decision, these have long since been cured by popular acquiescence and later decisions. Let me then begin this article by showing some difficulties in the way of this view.

The case of Marbury v. Madison arose upon an application by plaintiff to the Supreme Court for a writ of mandamus to the secretary of state to compel him to deliver a commission authorizing plaintiff to exercise the functions of an office to which he had been duly appointed. The Court, reversing the usual order of procedure,[7] went first into the merits of the question and from its review of these came to the conclusion that a mandamus, had it been sought in a tribunal having jurisdiction of the case, would undoubtedly have been the proper remedy. But this, it continued, had not been done. For though section 13 of the Act of 1789 purported to authorize the Supreme Court to issue "writs of mandamus in cases warranted by the principles and usages of law to . . . persons holding office under the authority of the United States,"[8] this provision transgressed Article III, section 2, paragraph 2, of the Constitution, the words of which describing the original jurisdiction of the Supreme Court must be interpreted as negativing any further power of the same order. Thereupon the Court pronounced section 13 null and void, and dismissed the case for want of jurisdiction.

Inevitably, the first question raised by Marshall's decision is as to the correctness of his construction of Article III, section 2, paragraph 2. In support of his position the chief justice might have quoted, had he chosen, the *Federalist*,[9] but against him was: first, the important evidence of the legislative

6. 1 Cranch 137 (1803).
7. On this point see 1 Cranch 91, 3 Cranch 171, 5 Cranch 221, 9 Wheat. 816, 10 Wheat. 20, 5 Pet. 190, 200.
8. For the Act of 1789, see 1 Statutes at Large 85ff. (Sept. 24, 1789, c. 20).
9. *Federalist* 81, at 507 (Lodge ed. 1888).

provision overturned, showing congressional opinion practically contemporaneous with the Constitution; secondly, the fact that anterior to Marbury v. Madison the Court itself had repeatedly taken jurisdiction of cases brought under that provision;[10] and thirdly, the fact that in other connections affirmative words of grant in the Constitution had not been deemed to infer a correlative negative. Thus, were the rule laid down in Marbury v. Madison to be followed, Congress would have power to enact penalties against only the crimes of counterfeiting, treason, and piracy and offences against the law of nations, whereas in fact it had, even as early as 1790, enacted penalties against many other acts, by virtue of its general authority under the "necessary and proper" clause.[11]

Yet it must be admitted that the rule of exclusiveness does often apply to cases of affirmative enumeration, so that the only question is whether Article III, section 2, paragraph 2, furnished such a case. Speaking to this point, the chief justice said:[12] "A negative or exclusive sense must be given them [the words of the paragraph in question] or they have no operation at all." But this is simply not so. For though given only their affirmative value, these words still place the cases enumerated by them beyond the reach of Congress,—surely no negligible matter. Nor does the chief justice's attempt to draw support from the further words of the same paragraph fare better upon investigation. "In all other cases," he quotes, the Supreme Court is given appellate jurisdiction, that is, as he would have it, *merely* appellate jurisdiction. Unfortunately for this argument the words thus pointed to are followed by the words—which the chief justice fails to quote—"with such exceptions . . . as the Congress shall make." But why should not the exceptions thus allowed to the appellate jurisdiction of the Supreme Court, have been intended to take the form, if Congress so willed, of giving the court original jurisdiction of the cases covered by them?

Moreover, the time was to come when Marshall himself was to abandon the reasoning underlying the rule laid down in Marbury v. Madison. This rule, to repeat, was that the Supreme Court's original jurisdiction is confined by the Constitution to the cases specifically enumerated in Article III, section 2, paragraph 2, and—though this was only dictum—that the Court's appellate jurisdiction is confined "to all other cases." But now it must be noted that jurisdiction is always *either original or appellate,*—that there is, in other words, no third sort. The rule laid down in Marbury v. Madison becomes therefore the logical equivalent of the proposition that the Supreme Court had *only* original jurisdiction of the cases enumerated in Article III, section 2, paragraph 2. In Cohens v. Virginia[13] nevertheless the Court took jurisdiction on appeal of a case which had arisen "under this Constitution," but was also a

10. See argument of counsel in 1 Cranch 137–53.
11. 1 Stat. L. 112ff. (April 30, 1790).
12. 1 Cranch 174.
13. 6 Wheat. 264 (1821).

case to which a state was party, on the basis of the rule, as stated by the chief justice, that "Where the words admit of appellate jurisdiction the power to take cognizance of the suit originally does not necessarily negative the power to decide upon it on an appeal, if it may originate in a different court."[14] And in further illustration of this rule, the chief justice instanced the right of the Supreme Court to take jurisdiction on appeal of certain cases which foreign consuls were allowed to institute in the lower federal courts.[15] He also insisted, and quite warrantably, upon the necessity of the rule in question to major purposes of the Constitution. Yet obviously if the rule is to be harmonized with that laid down in Marbury v. Madison, it must be by eliminating the word "all" from the opening clause of Article III, section 2, paragraph 2, and by inserting qualifying words in front of the word "those" of the same clause. Otherwise the line of reasoning taken in Marbury v. Madison is abandoned and the precise decision there left hanging in mid-air.[16]

Suppose however, we concede Marshall his construction of Article III, is his decision absolved of error thereby? By no means. This decision rests upon the assumption that it was the intention and necessary operation of section 13 of the Act of 1789 to *enlarge* the original jurisdiction of the Supreme Court, and this cannot be allowed. To begin with, in common law practice, in the light of which section 13 was framed, the writ of mandamus was not, ordinarily at least, an instrument of obtaining jurisdiction by a court, even upon appeal, but like the writs of habeas corpus and injunction, was a *remedy* available from a court in the exercise of its standing jurisdiction. This being the case, however, why may it not have been the intention of Congress in enacting section 13, not to enlarge the Supreme Court jurisdiction, but simply to enable the Court to issue the writ of mandamus to civil officers of the United States as auxiliary to the original jurisdiction which the Constitution conferred upon it? It is certain that the Court has more than once entertained motions by original suitors for injunctions to such officers,[17] and it is apparent that, so far as the question here discussed is concerned, an application for a writ of mandamus must rest on the same footing.[18]

---

14. *Id*. 395–402.

15. The validity of such appeals was considered by C. J. Taney in Gittings v. Crawford, 10 F. Cas. 447 (No. 5, 465) (1838). Referring to the precise clause under discussion in Marbury v. Madison, Taney said: "In the clause in question there is nothing but mere affirmative words of grant, and none that import a design to exclude the subordinate jurisdiction of other courts of the United States on the same subject matter." See also C. J. Waite's language in Ames v. Kansas, 111 U.S. 449 (1884).

16. The precise precedent in Marbury v. Madison has been applied several times. See 5 How. 176 (1847), 1 Wall. 243 (1863), 8 Wall. 85 (1868).

17. Miss. v. Johnson, 4 Wall. 475 (1867); Georgia v. Stanton, 6 Wall. 50 (1868). The grounds on which these cases were dismissed do not affect the view urged in the text.

18. Suppose Congress should transfer the business of interstate extradition to federal commissioners, as it would be within its power to do, there would be plenty of occasions when the Supreme Court would be asked for writs of mandamus to civil officers of the United States. See Kentucky v. Dennison, 24 How. 65 (1861).

Furthermore, the proposition that the writ of mandamus is not to be regarded ordinarily as a means of obtaining jurisdiction, but only of exercising it, was recognized and applied by the Supreme Court itself a few years later, in a case the exact parallel of Marbury v. Madison. By section 14 of the Act of 1789 the circuit courts of the United States were given the power, in words substantially the same as those employed in section 13, to issue certain writs "in cases authorized by the principles and usages of law." Yet in McIntire v. Wood,[19] where the issue was the validity of a writ of mandamus to a person holding office under the authority of the United States the Supreme Court ruled that before a circuit court could utilize the power given it in section 14 in a case, it must have jurisdiction of the case on independent grounds, and the same rule was later reiterated in McClung v. Silliman.[20] But clearly, had the Court followed this line of reasoning in Marbury v. Madison, it could not have questioned the validity of section 13. Indeed, had it but followed the, today at any rate, well-known maxim of constitutional law that of two possible interpretations of a statute, the one harmonious with the Constitution, the other at variance with it, the former must be preferred,[21] it could not have challenged the legislation in question. By its view of Article III, section 2, paragraph 2, it must still doubtless have declined jurisdiction of the case, but the ground of its action would have been, not the error of Congress, but the error of plaintiff.

In short there was no valid occasion in Marbury v. Madison for any inquiry by the Court into its prerogative in relation to acts of Congress. Why then, it will be asked, did the Court make such an inquiry? In part the answer to this question will appear later, but in part it may be answered now. To speak quite frankly, this decision bears many of the earmarks of a deliberate partisan *coup*. The Court was bent on reading the president a lecture on his legal and moral duty to recent Federalist appointees to judicial office, whose commissions the last administration had not had time to deliver, but at the same time hesitated to invite a snub by actually asserting jurisdiction of the matter. It therefore took the engaging position of declining to exercise power which the Constitution withheld from it, by making the occasion an opportunity to assert a far more transcendent power.

II

But from Marbury v. Madison we proceed to the question whether, and in what way, the Constitution itself sanctions judicial review. I have already indicated my opinion that no clause was inserted in the Constitution for the specific purpose of bestowing this power on courts, but that the power rests

---

19. 7 Cranch 504 (1813).
20. 6 Wheat. 598 (1821).
21. For a rather farfetched application of this rule see the "Commodities Clause" case, 213 U.S. 366 (1908).

upon certain general principles thought by its framers to have been embodied in the Constitution. I shall now endeavor to justify this opinion.

That the members of the Convention of 1787 thought the Constitution secured to courts in the United States the right to pass on the validity of acts of Congress under it cannot be reasonably doubted. Confining ourselves simply to the available evidence that is strictly contemporaneous with the framing and ratifying of the Constitution, as I think it only proper to do, we find the following members of the Convention that framed the Constitution definitely asserting that this would be the case: Gerry and King of Massachusetts, Wilson and Gouverneur Morris of Pennsylvania, Martin of Maryland, Randolph, Madison, and Mason of Virginia, Dickinson of Delaware, Yates and Hamilton of New York, Rutledge and Charles Pinckney of South Carolina, Davie and Williamson of North Carolina, Sherman and Ellsworth of Connecticut.[22] True these are only seventeen names out of a possible fifty-five, but let it be considered whose names they are. They designate fully three-fourths of the leaders of the Convention, four of the five members of the Committee of Detail which drafted the Constitution,[23] and four of the five members of the Committee of Style which gave the Constitution final form.[24] The entries under these names, in the Index to Farrand's *Records* occupy fully thirty columns, as compared with fewer than half as many columns under the names of the remaining members. We have in this list, in other words, the names of men who expressed themselves on the subject of judicial review because they also expressed themselves on all other subjects before the Convention. They were the leaders of that body and its articulate members. And against them are to be pitted, in reference to the question under discussion, only Mercer of Maryland, Bedford of Delaware, and Spaight of North Carolina, the record in each of whose cases turns out to be upon inspection of doubtful implication. For while Spaight, for instance, undoubtedly expressed himself, during the period of the

22. I Max Farrand, *Records of the Federal Convention* {hereinafter *Records*} (1913): I, 97 (Gerry, 109 (King); II, 73 (Wilson), 76 (Martin), 78 (Mason), 299 (Dickinson and Morris), 428 (Rutledge), 248 (Pinckney), 376 (Williamson), 28 (Sherman), 93 (Madison); III, 220 (Martin, in "Genuine Information"). *The Federalist:* Nos. 39 and 44 (Madison), No. 78 (Hamilton). Elliot's *Debates* (ed. 1836): II, 1898–99 (Ellsworth), 417 and 454 (Wilson), 336–37 (Hamilton); III, 197, 208, 431 (Randolph), 441 (Mason), 484–85 (Madison); IV, 165 (Davie). P. L. Ford, *Pamphlets on the Constitution* 184 (1888) (Dickinson, in "Letters of Fabius"). Ford, *Essays on the Constitution* 295 (1892) (Yates, writing as "Brutus"). Pinckney later, in 1799, denounced the idea of judicial review, thus: "On no subject am I more convinced than that it is an unsafe and dangerous doctrine in a republic ever to suppose that a judge ought to possess the right of questioning or deciding upon the constitutionality of treaties, laws, or any act of the legislature. It is placing the opinion of an individual, or two, or three, above that of both branches of Congress, a doctrine which is not warranted by the Constitution, and will not, I hope, long have any advocates in this country"; quoted from Wharton's State Trials, 412, by Mr. Horace A. Davis in {"Annulment of Legislation by the Supreme Court,"} *Am. Pol. Sci. Rev.* 551 (1913). Madison's later views are considered below.
23. Gorham, Rutledge, Randolph, Ellsworth, and Wilson.
24. Johnson, Hamilton, Morris, Madison, and King.

Convention, as strongly adverse to the theory of judicial review,[25] yet he later heard the idea expounded both on the floor of the Philadelphia Convention and the North Carolina convention without protest. The words of Bedford which are relied upon in this connection are his declaration that he was "opposed to every check on the legislature." But these words were spoken with reference, not to judicial review, but to the proposition to establish a council of revision.[26] Mercer of Maryland did not sign the Constitution and opposed its adoption. It is by no means impossible that one of the grounds of his opposition was recognition of the fact that the Constitution established judicial review.[27] Altogether it seems a warrantable assertion that upon no other feature of the Constitution with reference to which there has been considerable debate is the view of the Convention itself better attested.

Yet it must be admitted that, if we assume that the Convention did not finally incorporate its view in specific provisions of the Constitution, a difficulty that at first seems formidable opposes itself to the thesis that this view was secured by certain general principles thought to be embodied in the Constitution. The source of the difficulty I allude to is Article VI, paragraph 2, of the Constitution. This paragraph first announces the *supremacy* of the Constitution, the acts of Congress in pursuance thereof, and treaties made under the authority of the United States, as *law* of the land, and then proceeds to impose a specific mandate upon *state* judges to enforce this *supreme law,* anything in the law or constitution of any state to the contrary notwithstanding. The question therefore arises, Why did the Convention, if it believed general principles sufficient to secure judicial review of acts of Congress, deem it necessary to order the *state* judges to prefer what was described as *supreme* law of the land to subordinate law? Any doctrine of judicial review must rest in part upon the idea of one law superior to another, and if, to repeat the question just put, the fact of superiority of national law to state law furnished, in the estimation of the Convention, an insufficient security of the former as against the latter, why should not the analogous superiority of the Constitution itself to acts of Congress be similarly insufficient? But the answer to this question is, after all, plain enough: The judges to whom the mandate of Article VI is addressed are *state* judges, that is, judges of an independent jurisdiction. Their duty to take cognizance of national law *at all* had therefore to be declared in unmistakable terms. Indeed, once this fact is grasped, it is seen that the mandate in question, instead of opposing difficulty to the thesis I am presenting, furnishes it powerful confirmation. For the significant feature of that mandate now becomes the fact that it is addressed to state *judges,* who are thus assumed to be the *final* guardians of both state laws and state constitutions.

What, however, are the clauses usually represented as having been placed in

25. See 2 McRee, *Life and Correspondence of James Iredell* 169–76 (1857).
26. 1 Farrand, *Records* 100, 106.
27. 2 *id.* 298.

the Constitution for the purpose of giving the Supreme Court the power to pass upon the validity of acts of Congress? One is the "pursuance" clause of Article VI, paragraph 2. But obviously this clause, while perhaps making more explicit the fact that Congress' is a limited power, says nothing as to what agency is to say *finally* what of Congress' acts are, and what are not, "in pursuance of this Constitution." Moreover, the "pursuance" clause does not appear in Article III, where the judicial power of the United States is defined.

A clause more insisted upon, however, in this connection is the clause in this same Article III: "The judicial power of the United States shall extend to all cases arising under this Constitution." No doubt it must be allowed that cases involving the question of constitutionality with reference to acts of Congress are describable as "cases arising under this Constitution." Nevertheless, it must be insisted that the clause just quoted was not placed in the Constitution for the purpose of bringing such cases within the judicial power of the United States, and this for the simple reason that, *admitting the legal character of the Constitution,* they were already there. Thus we have just noted that the "pursuance" clause does not appear in Article III. But what this signifies is that the judicial power of the United States extends to *every* act of Congress whether made in pursuance of the Constitution or not; or, to quote the words of Chief Justice Taney in Ableman v. Booth, that it "covers every legislative act of Congress, whether it be made within the limits of its delegated power or be an assumption of power beyond the grants in the Constitution."[28] Had, therefore, the clause "arising under this Constitution" been inserted to extend the judicial power of the United States to cases involving the constitutionality of acts of Congress, it would be so far forth mere surplusage.

The explanation of the clause must then be sought in a class of cases to which *but for it* the judicial power of the United States could not possibly extend, even assuming the legal character of the Constitution. Nor, relying upon the guidance of Hamilton in the *Federalist* is it difficult to discover such a class of cases. Construing the clause under discussion in *Federalist* 80, Hamilton explains that it refers to cases arising in consequence of *state* enactments transgressing prohibitions of the Constitution upon *state* legislative powers, cases of which, therefore, but for this clause, would terminate in the *state* judiciaries. Hamilton's explanation is confirmed by Madison's analysis of Article III in the Virginia convention[29] and by Davie's language in the North Carolina convention,[30] but it is confirmed even more strikingly by the failure of the spokesmen for judicial review, while the Constitution was pending, to adduce the clause in question in support of their position.

But there are also some objections of a more general character to resting the power of the Supreme Court over acts of Congress upon the phrases under

28. 21 How. 506, 519–20 (1858).
29. 3 Elliot, *Debates* 484–85.
30. 4 *id.* 165.

discussion. For, if the framers wanted judicial review and still thought it necessary to provide for it specifically, why did they not choose language apt for the purpose, language as explicit and unmistakable as that describing, for example, the veto power of the president? A possible suggestion would be, of course, that they desired to conceal their intentions at this point, but the fact is, that they proclaimed them and that judicial review was universally regarded as a feature of the new system while its adoption was pending.[31] Moreover, their vagueness would have to be regarded as positively maladroit, since neither of the clauses just considered, taken by itself, secures the finality of the judicial view of the Constitution, which, however, is the very essence of judicial review. Furthermore, it may be queried, if these clauses are necessary to give the federal courts power to pass upon the constitutionality of acts of Congress, what becomes of the similar pretension of state courts with reference to state legislation under the state constitutions.

III

We are accordingly driven to the conclusion that judicial review was rested by the framers of the Constitution upon certain general principles which in their estimation made specific provision for it unnecessary, in the same way as, for example, certain other general principles made unnecessary specific provision for the president's power of removal.[32] What, then, are these general principles? The task of identifying them is, perhaps, at this date not an entirely simple one. For while the ideas that are essential to explaining and sustaining judicial review *as a matter of law,* which are the ideas we are in quest of, are relatively few, they have to be sifted from a more considerable stock of ideas which contributed to the rise of judicial review, *as a matter of fact,* or which have since been offered with the aim of curtailing its practical operation. It will be profitable to begin by criticizing some remarks by Professor McLaughlin in the course of his recent interesting study of the subject.

Thus, at the outset of his essay, writing with Marshall's argument in Marbury v. Madison in mind, Professor McLaughlin states the doctrine of judicial review as follows: "In theory any court may exercise the power of holding acts invalid; in doing so, it assumes no special and peculiar role; for the duty of the

31. See the evidence gathered by Mr. Horace Davis in the *Am. Pol. Sci. Rev.* for November 1913. Mr. Davis himself, however, endeavors to reject the obvious verdict of this evidence. The explanation of his strange attitude is that he confuses the question of whether judicial review of acts of Congress was believed to be a feature of the new system with the question whether it was expected to prove an effective limitation upon Congress. The absence of a Bill of Rights and the presence of the "general welfare" and "necessary and proper" clauses caused opponents of the Constitution to charge that the judges would never be able to stamp any act of Congress as invalid, that Congress' power was practically unlimited to begin with. See 1 Elliot, *Debates* 545; 2 *id.* 314–15, 318, 321–22; 4 *id.* 175; also, McMaster and Stone, *Pennsylvania and the Federal Constitution* 467, 611 (1888); also, Ford, *Pamphlets* 312; also and especially, *Federalist* No. 33.

32. The parallel is exact. See 1 Annals of Congress cols. 473 ff. and specially cols. 481–82 (Gales & Seaton eds. 1789).

court is to declare what the law is, and, on the other hand, not to recognize and apply what is not law.'' Further along, however, he sets himself the task of refuting the idea that the courts claim a superiority over the other departments in relation to the Constitution, and we then find him writing thus: ''This authority then in part arose . . . from the conviction that the courts were not under the control of a co-ordinate branch of the government but entirely able to interpret the constitution themselves when acting in their own field.'' And from this it is quite logically deduced that, ''If our constitutional system at the present time includes the principle that the political departments must yield to the decisions of the judiciary on the whole question of constitutionality, such principle is the result of constitutional development, and . . . . of the acquiescence of the political powers, because of reasons of expediency.'' Yet at the same time it is conceded that the political departments must ''accept as final'' ''the decision of the court in the particular case.'' Finally, it is urged that ''no one is bound by an unconstitutional law.''[33]

In other words, Professor McLaughlin presents the right of interpreting the Constitution that is enjoyed by the courts first, as a *judicial* power, and therefore one to be exercised by courts *as such;* secondly, as a departmental or official function, and therefore one to be exercised by all departments of government equally, *including the courts;* and thirdly, as an individual prerogative, and therefore one belonging to everybody, *including judges.* In the first place, there is an element of inconsistency among these three theories that should not escape our attention. For if the power of the judiciary to construe the Constitution, when acting in its own field, owes anything by way of *theoretical justification*—which is the point under discussion—to its position as an independent branch of the government, why is it necessary to insist on the legal character of the Constitution and the duty of courts to interpret the law? Likewise, if the position of the judiciary as an equal and co-ordinate branch of the government, or of judges as governmental functionaries, is an indispensible foundation of judicial review, why is it necessary to contend that ''no one is bound by an unconstitutional act''?

But a more important criticism is that the last two theories are either quite unallowable or totally insufficient to explain judicial review. Let us consider, first, the statement that ''no one is bound by an unconstitutional law.'' This may mean one of two things: either that no one is bound by a law that has been determined by proper authority to be unconstitutional, which leaves open the crucial question as to where this proper authority resides; or, that no one is bound by a law which *he* thinks is unconstitutional, which is nonsense. It is not open to contradiction that judicial review posits a constitutional system, complete in all points, and furnished with the machinery for determining all questions that arise out of it. But the right of revolution is a right external to

33. *The Courts, the Constitution, and Parties* 6, 51, 55, 56.

any constitution, and therefore to invoke it as a means of settling constitutional questions is to discard the Constitution at the outset.[34]

And similarly is the doctrine that the power to construe the Constitution is a departmental function allowable or unallowable according as one understands it. If what is meant by it is that all functionaries of government have to interpret the Constitution preliminary to performing their supposed duties under it, in the same way that the private citizen has to interpret the ordinary law whenever he performs an act having legal consequences—why the theory is correct enough, but obviously quite insufficient to explain the finality of the judicial view of the Constitution even in particular cases.[35] On the other hand, if what is meant is that the three departments have an equal right, when acting within their respective spheres, to determine the validity of their own acts, then it is untrue. This, of course, is apparent enough as respects the legislative department, for otherwise there would be no judicial review at all. It is true that the legislature is not arrested when it violates the Constitution, that the only legal disadvantage it suffers is to have its acts disallowed, in the same way as the private citizen who makes a contract contrary to the statute of frauds or a will contrary to the rule against perpetuities has *his* act disallowed. But a statute that has been disallowed is usually harmless, and so the remedy is ordinarily quite adequate.

Still there are those who have asserted that the advantage which the judiciary enjoys over the legislature is due merely to the accident that in the scheme of law-making and law-enforcement provided by the Constitution the judiciary has the later say, that it is, in other words, not one of *right* but of *position*.[36] The real test, therefore, of the departmental theory is supplied by the question whether it applies to the executive department, which occupies with reference to the judiciary the same favorable position that the latter does with reference to the legislature. Jackson, in his famous Bank Veto Message of 1832, claimed, it will be recalled, the benefit of the departmental theory to the fullest extent. His claim was met by Webster in the following terms: "The President is as much bound by the law as any private citizen. . . . He may refuse to obey the law and so may any private citizen, but both do it at their own peril and neither can settle the question of its validity. The President may *say* a law is unconstitutional, but he is not the judge. . . . If it were otherwise, there would be not

---

34. Vattel's apothegm that the legislature cannot "change the Constitution without destroying the foundation of its authority" was a commonplace in Massachusetts before the Revolution. See the Massachusetts Circular Letter of 1768 in W. MacDonald, *Documentary Source Book* 146–50 (1908). For interesting statements of basing judicial review on the right of revolution, see 2 Elliot, *Debates* 100–106 (Parsons in the Massachusetts convention), and 4 *id.* 93–94 (Steele in the North Carolina convention). See also note 59, below.

35. In an early Massachusetts case C. J. Parker has some very sensible words on this subject. At the moment of writing, however, I am unable to recover the reference.

36. Madison took this position tentatively in 1788; 1 *Letters and Other Writings* 195 (1865). His words on this occasion are considered below. Cf. *Federalist* No. 49.

government of laws, but we should all live under the government, the rule, the caprices of individuals; . . . The President, if the principle and reasoning of the message be sound, may either execute or not execute the laws of the land, according to his sovereign pleasure. He may refuse to put into execution one law, pronounced valid by all branches of government, and yet execute another which may have been by constitutional authority pronounced void." In brief, Webster concluded, the message converted "constitutional limitations of power into mere matters of opinion," denied "first principles," contradicted "truths heretofore received as indisputable"; *for it denied "to the judiciary the interpretation of the law."*[37] And he elsewhere inquired, with pertinent reference to a then impending issue: "Does nullification teach anything more revolutionary."[38]

The fact of the matter is that, while the principle of the independence and equality of the departments fortifies each department in the possession and use of the powers belonging to it, *it throws no light whatsoever upon the question as to what those powers are,* and that therefore it cannot be validly drawn to the support of judicial review. Moreover, we discover that at the critical moment Professor McLaughlin abandons this principle. For, as we have seen, he admits that the political departments are obliged "to accept as final . . . the decision of the court in the particular case." Yet he also contends that further acquiescence by these departments in the decisions of the judiciary on constitutional questions is not required by constitutional theory, but must be reckoned as "accommodation" on the part of these departments, based on reasons of expediency. With this contention I cannot agree. On the contrary, it seems to me that once we accept the doctrine of judicial review as a part of the Constitution, the acquiescence of the political departments in the judicial view of the Constitution is required by the Constitution itself. The question at issue may be put in this way: Is the legislature bound by judicial interpretations of the Constitution arising from past cases, when passing laws intended to govern future cases? It seems to me that there can be no doubt that it is, if the phrase "passing a law" be given its proper significance of endowing a legislative measure with the sanction and force of *law.* For this latter the legislature is simply incapable of doing when the measure runs counter to settled judicial interpretation of the Constitution, unless it possesses a constructive power over-riding that of the courts, which, however, would mean the end of judicial review. By the theory of judicial review a measure of the character described, although it may have been put through all the parliamentary stages, is not *law* and never was. Indeed, this result flows from Professor McLaughlin's own proposition that the courts do not "assume any special and peculiar role" in relation to the Constitution, different, that is, from their role in relation to the ordinary law. In both cases alike the courts are interpreting the law; and if those

37. Speech of July 11, 1832.
38. 2 *Works* {*sic.; Writings*} 122 (October 12, 1832) (National ed. 1903).

subject to the ordinary law are bound by the judicial interpretation of *it,* then those subject to the constitution are bound by the judicial interpretation of *it.* The unique element of the latter case is merely the fact that in the Constitution we have a law that binds the government itself.[39]

It is therefore submitted that judicial review rests upon the following propositions and can rest upon no others: 1—That the Constitution binds the organs of government; 2—That it is law in the sense of being known to and enforceable by the courts; 3—That the function of interpreting the standing law appertains to the courts alone, so that their interpretations of the Constitution as part and parcel of such standing law are alone authoritative, while those of the other departments are mere expressions of opinion. That the framers of the Constitution of the United States accepted the first of these propositions goes without saying. Their acceptance of the second one is registered in the Constitution itself, though this needs to be shown. But it is their acceptance of the third one which is the matter of greatest significance, for at this point their view marks an entire breach, not only with English legal tradition, but, for the vast part, with American legal tradition as well, anterior to 1787.

IV

The idea of judicial review is today regarded as an outgrowth of that of a written constitution, but historically both are offshoots from a common stock, namely the idea of certain fundamental principles underlying and controlling government. In Anglo-American constitutional history this idea is to be traced

39. A very explicit statement of the doctrine of departmental construction is that of Abraham Baldwin in the United States Senate, January 23, 1800: 3 Farrand, *Records* 383. For Jefferson's view as formulated late in life, see his 15 *Writings* 212 ff. (Mem. ed. 1903). Madison as president took the position that he had no discretion in the matter of enforcing, not only decisions of the judiciary, but acts of Congress: 2 Am. St. Papers Misc. 12 (1809). Jackson, on the other hand, is credited with the sentiment, with reference to Worcester v. Georgia (6 Pet. 515): "John Marshall has made his decision, now let him enforce it"; 1 Greeley, *American Conflict* 106 (1866). Lincoln's views expressed in criticism of the Dred Scott decision are contradictory. Professor McLaughlin refers approvingly to old Gideon Welles' attempt "to make General Grant see that he was not under constitutional obligation to obey an act if that act was unconstitutional. Grant maintained that he was under obligations to obey a law until the Supreme Court declared it unconstitutional. Such is the natural position of the layman." The illustration, however, falls down at the critical point, for even Welles had no idea of maintaining that the president would not be bound by a decision of the Supreme Court: 3 *Diary of Gideon Welles* 176–80 (1911). Furthermore, on the precise question in issue between Welles and Grant, I must express a preference for the views of the latter. Obedience to the mandates of the legislature till they are proved to be void is one of the risks of office under our system. The contrary view leads to irresponsibility and disorder. Bancroft, in his *History,* supports Professor McLaughlin's view on p. 350 (last revision): "The decision of the Court in all cases within its jurisdiciton is final between the parties to a suit and must be carried into effect by the proper officers; but as an interpretation of the Constitution, it does not bind the President or the legislature of the United States." This view is stated *ex cathedra* and without any attempt at argument, and three pages later (p. 353) is substantially contradicted. The position taken by President Taft and Congress with reference to the proposal to enact an income tax in the face of Pollock v. Farmers' Loan and Trust Co. (158 U.S. 601 {1895}) is fresh in mind.

to feudal concepts and finds its most notable expression in Magna Carta.[40] The notion was well suited to a period when the great institutions of mankind were thought to be sacred, permanent, immutable, and did in fact alter but slowly. The period of the Reformation, however, was a period of overturn, of defiance of ancient establishments, of revolution. Its precipiate for political theory was the notion, derived from Roman law, of *sovereignty*, of human authority in the last analysis uncontrollable, and capable accordingly of meeting the exigencies of the new *regime* of change.

But where did sovereignty rest? Sir Thomas Smith, in his *Commonwealth of England*,[41] reflecting Tudor ideas, attributed it to the crown in Parliament, and it is not impossible that English political theory would have remained from that day to this substantially what it is today but for the attempt of James Stuart to set up the notion, on the basis of divine right, of a kingly prerogative recognized but uncontrolled by the common law. The result was a reaction headed by Sir Edward Coke and having for its purpose, to quote the quaint words of Sir Benjamin Rudyard, "to make that good old, decrepid law of Magna Carta, which hath so long been kept in and bed-ridden, as it were, to walk again."[42] Coke took the position that there was no such thing as sovereign power in England, even for Parliament; for, said he: "Magna Carta is such a fellow as will have no sovereign." His famous dictum in Dr. Bonham's Case[43] that an act of Parliament "contrary to common right and reason" would be "void," was therefore quite in harmony with his whole propaganda. At the same time, it would be the height of absurdity to suppose that these words necessarily spell out anything like judicial review. They undoubtedly indicate Coke's belief that the principles of "common right and reason," being part of the common law, were cognizable by the judges while interpreting acts of Parliament. But for the rest they must be read along with Coke's characterization of Parliament as the "*Supreme* Court" of the realm. As he plainly indicated by his connection with the framing of the Petition of Right, Coke regarded Parliament itself as the final interpreter of the law by which both it, the king, and the judges were bound.

But it is the tendency of doctrines to strip themselves, so to speak, for action or else to disappear. A contemporary of Coke's, Hobart, early gave the dictum in Bonham's Case an interpretation which, had it been followed, might have meant something very like judicial review.[44] Hobart's doctrine in turn found its way to America through Bacon's *Abridgement*, where Otis found it an available

40. See C. H. McIlwain, *The High Court of Parliament and Its Supremacy* (1910); and G. B. Adams, *The Origin of the English Constitution* (1912).

41. F. W. Maitland, *Constitutional History* 255 (1908). Maitland expresses the emphatic opinion that the law-making power of crown and Parliament was from an early date unlimited.

42. 2 Cobbett, *Parliamentary History* col. 335 (1806–20); the remark quoted below is from the same debate.

43. 8 Reps. 107, 118 (1612).

44. Savadge v. Day, Hob. 85 (1615).

weapon for the moment in the Writs of Assistance Case in 1761.[45] More than a
century before this, however, the English judges in Streater's Case[46] had
decisively repudiated the dictum, while early in the 18th century Lord Holt,
minded to give his predecessor's words some meaning, had reduced their
application to the single case where an act of Parliament should be so
self-contradictory in terms as to be impossible of execution.[47] Just as the
Americans were about to frame their first constitutions, Holt's doctrine found
its way to them in the influential pages of Blackstone,[48] in company with the
notion of legislative sovereignty. Its initial effect, in co-operation with other
influences, was to give judicial review a set-back, though finally it was to
furnish the way of return thereto. Undoubtedly the most influential case in
which judicial review was broached before the Convention of 1787 was that of
Trevett v. Weeden,[49] in which in 1786 the Rhode Island judges refused enforcement to a rag-money law on account of its alleged "repugnancy," that
is self-contradictory character.

The influence of Blackstone, however, in excluding judicial review from the
early state constitutions was subordinate to two other considerations: first,
uncertainty whether these constitutions were law, and secondly, the position of
the legislature in them. There could, of course, be no doubt that the fundamental principles of right and reason invoked by Coke were law, since they were
part and parcel of the common law. They were, therefore, known to the judges
and enforceable by them, at least as principles of interpretation in applying
statute law. But the early state constitutions were of a different stamp,—they
were acts of revolution, social compacts, sprung from the pages of Locke rather
than of Coke. Undoubtedly they illustrated and realized the doctrine that all just
government rests upon the consent of the governed. Yet it was a corollary from
this doctrine, that a government established upon this foundation had the right
to *govern*, and that this was recoverable by the people only by another act of
revolution. The power of *enacting laws*, however, was a function of *government*.
How, then, could constitutions, bills or rights, frames of government, the work
of the people themselves, be regarded as laws in the strict sense of the term?

45. See my "Establishment of Judicial Review" in 9 *Mich L. Rev.* 104–6 (1910). For the spread
of the influence of Otis' argument, see the case of Robin v. Hardaway, Jefferson's Reports, 114.
Professor McMaster informs me that in 1765 the Stamp Act was declared unconstitutional by the
County Court of Northampton County, Va.

46. 5 State Trials 386 ff. (1653).

47. City of London v. Wood, 12 Mod. 669 (1701).

48. 1 *Comms.* 91. The case discussed by Hobart, Holt, and Blackstone in turn is that of an act
of Parliament making a man a judge in his own case. Such an act, says Hobart, would be against
the laws of nature and void, but Holt and Blackstone merely say it would be self-contradictory. The
discussion starts with Coke's citation of a case arising in the manor of Dales, where it was held
merely that an act of Parliament conferring in general terms upon a specific person the jurisdiction
of cases arising in the manor did not apply to a case to which that person was an interested party: 8
Rep. 118–20.

49. 1 J. B. Thayer, *Cases on Constitutional Law* 73–78 (1894–95); Brinton Coxe, *Judicial
Power and Unconstitutional Legislation* 234–48 (1893).

Their moral supremacy none doubted, nor yet that a breach of them by government destroyed its right to be, but until the *people* should be regarded as having an *enacting power,* exercisable directly and without the intervention of their legislative representatives, the *supremacy* of constitutions was a real barrier to their *legality.*[50]

But the second difficulty was even more formidable. A majority of the early state constitutions contained statements, sometimes in very round terms, of Montesquieu's doctrine of the separation of powers; and as against executive power, a supposed monarchical tendency in which was feared, this principle was given detailed application.[51] Not so, however, as against legislative power.[52] In the first place, all through colonial times, the legislature had stood for the local interest as against the imperial interest, which had in turn been represented by the governors and the judges. In the second place, the legislative department was supposed to stand nearest to the people. Finally, *legislative* power was *undefined* power. As applied against the legislative department, therefore, all that the principle of the separation of powers originally meant was that those who held seats in the legislature should not at the same time hold office in either of the other departments.[53] But the legislature itself, like the British Parliament and like the colonial legislatures before it, exercised *all kinds of power,* and particularly did it exercise the power of interpreting the standing law and interfering with the course of justice as administered in the ordinary courts,[54] and the only test deemed available to its acts was that they

50. On a constitution as an act of revolution, see the remarks of the judges in Kamper v. Hawkins, Va. Cases 20 ff.; also, Marshall in Marbury v. Madison. On the lodgment of the function of governing exclusively with the government, see Luther Martin's remarks in his "Genuine Information"; also, Dr. Benjamin Rush's remarks in his "Address to the People of the United States" (1787) in H. Niles' *Principles and Acts of the Revolution* 234–36 (1876). The idea, indeed, is fundamental to the concept of representative government.

51. See data in *Federalist* Nos. 47 and 48.

52. The position of the legislature in the early state constitutions is described at length by Morey, in 9 *Annals* 398 ff. {*sic;* W. C. Webster, "A Comparative Study of the State Constitutions of the American Revolution," 9 *Annals* 380, 398 (1897)}; also by Davis, "American Constitutions" in *Johns Hopkins University Studies,* 3rd Series.

53. The doctrine of the separation of powers receives recognition in the body of the first Virginia constitution in the following words: "That the legislative, executive, and judiciary departments shall be distinct; so that neither exercise the powers properly belonging to the other; nor shall any person exercise the powers of more than one of them at the same time," etc. See also the first New Jersey Constitution, Art. 20; the original North Carolina Constitution, Arts. 28–30; the first Pennsylvania Constitution, Sec. 23; the first South Carolina Constitution, Art. 10: Thorpe, *American Charters, Constitutions,* etc. (1909).

54. For Parliament's relation to the standing law in the seventeenth century, see the instructive pages in McIlwain, *High Court of Parliament,* etc., ch. 3, especially at 109–66. Said Harrington in his *Oceana:* "Wherever the power of making law is, there only is the power of interpreting the law so made": *loc. cit.* 163. See also Blackstone, 1 *Comms.* 160. For the case of the colonial legislatures, see 2 *Works of James Wilson* 50 (Andrews ed. 1896); 1 Minot, *History of Massachusetts* 29 (1798–1803); T. Hutchinson, *History of Massachusetts,* etc., I, 30, II, 250, 414; 15 *Harvard L. Rev.* 208–18 (1901–2); Massachusetts Acts and Resolves (to 1780), *passim;* Journal of Virginia House of Burgesses, *passim.* For the case of the early state legislatures, see *Federalist* Nos. 48 and

should be passed in the usual form.[55] In short, as both Madison and Jefferson put the matter later, legislative power was the *vortex* into which all other powers tended to be drawn. Obviously so long as this remained the case, there could be nothing like judicial review.

The period 1780–1787, however, was a period of "constitutional reaction," which mounting gradually till the outbreak of Shays' Rebellion in Massachusetts in the latter part of 1786, then leaped suddenly to its climax in the Philadelphia Convention. The reaction embraced two phases, that of nationalism against state sovereignty, that of private rights against uncontrolled legislative power; but the point of attack in both instances was the state legislature.[56] Yet it should not be imagined for a moment that those who discerned the central fault of "the

---

81, the latter of which is quoted below on this subject. See also Jefferson's "Virginia Notes" in 2 *Works {sic.; Writings}* 160–78 (Mem. ed.); also the Reports of the Pennsylvania Council of Censors of their sessions of November 10, 1783, and June 1, 1784, in The Proceedings Relative to the Calling of the Conventions of 1776 and 1790, etc. 66–128 (Harrisburg, 1825) {hereinafter Proceedings}. See also Langdon of New Hampshire's letters complaining of acts of the state legislature annulling judgments, in New Hampshire State Papers, XI, 812, 815, and XXII, 749, 756 (June 1790). For concrete instances in Massachusetts under the Constitution of 1780, see Acts and Resolves under following dates: 1780, May 5, June 9, September 19; 1781, February 12, April 28, October 10; 1782, February 13, 22, March 5, 7, May 6, 7, June 7, 18, September 11, October 4, November 2; 1783, February 4, 25; March 17, October 11; 1784, February 3; 1785, February 28, March 17; 1786, June 27, July 5; 1787, February 26, March 7, July 7; 1790, February 25, 26, March 9; 1791, February 24. See also Kilham v. Ward *et. al.,* 2 Mass. 240, 251; also, *Proceedings of the Massachusetts Historical Society* 231 (1893); also Story's *Commentaries* sec. 1367. Further testimony will be found in a speech by Roger Sherman in his contemporary essays on the Constitution; Moore's *History of North Carolina;* Jeremiah Mason's *Memories,* etc. {sic.; *Memoir and Correspondence of Jeremiah Mason* (1873)?}; Tucker's Edition of Blackstone (1802 {1803}), the appendix; Plumer's *Life of William Plumer* (1857); various judicial histories of Rhode Island,where the practice continued till 1842. The published Index to Rhode Island legislation to 1842 is immensely instructive in this connection. See also such cases as Rep. v. Buffington, 1 Dallas 61 (1781); Calder v. Bull, 3 Dallas 386 (1798); Watson v. Mercer, 8 Pet. 88 (1834); Satterlee v. Matthewson, 2 Pet. 380 (1829); Wilkinson v. Leland, *id.* 657 (1829). The overturn of this practice through a new interpretation of the principle of the separation of powers is traced below. See also my article in the February number of this *Review* on the doctrine of vested rights (12 *Mich. L. Rev.* 247–76 [1914]).

55. Consider, for example, Jefferson's words in his "Virginia Notes" (cited above): It is needless for the executive or the judiciary to attempt to oppose the legislature, he says, for then "they put their proceedings into the form of acts of assembly, which will render them obligatory on the other branches."

56. See criticisms passed in the Convention on the notion that the states were sovereign under the Articles of Confederation, in 1 Farrand, *Records* 313–33, 437–79. See also the present writer's *National Supremacy* ch. III (1913). For the revolt against legislative oppression of private (property) rights, see the elaborate criticism of the recent product of the state legislatures by Madison in 1786, 2 *Writings* 338 ff. (Hunt ed. 1900–1910). Also, see his statement on the floor of the Convention, June 6, and afterward repeated by him elsewhere, that "the necessity of providing more effectually for the security of private rights and the steady dispensation of justice" was one of the objects of the Convention. "Interferences with these," he declared, "were evils which had, more perhaps than anything else, produced this Convention. Was it to be supposed that republican liberty could long exist under the abuses of it practiced in some of the states?" See also *Federalist* Nos. 10 and 54.

American political system" gave themselves over merely to idle lamentation. Fortunately no one contended at that date that the existing American constitutions, wrought out as they had been under the stress and urgency of a state of warfare, were impossible of improvement.[57] Fortunately, too, American political inventiveness had by no means exhausted itself in its first efforts at constitution-building. Upon this latent talent the problems of the times acted as incentive and stimulant, eliciting from it suggestion after suggestion which it needed but the ripe occasion to erect into institutions composing a harmonious whole. Some of these suggestions it is pertinent to enumerate: (1) from Massachusetts and New Hampshire came the idea of an ordered and regular procedure for making constitutions, with the result inevitably of furthering the idea of an enacting power in the people at large and that of the legal character of the constitution;[58] (2) from New Jersey, Connecticut, Virginia, New Hampshire, and Rhode Island came the idea of judicial review, partly on the basis of the doctrine of the right of revolution and partly on the basis of the doctrine of certain principles fundamental to the common law that had found recognition in the state constitutions;[59] (3) from North Carolina, just as the Philadelphia Convention was assembling, came the idea of judicial review based squarely on the written constitution and the principle of the separation of powers;[60] (4) from

57. See Jefferson's apologia in his Virginia Notes, above cited; also Rush's "Address" in *Principles and Acts* 234–36.

58. On the making of the revolutionary state constitutions, see Davis in *Johns Hopkins University Studies,* 3rd Series, at 516 ff. The legal character of the Massachusetts constitution of 1780 was recognized and enforced by the Supreme Court of the state in a series of decisions, in 1780–81, pronouncing slavery unconstitutional. See G. H. Moore, *History of Slavery in Massachusetts* (1866). The writers on the subject of judicial review seem not to have discovered the importance of these cases.

59. The New Jersey case referred to is Holmes v. Walton, 1780, on which see Austin Scott in 4 *Am. Hist. Rev.* 456 ff. (1899). The case dealt with the question of trial by jury. The legislature complied with the court's view of the matter only very incompletely. The Connecticut case is the Symsbury Case, 1785, to which I first drew attention in my "Establishment of Judicial Review." The case, which is reported in Kirby (Conn.), 444 ff., dealt with the subject of vested rights. The Virginia case is Com. v. Caton, 1782 (4 Call 5), which is important for the dicta. However, it should be noted that the much quoted words of Chancellor Wythe in this case deal with the question of the duty of the court in the face of an attempt by one chamber of the legislature to usurp power, not that of its duty in face of a void act of the whole legislature. The case of Josiah Phillips, which Professor Trent tries to make out a precedent in this connection (1 *Am. Hist. Rev.* 444 ff.), is no precedent, Phillips was finally proceeded against in the regular way, rather than under the bill of attainder that had been voted against him because it was contended in his behalf that he was a British subject and, therefore, not capable of treason against Virginia. This is Jefferson's explanation of the matter, given repeatedly, and he was governor at the time. The mythical view of the case derives its chief support from a passage in 1 Tucker's Blackstone 293 (App.), cited by Haines, at 79. See also my article in 9 *Mich. L. Rev.* The Rhode Island case is Trevett v. Weeden. "The sole power of judging of the laws," said Varnum, belongs to the courts. The New Hampshire case is referred to in Plumer's *Life of William Plumer* and in Jeremiah Mason's *Memories {Memoirs?}*, but I cannot furnish the citations at this writing. It dealt with the subject of vested rights. The much cited case of Rutgers v. Waddington marked, as I pointed out in 9 *Mich. L. Rev.,* a triumph for the notion of legislative sovereignty.

60. Bayard v. Singleton, 1 Martin 42. See note 25, above. Mr. W. S. Carpenter finds from the

various sources came the idea that legislative power, instead of being governmental power in general, is a *peculiar kind of power*;[61] (5) from various sources came the idea that judicial power, exercised as it habitually was under the guiding influence of common law principles, was naturally conservative of private rights;[62] (6) from various sources came the idea that the judiciary must be put in a position to defend its prerogative against the legislative tendency to absorb all powers, and this idea was connected with the idea of judicial review both in the relation of means and of end;[63] (7) from the Congress of the Confederation came the idea that the Articles of Confederation and treaties made under them were rightfully to be regarded as part and parcel of the law of every state, paramount, moreover, to conflicting acts of the state legislatures and enforceable by the state courts.[64] Probably no one public man of the time shared all these ideas when the Philadelphia Convention met. But the able membership of that famous body was in a position to compare views drawn from every section of the country. Slowly, by process of discussion and conversation, these men, most of them trained in the legal way of thinking, discovered the intrinsic harmony of the ideas just passed in review; discovered, in other words, that the acceptance of one of them more or less constrained the acceptance of the others also, that each implied a system embracing all.

The Virginia Plan, introduced into the Convention at its outset, provided for the three departments of government. On the other hand, the same plan gave

---

contemporary newspapers that this case was decided in May, several days before the Philadelphia Convention had actually come together.

61. See, in this connection, the Reports of the Pennsylvania Censors, referred to in note 54, above. The earliest statement of the respective limits of legislative and judicial powers came from the royal governors, in an effort to check the former. See, for example, the message of Governor Fletcher to the New York Assembly, April 13, 1695: "Laws are to be interpreted by the judges," *i.e.*, the judges alone: 1 *Messages from the Governors* (of New York) 55 (Lincoln ed.). For later gubernatorial messages on the same subject, see *id.*, II, 250 (April 27, 1786), and IV, 532 ff. (April 10, 1850). For some early judicial statements of the motion {*sic; notion?*}, see Bayard v. Singleton; also Ogden v. Witherspoon and Ogden v. Blackledge, discussed below. Some later cases on the point are 5 Cow. (N.Y.) 346; 99 N.Y. 463; 159 N.Y. 362. See also Cooley, *Constitutional Limitations* 173–75 (2nd ed. 1871).

62. For the reception accorded Trevett v. Weeden, see 1 McMaster, *History* 338 ff. (1883–1927). At this same time William Plumer was writing (1786): "The aspect of public affairs in this state is gloomy. . . . Yet even in these degenerate days, our courts of law are firm," etc.: *Life of William Plumer* 166. It was at this time that the worship of the judiciary began, which was later to become so conspicuous a feature of the Federalist regime, leading indeed to the belief on the part of the judges themselves, that they were meant to be the moral guardians of society. See Henry Jones Ford, *Rise and Growth of American Politics* 112–13 (1914).

63. See the criticism by the Pennsylvania Council of Censors (November 1783) against the existing state constitution: "Because if the assembly should pass an unconstitutional law and the judges have the virtue to disobey it, the same could instantly remove them": *Proceedings* 70. See also, Hamilton in *Federalist* Nos. 78 and 80; also below on the debate of 1802. Madison's anxiety for judicial independence of legislative influence was extreme: 2 Farrand, *Records* 44–45.

64. 4 Secret Journals of Congress 185–287 (1821); 12 Journals of Congress (1801) under dates of March 21 and April 13, 1787. See also Bayard v. Singleton (above) and 6 *Writings of Jefferson* 98 (Mem. ed.).

evidence that its authors had but imperfect recognition of the implications of the doctrine of the separation of powers, for it associated members of the judiciary in a council with the executive to revise measures of the national legislature and it left to the national legislature the task of keeping state legislation subordinate to national powers. The first important step in the clarification of the Convention's ideas with reference to the doctrine of judicial review is marked, therefore, by its rejection of the council of revision idea on the basis of the principle stated perhaps most precisely by Strong of Massachusetts, "That the power of *making* ought to be kept distinct from that of *expounding* the laws." "No maxim," Strong added, "was better established," and the utterances of other members bear out his words.[65] For, in one form or another, the notion of legislative power as *inherently limited power,* distinct from and exclusive of the power of interpreting the standing law, was reiterated again and again and was never contradicted. When, therefore, the Convention adopted Article III of the Constitution vesting "the judicial power of the United States in one Supreme Court and such inferior courts as Congress shall from time to time establish," it must be regarded as having expressed the intention of excluding Congress from the business of law-interpreting altogether.

But a not less important step toward the final result was taken when the idea of a congressional veto of state laws was dropped and for it was substituted the small state proposition of giving the Constitution the character of supreme law within the individual states enforceable by the several state judiciaries.[66] Thus it was settled that as against state legislation at any rate the Constitution should be *legally* supreme. Why not then as against national legislation as well? When it was decided that the Constitution should be referred for ratification to conventions within the states, the question was probably determined for the majority of the members. Said Madison: "A law violating a constitution established by the people themselves would be considered by the judges as null and void.[67] Later the Convention proceeded to insert in the Constitution prohibitions upon congressional power in the same terms as some of those already imposed upon state legislative power.[68] The conclusion is unescapable that when Article VI, paragraph 2, designates the Constitution as *law* of the land in the same terms as it does acts of Congress made in pursuance of it, it does so by virtue of no inadvertence or inattention on the part of its framers. Moreover, as noted before, the same paragraph recognizes state constitutions as known to and enforceable by state courts.

65. 2 Farrand, *Records* 73–80.

66. Note particularly the significance of Sherman's words with reference to congressional veto: "Such a power involves a wrong principle, to wit, that a law of a state contrary to the Articles of Union would, if not negatived, be valid and operative." Yet as late as August 23, John Landon of New Hampshire said: "He considered it [the question of a congressional veto] resolvable into the question whether the extent of the national Constitution was to be judged of by the state governments": 2 Farrand, *Records* 391. The "arising" clause was adopted August 27.

67. 2 Farrand, *Records* 93.

68. Cf. sections 9 and 10 of Art. I.

But then was it upon the premises thus provided that the Convention did actually base its belief in judicial review of acts of Congress? The answer to this question is indicated in part by the fact that the function of judicial review is almost invariably related by the members of the Convention to the power of the judges as "expositors of the law." But a better rounded and a more satisfactory answer is furnished by Hamilton's argument in *Federalist* 78: "The interpretation of the laws is the proper and peculiar province of the courts. A constitution is in fact, and must be, regarded by the judges as a fundamental law. It therefore belongs to them to ascertain its meaning as well as the meaning of any particular act proceeding from the legislative body. If there should happen to be an irreconcilable difference between the two, that which has the superior obligation and validity ought of course to be preferred; in other words the Constitution ought to be preferred to the statute, the intention of the people to the intention of their agents." It cannot be reasonably doubted that Hamilton was here, as at other points, endeavoring to reproduce the matured conclusions of the Convention itself.[69] And not less certain is it that he was thus notifying those to whom the Constitution had been referred for ratification the grounds upon which its framers and supporters based the case for judicial review.

V

Our demonstration, however, of the views of the framers with reference to the basis of judicial review may also be profitably extended to the period between the adoption of the Constitution and the decision in Marbury v. Madison. For this was the period when the new system was set going, not only in the light of the views of its authors, but for the most part under their personal supervision. But the interest of the period also arises in part from the real paradox which judicial review has always presented in our system from the outset, the paradox namely of trying to keep a government based on public opinion within the metes and bounds of a formally unchangeable law. The dilemma thus created did not at first press, but with the rise of political opposition it became grave enough, and when this opposition finally triumphed, not only judicial review but even judicial independence was for the moment in peril.

But, indeed, the difficulty at the time of the adoption of the Constitution was hardly a new one, for some such objection had been forthcoming even earlier to judicial review within the states, where, however, the judges were generally much less secure of independence than under the United States Constitution,[70]

---

69. Note also the words of James Wilson in his "Lectures" (1792), where he presents judicial review as "the necessary result of the distribution of power made by the Constitution between the legislative and judicial departments": 1 *Works* 416–17 (Andrews ed.).

70. See 1 Annals of Congress col. 844 (Gales and Seaton eds. 1789).

and where, moreover, judicial power in the last resort often resided still within a branch of the legislature or with the whole of it. Furthermore, as I have already indicated, judicial review in the states had thus far rested upon a somewhat uncertain logic which put it in the light of a highly extraordinary, quasi-revolutionary remedy, or in best gave it sway within the limited area marking the intersection, so to speak, of the written constitution with certain fundamental principles of the common law, like trial by jury or the security of vested rights.

It is not surprising, therefore, to find Hamilton turning from his work of planting judicial review squarely within the Constitution and of rendering its field of operation co-extensive with the four corners of that instrument, to consider certain objections. Thus he recites: "The authority of the proposed Supreme Court of the United States, which is to be a separate and independent body, will be superior to that of the legislature. The power of construing the laws according to the spirit of the Constitution will enable that Court to mould them into whatever shape it may think proper; especially as its decisions will not be in any manner subject to the revision or correction of the legislative body. This is as unprecedented as it is dangerous. . . . The Parliament of Great Britain and the legislatures of the several states can at any time rectify by law the exceptionable decisions of their respective courts. But the errors and usurpations of the Supreme Court of the United States will be uncontrollable and remediless." Hamilton met these objections by denying that by the principle of separation of powers even a state legislature could reverse a judgment, and also by pointing to the power of impeachment.[71]

Madison, on the other hand, responded—characteristically—to the views of the alarmists more pronouncedly. On the floor of the Convention, as we have just seen, he had espoused the doctrine of judicial review in unmistakable terms. Again in the *Federalist* he had described the Supreme Court as the tribunal which was "ultimately to decide" the questions that would necessarily rise between the state and national jurisdictions.[72] And in the Virginia convention his point of view had still been the same: the national government was to be the final judge of its own powers through the Supreme Court.[73] Yet within six months he was writing a correspondent in Kentucky that neither the federal nor state constitutions made any provision "for the case of a disagreement in expounding them" and that the attempt of the courts to stamp a law "with its final characer" "by refusing or not refusing to execute it" made "the judicial department paramount in fact to the legislative, which was never intended and can never be proper."[74]

71. *Federalist* No. 81.
72. No. 39.
73. 3 Elliot, *Debates* 484–85.
74. Note 36, above. Madison, like many other Virginians of prominence, was angered at this time by the rather pedantic attitude taken by the state court of appeals toward an act of the

Still Madison was reluctant to abandon judicial review outright. What he really desired was a principle which, while saving to judicial interpretations of the Constitution their finality in certain instances, in others clad those of Congress with a like finality. He soon had an opportunity to attempt the formulation of such a principle. The bill introduced into the first Congress creating the Department of Foreign Affairs contained the clause, with reference to the secretary of state, "to be removable from office by the President of the United States." The clause was at once attacked by Smith of South Carolina in the following words: "What authority has this house to explain the law? . . . Sir, it is the duty of the legislature to make laws; your judges are to expound them." Madison sprang to the defense of the clause. He admitted that it represented an attempt by Congress to construe the Constitution *finally* at the point involved, but he asserted that it was within Congress' power to do this very thing in a case where the Constitution was silent and the question raised concerned an apportionment of power among departments. In other words an assumed incompleteness at points was to give Congress its opportunity. But, rejoined Gerry of Massachusetts, "I would ask, gentlemen, if the Constitution has given us the power to make declaratory acts, where is the necessity of inserting the Fifth Article for the purpose of obtaining amendments? The word amendment implies a defect, a declaratory act conceives one. Where then is the difference between an amendment and a declaratory act?" The protest against an "attempt to construe the Constitution" was also voiced by Sherman of Connecticut, Page and White of Virginia, and Benson of New York, with the result that eventually Madison himself joined in support of a motion striking out the exceptionable clause and substituting for it phraseology merely inferring that the president would exercise the power of removal and making provision for the event.[75] A little later the House passed the Judiciary Act almost without comment upon the 25th section of it, which recognizes the judicial prerogative in relation to the written constitution in the most explicit fashion.[76]

---

legislature imposing new duties on them without increasing their salaries. See the Case of the Judges, 4 Call. 139 ff. (1788). The case gave rise to a vigorous debate in the Virginia assembly. See Monroe to Madison, November 22, 1788: "Letters to Madison," MSS., Library of Congress.

75. For this debate, see 1 Annals of Congress col. 473 ff. (Gales and Seaton eds. 1789).

76. Professor Beard in his *Supreme Court,* etc. assumes that all who voted for the act of 1789 favored judicial review in 1787. The argument has little independent force, for judicial review was a rapidly spreading idea during this period. On the floor of the Convention itself there were several converts. Read, for example, in this connection the exact statements of Gerry, Wilson, and Dickinson, as reported by Madison. Compare Dickinson in his "Letters of Fabius." Compare Morris' words in 1785: 3 Sparks, *Life of Gouverneur Morris* 438 (1832). Also, the list is incomplete. Perfected, it would include the following names of those who attended the Philadelphia Convention and supported the Act of 1789: Ellsworth, Paterson, Strong, Bassett, and Few—all of whom were on the Senate Committee that drafted the act; Robert Morris and Read, also senators; and Madison, Baldwin, and Sherman in the House. Mr. Horace Davis on the November *Am. Pol. Sci. Rev.* seeks to prove, on the other hand, that those who supported the Act of 1789 thereby showed that they did not believe in the power of the Supreme Court to pass upon the validity of acts of Congress, except as the question was raised in cases coming up from the state courts. If Mr.

From this time on for nearly a decade the legalistic view of the Constitution passed substantially without challenge. It is true that when in the first Hayburn case the judges of the Middle Circuit refused to enforce the Pension Act of 1792 on the ground of its unconstitutionality, some "high-flyers in and out of Congress" raised the cry of impeachment; but they were speedily silenced. Upon the objections of the judges to the act being filed with the president, the latter forwarded them to Congress, which proceeded promptly to bring the act into conformity with the judicial view of constitutional requirements.[77] Four years later occurred the case of United States v. Hylton,[78] which is instructive of the established doctrine in a number of ways. The only question argued before the Court was that of the constitutionality of the act of Congress involved. In the argument for the United States, the attorney general was assisted by Alexander Hamilton, for whose services Congress appropriated a special fund. Neither side challenged the power of the Court in the premises.[79] The Court's decision upholding the act was based purely upon the merits of the case. Madison was plainly disappointed at the Court's not disallowing the act.[80]

And meantime, judicial review was also advancing within the states, and

---

Davis had turned to the debate, just reviewed, on the establishment of the Department of Foreign Affairs, he would have found at least half a dozen men championing the notion of judicial review who later voted for the Act of 1789. Also, I should like to ask where the state courts get their power to pass on the validity of acts of Congress save as it is intrinsic to judicial power under a constitution regarded as law. Mr. Davis' error consists apparently in the assumption that Congress, in the 25th section of the Act of 1789, conferred power upon the Supreme Court that it would not otherwise have had, instead of, as is the fact, organizing a particular branch of "the judicial power of the United States." For some later references in Congress to judicial review, see 2 Annals of Congress cols. 1978, 1988.

77. The materials for this account of the "Pension Case" are drawn from 2 Dallas 409; 1 Am. St. Papers, Misc. 49–52; 3 Annals of Congress cols. 556–57; 11 Annals of Congress (7th Cong., 1st sess.) cols. 921–25; United States v. Ferreira, 13 How. 40 (note) (1852). The statement with reference to the threat of impeachment is based on the following extract from *Bache's General Advertiser* (Camden, N.J.) for April 20, 1792:

> Never was the word 'impeachment' so hackneyed as it has been since the spirited sentence passed by our judges on an unconstitutional law. The high fliers, in and out of Congress, and the very humblest of their humble retainers, talk of nothing but impeachment! impeachment! impeachment! as if forsooth Congress were wrapped up in the cloak of infallibility, which has been torn from the shoulders of the Pope; and that it was damnable heresy and sacrilege to doubt the constitutional orthodoxy of any decision of theirs, once written on calf skin! But if a Secretary of War can suspend or reverse the decision of the Circuit Judges, why may not a drill sergeant or a black drummer reverse the decisions of a jury? Why not abolish at once all our courts, except the court martial? and burn all our laws, except the articles of war? . . .
>
> But when those impeachment mongers are asked how any law is to be declared unconstitutional, they tell us that nothing less than a general convention is adequate to pass sentence on it; as if a general convention could be assembled with as much ease as a party of stock jobbers.

I am indebted for this extract to my friend Mr. W. S. Carpenter, who is preparing a volume on judicial tenure in the United States.

78. 3 Dallas 171 (1796).

79. 11 Annals of Congress cols. 925–26.

80. It was also during this period that, in 1793, the Supreme Court refused Washington's request

what is an even more significant development, was being transferred from the earlier basis of fundamental principles to the written constitution. Two illustrative cases are Bowman v. Middleton,[81] and Kamper v. Hawkins.[82] In the former, decided in 1789, the South Carolina supreme court pronounced an early colonial statute to have been void *ab initio* as contrary to "common right" and "Magna Carta." In the latter, four years later, the Virginia court of appeals pronounced an act of the state legislature void as in conflict with the letter and spirit of the Virginia constitution, which was described as an ordinance of the people themselves and therefore superior to an ordinary statute, but as nonetheless a source of rules determinative of the rights of individuals.[83]

One thing that retarded the growth of judicial review in the states was the continuing influence of Blackstone, with his notions of parliamentary sovereignty,[84] but a more potent factor was the retention of the doctrine that legislative power extended to the interpretation of the standing law. Thus as late as 1798 we find Justice Chase of the United States Supreme Court declaring that only in the Massachusetts constitution were the *powers* of government *distributed;* and two years later the same judge announced his opinion that the mere statement of the general principle of the separation of powers in a state constitution did not serve to restrict the legislative powers, that such general principles were "not to be regarded as rules to fetter and control, but as matter merely declaratory and directory."[85] But in Ogden v. Witherspoon,[86] which was a North Carolina case falling within federal jurisdiction because of the diverse citizenship of the parties to it, and in which therefore the federal court stood in the same relation to the state constitution that the State court would have, Chief Justice Marshall

---

to advise him with reference to the operation of the treaties of 1778 with France, basing its refusal upon the strictly judicial character of their office: Baldwin, *American Judiciary* 33 (1905). In the debate on the Department of Foreign Affairs in 1789, Gerry had expressed the idea that the president could require opinions of the judges on constitutional questions and that these would be binding on Congress: 1 Annals of Congress col. 524 (Gales & Seaton eds. 1789).

81. 1 Bay (S.C.) 93.

82. Va. Cases, 20.

83. Note J. Nelson's words, at 131 of the volume: For the legislature to decide whether its own act is void or not would be unconstitutional, "since to decide whether the plaintiff or defendant under the existing law have a right is a judicial act."

84. For an illustration of the Blackstonian influence, see Z. Swift, *The System of Laws of Connecticut* 16–17, 34–35, 52–53 (1795). Also, in the same connection, see arguments of attorneys in 4 Halstead (N.J.) 427 and 1 Binney (Pa.) 416. For a decidedly disingenuous and somewhat amusing attempt to explain Blackstone's words away, see 2 *Works of James Wilson* 415 (Andrews ed.). Note also, Marshall's words, as attorney in Ware v. Hylton, 3 Dallas 199, 211: "The judicial authority have no right to question the validity of a law unless such a jurisdiction is given expressly by the Constitution."

85. The cases referred to are Calder v. Bull, 3 Dallas 386, and Cooper v. Telfair, 4 Dallas 13. Justice Chase indicates by this remarks in these cases, significantly, reluctance to admit judicial review save on the basis of natural rights and the social compact. His remarks in the latter case, however, contain interesting testimony as to the unanimity of opinion on the subject among bench and bar, both in 1800 and at the time of the adoption of the Constitution.

86. 3 N.C. 404 (1802).

on circuit reversed this position; and in Ogden v. Blackledge[87] the Supreme Court itself sustained his course. In the latter case the question at issue was whether a North Carolina statute of limitations, passed in 1715, had been repealed in 1789, the state legislature having declared in 1799 that it had not been. Said attorneys for plaintiff: "To declare what the law is or has been is a judicial power, to declare what it shall be is legislative. One of the fundamental principles of all our governments is that the legislative power shall be separated from the judicial." The Court stopped counsel and decided that, "under all the circumstances stated, the act in question had been repealed in 1789." The service thus rendered to the cause of judicial review under the state constitutions by the federal courts acting in their vicarious capacity cannot be overestimated. By 1820, the spread of the legalistic interpretation of the principle of the separation of powers had effected the establishment of judicial review on the basis of the written constitution in every state in the Union save only Rhode Island, which exception moreover only proves the rule, since it is explained by the fact that till 1842 Rhode Island continued its colonial charter as a constitution and that by this instrument legislative power remained undefined.[88]

VI

It thus becomes apparent once more that judicial review in all its branches rests upon a common basis, that its cause in one jurisdiction is its cause in all. The reflection becomes especially pertinent as we turn to consider the challenge made to the finality of the Supreme Court's interpretation of the Constitution in relation to acts of Congress by Jefferson and his more radical followers in the years 1789–1802. For it was in part at least some such understanding that accounts for the entire failure of this challenge even while its authors were borne into higher office by an overwhelming political triumph.

The debate and vote on the Judiciary Act of 1789 prove that originally the advocates of state rights—for they existed from the beginning—were nothing loath to accept the Supreme Court's view of the Constitution as final, both in

87. 2 Cranch 272 (1805).

88. By 1803, the following states had either been definitely committed to the doctrine of judicial review by judicial decision or practically so by judicial dicta: North Carolina (1787), South Carolina (1792), Virginia (1788, 1793), Pennsylvania (1793, 1799), New Jersey (1796), Kentucky (1801), Maryland (1802). The Kentucky Constitution of 1792, Art. XII, at 28, says: "All laws contrary . . . to this Constitution shall be void." Professor Thayer, in an article in 7 *Harvard Law Rev.* 129 ff. (1893), contended that this article specifically authorized judicial review; but the Pennsylvania constitution of 1776 and the Massachusetts constitution of 1780 contained equivalent provisions without producing judicial review. See a valuable list of cases in Professor Haines' volume, 90 ff. Also, the opinion of the judges of the Pennsylvania Supreme Court of December 22, 1790, to Governor Mifflin, holding that certain offices had been vacated by the new Constitution, is worth notice. The ground of the opinion is indicated by the following words: "We think the Constitution to be paramount [to] the acts of the legislature": Pennsylvania Archives, 1st ser., XII, 36.

relation to national and to state power. When, however, the federal judges showed themselves disposed to uphold and enforce the Alien and Sedition Laws of 1798, and some of them indeed to entertain prosecutions for sedition under a supposed common law of the United States, the state-rights champions began to appreciate for the first time the added sanction given to national authority by judicial decision. The Virginia and Kentucky Resolutions of 1798 and 1799 were framed primarily with the design of breaking through this subtle control, on the warrant of the propositions, first that the Constitution was a compact of sovereign states and, second, that the organ of sovereignty within a state was its legislature, from which propositions the conclusion was drawn that the final word in construing the national Constitution lay with the individual state legislatures.[89] But the final outcome of the propaganda thus undertaken was not merely a further vindication of the prerogative of the Supreme Court of the United States, but of *all* courts. Thus having been forwarded to the other legislatures, the resolutions elicited from the seven northern of them unequivocal declarations of the right of the "Supreme Court of the United States ultimately" to decide "on the constitutionality of any act" of Congress.[90] In his famous Report of 1799 to the Virginia legislature, Madison endeavored at first to meet these responses by reiterating the doctrine of the original resolutions, but even in so doing he admitted the finality of judicial constructions of the Constitution as against the *other* branches of the national government, and in the end he abandoned his case completely.[91] The Resolutions, he contended, taking a defensive tone, were entirely proper, since they were designed merely "to excite reflection," whereas, he added, decisions of the judiciary, *"are carried into immediate effect by force."* It would be hard to imagine a more complete retreat. The probability is that he and those for whom he spoke had begun to realize that to make the state legislature the final interpreter of the national Constitution was also to make it the final interpreter of the state constitution, which in turn meant either the setting up of a legally uncontrolled power within the state itself or—what *practically* would have been the same thing—return to the idea now rapidly becoming obsolete of a legislative function of *jus dicere*.

Two years later, nevertheless, the question of the finality of the judicial view of the Constitution was again to the front, though on a somewhat altered footing. By the election of 1800 the Republicans had captured the presidency and both Houses of Congress, but the judiciary still withstood them. Now, at the very moment of retiring from power the Federalists proceeded by the Act of February, 1801, substantially to double the number of inferior federal courts, while President Adams at once set to work, with the cooperation of the Senate,

---

89. MacDonald, *Select Documents* 148–60 (1901); 4 Elliot, *Debates* 528–32, 540–45.
90. H. V. Ames, *State Documents on Federal Relations* 16–26 (1911).
91. 6 *Writings* 341–406 (Hunt ed.).

to fill the newly created offices with Federalists. The federal judiciary, exclaimed Randolph wrathfully, has become "a hospital of decayed politicians!" Jefferson's concern went deeper. Writing Dickinson he said: "They have retired into the judiciary, from which stronghold they will batter down all the works of Republicanism."

Naturally the first step attempted was the repeal of the Act of 1801, but from the point of view of a possible larger program of definitely subordinating the judiciary to the political branches of the government, the repeal voted was indeed a Pyrrhic victory.[92] In the debate on the question the Federalists speedily developed the argument that, inasmuch as the Constitution designed the judiciary to act as a check upon Congress, the latter was under constitutional obligation not to weaken the independence of the former in any way. To meet this argument Breckenridge of Kentucky, the Republican leader in the Senate— and one of the authors of the Kentucky Resolutions—brought forward for the first time the theory of the equal right of the three departments, when acting within their respective fields, to construe the Constitution for themselves, and from it deduced the exclusive right of the legislature "to interpret the Constitution in what regards the law-making power" and the obligation of the judges "to execute what laws they make." In other words, the notion of a departmental right of constitutional construction takes its rise not from the effort to establish judicial review but from an attempt to overthrow it. But the feeble disguise which this doctrine affords legislative sovereignty made it little attractive even to Republicans, who for the most part either plainly indicated their adherence to the legalistic view of the Constitution, or following a hint by Giles of Virginia, kept silent on the subject. The Federalists on the other hand were unanimous on the main question, though of divergent opinions as to the grounds on which judicial review was to be legally based, some grounding it on the "arising" and "pursuant" clauses, some on the precedents of the Pension and Carriage cases, some on the nature of the Constitution and of the judicial office, some on "the contemporary use of terms" and "the undisputed practice under the Constitution" "of all constitutional authorities." And undoubtedly, at this date, all these grounds were fairly available save the first. For the rest, said the Federalist orators, judicial review was expedient, since the judiciary had control of neither the purse nor the sword; it was the substitute offered by political wisdom for the destructive right of revolution; "to have established this principle of constitutional security," "a novelty in the history of nations," was "the peculiar glory of the American people;" the contrary doctrine was "monstrous and unheard of."[93]

92. Jefferson and Giles were originally of the opinion that the act was irrepealable. They were converted to their later view by the dialectics of John Taylor of Caroline. These statements are based on documents from the Breckenridge MSS. which are given in Mr. W. S. Carpenter's thesis on judicial tenure in the United States.
93. 11 Annals of Congress cols. 26–184 (Senate), cols. 510–985 (House). Breckinridge of

A few months later occurred the decision in Marbury v. Madison, which against this background assumes its true color. Yet Marshall's performance is by no means to be regarded as a work of supererogation. In the first place, vested as it was with the apparent authority of a judicial decision, it brought to an end a discussion which, for all that it had been highly favorable to judicial review, might in the end have proved unsettling. Again, it threw the emphasis once more upon the great essential considerations of the character of the Constitution, as "fundamental and paramount law" and "the province and duty of the judicial department to say what the law is." Finally, in the very process of vindicating judicial review, it admitted to a degree the principle that had thus far been contended for only by opponents of judicial review. Thus, discussing the amenability of the president and his agents to mandamus, the chief justice says: "By the Constitution of the United States the President is vested with certain important political powers in the exercise of which he is to use his own discretion and is accountable only to his country in his political character and to his own conscience."[94] Later of course, this doctrine, which we may call the doctrine of *departmental discretion,* was supplemented by the doctrine that the powers of Congress must be liberally construed,[95] and later still by the doctrine of the immunity of the president from judicial process.[96] The first two of these doctrines at least may be readily harmonized with the theory of judicial review. At the same time, they are not constrained by that theory, but are plainly concessions to the necessity of making the Constitution flexible and adaptable while still keeping it legal. They prove therefore that "the spirit of accommo-

---

Kentucky did not at first attack judicial review, *id.* 92–99; but was finally prodded to it, *id.* 178–80. In the Senate two advocates of repeal attacked judicial review (Breckinridge and Stone of North Carolina), while two (Jackson of Georgia and Wright of Maryland) accepted it. In the House, three advocates of repeal attacked judicial review (Randolph of Virginia, Williams of North Carolina, and Thompson of Virginia); two endeavored to discover a compromise position, along the line of the doctrine of departmental equality (Davis of Kentucky and Bacon of Massachusetts); but five, impliedly at least, accepted judicial review without making such qualifications (Smith of Vermont, Nicholson of Maryland, Gregg of Pennsylvania, Holland of North Carolina, and Varnum of Massachusetts). Their remarks can be easily located through the Index. Those of Randolph and Bacon are most instructive. In the Senate seven opponents of repeal championed judicial review (see, especially, the speeches of Morris of New York and Chipman of Vermont). In the House, fifteen of the same party performed this service. The remarks quoted in the text are from the speeches of Stanly and Henderson of North Carolina, Rutledge of South Carolina, and Dana of Connecticut: cols. 529–30, 542–43, 574–76, 754–55, 920, 932. Other notable speeches were those of Goddard and Griswold of Connecticut and Hemphill of Pennsylvania. Giles' case is interesting. In the debate on the first Bank, 1791, he had answered an argument in behalf of the proposition, that was drawn from the fact that the Congress of the Confederacy had chartered "the Bank of North America" thus: "The act itself was never confirmed by a judicial decision." In other words, adjudication is made the final test of constitutionality. But in 1804, we find him holding that Congress might impeach a judge for declaring one of its acts unconstitutional: 1 J. Q. Adams, *Memoirs* 321ff. (1874–77).

94. 1 Cranch 165–66.
95. McCulloch v. Maryland, 4 Wheat. 316 (1819).
96. Miss. v. Johnson, 4 Wall. 475 (1867).

dation" with which Professor McLaughlin credits the political departments has been met by a similar spirit on the part of the judiciary.

At the outset of this paper I raised the question of the legal basis of judicial review. The answer to this question I have already reiterated more than once. The legal basis of judicial review is supplied by the view of the Constitution as law enforceable by the courts, which is verbally recognized by the national Constitution, and by that view of the principle of the separation of powers which sharply distinguishes law-making from law-interpreting and assigns the latter exclusively to the courts, the view which was demonstrably held by the framers of the Constitution when they drafted Article III. But in the last analysis judicial review rests upon the assumption, hardly concealed by this interpretation of the principle of the separation of powers, that the judges alone really *know* the law. To a generation born and bred under the *regime* of the common law this was a natural assumption to make. Today, however, the activity of the legislatures in the field of social reform imparts to the law more and more the character of an assertion of authority, with the result that the possibility of a purely mechanical interpretation of it comes to be denied.[97] At the same time, with the rise of administrative bodies, the courts are losing the role which once was theirs almost exclusively, of mediating between the state and the individual, with the result that men today find it requisite to look to them for their rights less frequently than in the past. On both these accounts the theoretical argument for judicial review tends to lose touch with the nourishing earth of solid facts and congenial ideas, and its persuasiveness to weaken. But on the other hand it is by no means certain that this will always be the case. The doctrine of due process of law, while it has enlarged the scope of judicial review enormously, has also rendered it correspondingly flexible. Granting the judges due wisdom, there is today no good reason why the aegis of the Constitution may not be thrown about almost any sensible measure of social reform, to give it legal stability. Who can doubt, then, that history will repeat itself, and that the muck-rakers of today will become the stand-patters of tomorrow?

97. See especially John Chipman Gray's *Nature and Sources of the Law* (1909).

II.

THE DEVELOPMENT OF
JUDICIAL SUPREMACY

4. The Supreme Court and the Fourteenth Amendment

I‍t was formerly the wont of legal writers to regard court decisions in much the same way as the mathematician regards the x of an algebraic equation: given the facts of the case and the existing law, the outcome was inevitable. This unhistorical standpoint has now been largely abandoned. Not only is it admitted that judges in finding the law act not as automata, as mere adding machines, but creatively, but also that the considerations which determine their decisions, far from resting exclusively upon a narrowly syllogistic basis, often repose very immediately upon concrete and vital notions of what is desirable and useful. "The very considerations," says Holmes in his *Common Law*, "which judges most rarely mention and always with an apology, are the secret root from which the law draws all the juices of life. I mean, of course, considerations of what is expedient to the community concerned. Every important principle which is developed by litigation is in fact and at bottom the result of more or less definitely understood views of public policy; most generally, to be sure, under our practice and traditions, the unconscious result of instinctive preferences and inarticulate convictions, but none the less, traceable to views of public policy in the last analysis."

Holmes has in mind of course the common law, but his argument is equally to the point in the study of our American constitutional law. A great and growing part of this law is, like the common law, judge made. It is true that constitutional limitations are generally referred to some clause or other of the written Constitution. But this after all is a circumstance of which too much may

From 7 *Michigan Law Review* 643 (1909). Reprinted by permission.

This article is a summary of Part III of a volume which the writer has in preparation, to be entitled *The Growth of Judicial Review*. Naturally the article has all the faults of a summary, and this is to be regretted particularly, since footnotes have had to be sacrificed to make way for the text. For this reason the writer has not the opportunity to justify at length certain statements which may seem to demand qualification.

be made very easily. Given a sufficient hardihood of purpose at the rack of exegesis, and any document, no matter what its fortitude, will eventually give forth the meaning required of it. Nor does this necessarily mean that the law is a nose of wax, to be moulded according to the caprice of the hour. What it does mean is that the institutional character of the law rests, partly upon the conception of precedent as binding, but much more largely—and it may be added much more securely—upon the fact that views of policy themselves tend to become institutional in social and political theories.

The police power we may define for our purposes as that power of government under the control of which private rights fall. From the time of the decision in Barron v. Baltimore, (7 Pet. 243), in which the Supreme Court of the United States, after some vacillation, finally decided that the first eight amendments to the Constitution bind only the federal government, down to the adoption of the Fourteenth Amendment in 1867, it was generally admitted that this ample realm of governmental competence belonged to the states, limited only by Congressional regulation of interstate and foreign commerce, and by the necessity of not impairing the obligation of contracts. The Fourteenth Amendment however is directed explicitly to the states. "No *State* shall make or enforce any law which shall abridge the privileges or immunities of citizens of the United States; nor shall any *State* deprive any person of life, liberty, or property without due process of law; nor deny to any person within its jurisdiction the equal protection of the laws." Such is the language of the first section of the Fourteenth Amendment. There can be no kind of doubt that its authors designed that, at the very least, it should make the first eight amendments binding upon the states as well as the federal government and that is should be susceptible of enforcement both by the federal courts and by Congress. But now to give such scope to the Fourteenth Amendment obviously meant to bid farewell to the old time federal balance which before the war had seemed the very essence of our constitutional system. It meant, in the language of contemporary protest "the institution of a solid sovereignty instead of a government of limited powers," "the transfer of municipal control of the State governments over their internal affairs into the hands of Congress," the subordination of the "State judiciaries to Federal supervision and control," the annihilation of the "independence and sovereignty of the State Courts in the administration of State laws"—in short, "a deep and revolutionary change in the organic law and genesis of the government." But as often happens, the large issue thus raised was obscured by numerous lesser ones. Popular attention was riveted upon the second, third and fourth sections of the Fourteenth Amendment, and thus what was potentially a revolution in our constitutional system was effected entirely incidentally.[1]

Nor did this vast change seem likely to remain long a mere possibility. The

1. See Flack, *Adoption of the Fourteenth Amendment* chs. 2 and 3 (1908).

Fourteenth Amendment authorizes Congress to enforce its provisions by appropriate legislation. In pursuance of what it deemed to be the authority thus bestowed, Congress in May, 1870, passed the so-called Enforcement Act, which enacted severe penalties not only against state officers and agents, but also against any *person* within the states who should under the color of any statute, ordinance, regulation, or custom deprive any other person of his civil rights and civil equality. This act was followed a year later by the Ku Klux Act which was of the same general purport but more stringent in its provisions and somewhat wider in its pretensions. Finally in 1875 Congress passed the Civil Rights Act which decreed the "equal enjoyment of the accommodations . . . of inns, public conveyances . . . theatres, and other places of public amusement . . . to citizens of every race and color regardless of any previous condition of servitude," and imposed penalties upon all persons violating these provisions. The theory of these enactments comprises three points: 1. that the rights to which citizens of the United States are entitled by the Fourteenth Amendment comprehend all the rights which the ordinary person enjoys in his community; 2nd, that a denial of the equal protection of the law may be effected as much by acts of omission on the part of a state and its functionaries as by acts of commission; and that therefore, 3rdly, the power of Congress to enforce the provisions of the Fourteenth Amendment extends not merely to remedial measures in rectification or disallowance of adverse state legislation, but also to affirmative legislation, designed to supply the inadequacies of state legislation and directly impinging upon private individuals as well as upon official representatives of the state. It is true that the intention of all this legislation was to secure an equality of black and white races before the law, but it was enacted under color of sanction by the first section of the Fourteenth Amendment, the provisions of which are not specifically limited to such an end. To allow Congress's competence in this one case was, therefore, it could be contended, to allow it in all and to allow it in all was to make actual the revolution which the Fourteenth Amendment had been held to menace.

So far so good, but at this point it became evident that one element of the situation had yet to be dealt with, viz.: the power of the Supreme Court of the United States to pass upon the constitutionality of both state enactments and of congressional enactments, and with the Supreme Court the federal theory was still dominant. In the following pages, therefore, I shall show how the Supreme Court, out of devotion to this theory, at first proceeded to eliminate the Fourteenth Amendment from the law of the land. This, however, will comprise but the preliminary part of my task. For the questions raised by the outcome of the war were presently in a manner disposed of and a new set of problems— those namely arising from the growth of capital and the development of corporate industry—confronted government and particularly the state legislatures, which are still—thanks to the Supreme Court itself—the repositories of the police power. These now began to exercise this power more aggressively

than ever before, with the natural result of arousing that jealousy of governmental control in which our constitutional system was initially conceived and
which had, years before the Fourteenth Amendment had been thought of, found
enduring expression, not only in our political theory, but also to a great degree
in the constitutional jurisprudence of the states themselves, in the days when
constitutional limitations fell largely to the device and enforcement of the local
judiciaries. To this viewpoint the Supreme Court of the United States was the
spiritual heir. Dismissing, therefore, its earlier concern for the federal equilibrium, this tribunal began a reinterpretation of the Fourteenth Amendment in the
light of the principles of Lockian individualism and of Spencerian laissez faire,
which traverses the results it had previously reached at every point. To
demonstrate this, then, is my task. In its discharge I shall naturally interest
myself principally in those cases which have arisen under the Fourteenth
Amendment in connection with state legislation affecting property and business.

Two decisions of the Supreme Court are of prime importance as illustrating
the point of view from which the Fourteenth Amendment was first interpreted:
the decision in the Slaughter House Cases, (16 Wall. 36) and the decision in
Munn v. Illinois (94 U.S. 113). In the Slaughter House Cases, which were
decided in 1873, the issue was the validity under the Fourteenth Amendment of
defendant's charter, which, in the supposed interest of the public health,
granted defendant a certain degree of control over its competitors in the
business of slaughtering cattle, and certain exclusive and, so it was alleged,
monopolistic privileges. Complainants in error contended that inasmuch as they
were engaged in a lawful pursuit, it was their privilege as citizens of the United
States to continue in that pursuit unhampered by the legislation in question. The
Court, however, considered the invitation to interfere equivalent to an invitation
to set up a new and comprehensive system of national jurisdiction, within
which should be brought the sum total of the rights of citizenship and of the
powers of government to deal with those rights; and it declined to commit itself
to so "revolutionary" a course. A straight line was drawn between citizenship
of the United States and the citizenship of a state; and only the rights of the
former, relatively few in number and already secured by the Constitution
against adverse state action, even before the adoption of the Fourteenth
Amendment, were held to be beneath the protecting aegis of the Court. The
opposing view, said Justice Miller, speaking for the Court, "would constitute
this Court a perpetual censor upon all legislation of the States, on the civil
rights of their own citizens with authority to nullify such as it did not approve
as consistent with those rights as they existed at the time of the adoption of this
amendment." And the effect of doing this would be "to fetter and degrade the
State governments by subjecting them to the control of Congress in the exercise
of powers heretofore universally conceded to them of the most ordinary and
fundamental character" and thus to change radically "the whole theory of the
relations of the State and Federal Governments." "We are convinced that no

such results were intended by the Congress which proposed these amendments, nor by the legislatures of the States which ratified them.''

But the argument was also offered that the legislation under review deprived complainants of their property "without due process of law" and that it denied them the "equal protection of the laws." Significantly enough, these arguments were not much pressed, although the Court thought it necessary to animadvert upon them briefly. The prohibition of a deprivation of property without due process of law, it said, "has been in the Constitution since the adoption of the Fifth Amendment, as a restraint upon the Federal power. It is also to be found in some form of expression in the Constitutions of nearly all the States, as a restraint upon the power of the States. . . . We are not without judicial interpretation therefore both State and National of the meaning of this clause. And it is sufficient to say that under no construction of that provision that we have ever seen, or any that we deem admissible, can the restraint imposed by the State of Louisiana upon the exercise of their trade by the butchers of Louisiana be held to be a deprivation of property within the meaning of that provision.'' The other objection he dismissed even more curtly: "We doubt very much whether any action of a State not directed by way of discrimination against the negroes as a class or an account of their race will ever be held to come within the purview of this provision.''

The task of the Court in the Slaughter House decision was to draw the line between its own power under the Fourteenth Amendment and the police power of the states. Still more immediately was this its task in Munn v. Illinois, the most important of the Granger cases, in which the validity of state enactments designed to establish a uniform rate for the transportation and warehousing of grain and other classified products was challenged on the ground again of their alleged conflict with the Fourteenth Amendment. The opponents of this legislation urged in Munn v. Illinois, that on two accounts it effected a "deprivation of property without due process of law:" first because it attempted to transfer to the public an interest in a private business, and secondly, because the owner of property is entitled to reasonable compensation for its use and "what is reasonable is a judicial and not a legislative question." The Court, speaking through Chief Justice Waite, overruled both contentions. Business, it said, is subject to the police power, and a well recognized item of that power is the right to regulate the charges of businesses "affected with a public interest." It is true that the Court does not at first sight seem to accept the enactment under review as evidence conclusive of the public character of complainant's business, but appears to canvass the subject anew of its own initiative. The purport of this inquiry is, however, quite different from what it has often been entirely misconceived to be. A careful examination of the language of the Court will show that this inquiry is entered upon not with the design of insinuating that the Court might, if it chose, overrule the legislative determination as to the public character of a particular pursuit, but in order to ascertain whether the field which the legislature in this instance had assumed to occupy was one which a legislature might ever enter legitimately. There is, the Court finds, a category of businesses "affected with a public interest," and secondly, a line of precedents demonstrating the right of the legislature to regulate the charges of such businesses. "For us," it says, "the question is one of power, not of expediency. If *no* state of circumstances *could* exist to justify such a statute, then we may declare this one void, because in excess of the legislative power of the State. *But if it could, we must presume it did.* Of the propriety of legislative interference within the scope of legislative power the legislature is exclusive judge."

The allocation of the power in question to the police power made easy the answering of a second objection to the enactment under review, viz.: that the question of what is a reasonable compensation for the use of property is a judicial and not a legislative one. Said the Court: "The practice has been otherwise. In countries where the Common Law prevails it has been customary from time immemorial for the legislature to declare what shall be a reasonable compensation under such circumstances, or perhaps more properly speaking, to fix a maximum beyond which any charge made would be unreasonable. . . . In fact, the Common Law rule which requires the charge to be reasonable is itself a regulation as to price. . . . But mere Common Law regulation of trade or business may be changed by statute. A person has no property, no vested interest, in any rule of the Common Law. That is only one of the forms of municipal law and is no more sacred than the other. Rights of property which have been created by the Common Law cannot be taken away without due process, but the law itself, as a rule of conduct, may be changed at the will or even at the whim of the legislature, unless prevented by constitutional limitation. Indeed the great office of statutes is to remedy the defects in the Common Law as they are developed, and to adapt it to the changes of time and circumstances. . . . We know that this power (of rate regulation) may be abused, but this is no argument against its existence. For protection against abuses by legislatures the people must resort to the polls, not to the Courts."

Both in the decision in Munn v. Illinois and in the Slaughter House decision the Supreme Court is dominated by the view that the states ought to be left to enjoy the same scope of police power which was theirs before the Civil War, unrestricted by the Fourteenth Amendment or the federal judiciary in the interpretation of that amendment, except in so far as they might attempt to discriminate against persons on account of race or previous condition of servitude. Let us summarize the leading principles started in these decisions which plainly flow from this view: 1—The phrase "privileges and immunities of citizens of the United States" comes to signify those privileges and immunities which are secured to citizens of the United States by the United States Constitution independently of this phrase, which therefore becomes entirely gratuitous and unnecessary. 2—The phrase "equal protection of the laws" is construed to prohibit only legislation directed against racial classes. 3—The phrase "due process of law" is scarcely allowed any efficacy at all as a limitation upon legislative power, at the mercy of which the common law lies as completely as statute law. These principles receive moreover not merely reiteration but enlargement in adherent decisions, some of which, since we shall have occasion to refer to them later on, we may briefly mention at this point. In the Bradwell case (16 Wall. 130) the Court upheld the exclusion of women from practice of the law in the courts of Illinois. In the Bartemeyer case (18 Wall. 129) it was similarly held that the right to manufacture and sell intoxicants is not a privilege of United States citizenship. In a number of cases it was held that the legislature cannot divest itself of its power of police, and that all rights, including those of contract, are subject to that power. (E.g. 101 U.S. 814 and 109 U.S. 527.) In Barbier v. Connelly (113 U.S. 27) the Court upheld a municipal ordinance regulating the hours of labor in a laundry, which it was charged, was "class legislation." Said Justice Field, speaking for the Court,: "Special burdens are often necessary for general benefits;" nor do they "furnish just ground of complaint if they operate alike upon all persons and property under the same circumstances and conditions, . . . and it would be a most extraordinary usurpation of the authority of a municipality if a federal tribunal should undertake to supervise such regulations." On the other hand, in Yick Wo v. Hopkins (118 U.S. 356) the Court reiterated its intention not to allow legislative discriminations on account of race. But the phrase "equal protection of the laws," which is construed in these cases, was apt to be invoked rather less often by those seeking the downfall of state legislation than the phrase "due process of law." Says Justice Miller in Davidson v. New Orleans (96 U.S. 97): The phrase "due process of law" remains to this day "without that satisfactory precision of definition which judicial decisions have given to nearly all the other guarantees of personal rights found in the Constitutions of the several States and of the United States." What is the result? Though as a restraint upon the states the phrase in question has been a part of the Constitution only a few years, yet "the docket of this court is crowded with cases in which we are asked to hold that State courts and State legislatures have deprived their own citizens of life, liberty and property without due process of law." "There is here abundant evidence," he continues, "that there exists some strange misconception of the scope of this provision as found in the Fourteenth Amendment. In fact it would seem . . . that the clause under consideration is looked upon as a means of bringing to the test of the decision of this court the abstract opinion of every unsuccessful litigant in a State court of the justice of the decision against him and of the merits of the legislation on which such decisions may be founded." In this same case of Davidson v. New Orleans complainant was urging that in cases of eminent domain "due process of law" meant "just compensation." The Court, however, arguing strictly from the *usus loquendi* of the Fifth Amendment in which "just compensation" and "due process" appear as distinct phrases, overruled the contention. This was in 1877. Somewhat earlier than this in the United States v. Cruikshank (92 U.S. 542) the Court repelled the argument that the Fourteenth Amendment makes the first eight amendments binding upon the states, and somewhat later in Hurtado v. California (110 U.S. 516), upon the basis of Webster's definition of "due process of law" in his argument in the Dartmouth College case, showed itself indisposed to interfere with the right of a state to elaborate its own judicial processes. Rather broader was the issue raised in Powell v. Pennsylvania (127 U.S. 678), in which an anti-oleomargarine law was attacked upon the ground that it did not further the public health or public morals and was therefore not within the scope of the police power. The Court refused to make a hypothetical definition of the police power a judicially enforceable limitation upon that power. "Whether" said Justice Harlan, "the manufacture of oleomargarine . . . involves such danger to the public health as to require . . . the entire suppression of business . . . are questions of fact and public policy which belong to the legislative department to determine. And as it does not appear upon the face of the statute or from any facts which the Court may take cognizance of that it infringes rights secured by the fundamental law, the legislative determination of those questions is conclusive upon the courts. It is not a part of their functions to conduct investigations of facts entering in questions of public policy merely and to sustain or frustrate the legislative will, embodied in statutes, as they happen to approve and disapprove their determination of such questions. The legislature of Pennsylvania, upon the fullest investigation, we must conclusively presume . . . has determined that the prohibition of the sale (of oleomargarine, etc.) . . . will promote the public health and prevent fraud in the sale of such articles."

Thus again and again is the point of view from which the Fourteenth Amendment was at first construed by the Supreme Court brought to light. But we have dwelt too long already upon this phase of the subject. Today, as we know, this point of view has been abandoned. What we have to do now, therefore, is to inquire how this change has come about. The truth is that the Court was committed by the traditions at its back even from the outset to a theory of the relation of government to private rights which was gradually discovered, with the developing self-assertion of state legislatures, to be utterly incompatible with the intention of leaving to those bodies the range of power that had been theirs before the Civil War. Is the legislature or is the United States Supreme Court the final guardian of individual rights?—This was, in all the cases above reviewed, the ultimate question before the Court. In the decisions rendered in these cases the victory rested with the cause of legislative autocracy, but this victory was not uncontested and much less was it final. With each decision upholding the power of the legislature in the particular case at issue, there usually went forth one or more dissenting opinions, wherein was bespoken for a minority of the Court its allegiance to the idea of judicial supervision. How have these dissents become finally incorporated in the law of the land? This really is the question before us.

To Justice Field, vehement and dogmatic exegete, fell the task of developing primarily the canons of an individualistic interpretation of the Fourteenth Amendment. To Justice Miller's identification, in his Slaughter House decision, of "the privileges and immunities of the citizens of the United States" with the relatively few and meager rights that arise because of the existence of the United States as a government, Field responded by identifying the rights of citizens of the United States with "the natural rights of man." "The question presented," says he, "is . . . nothing less than the question whether the recent amendments to the Federal Constitution protect the citizens of the United States against the deprivation of their common rights by State legislation." His own answer to this question is as follows: "That amendment was intended to give practical effect to the declaration of 1776 of inalienable rights, rights which are the gift of the Creator, which the law does not confer, but only recognizes." Unless the amendment referred "to the natural and inalienable rights which belong to all citizens," its inhibitions were needless. Though concurring in the Bartemeyer decision, Justice Field nevertheless found an opportunity to reiterate these views and to elaborate upon them. The Fourteenth Amendment was not, as the majority insisted in the Slaughter House case, primarily "intended to confer citizenship upon the negro race. It had a much broader purpose; it was intended to justify legislation, extending the protection of the national government over the common rights of all citizens of the United States. . . . It therefore recognized, if it did not create, a national citizenship and made all persons citizens . . . and declared that their privileges and immunities, which embraced the fundamental rights belonging to the citizens of all free governments, should not be abridged by any State." Field refused, however, to admit that this view took from the states their power of police; but it did take from them "the power to parcel out to favorite citizens the ordinary trades . . . of life. . . . It was supposed that there were no privileges or immunities of citizens more sacred than those which are involved in the right to the pursuit of happiness which is usually classed with life and liberty; and that in the pursuit of happiness, since that amendment became part of the fundmental law, everyone was free to follow any lawful employment without other restraints than such as equally affect all other persons."

The view embodied in this final sentence Field himself subsequently rejected in Barbier v. Connelly, in which he upheld the propriety of so-called class legislation. It will be interesting therefore to observe the Court at a still later period blinking the view set forth in his decision, which is precedent, in order to draw for support upon his dicta just quoted, which are not precedents. But this is a later story. Meantime we find Field renewing his protest in Munn v. Illinois, declaring that that decision left "all property and all business . . . at the mercy of the majority of the legislature." It will be remembered that the

Court's chief task in Munn v. Illinois was to ascertain what constituted a deprivation of "life, liberty, and property without due process of law." Naturally, therefore, it is to this task that Field also addresses himself in his dessenting opinion. Life, he contends, signifies not merely animal existence but "whatever God has given" for its growth and enjoyment; liberty means freedom of pursuit; property connotes the use and income of property as well as its title and possession. These terms, however, have no efficacy independently of the term "due process of law" and this term Justice Field defines only by implication. Thus he complains that the police power is too often spoken of as if it were an irresponsible element of government, whereas, he insists, it is limited to the prevention of injury and quotes the maxim of the common law; *Sic utere tuo ut alienum non laedas,* as its controlling principle. It assuredly does not comprise the right, he declares, to regulate compensation unless a business is affected with the public interest. But who is to decide these questions—the question of *when* an injury exists and the other question of *when* a business is affected with the public interest? Again Justice Field fails of explicitness, but the unavoidable inference from all that he says is that, while primarily these are questions of policy calling for legislative determination, yet ultimately they are questions to be determined by the Court, to whose determination that of the legislature must of course succumb in case of conflict.

Justice Field then is the pioneer and prophet of our modern constitutional law, but this is so not because his natural law creed was his own peculiar possession, but on the contrary because, though none of them was so ready to proclaim the faith that was in him both in season and out, it was shared none the less by almost all of his associates on the Supreme Bench. Thus in the Slaughter House case Justice Field spoke not only for himself but also for at least two other associates, and in Munn v. Illinois for one other associate. Then, in the Bartemeyer case the tone of the decision itself which the Court was glad to make turn upon a technical point, was strongly indicative of the conflict going on in *gremio judicis* between the Court's sense of duty to private rights and the allegiance it had pledged to the menaced dignity of the states. But the most impressive example of the strength of theoretic individualism upon the Supreme Bench at this time is furnished by the decision in the Loan Association v Topeka (20 Wall. 655), in which an all but unanimous Court, speaking moreover through the author of the Slaughter House decision, adopted the notion, that a tax must be for a public purpose, as a limitation upon the state's power of taxation. It is not the outcome of the Court's reasoning, however, to which I desire to call particular attention—for the principle above stated is simply one of several dubious restrictions upon legislative authority that the courts have from time to time created out of hand; it is the reasoning itself that is the important consideration. "It must be conceded," says Justice Miller, "that there are . . . rights in every free government beyond the control of the State. A government which recognized no such rights, which held the lives, the liberty, and the property of its citizens subject at all times to the absolute disposition and unlimited control of even the most democratic repository of power is after all but a despotism. . . . The theory of our governments, State and National, is opposed to the deposit of unlimited power anywhere. . . . There are limitations on such power which grow out of the essential nature of all free governments, implied reservations of individual rights without which the social compact could not exist." From this view Justice Clifford alone dissented, contending that, "except where the Constitution has imposed limits upon the legislative power the rule of law appears to be that the power of the legislature must be considered as practically absolute, whether the law operates according to natural justice or not in any particular case"; and this "for the reason that the Courts are not the guardians of the rights of the people of the State save where those rights are secured by some constitutional provision which comes within judicial cognizance," otherwise the courts would become "sovereign over both the Constitution and the people and convert the government into a judicial despotism." Despite the obvious weight of this protest it passed unheeded. The champions of the view that the social compact and natural rights imposed judicially ascertainable and enforceable limitations upon legislative power stood eight strong against Justice Clifford's sole advocacy of legislative independence within the limits set by the written Constitution.

But now it may well be asked, why did not the Court, since it was willing to do so at this time, enforce its views of natural rights in the other cases we have reviewed? Two duties, more or less in conflict, confronted the Court, it is true; but if it could be loyal to both, as it was apparently persuaded it could, on the one occasion, why not on the other occasions as well? The answer is to be sought in the queston of jurisdiction as it was raised before the Court on these several occasions. The Loan Association case was one of those cases that fall within federal jurisdiction not because of the nature of the issue involved but because of the character of the parties to the suit: thus the Court's jurisdiction was unmistakable and could by no means be represented as an act of aggression against the prerogative of the state legislature. The Court accordingly felt perfectly free, as Justice Miller afterwards explained in Davidson v. New Orleans, to enforce "general principles of constitutional law" in that case. Quite otherwise was it in the Slaughter House cases and the other kindred litigation. If the Court was to assume jurisdiction in those cases—and whether it should or not was the entire issue—it must do so under the Fourteenth Amendment, and under an interpretation of that amendment moreover which would, in Justice Miller's language, not only constitute the federal judiciary "a perpetual censor upon all legislation of the States" but would also enable Congress "to degrade and fetter" the state governments in the exercise of "their most ordinary powers." It was not unnatural that the Court should be reluctant to take a step the consequences of which might turn out to be so revolutionary.

But again the question that we are discussing obtrudes itself upon our inquiring minds in a new form. We know that eventually the Court's reluctance was overcome: How was this brought about? Three circumstances may be adduced in partial satisfaction of this inquiry:

First. The first circumstance to which I allude is the pressure upon the Court of which Justice Miller speaks in Davidson v. New Orleans, to adopt a definition of "due process of law" which would cancel the effect of the narrow construction given to the phrase "privileges and immunities of citizens of the United States." This pressure was the more formidable in that, notwithstanding Justice Miller's assertion in the Slaughter House decision, the definition that the attorneys were contending for was well warranted by certain results that had been arrived at by the state courts before the Civil War. It must moreover always be borne in mind that, as Judge Baldwin puts it, it is counsel rather than judges that make the law, the later interposing only to winnow counsel's results. The insistence of counsel upon a broad view of "due process of law" was bound eventually to bear fruit.

Second. In an earlier paragraph I referred to a series of congressional enactments between the years 1870 and 1875 by which the independence and indeed the continuance of the legislative authority of the states seemed seriously menaced. In 1883, however, the last of these enactments was erased from the statute book, by the concluding one (109 U.S. 3) of a line of decisions by which they were, one after the other, brought under the ban of unconstitutionality. In these decisions the Court held that the Fourteenth Amendment prohibited only discriminatory action on the part of the state itself or its functionaries. From this it followed that Congress's power under the fifth section of the amendment was merely remedial: in other words, was of the same scope essentially as that of the Court itself to set aside discriminatory state legislation. But what was this except to condemn constitutional action by Congress as gratuitous meddling? The Civil Rights Act eliminated and the equality of the two great political parties once more restored in the national government, the Court had little further reason to apprehend the substitution of congressional legislation for state legislation.

Third. Meantime, in 1883, in the Butchers Union Company v. Crescent City Company (111 U.S. 746), the opportunity was afforded the dissenting minority in the Slaughter House cases to appear as a concurring minority and to give their views thereby something of the guise of Court doctrine. The question at issue before the Court in this case was the right of the legislature of Louisiana to limit the grant of privileges upheld in the earlier litigation. The majority of the Court again rested its case upon the latitudinarian view of legislative power. The minority, on the other hand, preferred to look upon the legislation under review as vindicating the private rights that were, to their way of thinking, transgressed by the original charter of the Crescent City Company. Again it is Justice Field who heads the minority, renewing his allegiance "to those inherent rights which lie at the foundation of all action'' and to ''that new evangel of liberty to the people,'' the Declaration of Independence. It is, however, Justice Bradley's opinion that subsequent use has made most impor- tant. Summarizing his views under three captions, he holds, first, ''that liberty of pursuit . . . is one of the privileges of a citizen of the United States,'' and again enters a protest against the Slaughter House decision. Still he is willing to abandon this contention; for, secondly, if the law creating the monopoly ''does not abridge the privileges and immunities of a citizen of the United States . . . it certainly does deprive him—to a certain extent—of his liberty. . . . And, if a man's right to his calling is property, as many maintain, then those who had already adopted the prohibited pursuits in New Orleans were deprived, by the law in question, of their property, as well as their liberty without due process of law.'' And thirdly, ''Still more apparent in the violation by this monopoly of the last clause of the section, 'no State shall deny to any person equal protection of the laws.' ''

As we shall discover presently, one of the central canons of present day interpretation of the Fourteenth Amendment is the concept of ''class legisla- tion.'' When a particular class of the community is selected by the legislature for additional privileges or duties, the Court's approval of the legislation whereby this selection is effected is necessary to meet the requirement of ''due process of law'' and ''equal protection of the laws.'' In most of the cases which we shall subsequently review, therefore, these phrases attend upon each other in an interesting and significant fashion. But now it is in Bradley's opinion as given above that this concomitance is first suggested. Likewise in this same opinion, as well as in Field's various opinions recited above, the terms ''liberty'' and ''property'' take on the meaning of liberty of pursuit and freedom of contract, which also are today leading ideas with attorneys and with the Court. It is true that Bradley's opinion in the Bartemeyer case shows that his views in the Slaughter House case were determined by the fact that he regarded the Crescent City Company as a monopoly; and it is equally evident that this was still his attitude in the Crescent City case. Nevertheless, we have in his utterance given above a form of words, so to say, which is capacious of varied use and of which, it is a fact, that the very greatest use has been made in the elaboration of present day constitutional law. These then are the circumstances which made it easy for the Court to assume a supervisory power over state legislation, in the pretended enforcement of the Fourteenth Amendment. In the first place, the pressure upon the Court to do so by adopting a view of due process of law that would settle the question of jurisdiction in its own favor was constantly increasing. In the second place, after the Civil Rights decision, all danger that Congress would take advantage of a broad construction of the Fourteenth Amendment to assert its own authority aggressively seemed at an end. Finally, the doctrine by which the Court was to assert its juridiction was already at hand in a form that bore the guise of an adequate precedent. But even now the Court still held back from occupying at one stroke the whole region of jurisdiction that lay before it. It must proceed step by step. And in this connection the downfall of Munn v. Illinois is important.[2]

Interesting enough, it was Chief Justice Waite himself who laid the ax to the tree. In the Railroad Commission cases (116 U.S. 307), in 1886, the Court again declared the right of the legislature to regulate railroad charges, but in the very body of the opinion is to be found this warning of a veering in the judicial mind: "From what has thus been said it is not to be inferred that this form of limitation or regulation is itself without limit. This power to regulate is not a power to destroy, and limitation is not the equivalent of confiscation. . . . The State cannot . . . do that which in law amounts to a taking of private property for public use without just compensation or without due process of law." The important feature of this utterance is the use of "just compensation" and "due process of law" as equivalent phrases,—a usage involving two assumptions, each of which contradicts flatly the previous pronouncement of the Court. The first of these assumptions is that the power to regulate carrier's charges is an item, not of the state's police power, but of that much more special branch of the state's power, the power of eminent domain. The second assumption is that this power of eminent domain is limited by the Fourteenth Amendment. This assumption is of course to the entire derogation of Davidson v. New Orleans, as the other is both of historical fact and of Munn v. Illinois. Nevertheless we find Justice Gray in Dow v. Beidelman (125 U.S. 680) ratifying Waite's dictum in the Commission cases as the "general rule of laws." Gray's utterance is also obiter dictum, but it warrants the assertion that the identification of a branch of the police power with the power of eminent domain and the overruling of Davidson v. New Orleans together comprise the initial step in the overthrow of Munn v. Illinois.

But only the first step. To his acquiescence in Waite's dictum Justice Gray adds: "Without proof of the sum invested (by complainant in error) . . . the Court has no means, *if it would under any circumstances have the power,* of determining that the rate fixed by the legislature is unreasonable." How is the doubt thus expressed to be reconciled with the reiteration of the general rule of law which it follows so immediately? The answer is to be found in the argument for counsel for complainant in error in the Dow case. This argument reveals the fact that the railroads were by no means satisfied with the limitation which Chief Justice Waite had suggested in the Commission cases upon the power of rate regulation; for that limitation still left the power of the legislature very ample. The legislature must not impose a confiscatory rate, a rate in other words that might mean positive loss to the carrier; for such loss would amount to a taking of the physical property of the railroad for public use without compensation: this, it seems, is the sum and substance of Chief Justice Waite's

2. In tracing the downfall of Munn v. Illinois, I have made large use of Smalley's *Railroad Rate Control.*

thinking in the Commission cases. In the Chicago and Northwestern Railway v. Dey, moreover, we find Judge Brewer, then of the United States Circuit Court, applying Waite's principle as follows: "Counsel for complainant urge that the lowest rates the legislature may establish must be such as will secure to the owners of the railroad property a profit on their investment at least equal to the lowest current rate of interest, say three per cent. Decisions of the Supreme Court seem to forbid such a limit to the power of the legislature in respect to that which they apparently recognize as a right of the owners of the railroad property to some reward; and the right of judicial interference exists only when the schedule of rates established will fail to secure to the owners of the property some compensation or income for their investment. As to the amount of such investment, if some compensation or reward is in fact secured, the legislature is the sole judge." Put more concisely, Judge Brewer's idea seems to be that legislatively imposed rates must not be confiscatory, and to secure that they shall not be, the Courts may interfere, but farther than that they must keep their hands off. But certainly to have secured such an illusory restraint as this upon legislative power was an empty triumph for the railroads, and so they regarded it. Accordingly we find them urging a stricter pinioning of the legislature's hands and devising a new argument, or rather perfecting an old one, upon which to base their contention.

In brief compass this argument is simply that when the reasonableness of legislative rates is questioned, "due process" requires that the courts shall finally decide the matter; that is, that the question of the reasonableness of legislative rates is a judicial one, under the Fourteenth Amendment's guaranty of "due process of law." This argument had been met directly and resolutely repulsed by Judge Brewer in the Chicago and Northwestern case, which occurred in 1886. Justice Gray's dictum in the Dow case is perhaps evidence that, three years later, the Supreme Court was also adversely minded, but the year following the Court yielded to the inevitable and adopted the argument of the railroad attorneys, making it the basis of their decision of the decisive case of the Chicago, St. Paul and Milwaukee Railroad v. Minnesota (134 U.S. 418). Complainant in error asserted its rights under the Fourteenth Amendment to contest the reasonableness of certain rates imposed by the Railroad Commission of defendant state. The law establishing this commission made the rates fixed by it conclusively reasonable. The constitutionality of this law under the Fourteenth Amendment was therefore the question before the Court, and it was held to be unconstitutional. Said Justice Blatchford, delivering the opinion of the Court: "The question of the reasonableness of a rate of charge for transportation by a railroad company, involving as it does *the element of reasonableness both as regards the company and as regards the public,* is eminently a question for judicial investigation, requiring due process of law for it determination. If the company is deprived of the power of charging rates for the use of its property, and such deprivation takes place in the absence of an investigation by judicial machinery, it is deprived of the lawful use of its property and thus, in substance and effect, of the property itself, without due process of law, and in violation of the Constitution of the United States, and in so far as it is thus deprived, while other persons are permitted to receive reasonable profits upon their invested capital, the company is deprived of the equal protection of the laws.''

Thus was the doctrine of judicial review of legislative rates brought forth. Its appearance marks a complete volte-face on the part of the Court that fourteen years before pronounced the decision in Munn v. Illinois. The completeness of the change of view is well indicated in the dissenting opinion delivered by Justice Bradley for himself and Justices Gray and Lamar. "It is urged," says Bradley, "that what is a reasonable rate is a judicial question. On the contrary, it is preeminently a legislative one, involving considerations of policy as well as of remuneration. The legislature has the right and it is its prerogative, if it chooses to exercise it, to declare what is reasonable. This is just where I differ from the majority of the Court. They say in effect, if not in terms, that the final tribunal of arbitrament is the judiciary; I say it is the legislature . . . unless the legislature . . . has made it judicial. . . . By the decision now made we declare in effect, that the judiciary, and not the legislature, is the final arbiter in the regulation of fares and freights of railroads. . . . It is an assumption of authority on the part of the judiciary which it seems to me, with all due deference to the judgment of my brethren, it has no right to make."

Justice Bradley's protest fell on deaf ears. In Budd v. New York, Justice Blatchford attempted to reconcile his decision in the Chicago, Milwaukee and St. Paul case with Munn v. Illinois by confining the operation of the former to cases where rates had been fixed by commission and denying its application to rates directly imposed by the legislature. This attempt is important as showing the step that still lay between the Chicago, Milwaukee and St. Paul decision when it was first pronounced and the doctrine at which the Court was finally to arrive. Otherwise this distinction has long since dropped out of judicial ken, while the decision it was meant to limit has been progressively expanded. We shall, however, have to be brief with the record. "It has always been recognized," says Justice Brewer in Regan v. The Farmers' Loan and Trust Co. (154 U.S. 362, 397), "that if a carrier attempted to charge a shipper an unreasonable sum, the Courts had jurisdiction to inquire into that matter and to award the shipper any amount exacted from him in excess of a reasonable rate. . . . The province of the Courts is not changed, nor the limit of judicial inquiry altered because the legislature instead of the carrier prescribes the rates." This language, besides setting forth in a very illuminating manner the theory which the courts of this country entertain of their position in the state, marks the final definition of "due process of law" in this species of cases, viz.: law which the Court has pronounced reasonable. The same doctrine finds reiteration in Smyth v. Ames (169 U.S. 466), but at the same time it is assimilated to the doctrine of Chief Justice Waite's dictum in the Commission cases, with the result that the distinction between confiscatory and unreasonable rates, against which the railroad attorneys had waged war from the outset, disappears. "What the company is entitled to ask," says Justice Harlan, "is a fair return upon the value of that which it employs for the public convenience." Finally, in the recent Consolidated Gas Company case the Court stipulates six per cent as its idea of a "fair return."

At this point we may dismiss the railroad decisions, our concern with which has been simply to trace the development through them of the doctrine of due process of law. With the results obtained in mind we return to the larger subject of the relation of the police power of the state, as a whole, to the Fourteenth Amendment as interpreted today. The first matter that we have to take note of is this. While the Supreme Court of the United States was engaged in the obliteration of Munn v. Illinois, the state judiciaries had seized upon Bradley's dissent in the Crescent City case and, divesting it of all its original qualifications, had elevated it to the position of an authoritative canon of constitutional law, applying it moreover in a manner against which Bradley himself would have been the first to protest. These decisions we have no space within the limits of this article to review. Instead we shall content ourselves with sketching their ratification by the Supreme Court, under the following topics: 1. Due process of law; 2. Class legislation; 3. Liberty and property; 4. Judicial cognizance; 5. Legal presumption.

1. The constitutional requirement of "due process of law" is recognized as a limitation upon legislative power from the outset of our constitutional history, but in a very definite sense: the legislature must provide "due process" for the *enforcement* of the law.[3] But what is due process in the *enforcement* of the law? One indispensable element, it came to be held, was a hearing: wherefore, it followed that a visitation of pains and penalties or other inconveniences upon selected individuals by direct legislative action, as in bills of attainder or in acts of confiscation, is not allowable. This view of the matter finds expression with some enlargements, in Webster's definition of "due process of law" in his argument in the Dartmouth College case, which definition is adopted by the Supreme Court in Hurtado v. California. Nor is it evident that Justice Bradley thought that he was going beyond this view of the matter when, in the Crescent City case, he protested against the monopoly which, he alleged, had been created by legislative enactment, at the expense of particular persons engaged in a business which the law itself viewed as legitimate. Nevertheless the connection between this view of "due process of law" and the present very sweeping view is palpable enough. Suppose, for example, that the legislature, while providing satisfactory machinery for the *enforcement* of a particular

---

3. This is a subject I go into at great length in Part II of my study, where I trace the development of "due process of law," principally at the hands of the state courts, before the Civil War.

statute should by that same statute impose pains and penalties for the performance of an act generally deemed harmless or even beneficial; in such a case the question of the method by which the act was to be enforced would be a very trivial consideration as compared with the requirements visited by the act upon those to whom it was addressed. It is still, I believe, a maxim formally recognized by the courts in constitutional cases, that the possibility that power may be abused is no argument against its existence. In point of fact, however, this maxim has been entirely cast aside. In the matter under review, therefore, the courts, moved by some such consideration as finds illustràtion in the hypothesis just given, have set up, in the first place, certain purposes which it is assumed the police power ought always to subserve and, in the second place, their own opinions as to the reasonableness of legislation viewed from the standpoint of these purposes, as limitations answering to the constitutional requirement of "due process of law" and therefore as judicially enforceable limitations upon legislative power. "Due process of law," therefore, comes to mean reasonable law, in the Court's opinion. This view is first deduced by the state courts from Bradley's dissent in the Crescent City case. Meantime, the Supreme Court itself was elaborating a kindred doctrine out of Blatchford's opinion in the Chicago, Milwaukee and St. Paul case. It was quite ready, therefore, to appreciate and, when the time came, to ratify the more broadly applicable doctrine of the state courts. This it does for the first time in Mugler v. Kansas (123 U.S. 623). Later cases will be noted below.

2. But the view that the courts today hold of "due process of law" is intimately involved with their view of what is called "class legislation." Most police legislation, as was insinuated in Barbier v. Connolly, indicates some class in the community for special privileges or special burdens. Such legislation therefore tends to approximate, if the question of its reasonableness be eliminated from the discussion, to that type of legislation in which the legislature, without the intervention of the courts, designates certain persons for unfavorable treatment and which was brought under judicial condemnation long before the Fourteenth Amendment had been framed. This being the case, it is easy to see that that amendment's requirement of "an equal protection of the laws" for all persons greatly assisted the Court in arriving at its final view of "due process of law." Again, however, there was no sudden evolution by a step by step development. In the Slaughter House cases this clause was construed to require merely that here should be no legislative discrimination against the Negro, but in Yick Wo v. Hopkins, the Chinese were also brought within its contemplation. The first great step toward the modern view was taken in the county of Santa Clara v. the Southern Pacific Railroad Company (118 U.S. 394). In this case the issue raised by defendant was the validity of a law which certain corporations were subjected to a special method of assessment for purpose of taxation. The Court refused, much to Justice Field's disappointment, to pass upon the constitutional question. At the same time, however, it

ruled unanimously, and without listening to argument on the point, that a corporation is a "person" in the sense in which that term is used in the final clause of the first section of the Fourteenth Amendment. Meantime, in Munn v. Illinois, an idea had cropped up of which the Court was years later to make the greatest possible use; viz.: the application of the historical test of the common law in the partial determination of what are reasonable legislative classifications. Thus in Holden v. Hardy (169 U.S. 366), where the Court assumes its final position, and in later related cases, it comes out that there is an important difference in the mind of the Court between what it calls persons *sui juris,* meaning adult males, and dependent persons, such as women and children. In some of the state decisions in which this distinction is first utilized, the right of the legislature to go further and distinguish classes of persons *sui juris,* for the purpose of placing special duties upon some or bestowing special privileges upon others, is totally denied. The Supreme Court does not go that far, but contents itself with thrusting upon the state the burden of showing the reasonableness of such legislative classifications.

3. The third topic is the phrase "liberty and property" in the constitutional requirement that no state "shall deprive any person of life, liberty or property without due process of law." The evident assumption underlying the attempt in the Commission cases to identify "due process of law" with "just compensation" is that property is tangible property, or evidences thereof, and this indeed is the view of the common law, where similarly liberty means simply freedom from physical distraint, a violation of which would be remediable by an action in damages for false imprisonment. The whole tendency, however, of the effort succeeding the Civil War to put the Negro on a parity with the white race was, in the first place, to enlarge very greatly the significance of both these terms, and, secondly, by investing civil rights with the sanctity of property rights, to merge them and thus to confer upon property something of the broad connotation that it bears in the pages of Locke. Justice Field, in his various dissents, accepts these enlarged but decidedly vague notions of liberty and property apparently without qualification. Bradley's tone, on the other hand, even in his monumental Crescent City opinion, is noticeably diffident and tentative. Naturally the more confident view won its way, first with the state courts, and then with the Supreme Court. In Allgeyer v. Louisiana (165 U.S. 578) the Court was confronted with the task of obviating an uncomfortable precedent without incurring the responsibility of overturning it. This is does by adopting Justice Field's definition of liberty and then applying it in a totally illogical fashion to the case under review. In Holden v. Hardy, Justice Brown seeks for a definition of "due process of law," and finally fastens upon the definition of liberty given in the Allgeyer case.

4. Thus far we have been dealing with phrases. The law, however, is not a mere matter of phrases: it has to be applied by the Court to facts. And what sort of facts? In constitutional cases the answer given to this question will depend

upon the theory held of the nature of the power of judicial review. Is it, as is often asserted, a power analogous to that of the courts at the common law to pass upon the validity of executive commissions, or is it a broader power and analogous rather to that of equity, to set aside a rule of law which it finds productive of injustice in a particular case? This at bottom is the point in a dispute that arose very early in the judiciary itself. Ostensibly the former of these two views won out, but actually it is the latter that has triumphed, the best proof of which is the doctrine of due process of law which we have been tracing. Accordingly a part of the process by which this doctrine has become established has been a concomitant change of view upon the part of the Court as to the sort of facts of which it could take "judicial cognizance" in deciding constitutional cases. In Munn v. Illinois, the Court sets about to canvass only facts of law, the only question for determination being the question of legal power. In Powell v. Pennsylvania the same point of view is adhered to with emphasis. Meantime, however, the state courts, in setting up their views of what is conducive to the public health, etc., as a limitation upon the police power, had adopted a different practice, and in the Jacobs case the New York Court of Appeals had taken "judicial cognizance" of the effect of tobacco upon the human system. The ratification of this method by the Supreme Court of the United States takes place in Mugler v. Kansas. Powell v. Pennsylvania, which comes shortly after, is therefore a retreat, but only a temporary one, for the lost ground is recovered and new territory gained in Holden v. Hardy.

5. The Court, then, in passing upon constitutional cases, judges of both the law and the facts: but even this is not the whole story. For in judging of the law and the facts the Court sets out with certain presumptions in mind whereby it directs its inquiries. No judicial maxim is more venerable than that a legislative enactment must be *presumed* to be valid until it is shown to be the contrary. The inevitable implication, however, from the distinction drawn by the Court, in cases affecting their liberty or property, between persons *sui juris* and dependent persons, is that legislation touching these matters stands upon a diverse footing; that, in short, the presumpton shifts from the side of the state to that of private rights, or vice versa, according as the persons affected by the legislation are adult males or not. In Holden v. Hardy the burden of proof is still held to rest upon the opponents of the legislation under review, despite the principle just stated. In Lochner v. New York (198 U.S. 45) the burden of proof is shifted.

All this, however, is a very abstract statement of the development of the law. Let me therefore review a decision that furnishes illustration of the various points made above, and of the present state of the law. In Lochner v. The People of the State of New York the issue was the validity of a statute limiting employment in bakeries to sixty hours a week and to ten hours a day. Complainants in error contended that this statute comprised an unreasonable and arbitrary regulation of an innocuous trade and was therefore not within the police power; and they propounded the following questions, which, they contended, the state must answer satisfactorily, in order to justify such an enactment as the one in question. "Does a danger exist which the enactment is designed to meet? Is it of sufficient magnitude? Does it concern the public? Does the proposed measure tend to remove it? Is the restraint or requirement in proportion to the danger? Is it possible to secure the objects sought without impairing essential rights and principles? Does the choice of a particular measure show that some other interest than safety or health was the actual motive of legislation?" These questions are interesting as showing counsel's estimate of the present state of the law. Judged by the standard set by the court in Powell v. Pennsylvania, none of them is pertinent. But much water had poured over the judicial mill wheel since that decision. The extremest proposition that the defenders of the statute could adduce with which to ward off this fusilade of questions was the equivocal maxim that "the propriety of the exercise of the police power within constitutional limits is purely a matter of legislative discretion with which the courts cannot interfere," thus leaving it still to be determined, it is obvious, what such constitutional limits are.

Justice Peckham, speaking for a bare majority of the Court, pronounced the statute void as in transgression of the right of contract safeguarded by the Fourteenth Amendment. His statement of the law governing the case is far from clear, and deals very freely in those ambiguous platitudes the constant reiteration of which, without attempt at definition, has from the outset of the development we are tracing, constituted the Court's most formidable weapon in its struggle for jurisdiction. The assertion is ventured that under the Fourteenth Amendment "no State can deprive any person of life, liberty and property without due process of law"; also that the police powers "relate to the safety, health, morals and general welfare of the public"; that "both property and liberty are held on such reasonable conditions as may be imposed by the governing power of the States, in the exercise of those powers, and with such conditions the Fourteenth Amendment was not designed to interfere"; that "the State therefore has the power to prevent the individual from making certain kinds of contracts, and in regard to them the Federal Constitution offers no protection"; that "if the contract be one which the State, in the legitimate exercise of its police powers, has the right to prohibit, it is not prevented from prohibiting it by the Fourteenth Amendment." All of which seems fairly indisputable but gets us no further. The next statement is more illuminating: "When the State," it runs, "by its legislature, in the assumed exercise of its police powers, has passed an act which seriously limits the right to labor or the right to contract in regard to their means of livelihood between persons who are *sui juris*—both employer and employee—it becomes of great importance to determine which shall prevail—the right of the individual to labor for such time as he may choose, or the right of the State to prevent the individual from laboring, or from entering into any contract to labor, beyond a certain time prescribed by the State." "It must of course be conceded," the opinion continues, "that there is a limit to the valid exercise of the police power by the State. . . . Otherwise the Fourteenth Amendment would have no efficacy in the legislatures, and the legislatures of the States would have unbounded power, and it would be enough to say that any piece of legislation was enacted to conserve the morals, the health, or the safety of the people; such legislation would be valid no matter how absolutely without foundation the claim might be. The claim of the police power would be a mere pretext,—become another and elusive name for the supreme sovereignty of the State, to be exercised free from constitutional restraint. . . . In every case that comes before this Court, therefore, where legislation of this character is concerned and where the protection of the Federal Court is sought, the question necessarily arises: Is this a fair, reasonable, and appropriate exercise of the police power of the State, or is it an unreasonable, unnecessary, and arbitrary interference with the right of the individual to his personal liberty?" This does not mean, however, Justice Peckham insists, that the Court is substituting its own judgment for that of the legislature. "If," he asserts, "the act be within the power of the State it is valid, although the judgment of the Court might be totally opposed to the enactment of such a law. But the question would still remain: Is it within the police power of the State? And that question must be answered by the Court." But certainly this is a rather dark saying, since, taken in its literal and grammatical sense, it means that the question of whether it is within the police power of the states may be raised even of an entirely valid statute. Probably, though, Justice Peckham does not mean that, but is contending simply that the validity, which in this connection means reasonableness, of a law is something absolute. But if this be true, why was the statute in this particular litigation overturned by the Supreme Court of the United States by a vote of five to four after having been sustained by the New York Court of Appeals by a vote of four to three?

But to return to the decision itself, we find Justice Peckham animadverting upon the statute under review in this fashion: "In looking through statistics regarding all trades and occupations it may be true that the trade of a baker does not appear to be as healthy as some trades, and is also vastly more healthy than still others. To the common understanding the trade of a baker has never been regarded as an unhealthy one. Very likely physicians would not recognize the exercise of that or of any other trade as a remedy of ill health. . . . It might be safely affirmed that almost all occupations more or less affect the health. . . . But are all on that account at the mercy of legislative majorities. . . . Not only the hours of employees, but the hours of employers could be regulated, and doctors, lawyers, scientists, or professional men, as well as athletes and artisans, could be forbidden to fatigue their brain and body by prolonged hours of exercise lest the fighting strength of the State be impaired." This method of proceeding by the *reduction ad adsurdum* is scarely convincing, since the whole question at issue is whether the statute under consideration is reasonable or unreasonable; and to the query, whether all trades are to be at the mercy of legislative majorities, inquiry may be returned, whether they are to be at the mercy of judicial majorities.

Justice Peckham's mode of arguing nevertheless has its value; for it brings out the fact that this decision rests, immediately, upon considerations of policy with regard to which there is ample room for debate, and, ultimately, upon a highly controversial view of public policy in general. Addressing himself to the former of these topics, Justice Harlan, speaking in dissent for himself and Justices White and Day, adduces the *Eighteenth Annual Report by the New York Bureau of Statistics of Labor,* a Professor Hirt's treastise on the *Diseases of the Workers,* and "another writer," who testifies to the chronic suffering of bakers from inflamed lungs and bronchial tubes and sore eyes, and to their lack of resisting power to diseases, and short average life. Thus the reasonableness of the enactment under consideration is at any rate open to discussion, and that fact of itself makes it, under Holden v. Hardy and kindred precedents, within legislative discretion. "Responsibility," Harlan concludes, "therefore rests upon legislators, not upon the courts. No evils arising from such legislation could be more far reaching than those that might come through our system of government if the judiciary, abandoning the sphere assigned to it by the fundamental law, should enter the domain of legislation, and upon grounds merely of justice or wisdom annul statutes that had received the sanction of the people's representatives. We are reminded by counsel that it is the solemn duty of the courts in cases before them to guard the constitutional rights of a citizen against merely arbitrary power. That is unquestionably true. But it is equally true—indeed the public interests imperatively demand—that legislative enactments should be recognized and enforced by the courts as embodying the will of the people, unless they are plainly and palpably beyond all question in violation of the fundamental law of the Constitution."

Justice Holmes' dissent is still more trenchant, cutting as it does through the momentary question of policy to the deeper, though inarticulate, major premise underlying all preference for or against the political will when it appears arrayed against private rights. "This case," says Holmes, "is decided upon an economic theory which a large part of the country does not entertain. If it were a question whether I agreed with that theory, I should desire to study it further and long before making up my mind. But I do not conceive that to be my duty, because I strongly believe that my agreement or disagreement has nothing to do with the right of a majority to embody their opinions in law. It is settled by various decisions of this Court that State constitutions and State laws may regulate life in many ways which we as legislators might think as injudicious or, if you like, as tyrannical as this and which, equally with this, interfere with the liberty of contract. . . . The Fourteenth Amendment does not enact Mr. Herbert Spencer's *Statics.* . . . A constitution was not intended to embody a particular economic theory, whether of paternalism and the organic relation of the citizen to the State or of *laissez faire*. It is made for people of fundamentally differing views, and the accident of our finding certain opinions natural and familiar, or novel and even striking, ought not to conclude our judgment upon the question whether statutes embodying them conflict with the Constitution of the United States. . . . I think that the word 'liberty' in the Fourteenth Amendment is perverted when it is held to prevent the natural outcome of a dominant opinion, unless it can be said that a rational and fair man necessarily would admit that the statute proposed would infringe fundamental principles as they have been understood by the traditions of our people and of our law.''

The value of these dissenting opinions is that of most of the other dissenting opinions that we have noted, viz.: that they serve to measure the advance that the law receives in a given direction from the decision dissented from. On the other hand, they are both of them open to criticisms of a rather obvious sort. Thus Justice Harlan was himself the author of Mugler v. Kansas and the line connecting that decision with the one in Lochner v. New York is both direct and logical. Much the same criticism has to be levelled against Justice Holmes' dissent also. For it is to be noted that he accepts in toto the present day view of due process of law. Moreover his ''rational and fair man'' without a social philosophy of some kind and, equally, his constitution devoid of preconceptions are the veriest fictions. And certainly it was ungracious on Justice Holmes' part to imply a lack of rationality on the part of his majority brethren. The truth is that, the moment the Court, in its interpretation of the Fourteenth Amendment, left behind the definite, historical concept of ''due process of law'' as having to do with the *enforcement* of law and not its *making,* the moment it abandoned, in its attempt to delimit the police power of the state, its ancient maxim that the possibility that a power may be abused has nothing to do with its existence, that moment it committed itself to a course that was bound to lead, however gradually and easily, beyond the precincts of judicial power, in the sense of the power to ascertain the law, into that of legislative power which determines policies on the basis of facts and desires. Moreover, and this is another point at which Justice Holmes seems to blink the truth, the feeling instigating the first step was the same as that which prompted the last, viz.: a fear of popular majorities, which fear, however, lies at the very basis of the whole system of judicial review, and indeed of our entire constitutional system.

Thus it comes about that Justice Miller's apprehension of a perpetual censorship of state legislation by the Supreme Court has been realized, and Chief Justice Waite's counsel that the remedy for abuses of legislative power is to be sought at the polls and not in the court has been rendered obsolete: and this in brief is the theme I have been pursuing. I desire to add but two remarks. In the first place, this development which we have been tracing is often represented as a centralizing movement in our government, and the cry of ''states rights'' has been recently revived in consequence. Is this protest a really relevant one? On the one hand, in support of the view which it represents, the following facts may be adduced: the "Twilight Zone," which also is a creation of the federal judiciary at the expense of state power; the increased use of the injunction by the federal courts in constitutional cases, the enlarged view held by these tribunals today of their power under the Eleventh Amendment (*Ex parte* Young, U.S. Sup. Ct. Reps., 52 L. ed. 714), the recent action of the Supreme Court in sweeping aside the line drawn by the new Virginia constitution between legislative and judicial power in the creation of a railroad commission (Virginia R.R. Commission cases, 211 U.S. 210). But on the other hand these facts are equally obvious: the general extension of their equity jurisdiction of all American courts today, whether state or federal; the indebtedness of the Supreme Court of the United States to state jurisprudence for its present view of the pregnant phrases of the Fourteenth Amendment; the evident readiness of the Supreme Court to enforce the same ideas against federal legislation under the sanction of the first eight amendments (Adair v. United States, 208 U.S. 161), and indeed the "general principles of constitutional law," where these may be needed to piece out the written Constitution (dicta in the Insular and related cases); and finally the fact that the Supreme Court of the United States has never in the course of its existence bestowed authority upon the political branches of the federal government, though it has often been called upon to ratify an assumption of authority by those branches after the act. The truth of the matter is that the alleged issue between state power and federal power is largely imaginative, and in this connection at least quite pointless. The real issue is far different and traverses both state and federal governments. It is the issue between two theories of government, one of which, centering around the notion of sovereignty, regards government as the agent of society; the other of which, centering around the notion of natural rights, regards government as somewhat extrinsic to society. It is the issue also between two theories of law, the one of which regards law as an emanation from authority and as vested with a reformative function, the other of which holds that law ought to be conservative and ought to represent no more than a ratification of the custom of the community. The latter is plainly shown, for example, by the language of Justice Holmes dissent just quoted to be the theory of our American courts, which indeed seem disposed to reduce legislative power to the function of finding the law rather than of making it. Nor is it impertinent to add in this connection that the maxim *sic utere tuo ut alienum non laedas,* which the courts today make the controlling principle of the police power, is the norm which the common law sets to private action.[4]

My second remark I can put more briefly. The Court in its early fear for the federal balance denied the Fourteenth Amendment practically all efficacy as a limitation upon state power, save in the interest of racial equality before the

4. The topics referred to in this paragraph, I treat of at length in Part IV of my study *The Growth of Judicial Review.*

law. Subsequently, however, the Court found reason to abandon its early conservative position and in the interest of private and paricularly of property rights to take a greatly enlarged view of its supervisory powers over state legislation. As we have seen, the history of this change is the history particularly of the development of the phrase "due process of law." But now an interesting thing is to be noted. The Berea College decision makes it perfectly plain that the enlarged view of "due process of law" is not available against legislative classifications based on racial differences, such classifications being deemed prima facie reasonable. Thus it comes about that property, or, calling to mind the Santa Clara case, the corporations succeed to the rights which those who framed the Fourteenth Amendment thought they were bestowing upon the Negro. The outcome is not entirely devoid of irony, but neither on the other hand, as I have above emphasized, is it devoid of historical justification, from our constitutional jurisprudence antedating the Fourteenth Amendment.

5. The Doctrine of Due Process of Law before the Civil War

DURING the last court year the United States Supreme Court decided sixty-five constitutional cases; eight of these arose under the obligation of contracts clause, twenty-one under the commerce clause, and twenty-four under the Fourteenth Amendment, or, more specifically, under that clause of the Fourteenth Amendment which declares that no state shall "deprive any person of life, liberty, or property without due process of law."[1] In other words, the most important clause of the United States Constitution judged as a restriction upon the legislative power of the states is the due process of law clause of the Fourteenth Amendment. Equally interesting is the fact that this importance is comparatively recent. The Fourteenth Amendment was added to the Constitution in 1868. Between 1868 and 1889 seventy-one cases arose under the entire amendment. Between 1890 and 1901, on the other hand, 197 cases arose under the amendment, and that amounts to saying under the clause just quoted.[2] Again, while the *American Digest* in 1887 contains but 11 items upon due process of law out of 274 items upon the subject of constitutional law, the same publication for 1902 contains 109 items upon due process of law out of a total of 470 items upon constitutional law; and furthermore, a large proportion of the remainder of these 470 items are upon topics related to and growing out of the modern concept of due process of law.[3]

Nor is the significance of these statistics difficult to discover when we understand what the modern concept due process of law is. In the now famous case of Lochner v. State of New York[4] the issue was the validity of the statute

From 24 *Harvard Law Review* 366, 460 (1911). Reprinted by permission. Copyright 1911 by the Harvard Law Review Association.

1. E. Wambaugh, "Constitutional Law in 1909–10," 4 *Am. Pol. Sci. Rev.* 483–97.
2. See the Annotated Constitution of the United States in any House or Senate Manual.
3. *Am. Dig.* of dates mentioned, Tit. "Constitutional Law."
4. 198 U.S. 45 (1905).

limiting employment in bakeries to sixty hours a week and ten hours a day. Complainants in error contended that this statute comprised an unreasonable and arbitrary regulation of an innocuous trade and was therefore not within the police power; and they propounded the following questions, which, they contended, the state must answer satisfactorily, in order to justify such an enactment as the one in question: "Does a danger exist which the enactment is designed to meet? Is it of sufficient magnitude? Does it concern the public? Does the proposed measure tend to remove it? Is the restraint and requirement in proportion to the danger? Is it possible to secure the objects sought without impairing essential rights and principles? Does the choice of a particular measure show that some other interest than safety or health was the actual motive of legislation?" The range of inquiry which the Court is thus invited to enter into is obviously almost indefinite. Nevertheless it would seem from the language of Justice Peckham's opinion, pronouncing the statute under review void, that the Court accepted the invitation. A salient passage of this opinion runs as follows:

> It must of course be conceded that there is a limit to the valid exercise of the police power by the state . . . otherwise the Fourteenth Amendment would have no efficacy in the legislatures, and the legislatures of the state would have unbounded power, and it would be enough to say that any piece of legislation was enacted to conserve the morals, the health, or the safety of the people; such legislation would be valid no matter how absolutely without foundation a claim might be. The claim of the police power would be a mere pretext,—become another and elusive name for the supreme sovereignty of the state, to be exercised free from constitutional restraint . . . In every case that comes before this Court, therefore, where legislation of this character is concerned and where the protection of the federal court is sought, the question necessarily arises: Is this a fair, reasonable, and appropriate exercise of the police power of the state, or is it an unreasonable, unnecessary, and arbitrary interference with the right of the individual to his personal liberty?

It is true that the decision in the Lochner case was rendered by a vote of five to four, but it would seem from a careful examination of their language that the dissenting judges were not protesting so much against the idea that due process of law means reasonable law, or, in other words, the Court's opinion of reasonable law, as against the view that the statute before them was unreasonable.

I have elsewhere traced the development of the due process of law clause of the Fourteenth Amendment.[5] That development, however, has a certain background in the history of our constitutional law anterior to the Civil War. My purpose in this paper is to show what that background is.

I

The phrase "due process of law" comes from Chapter 3 of 28 Edw. III, which reads as follows:

5. 7 *Mich. L. Rev.* 642.

"No man of what state or condition he be, shall be put out of his lands or tenements, nor taken, nor imprisoned, nor disinherited, nor put to death, without he be brought to answer by due process of law."

This statute in turn harks back to the famous Chapter 39 of Magna Carta, which the Massachusetts Constitution of 1780 paraphrases thus:

"No subject shall be arrested, imprisoned, despoiled, or deprived of his property, immunities, or privileges, put out of the protection of the law, exiled, or deprived of his life, liberty, or estate, but by the judgment of his peers or the law of the land."[6]

The important phrase in this passage for our purposes is of course "by the law of the land," which is made by Sir Edward Coke in his *Institutes* synonymous with the later phrase, "by due process of law," and that in turn to signify "by due process of the common law," that is, "by the indictment or presentment of good and lawful men . . . or by writ original of the common law."[7] It must not be thought, however, that in writing thus Coke is recording the facts of history. Rather, to quote a recent authority upon Magna Carta, he was but "following his vicious method of assuming the existence in Magna Carta of a warrant for every legal principle established in his own day," a method which has enabled him to mislead utterly "several generations of commentators."[8] Among those thus misled are the three great commentators on American constitutional law, Kent, Story, and Cooley,—willing dupes no doubt, yet dupes nonetheless.[9]

It will not be amiss perhaps to raise the question whether Coke regarded "the law of the land," as he defined it, as beyond the power of parliamentary alteration, an inquiry which leads us to the great parliamentary inquest upon "the liberty of the subject" which, growing out of the arrest of the five knights, found ultimate fruition in the Petition of Right of 1628.[10] The question at issue at this time between Parliament and the king was whether the latter in ordering an arrest must assign a cause the validity of which it would accordingly devolve upon the judges finally to determine. The parliamentary lawyers, among whom was Coke, in support of their contention that such assignment of cause must be made, propounded the following argument: "And for the words *'per legem terrae'* original writs only are not intended, but all other legal process, which comprehended the whole proceedings of the law upon a cause other than trial by jury . . . and no man ought to be imprisoned by special command without indictment, or other due process to be made by the law."[11]

6. Declaration of Rights, Art. XII.

7. II Inst. 50–51.

8. McKechnie, *Magna Carta* 447 (1905); *id.,* generally on "Chapter 39."

9. 2 Kent, *Comm.* 13 (2 ed. 1832); Story, *Comm.* sec. 1789 (4 ed. 1873); Cooley, *Const. Lim.* 351 *et seq.* (2 ed. 1871).

10. 2 *Parliamentary History,* especially cols. 262–362 (1806–20).

11. *Id.,* cols. 263–64. See also "Mr. Attorney," at col. 306, with reference to a "precise statute"; also Littleton, at cols. 319–20; also same at col. 323.

The phrase "to be made by the law," taken in connection with the purpose of Parliament's protest, which was to keep "the regal power," seems plainly to leave Parliament itself unhampered.

There is, however, another phase of the matter which demands brief consideration. By "law of the land" Coke and his associates meant apparently merely such way of proceeding on the part of the monarch, when moving against individuals, as the law, whether ancient custom, the common law, or statute, ordained and established. But now the source of the guaranty that the monarch should thus proceed was Magna Carta. It therefore behooved the parliamentarians to exalt Magna Carta as much as possible, or, to quote Sir Benjamin Rudyard, to make "that good old decrepit law of Magna Carta, which hath been so long kept in and bed-ridden, as it were, . . . walk abroad again."[12] Magna Carta is accordingly pronounced the source of the fundamental rights of English subjects, is treated as irrepealable, and, finally, as incompatible with the notion of sovereignty anywhere in the realm: "Magna Carta is such a fellow that he will have no sovereign."[13] Years earlier than this, moreover, Coke himself had in Dr. Bonham's Case[14] declared specifically that the common law would on occasion control an act of Parliament if the latter were contrary to common right and reason, and adjudge it to be utterly void. From the general idea, however, of Parliament's power as limited by a fundamental law which had found embodiment in Magna Carta as a whole to the more definite proposition that it was limited by the "law of the land" clause of Chapter 39 was but a step; and it is interesting to note that that step was actually taken by some of Coke's contemporaries, to wit, in the case of Captain John Streater,[15] who, having been arrested by order of the Commonwealth Parliament, set up the contention in an application for a writ of *habeas corpus*, that such an order was not "law of the land." The argument was rejected by the court: "If the Parliament should do one thing and we the contrary here," said the judges, "things would run round. We must submit to the legislative power." But though rejected, Streater's argument, which is based almost exclusively upon passages drawn from Coke's various writings, serves to show what construction Coke's language is susceptible of when viewed from the proper angle.

II

The early state constitutions did not contemplate judicial review, but they were considered nonetheless as setting certain limitations upon legislative

---

12. *Id.*, col. 335. In same connection, see Edward Jenks, "The Myth of *Magna Carta*," *Independent Review* (March 1904).

13. *Parliamentary History*, col. 357. For Pym's point of view, see McIlwain, *High Court of Parliament* 83 (1910).

14. 8 Rep. 118.

15. 5 *State Trials* 386 *et seq.*

power, the transgression of which by the legislature would destroy, to use an oft-quoted phrase from Vattel, "the basis of the legislature's own existence,"[16] thus giving rise to the right of revolution on the part of the people. Did, then, the phrase "law of the land," which is the universal form in these constitutions, import any limitation upon legislative power? There are three good reasons for thinking not. In the first place, "the judgment of peers," signifying in our constitutional usage trial by jury, which is usually alternative to "law of the land" and therefore apparently displaceable by it,[17] is often further safeguarded by a clause rendering it inviolable in all cases in which it had hitherto been used,[18] a clause to which the members of the legislature were sometimes required to take special oaths of fidelity.[19] In the second place, moreover, if "law of the land" meant something else than statutory enactment, that something could have been only the common law, which, however, is adopted in these same constitutions, when specific mention is made of it, only until the legislature may choose to alter it.[20] Finally, in the early days of judicial review, a number of cases arose in which the law of the land clause would certainly have been brought forward had it been deemed available as a constitutional restriction upon legislative power.[21] The argument from silence is often of dubious value, but in a case of this sort it is almost conclusive.

One of the two earliest constitutional cases under the law of the land clause arose in North Carolina in 1794,[22] in connection with the statute authorizing the attorney general of the state to take judgments against the receivers of public moneys upon motion and without notice to the delinquents. At first the opinion of the single judge sitting was adverse to the statute, but "next day at the sitting of the court, Haywood, Attorney General, moved the subject again," contending that the clauses of the constitution that had been invoked were

16. See Massachusetts' Circular Letter of 1768, MacDonald, *Documentary Source Book* 146–50 (1908).

17. *American Charters, Constitutions, and Organic Laws* 569, 1687, 1891, 2455, 2473, 2788, 3277 (F. N. Thorpe ed. 1909). See also, for existing provisions of this character, Cooley's *Const. Lim.* 351–53, note 1; and F. J. Stimson, *Federal and State Constitutions* sec. 130–31 (1908).

18. The original Maryland, New Hampshire, North Carolina, and South Carolina constitutions answer this description: *American Charters,* above, 1687 and 1688, 2455 and 2456, 2787 and 2788, 3277 and 3278; the Pennsylvania Constitution of 1766 is similiar, at 3083. See also *id.* 785, 2598, and 2637; Stimson, above, sec. 72.

19. This was the case in the original New Jersey Constitution, *American Charters,* above, 2598.

20. The original Delaware, New Jersey, and New York constitutions contain this sort of provision. *American Charters,* above, 566, 2598, 2635. The absence of a similar provision from the other contemporary constitutions is acknowledgment that the power of sifting, continuing, or repealing the common law lay with the legislature. See also *id.* 680, 1713, 1742, 1780, 2613, 2649, 2655.

21. Bayard v. Singleton, 1 Martin (N.C.) 42, 47 (1787); Bowman v. Middleton, 1 Bay (S.C.) 282 (1792); Van Horne v. Dorrance, 2 Dallas (U.S.) 309 (1795); Cooper v. Telfair, 4 Dallas (U.S.) 14 (1800).

22. —— [sic] v. State, 2 Hayw. (N.C.) 29, 38.

"declarations of people thought proper to make of their rights, not against a power they supposed their own representatives might usurp, but against oppression and usurpation in general." Historically, he argued, the term "law of the land" had a double significance: first, it was a protest on the part of those who drafted Magna Carta against the attempt of King John to introduce the civil law into England, and secondly, it was a protest against royal action "by a pretended prerogative against or without the authority of law." In the North Carolina constitution therefore the *lex terrae* signified simply "a law for the people of North Carolina, made or adopted by themselves by the intervention of their own legislature." After some hesitation two of the three judges accepted the attorney general's point of view.

The result arrived at by the North Carolina Superior Court in 1794 was reached independently by the New Hampshire Supreme Court nearly a quarter of a century later in Mayo v. Wilson,[23] in which a statute authorizing selectmen and tything-men to arrest persons suspected of traveling unnecessarily on the Sabbath was challenged upon the ground that under the law of the land clause of the state constitution arrests could be made only by virtue of writs of duly constituted courts or warrants under the hand and seal of the magistrates. Said the court: "If this be the true construction of the constitution, the law in question is most clearly invalid, for it certainly purports to authorize an arrest without writ and without warrant from the magistrate." But is this the true construction? First, upon the basis of a review of Coke's and Sullivan's treatment of the same clause in Magna Carta, and secondly, upon the basis of an examination of the general principles upon which society is founded, the court comes to the opinion that "the fifteenth article in our Bill of Rights was not intended to abridge the power of the legislature, but to assert the right of every citizen to be secure from all arrests not warranted by the law," expressing "the will of the whole." It should be noted in passing that the entire objection to the New Hampshire statute was to the method of its enforcement and not at all to its substance.

By admitting the law of the land clause to limit the power of the legislature, when would it limit it? The context in which the clause is invariably found in the early state constitutions signifies that its reference is to procedure in the enforcement of penalties.[24] If therefore it limited the power of the legislature, it was when the legislature was delineating the process by which its measures, imposing penalties for their violation, were to be enforced. At this point the choice of the legislature would be restricted: it must select those methods of procedure which were known to "the law of the land." Such is the point of view of the South Carolina Supreme Court in the case of Zylstra v. Corporation of Charleston,[25] which was decided in 1794, the same year as the North

23. 1 N.H. 58.

24. See references in note 17, above. See also the opinion of Attorney General Rawlin of Barbadoes (1720?), Chalmer's *Opinions* 373–82 (1814).

25. 1 Bay (S.C.) 384.

Carolina case just reviewed. The plantiff Zylstra had been arrested for violating a city ordinance which forbade the keeping of a tallow-chandler's shop within the corporation limits and, being subsequently convicted by the court of wardens without the intervention of a jury, had been fined £100. Again, it should be observed that plaintiff's objections are leveled not at all against the body of the ordinance in question, that is, against the prohibition enacted against the further pursuit of his livelihood within the city limits, but solely against the manner in which that prohibition was enforced. Even so, the court was hesitant to pass upon the constitutional issue, half of the bench basing their decision in favor of plaintiff upon the terms of the municipal charter. Waties, J., was more audacious, and construing the law of the land clause to consecrate the procedure known to the common law, pronounced the jurisdiction of the court of wardens unconstitutional. This view turned out, however, to be too stringent for any practical use, wherefore it was ultimately so far modified as to sanction the procedure that has been in existence at the time of the adoption of the state constituton,[26]—an illogical doctrine surely, since on the one hand it admits the necessity of legal development, but on the other hand cuts it short at a point which, from the standpoint of such necessity, is a perfectly arbitrary one.

"Law of the land" and "due process of law," however, derive their great contemporary importance not from their character as restrictions upon the power of the legislature in the enactment of procedure merely, but from their character as restrictions upon the power of legislation in general.[27] Not everything that is passed in the form of law is "law of the land," say the courts, not only with reference to enactments which have nothing to do with the subject of procedure, but even with reference to enactments sanctioned by methods of enforcement admittedly unexceptionable, as, for example, the statute involved in the Lochner case. How has this come about? The essential fact is quite plain, namely, a feeling on the part of judges that to leave the legislature free to pass arbitrary or harsh laws, so long as all the formalities be observed in enforcing such laws, were to yield the subtance while contending for the shadow. But such a feeling is of course not in itself constitutional law: the question is, therefore, how did it become such? Before we can take up his question we have to dispose of some collateral matters.

The first great achievement of the courts in the interpretation of the written constitution was the establishment of judicial review; but that being done, the great problem toward the solution of which this same achievement is but the

26. See particularly State v. Simons, 2 Spears 761 (1836); the definition there given at 767 by O'Neill, J., anticipates Justice Curtis' definition in Murray v. Hoboken Land and Improvement Co., below.

27. Such use was originally suggested for the trial by jury and due compensation clauses; see Madison on paper money, November, 1786, 2 *Writings* 280 (Hunt ed. 1900–1910). Also see notes 81 and 106, below.

first contribution still remained, namely, the problem of the rightful limits of legislative power, particularly in dealing with property rights. During the Revolution and the years immediately following, the state legislatures had put through a number of reforms that had borne down upon various proprietary interests rather severely: the northern legislatures had adopted measures looking to the gradual abolition of slavery within their respective jurisdictions; the southern legislatures had abolished primogeniture; the reforming legislature of Virginia, after first disestablishing the Episcopal church in that state, had twice reorganized it and had concluded, in 1801, by appropriating certain of its lands to the state.[28] Meantime, other exigencies than reform had, in the course of the years 1785–87, produced still more drastic legislation—"rag money" measures in a majority of the states and laws impairing the obligation of private contracts in still more;[29] so that when the Constitutional Convention met in Philadelphia in May, 1787, Madison atttributed its convening less to the necessity of remedying the deficiencies of the Articles of Confederation for national purposes than to the necessity of providing some effective security for private rights against legislative attack.[30] Finally, in virtue of notions inherited from colonial days, which were further confirmed by the prevalent analogy between the state legislatures and the British Parliament, these bodies were prone, during the early years of our constitutional history, and some of them for years afterward, to all sorts of "special legislation" so called; this is, enactments setting aside judgments, suspending the general law for the benefit of individuals, interpreting the law for particular cases, and so on and so forth.[31] So long, of course, as there were Tories to attaint of treason this species of legislative activity had some excuse, but hardly was this necessity past than it came into great disrepute even with some of the best friends of democracy, by whom it was denounced not only as oppressive but as not properly within legislative power at all.[32]

But how was criticism upon legislative power converted into effective constitutional law? The answer is to be found in the doctrine of *vested rights*, which is the foundational doctrine of constitutional limitations in this country, and which in turn rests, not upon the written constitution, but upon the theory

28. For a general account of this legislation see Fiske, *Critical Period* 70–82 (1890). For a sketch of the Virginia Church Acts see Terrett v. Taylor, 9 Cranch (U.S.) 43, at 47–48 (1815).

29. See Fishke, *Critical Period* 168–86; A. C. McLaughlin, *Confederation and the Constitution* ch. 9 (1905); 1 McMaster, *History of the People of the United States* ch. 3 (1883–1927); Story, *Comm.* sec. 1371; Marshall in Sturges v. Crowninshield, 4 Wheat. (U.S.) 122 (1819).

30. See Madison's long speech of June 6 in the Convention, in his Notes; also his letter of October 24, 1787, to Jefferson, giving an account of the Convention; also *Federalist* 44 (Lodge ed.).

31. For examples note the following cases, cited below, Calder v. Bull, Cooper v. Telfair, Holden v. James, Merrill v. Sherburne, Dash v. Van Kleek, Van Horne v. Dorrance's Lessee, Satterlee v. Matthewson, Norman v. Heist, and others referred to in footnotes.

32. See *Federalist* 48, quoting from Jefferson's notes on Virginia.

of fundamental and inalienable rights. Setting out with the definition of a vested right as a right which a particular individual has equitably acquired under the standing law to do certain acts or to possess and use certain things, the doctrine of vested rights regards any legislative enactment infringing such a right, whether by direct intent or incidentally, without making compensation to the individual affected, as inflicting a penalty *ex post facto*.[33] Article I, section 10, of the federal Constitution prohibits the states from passing *ex post facto* laws, and there is good evidence for believing that some of those who were instrumental in framing this provision intended it to forbid practically all sorts of retrospective laws.[34] In Calder v. Bull,[35] however, partly upon the strength of Blackstone's authority and partly for reasons of expediency, the Supreme Court ruled that the prohibition in question extended not to civil cases but to penal cases only. But now it is exactly the purport of the doctrine of vested rights to obliterate this very distinction between civil and penal legislation; and what is more paradoxical still, the first difficult step to this end was taken in the leading opinion in Calder v. Bull, that of Chase, J., who set forth in a *dictum* that must be regarded as stating the leavening principle of American constitutional law, the notion that legislative power, quite independently of the written Constitution, is not absolute, but is constrained both by its own nature and by the principles of republican government, natural law, and the social compact. It is true that these views did not pass unchallenged, for Iredell, Chase's own associate, pronounced them those of a "speculative jurist," insisting that in a constitution which should contain no other provisions than those organizing the three branches of government, the legislative would be omnipotent. But, Iredell's disparaging tone to the contrary notwithstanding, Chase is to be regarded as foreshadowing the doctrine of Kent, Story, and, to some extent, that of Marshall, besides that of a host of lesser contemporaries,—in a word, the main trend of American constitutional decisions for a generation.

And indeed from the very moment, as Chase shortly afterwards testified without contradiction in Cooper v. Telfair,[36] state legislation began to be subjected generally to "new and more rigorous tests," which, a few years anterior, little of it that was of major importance could have survived. An

33. The definition of a "vested right" is essentially that given by Chase, J., in Calder v. Bull, modified by Parker, C. J., in Foster v. Essex Bank, 16 Mass. 235 (1819), that there is no such thing as a "vested right to do wrong." Special legislative exemptions for which consideration is lacking should also be excepted from the definition. See Beers v. Ark, 20 How. (U.S.) 527 and cases cited. Also certain remedial statutes, 1 Kent, *Comm.* 455. In general, see T. M. Cooley in 12 *Cent. L. Journ.* 2–4: Cooley admits that the validity of legislation in this class of cases [retrospective laws] depends upon the view the court may take of its justice, and thinks this an unsatisfactory state of the law. Cooley follows the early cases largely. On the general subject see W. G. Meyer, *Vested Rights* (St. L. 1891). See also H. C. Black in 25 *Am. L. Reg.* N.S. 681 *et. seq.*

34. See Madison's Notes, under the dates of August 22 and 28; Dickinson's speech on the subject, August 29; Mason's, on September 14. Also see *Federalist* No. 44.

35. 3 Dallas (U.S.) 386 (1798).

36. 4 Dallas (U.S.) 14 (1800).

excellent illustration is furnished by the conversion of the Court of Appeals of Virginia, which between the years 1797 and 1802 advanced the doctrine of vested rights from a mere interpretative principle of general statutes[37] to a positive limitation upon legislative power and passed from giving, in the earlier of these years, the most sweeping possible application to the law forbidding entails[38] to the very verge of overturning the law disposing of the church lands, which was saved by the merest accident.[39] Another interesting illustration of the same character is afforded by the argument of the Supreme Court of Massachusetts in the case of Wales v. Stetson,[40] which gives the doctrine of vested rights the same effect as Marshall later gave the obligation of contract clause in the Dartmouth College case. This was in 1806. Eight years later the same court decided in Holden v. James[41] that notwithstanding the fact that the twentieth article of the state constitution contemplates a power inhering in the legislature to suspend the laws, such suspensions must be general, it being "manifestly contrary to the first principles of civil liberty, natural justice, and the spirit of our constitution and laws, that any one citizen should enjoy privileges and advantages which are denied to all others under like circumstances." Five years later the New Hamphire Supreme Court laid down a similar doctrine upon the basis of the theory of the separation of powers, which had found clear and dogmatic expression in the New Hampshire Constitution of 1784.[42] Meanwhile, in 1811 the doctrine of vested rights was given its classic statement by Chancellor Kent in the famous case of Dash v. Van Kleek,[43] which was bottomed squarely upon Chase's *dictum* in Calder v. Bull.

But it is most important for our purposes to note the constrictive effect of the doctrine of vested rights, pariculary in the New York courts, upon the large acknowledged powers of eminent domain and police regulation, and, contrariwise, its expansive effect in the Supreme Court of the United States upon the prohibitions upon state power in the Constitution of the United States. The state had, it was always recognized, the power of eminent domain and also the power to regulate the use of property in the interest of the security, health, and comfort of its citizens,[44] that is to say, the police power, but to both these powers fundamental principles were now found to set very definite limits. Thus in Gardner v. Newburgh[45] Chancellor Kent ruled, upon the authority of

37. See Elliott v. Lyell, 3 Call (Va.) 268 (1802), following Lord Mansfield in Couch v. Jeffries, 4 Burr 2460 (1769).

38. Carter v. Tyler, 1 Call (Va.) 165 (1797).

39. Turpin v. Lacket, 6 Call (Va.) 113 (1802). The accident referred to was the death of Pendleton, J., the night before the day of the decision. Had he survived, the court would have stood 3 to 2 against the statute.

40. 2 Mass. 145. Cf. 1 Yeates (Pa.) 260 (1793).

41. II Mass. 396.

42. Merrill v. Sherburne, 1 N.H. 204 (1819). Bill of Rights, Art. 37. See also Arts. 23 and 29.

43. 7 Johns. (N.Y.) 498. See also 1 *Comm.* 455–56 and notes.

44. 2 *Comm.* 340.

45. 2 Johns. Ch. (N.Y.) 162 (1819).

Grotius, Puffendorf, and Bynkershoek,[46] and that of Blackstone, whom he quotes to the effect that in exercising the power of eminent domain the state is "an individual treating with an individual for an exchange,"[47] that compensation was due the owner of property taken by the state even in the absence of any constitutional provision to that effect; furthermore that similar compensation was due one whose property, though not taken, was damaged by the state, and finally, by way of *dictum,* that the power of eminent domain is exercisable for "public purposes *only.*"[48] The police power was similarly delimited. In the first place Kent was careful to point out that it did not extend to sumptuary legislation.[49] Again, by the followers of Kent, more zealous perhaps than their master, a distinction was drawn, upon the authority of Vattel, between regulation on the one hand, which was the true function of the police power, and on the other hand destruction, which lay without it.[50] True, the state could abate a nuisance, but only in those cases in which at the common law a private person, "taking the law into his own hands," could do so.[51] If it would go farther than this, the state could rely only upon its power of eminent domain and, by the doctrine of consequential damages, must render adequate compensation for any valuable use abolished by its action.

Lastly, the doctrine of vested rights was infused by the Supreme Court into the obligation of contracts clause of the federal Constitution. The channel through which the doctrine was conducted to this use was furnished by the circuit courts, which in cases falling to the jurisdiction of the national judiciary because of diversity of citizenship stand in the place of the state courts and so have, from the outset, felt free to pass upon the constitutionality of state laws under the state constitution and such "general principles" as they have found those constitutions to recognize.[52] This is the explanation of such decisions as that of Patterson, J., in Van Horne v. Dorrance,[53] of Story in Society v. Wheeler,[54] and of the Supreme Court itself, speaking through Story, in Terrett v. Taylor.[55] But the benefits of such decisions, after all, were not widespread. It

46. See Grotius, *De Jure Belli ac Pacis* bk. 8, ch. 14, sec. 7; Puffendorf, *De Jur. Nat. et. Gent.* bk. 8, ch. 5, sec. 7; Bynkershoek, *Quaest. Jr. Pub.* bk. 2, ch. 15.

47. 1 *Comm.* 138.

48. On this point see also 2 Kent, *Comm.* 339–40; also Varick v. Smith, 5 Paige (N.Y.) 146.

49. 2 *Comm.* 328–30. For an instructive passage, setting forth Kent's point of view, see *id.* 325–26. Here Kent demurs to Blackstone's doctrine that the descent and transfer of property "are political institutions and creatures of municipal law, and not natural rights." See also *id.* 1.

50. See particularly Attorney Griffin's argument in 7 Cowen (N.Y.) 592; the passage from Vattel in bk. I, ch. 20, sec. 246.

51. See also Justice Comstock's opinion in the Wynehamer case, reviewed below, and citations given. Cf. 2 Kent, *Comm.* 339–40.

52. See particularly Cushing, J., upon this point in Cooper v. Telfair; also Miller, J., in Loan Association v. Topeka, 20 Wall. (U.S.) 655 (1874), and Davidson v. New Orleans, 96 U.S. 97 (1877).

53. 2 Dallas (U.S.) 309 (1795).

54. 2 Gal. (U.S.C.Ct.) 103 (1814).

55. 9 Cranch (U.S.) 43 (1815).

was necessary, if the doctrine of vested rights was to do its full work, to enter the states themselves, and particularly was it necessary to extend the protection of the federal judiciary to legislative grants, whether of lands or charters, which, even in the states whose courts generally enforced the doctrine of vested rights, was sometimes left to the mercy of the legislatures; it being held, apparently, that what the legislature had given, the legislature could take away. In Fletcher v. Peck,[56] a case coming up from the circuit, Marshall achieves the deftest kind of blending of the doctrine of vested rights with the prohibition of the national Constitution of state laws as impairing the obligation of contracts. In the Dartmouth College case,[57] which came up on a writ of error from a state supreme court, the same doctrine is upheld. The step was an easy one, and it was furthermore assisted by Webster's argument, a large part of which comprised Jeremiah Mason's earlier argument before the state court, invoking the doctrine of vested rights.[58] A decade later, in 1829, Johnson, J., made an interesting confession of the motives that had guided the Court in this, the most important, class of its decisions, throughout the period that was then drawing to a close. He writes:

> This court has had more than once to toil up hill in order to bring within the restriction of the states to pass laws violating the obligation of contracts, the most obvious cases to which the Constitution was intended to extend its protection; a difficulty which it is obvious might often be avoided by giving to the phrase *ex post facto* its original and natural application.[59]

The suggestion of Johnson, J., fell upon stony ground; but today it would be easy to imagine that the Supreme Court, in the interpretation that it began giving the due process of law clause of the Fourteenth Amendment in 1890, had heard and heeded the warning of sixty years before.

But now for the purpose of this digression, which is twofold: first to indicate the point of view of the period during which the law of the land clause of the written constitution was first invoked as a protection of private rights against legislative power in general, and secondly, to point out that even where available, as, for example, it always was to the Massachusetts[60] and New York courts, it was not so invoked by the courts above mentioned, which instead contented themselves with drawing upon the principles of natural law and the social compact, at least so far as these principles render private property inviolate. But, of course, there

56. 6 Cranch (U.S.) 87 (1810); see Justice Johnson's opinion in this case.

57. 4 Wheat. (U.S.) 518 (1819).

58. For Mason's argument and collateral matter of great interest, see Shirley, "Dartmouth College Causes," in 2 *So. L. Rev* N.S. 22 *et seq.* and 246 *et seq.* Webster significantly enough desired to bring the case up through the Circuit Court.

59. Note appended to his concurring opinion in Satterlee v. Matthewson, 2 Pet. (U.S.) 380, 681 *et seq.* (1829).

60. Marcy v. Clark, 17 Mass. 330 (1821), furnishes a good example of a case in which the phrase "law of the land" might have been used in the derived sense but is, as a matter of fact, used only in the narrow sense of procedure. In the same connection see also Rice v. Parkman, 16 Mass. 326.

had to be the notable exception to this general rule, for without it the law of the land clause would have had as short and inglorious a history as the initially much more promising provision respecting *ex post facto* laws.

III

The exception was furnished by the supreme court of North Carolina. At first glance this circumstance appears remarkable in view of the attitude taken by that court in 1794, but upon a little investigation it is easily comprehended. In North Carolina, as in Pennsylvania, Rhode Island, and a number of the western states, at the time judicial review was coming into general practice the creed of popular sovereignty was already in high favor;[61] accordingly it soon came to be understood in these states that judicial review rested not upon the doctrine of natural rights, its original foundation, but exclusively upon the written constitution, which was represented as an enactment of the sovereign people. But while in Pennsylvania and Rhode Island the courts, in consequence of the unavailability of such standards, felt themselves obliged to uphold all enactments of the legislature not transgressing some specific provision of the written constitution,[62] the Supreme Court of North Carolina, possessed of a more enterprising spirit, set about to discover some clause of the written instrument of sufficiently indefinite content, to accomplish the task that in Massachusetts, New York, and New Hampshire had fallen to doctrine drawn from abroad.

The pioneer case in North Carolina was that of the University of North Carolina v. Foy,[63] in which the constitutional issue was furnished by an act of the legislature of North Carolina repealing an earlier grant of lands to the university. In part the court rendered its decision in favor of the university upon the ground that that institution was erected in accordance with a mandate from the constitution itself and therefore stood on "higher grounds than any other aggregate corporation," but in part it relied upon the law of the land clause of the state bill of rights, which it found binding upon the legislature exclusively and which it defined to mean that no one should be deprived of his liberties or property without the intervention of the court of justice acting with a jury. The court says:

> The property vested in the trustees must remain, therefore, for the uses intended for the university, until the judiciary of the country in the usual and common form

61. See 2 G. J. McRee, *Life and Correspondence of James Iredell* 145–49, 169–76 (1857–58). Iredell's own later change of heart is shown by his opinion in Calder v. Bull, above.

62. Under C. J. Tilghman's leadership the Pennsylvania Supreme Court enforced the doctrine of vested rights, but under Gibson, C. J., rejected it for the doctrine of a plenary legislature power, save so far as limited by specific prohibitions of the written Constitution. Cf. Bedford v. Shilling, 4 Serg. & R. (Pa.) 401 (1818), and Eakin v. Rauh {*sic;* Raub}, 12 Serg. & R. (Pa.) 330 (1825), with Watson v. Mercer, 1 Watts (Pa.) 330 (1833), and Menges v. Wertman, 1 Pa. St. 218 (1845), and note cases decided in the last case.

63. 2 Hayw. (N.C.) 310 (1804).

pronounce them guilty of such acts as will in law amount to a forfeiture of their rights or a dissolution of their body.

University of North Carolina v. Foy is susceptible of two interpretations, a narrow one and a broad one. On the one hand emphasis may be laid upon the special character of the enactment overthrown and the decision classified accordingly with those reviewed above, in which the judges were endeavoring to rid legislative power of its element of prerogative by emphasizing the general character of legislation. This is the interpretation which Webster makes of the case in his argument in the Dartmouth College litigation, where he defines "law of the land" to mean the "general law," and prohibitive therefore of "acts of attainder, bills of pains and penalties . . . legislative judgments, degrees and forfeitures."[64] A decade later Webster's language is in turn similarly interpreted by the Supreme Court of Tennessee, in the case of Van Zant v. Waddell,[65] in which the law of the land clause of the Tennessee constitution is defined to mean "a general public law equally binding upon every member of the community . . . under similar circumstances." In 1832 similar doctrine is voiced by the supreme court of South Carolina in the case of State v. Heyward,[66] where it supplements the doctrine of vested rights and the obligation of contracts clause of the federal Constitution; and in 1838 the performance of the South Carolina court is exactly repeated by the Supreme Court of Maryland in the case of Regents v. Williams.[67] Finally, in 1843, Gibson, C. J., of Pennsylvania, who had begun his judicial career a firm believer in legislative sovereignty,—going even to the length of denying the doctrine of judicial review,—and who had always shown himself hostile to the doctrine of vested rights, was driven in Norman v. Heist,[68] in order to avoid too outrageous consequences from a special act of the legislature, to avail himself, if only temporarily, of the law of the land clause of the Pennsylvania constitution, which he defined as signifying "undoubtedly a preexistent rule of conduct, declaratory of a penalty for a prohibited act, not an *ex post facto* rescript or decree made for the occasion."

The broad interpretation of University of North Carolina v. Foy is to be had by disregarding the special character of the act under review and attending only to its operation upon private rights; that is, by identifying the doctrine of that decision with the general doctrine of vested rights, and so translating the law of the land provision into a prohibition of all retrospective legislation. In the case

64. 4 Wheat. (U.S.) 575 *et seq.* See also *id.* 582, a question from Burke; Lache's {*sic;* Locke's?} *Second Treatise on Civil Government* par. 142.
65. 2 Yerg. (Tenn.) 260. See also *id.* 554; 10 Yerg. (Tenn.) 59.
66. 3 Rich. (S.C.) 389.
67. 9 Gill & J. (Md.) 362. The court cites University of North Carolina v. Foy. Cf. 7 Gill & J. (Md.) 191. In the latter case a special act of the legislature was overturned under the Sixth Article of the Bill of Rights, but no mention is made of "law of the land" clause of the Constitution.
68. 5 W. & S. (Pa.) 171.

of Hoke v. Henderson,[69] moreover, decided in 1833, the Supreme Court of North Carolina itself puts exactly this interpretation upon its precedent. In that case the act in question was a statute which, in providing for the future election of court clerks, operated in some cases to displace previous incumbents by appointment. In behalf of the statute it was urged, first, that it was general in terms, "wanting in the precision and direct operation usually belonging to and distinguishing judicial proceedings," and secondly, that it was—ostensibly at least—enacted from the standpoint of the legislative view of the public interest and without any intention of passing sentence upon those detrimentally affected by it, who in fact were not charged with any delinquency: that the measure therefore was not a bill of pains and penalties and that any discussion of procedure was impertinent to the issue. Ruffing, C. J., was not much moved by these objections, but brushing them aside, proceeded to define "law of the land" to require that, before anyone shall be deprived of property, he shall have a judicial trial "according to the mode and usages of the common law" "and a decision upon the matter of rights as determined by the law under which it [the property] vested." The final clause of this definition is the notable part of it; for if it be taken literally it means that, with reference to any particular property right, the existent law is elevated to the position of a constitutional limitation upon the body which enacted it and can never be altered to the diminution of that right. Nor does the court apparently shrink from this result; for it says, it is true that "the whole community may modify the rights which persons can have in things or at its pleasure abolish them altogether," but it hastens to add that the community speaks only through the constitution.

Some five years following Hoke v. Henderson occurred the Alabama case of *Ex parte* Dorsey,[70] which is notable for a number of reasons: First, because by the decision in it the doctrine of the Tennessee court in Van Zant v. Waddell is expanded, under color of warrant from the first article of the Alabama Bill of Rights, into a condemnation of legislation affecting detrimentally, not merely particular persons, but particular classes; secondly, because in the opinion of Ormond, J., the much more precise phrase "due course of law" is used as the equivalent of the phrase "law of the land"; and thirdly, because in the same opinion the term "property" in the due course of law provision takes on a greatly expanded meaning, connoting not merely, like the phrase "vested rights," tangible property or specific franchises or remedies, but the general rights of an individual as a member of the community. The act under review in *Ex parte* Dorsey provided among other things that an attorney at law should be required, as a prerequisite condition to his practicing in the courts of the state, to take an oath asserting not only that he would not in the future participate in a duel in any capacity, but that he had not done so in the past. This rather harsh

69. 2 Dev. (N.C.) 1.
70. 7 Porter (Ala.) 293.

provision was placed by its defenders upon one or more of three grounds: first, that attorneys were public functionaries and that therefore the legislature has, under the constitution, the express right to prescribe their qualifications; secondly, upon the ground that it was penal legislation such as the constitution explicitly required the legislature to enact for the suppression of duelling; thirdly, upon the ground that the legislature had enacted it by virtue of its general power to provide for the moral welfare of the community. The point of view of the majority of the court in overturning the provision in question is indicated by its use of the final clause of the bill of rights, containing the usual *caveat* that enumeration of certain rights should not be construed to disparage other rights not so enumerated, in such a way as virtually to convert the constitution of the state into a grant of powers. They therefore insist upon treating the act under review—having swept aside the contention that attorneys are public functionaries—as a bill of pains and penalties, aimed at a particular class in the community. The measure is held, therefore, to fall under the condemnation of the first article of the bill of rights and the constitutional guaranty of a trial by jury, and by Ormond, J., who is sure that the right to practice law is "as deserving of protection as property," or at least is an element of the inalienable right to pursue happiness, under that of the "due course of law" clause. Collier, J., dissented, upon the ground that the state constitution is not a grant of powers but an organization of inherent powers, which accordingly are available to the legislature unless specifically withheld. The "due course of law" clause has therefore no independent force as a limitation upon the power of the legislature. It means such "forms of arrest, trial, and punishment" as are "guaranteed by the Constitution, or provided by the common law, or else such as the legislature, in obedience to constitutional authority, have enacted to insure public peace or elevate public morals." Two years later we find Ormond, J., essentially disavowing his doctrine in this case and adopting that of his dissenting associate.

IV

It was not destined, therefore, that the doctrine of due process of law should enter the general constitutional jurisprudence of the United States through the Supreme Court of Alabama. Some court more zealous for private rights must be the one to receive the torch from the North Carolina court, and indeed one more generally conspicuous in the world of citation and precedent than either of the southern courts. At the same time, the final fate of *Ex parte* Dorsey teaches us the character of the exigency that would force such a tribunal as the one described to take up with the doctrine of due process of law, namely, the advance of Iredell's doctrine of the plenary power of the legislature within the written constitution and the consequent gradual retirement into disuse of constitutional limitations based upon extra-constitutional grounds.

The accession of Taney to the chief justiceship of the Supreme Court marks an epoch in the history of American constitutional law, though perhaps somewhat less distinctly than is often supposed.[71] Marshall's guiding notion with respect to the national Constitution was, that it was intended to provide a realm of national rights subject to national control, a point of view from which state legislation limiting individual action became impertinence. Had the political branches of the national government been of Marshall's way of thinking all along, and willing, therefore, to assert the necessary degree of national control, perhaps this theory would have worked out very well even at that period. With the election of Jackson, however, the doctrine of states' rights and strict construction laid a paralyzing hand upon the sources of national power. On the other hand, at the very same moment, what with the revival of revolution abroad and the rise of transcendentalism at home, and last, but not least, the phenomenal success of the Erie Canal, the demand went forth for a large governmental program: for the public construction of canals and railroads, for free schools, for laws regulating the professions, for anti-liquor legislation, for universal suffrage and for the abolition of slavery. I say "governmental program," but what government? Necessarily the state governments, which must, therefore, be furnished with the adequate constitutional theory to carry it forward. It is true that the panic of 1837 struck off the first item of this program, but, save in a way presently indicated, it does not seem to have affected permanently the development of constitutional theory. Taney became chief justice in 1836, bringing with him to the Supreme Bench the fixed intention of clothing the states, so far as a faithful adherence to precedent would allow, with the sovereign and complete right to enact useful legislation for their respective populations. In his great Charles River Bridge[72] decision, accordingly, Taney laid down the maxim that in a public grant nothing passes by implication, a doctrine which, as Story showed conclusively in his dissent, would have made the decision in the Dartmouth College case originally impossible, and which did in point of fact, in the decades following, pave the way for the great but necessary curtailment of the efficacy of that decision.[73] Again, in the License Cases,[74] Taney reveals his point of view by refusing to extend to the field of interstate commerce the principle of Marshall's decision in Brown v. Maryland[75] with reference to Congress' power over foreign commerce, namely, that the power is exclusive, and this Taney did in the very

---

71. See Marshall in Wilson v. Blackbird Creek Marsh Co., 2 Pet. (U.S.) 245 (1829); and in Providence Bank v. Billings, 4 Pet. (U.S.) 514, 563 (1830).

72. 11 Pet. (U.S.) 420 (1837).

73. See particularly West River Bridge Co. v. Dix, 6 How. (U.S.) 507 (1848); Beer Co. v. Massachusetts 97 U.S. 25 (1878); Fertilizing Co. v. Hyde Park, *id.* 659; Stone v. Mississippi, 101 U.S. 814 (1880), and Butchers Union C. v. Crescent City Co., 111 U.S. 746 (1884); also see Murray v. Charleston, 96 U.S. 432 (1878).

74. 5 How. (U.S.) 504 (1846).

75. 12 Wheat. (U.S.) 419 (1827).

face of Marshall's dictum to the contrary. Finally, in this and in other opinions and decisions Taney diluted Marshall's doctrine of the paramountcy of national power within the sphere of its competence with the doctrine of the reserved sovereignty of the states, whereby he meant not merely that the states have left to them certain powers in consequence of their not being granted to the national government, which is all that the Tenth Amendment says, but that the states had an area of power which was positively reserved to them and which therefore no legitimate exercise of federal power could ever invade.[76]

But what was happening on the Supreme Bench was the index of what was happening also in the state judiciaries, where popular sovereignty and states' rights united to force a recognition of the plenitude of legislative power. One illustration of this I have already referred to, the disavowal by Ormond, J., of the Alabama Supreme Court in 1841 of his own line of reasoning of three years earlier. The case referred to was that of Mobile v. Yuille,[77] in which the question was the power of the legislature to authorize a municipality to regulate the weight and price of bread. The attorney for defendant in error was the reporter of *Ex parte* Dorsey, who, upon the basis particularly of Justice Ormond's opinion in that case, now "strenuously contended" "that no such power exists because [as he contends] it would interfere with the right of a citizen to purse his lawful trade or calling in the mode his judgment might dictate," and also because such by-laws, being in restraint of trade, are void under the common law. But, rejoined Ormond, J., sweeping aside defendant's interpretation of *Ex parte* Dorsey, "in this case the power is expressly given by the statute to do the act complained of," wherefore what the common law ordains is not in point. For the rest,

> the legislature having full power to pass laws as is [*sic*] deemed necessary for the public good, their acts cannot be impeached on the ground that they are unwise or not in accordance with just and enlightened view of political economy, as understood at the present day . . . arguments against their policy must be addressed to the legislative departments of government.

Mobile v. Yuille, however, is a comparatively late case, and more than a decade earlier, some years even before Taney had become chief justice, a similar doctrine was struggling for recognition in the New York courts, whose dilemma, comprising as it did the tradition of judicial review created by Kent on the one hand, and the victorious principles of Jacksonian Democracy on the other, if it was rather painful, was also of the greatest possible importance in connection with the history of due process of law.[78] For the problem before the New York courts, from 1830 on, was precisely the problem that had confronted

76. See particularly the chief justice's opinions in Groves v. Slaughter, 15 Pet. (U.S.) 449 (1841), and Pollard v. Hagan's Lessee, 3 How. (U.S.) 212 (1845).

77. 3 Ala. 137 (1841). See also State v. Maxey, 1 McMul. (S.C.) 501 (1837).

78. For an excellent illustration of the difficulty created by the dilemma referred to, read Justice Nelson's opinion in People v. Morris, 13 Wend. (N.Y.) 329 (1835).

the North Carolina court a quarter-century earlier, namely, the problem of reconciling an adequate supervision over legislative power with due deference to the principle of legislative sovereignty within the written constitution. Naturally the North Carolina solution of this difficult problem seemed much to the point.

More specifically, the situation that confronted the New York courts was this: the power of eminent domain is rather the most invidious branch of governmental authority, even when exercised by the state directly. Within a very few years, however, hundreds and hundreds of private corporations organized for the business of transportation had been endowed by the state with this power. Kent's doctrine of consequential damages and the resultant blending, at their outer edges, of the police power and that of eminent domain, had already gone by the board in 1827 in the cases of Vanderbilt v. Adams[79] and Stuyvesant v. New York.[80] Kent's other doctrine, that the power of eminent domain is exercisable for a public purpose only, that is to say, for what the courts may regard as a public purpose, was also in grave danger of extinction, being first rested, by Chancellor Walworth, upon the untenable basis of the obligation of contracts clause of the federal Constitution[81] and then transferred again to its original position upon the doctrine of "natural rights" and the "spirit of the constitution."[82] But the doctrine of natural rights no longer sufficed either. What, then, was to be done? In Taylor v. Porter[83] an act authorizing a private road under the eminent domain power was under review. The act was overturned; and Bronson, J., speaking for the majority of the court, annexed the doctine of natural rights and of limitations inherent to legislative power to the written constitution by casting around that doctrine the phrase "law of the land" and the phrase "due process of law," which had also since 1821 been a part of the New York constitution.

Justice Bronson's line of argument is most instructive. Setting out with the proposition that the people alone are absolutely sovereign, he follows it up with the assertion that the legislature can exercise only such powers as have been delegated it, which is evidently either a restatement of the doctrine of limita-

---

79. 7 Cowen (N.Y.) 349.

80. *Id.* 585. For the derivation of the doctrine of these cases from the common law, see 12 Mass. 220 (1815) and 1 Pick. (Mass.) 417 (1823), decisions which Kent pronounces "erroneous." 2 *Comm.* 339, note c. See also in condemnation of the same doctrine, Story, J., in his dissent in the Charles River Bridge Case, 11 Pet. (U.S.) 638, 641 (1837). See also Baker v. Boston, 12 Pick (Mass.) 184 (1831), in which the doctrine of 7 Cow. (N.Y.) 349 and 585 is applied.

81. Beekman v. Saratoga, etc. R.R., 3 Paige (N.Y.) 45 (1831).

82. Albany Street Matter, 11 Wend. (N.Y.) 149 (1834); Bloodgood v. Mohawk, etc. R.R., 18 Wend. (N.Y.) 1 (1837).

83. 4 Hill (N.Y.) 140; preceded in 1839 by the Matter of John and Cherry Sts., 19 Wend. (N.Y.) 676. Besides the fact that the line of argument is more clearly cut in Taylor v. Porter, citation also makes it the more important case by far. Cf. Harvey v. Thomas, 10 Watts (Pa.) 63, and the Pacopson Rd. Case, 16 Pa. St. 15 (1851). For Kent's view of Hoke v. Henderson, quoted immediately below, see 2 *Comm.* 13, note b (ed. of 1840).

tions inherent to legislative power or an assertion that a state constitution, like the federal Constitution, is a grant of powers. Quotations from Story's opinion in Wilkinson v. Leland[84] make it evident that it is the former, as does also the invocation of the social compact at this point. But it is a phrase of the written constitution that Bronson, J., is in particular search of. Fortunately the decision in Hoke v. Henderson is at hand, recommended by Kent in a recent edition of his *Commentaries* as "replete with sound constitutional doctrines." On the strength of Hoke v. Henderson, accordingly, "law of the land" is asserted to mean that before a man can be deprived of his property "it must be ascertained judicially that he has forfeited his privileges, or that someone else has a superior title to the property he possesses." But it there is doubt as to the meaning of the phrase "law of the land," at least there can be none as to that of "due process of law" of the same article of the Constitution; for this means nothing "less than a proceeding or suit instituted and conducted according to prescribed forms and solemnities for ascertaining guilt or determining the title to property." One exception to this definition is indeed furnished by the case of an exercise of the power of eminent domain, when due process of law means due compensation. The eminent domain power, however, can be exercised only for a public purpose. But who is to ascertain whether a given purpose is a public one or not? Justice Bronson's evident assumption—and it is only assumption—is that it is the courts, as preliminary to their task of determining whether due process of law has been observed. Nelson, J., dissented; at the same time, however, he accepted the general principle of the decision, but confessed that he was uncertain as to what grounds it rested upon.

Taylor v. Porter, on account of the special character of the enactment there reviewed, is to be classified with University of North Carolina v. Foy. It was followed in 1849 by White v. White,[85] in which a general statute was pronounced void and which therefore stands very closely coincident with Hoke v. Henderson. The statute in question removed the disability of married women under the common law in the control of their property. As an exercise of legislative power it was closely analogous to the statutes enacted early in our national history abolishing the right of primogeniture, statutes which, as we have seen, received enforcement even against rights of succession vested at the time of their passage. But the *virus* of natural law had spread since those days. In the first case, Holmes v. Holmes,[86] in which the Married Women's Act is challenged successfully, the decision was put upon the obligation of contract clause of the federal Constitution. But Mason, J., who decided White v. White, was very justifiably skeptical of the reasoning by which this result was attained. He accordingly decided to avail himself of the due process of law clause and the doctrine of natural rights, citing the Albany Street case, Wilkinson v.

84. 2 Pet. (U.S.) 657 (1829).
85. 5 Barb. (N.Y.) 474.
86. 4 Barb. (N.Y.) 295.

Leland, and Taylor v. Porter indifferently. Eventually this decision also was superseded by decisions upholding the Married Women's Act but confining its operation to property acquired subsequently to the passage of the act. The cases in question were those of Perkins v. Cottrell[87] and Westervelt v. Gregg,[88] in the former of which the decision was based upon the doctrine of vested rights, the obligation of contracts clause of the federal Constitution, and the "spirit of the constitution which declares" that no person shall be deprived of life, liberty or property without due process of law; and in the latter, explicitly upon the due process of law clause: "Such an act as the legislature may, in the uncontrolled exercise of its power, see fit to pass, is in no sense," said the court, "the due process of law designated by the constitution." Similar acts were similarly construed in other states, but generally upon the ground that their prospective operation had been plainly intended by the legislature itself.[89]

V

And thus by adopting the North Carolina doctrine of "law of the land" *pro tanto,* the New York courts, in 1843, rescued from disuse the doctrine of public purpose in connection with the power of eminent domain, and ten years later succeeded in drawing the teeth of the Married Women's Property Act. The real tussle with the reforming tendencies of the period was, however, yet to come. During the decade 1846 to 1856 no fewer than sixteen states passed anti-liquor laws of a more or less drastic character. Never since the doctrine of vested rights had been formulated had such reprehensible legislation, from the standpoint of that doctrine, been enrolled upon the statute books. How was it to be withstood? Some of the earlier of these laws took the form of local option measures, and to meet these a new dogma of constitutional law, drawn originally from John Locke's *Second Treatise on Civil Government,* was invented, namely, the doctrine that the legislature cannot delegate its power,— an utterly absurd doctrine, at least in this application of it, and one which was in singular contradiction both with legislative practice anterior to 1846, and with judicial decision.[90] Furthermore, as was immediately shown, it was

87. 15 Barb. (N.Y.) 446 (1851).

88. 12 N.Y. 209 (1854). See also the case of Powers v. Bergen, 6 N.Y. 358, in which use is made of the law of the land clause of the Constitution to overturn a special act of legislation.

89. Cf. 24 Ala. 386 (1854); 43 Ill. 52 (1857); 28 N.J.L. 219 (1860); 20 Oh. St. 128; with 34 Me. 148 (1852), and 8 Fla. 107 (1858); in the latter two cases the doctrine of vested rights plays its part.

90. The courts to whose fertility of mind is due this doctrine were those of Delaware and Pennsylvania. See Rice v. Foster, 4 Harr. (Del.) 479 (1847), and Parker v. Commonwealth, 6 Pa. St. 507 (1847). The doctrine is refuted in People v. Reynolds, 10 Gilman (Ill.) (1848), and in Bull *et al.* v. Read, 13 Gratt. (Va.) 78 (1855). Also in Johnson v. Rich, 9 Barb. (N.Y.) 680 (1848), with which, however, cf. Barto v. Himrod, 8 N.Y. 483. For the contradictory position of the Delaware and Pennsylvania courts cf. Rice v. Foster with 3 Harr. (Del.) 335 and 4 Harr. (Del.) 82; and Parker v. Commonwealth with 8 Barr (Pa.) 391 and 10 Barr (Pa.) 214. The Pennsylvania court

generally an utterly futile doctrine; for the easy retort of the reforming legislatures was statewide prohibition.

Such a law was enacted by the New York legislature in 1855. It forbade all owners of intoxicating liquors to sell them under any conditions save for medicinal purposes, forbade them further to store such liquors when not designed for sale in any place but a dwelling house, made the violation of these prohibitions a misdemeanor, and denounced the offending liquors as nuisances and ordained their destruction by summary process. In the great case of Wynehamer v. State of New York,[91] which comprises a new starting point in the history of due process of law, this act was overturned, the essential ground of the decision being that the harsh operation of the statute upon liquors in existence at the time of its going into effect comprised an act of destruction not within the power of government to perform, *"even by the forms which belong to due process of law."*[92] The significance of this statement of the matter is this: in every previous case of due process of law the court had had its opportunity in treating a civil enactment as, in certain applications, a bill of pains and penalties. In Wynehamer v. State of New York, however, the court was confronted with a frankly penal statute which provided a procedure, for the most part unexceptionable, for its enforcement. That statute was nonetheless overturned under the due process of law clause, which was thereby plainly made to prohibit, regardless of the matter of procedure, a certain kind and degree of exertion of legislative power altogether. The result is obvious, even if somewhat startling, and it serves to bring into strong light once more the dependence of the derived notion of due process of law upon extra-constitutional principles; for it is nothing less than the elimination of the very phrase under construction from the constitutional clause in which it occurs. The main proposition of the decision in the Wynehamer case is that the legislature cannot destroy by any method whatever what by previous law was property. But why not? To all intents and purposes the answer of the court is simply that "no person shall be deprived of life, liberty or property."

But how can the elimination of the phrase "due process of law" from the constitutional clause be regarded as furnishing a new starting point in the history of the development of that clause? The answer is that from now on the

---

subsequently abandoned the dogma, in connection with local option legislation, in Locke's Appeal, 72 Pa. St. 491. For a very early Pennsylvania case in which the doctrine was offered to the court but ignored, see 2 Yeates (Pa.) 493 (1799); a later Massachusetts case in which the same idea was brought forward but specifically repelled by the court is that of Wales v. Belcher, 3 Pick. (Mass.) 508 (1827). The immediate responsibility for this absurdity must fall to Gibson, C. J., in which connection see 5 W. & S. (Pa.) 281 (1843). The passage from Locke's work is par. 141. On the history of the referendum, see E. P. Oberholtzer, *Referendum in America* (1893).

91. 13 N.Y. 378 (1856).

92. A. S. Johnson, J., 420: "The legislature cannot make the mere existence of the rights secured the occasion of depriving a person of them even by the forms which belong to 'due process of law.'"

attention of the courts is drawn to the other words of the clause; more particularly to the words "liberty" and "property" and the word "deprive." Indeed the attention is seen to shift to these terms on this very occasion, in the case of the dissenting opinion of T. A. Johnson, J., who bases his argument against the decision partly upon his construction of the word "deprived" and partly upon a *reductio ad absurdum* involving the term "liberty." The word "deprive," he contends, is used in the constitutional clause,

> in its ordinary and popular sense, and relates simply to divesting of, forfeiting, alienating, taking away property. It applies to property in the same sense that it does to life and liberty and no other. . . . When a person is deprived of his property by due process of law the thing itself . . . with the legal title is taken away. . . . The act itself does indeed . . . directly provide for depriving the owner of his property by forfeiture and destruction, but that is where it is kept for an unlawful purpose and after trial and judgment. That provision has no bearing upon the question under consideration. When property is taken from the owner and destroyed, he is deprived of it by virtue of the act, not before. It might be urged with precisely the same pertinency and force, that a statute which prohibits certain vicious actions and declares them criminal deprives persons of their liberty and is therefore in derogation of the constitution.

Undoubtedly Johnson, J., reveals a grave danger attending the decision he is criticizing. For the moment the danger was not practically serious on account of the conservative view taken by the court of "property," which is defined by implication as the valuable use of the thing possessed. But let "property" come to mean—as indeed it does in this very case with one or two of the judges—any particular item of such right, for example, the right of sale; let "liberty" be made to signify the rights which one enjoys in the community under the standing law, and the decision in this case, together with the distinction between regulation and destruction upon which it is based, becomes immediately untenable and a new solution of the eternal issue between legislative sovereignty and private rights at once imperative. But what line is this solution to take? Must outright choice be made between, on the one hand, allowing the legislature to destroy or even to regulate at discretion or, on the other hand, absolutely tying the hands of the legislature as in Hoke v. Henderson? Or is there a midway course? By construing the word "deprive," Johnson, J., pointed the way, though no doubt unintentionally, to such a midway course and so provided an escape from the difficulty which it was his purpose merely to expose.

But at another point also is the Wynehamer decision a starting point. As we have just seen, the decision rests upon an alleged distinction between regulation and destruction: but are regulation and destruction two such different things, or is the latter often merely consequential upon the former? Common sense inclines to the latter view. Yet admit this view and what becomes of Marshall's famous maxim, that "questions of power do not depend upon the degree to which it is exercised?" In this connection a remark of Comstock, J., becomes of greatest significance in view of modern developments. "We," he contends, "must be allowed to know what is known by all persons of common intelligence, that intoxicating liquors are produced for sale and consumption as a beverage." Here is the first assertion of that doctrine of "judicial cognizance" which lies at the very basis of the modern flexible idea of "due process of law."[93] Questions of power do today emphatically depend upon the degree to which it is exercised, and this because the courts are able to take cognizance of facts which make different degress of power harmonious with the "due process of law" requirement in different cases.

The last feature of the Wynehamer decision that I desire to call attention to is the fact that by it the New York Court of Appeals finally dismisses the doctrine of natural rights from the firing line as a defender of property. The ungracious task falls to Comstock, J., whose opinion heads the others, and he performs it with great considerateness. He says:

> It has been urged upon us that the power of the legislature is restricted not only by the express provisions of the written constitution but by limitations implied from the nature and form of our government; that aside from all special restrictions the right to enact such laws is not among the delegated powers of the legislature, and that the act in question is void as against the fundamental principles of liberty and against common reason and natural rights.

Moreover, he admits that "high authority has been cited" for these views, and himself quotes at length from Justice Chase's opinion in Calder v. Bull, which quotation he follows up with citations of Fletcher v. Peck, Dash v. Van Kleek, and Taylor v. Porter. He then proceeds to furnish us with his own point of view in the following words:

> I entertain no doubt that, aside from the special limitations of the constitution, the legislature cannot exercise powers which are in their nature essentially judicial or executive. These are by the constitution distributed to the other departments of the government. It is only 'legislative power' which is vested in the Senate and Assembly. But where the constitution is silent and there is no clear usurpation of the powers distributed to the other departments, I think there would be great difficulty and great danger in attempting to define the limits of this power. Chief Justice Marshall said [Fletcher v. Peck]: 'how far the power of giving the law may involve every other power in cases where the constitution is silent never has been and perhaps never can be definitely stated.' That very eminent judge felt the difficulty; but the danger was less apparent then than it is now when theories, alleged to be founded in natural reason and inalienable rights, but subversive of the just and necessary powers of government attract the belief of considerable classes of men, and when too much reverence for government and law is certainly among the least of the perils to which our institutions are exposed. I am reluctant to enter upon this field of inquiry, satisfied as I am that no rule can be laid down in terms which may not contain the germs of great mischief to society, by giving to private opinion and speculation a license to oppose themselves to the just and

93. See the Lochner case, above; also In re Jacobs, 98 N.Y. 98 (1885). Cf. Powell v. Pennsylvania, 127 U.S. 678 (1887).

legitimate powers of government. Nor is it necessary to push our inquiries in the direction indicated. There is no process of reasoning by which it can be demonstrated that the 'act for the prevention of intemperance, pauperism and crime,' is void upon principles and theories outside the constitution, which will not also and by an easier deduction, bring it in direct conflict with the constitution itself.

This surely is a remarkable passage betwixt the Scylla and Charybdis of tweedle-dee and tweedle-dum. What it all comes to is this: Comstock, J., dismayed by the abolitionists' quoting the same scripture to their purpose, refuses to annex the doctrine of natural rights to the written constitution, save only as a protection of property rights, that is to say, of vested rights; and generally speaking, this is always the significance of the doctrine of due process of law.

VI

But now let us inquire how the doctrine of the Wynehamer decision accorded with the general constitutional law of the period. Within a year or two either side of the New York case similar cases involving similar questions arose in an even dozen states, and in all these states, save one, laws very closely analogous to the New York statute, or indeed sometimes more drastic in their provisions than that statute, were sustained. With reference to these cases two facts of foremost importance immediately present themselves. The first is that in only one case, and that occurring subsequently to the New York decision, is any argument against the body of the statutes under review based upon the due process of law, or law of the land clauses of the constitution involved. The second is that the decisions, save in two or three instances, are based upon views of the police power which leave the definition of that power essentially to legislative discretion. Both these facts demand illustration from the cases themselves.

In State v. Noyes,[94] a New Hampshire case, a municipal ordinance pronouncing bowling alleys a nuisance and discontinuing those in existence was under review. The constitutional question raised is precisely the same as that raised by the provision of the New York statute which pronounced existing stocks of liquors nuisances. The attorney for Noyes urged that the question of what is a nuisance is a question of law and therefore for the courts. But, said the court, we have the law before us.

> The legislature do not exceed their legitimate authority when they make a change of laws and constitute that an offense which was not such before. . . . There may be an apparent unfitness sometimes in such legislation, but its validity has never been questioned.

94. 10 Foster (N.H.) 279 (1855). See also *id.* 286, also 289.

In all the other cases the statutes involved were anti-liquor enactments, the arguments against which were based either—though but timidly on account of the attitude of the United States Supreme Court—on the commerce clause of the federal Constitution or on the doctrine of natural rights. The latter argument was used in Beebe v. State,[95] an Indiana case, and the statute was overturned, Perkins, J., holding in a remarkable opinion that the right to manufacture, the right to sell, and the right to drink, spirituous liquors were inalienable rights. This decision, however, accompanied as it was by a well-argued dissent, marked the exception to the rule. In Lincoln v. Smith,[96] a Vermont case, a similar line of argument was taken by attorneys but was decisively rejected by the court. "Every member of society," runs the first article of the Vermont Bill of Rights, "hath a right to be protected in the enjoyment of life, liberty and property." But said the court in comment, "We do not well see how it can be claimed that the act in question is a violation" of this article, "unless it be assumed that the law is invalid, which is the very thing in question." Natural rights, the court continues, are subject to the civil law, and quotes Blackstone to the effect that certain rights are "absolute and inherent" and "without any control or limitation save only by the laws of the land." But the statute under review is law of the land unless invalid. The court proceeds to point out,

> The right to life, liberty, and property are all placed in the same connection; and certainly the two former are as sacred as the latter; although they have not seemed at all times to have called out the same legal acumen in their behalf as the latter.

Of similar purport is the decision of the Supreme Court of Illinois in Goddard v. Jacksonville.[97] Natural rights are surrendered or modified upon entering into the social compact. This surrender and modification, such as are indispensable to good government and the well-being of society, are comprehended under the police power of the government. "The framers of Magna Carta and the constitutions of the United States and of the states never intended to modify, abridge, or destroy the police powers of government. They only prohibited its exercise by *ex post facto* laws and regulated the mode of trial for offenses." Finally, the court argues, the police power must be recognized as a developing power, a power which unfolds with the increasing complexity of society and the advance of social needs. These decisions belong to the years 1854 and 1855. That of State v. Gallagher,[98] however, in which the Michigan Supreme Court defines legislative power even more broadly if possible, was rendered in 1856 and some weeks after the Wynehamer decision. The attorneys for Gallagher based their argument both upon the doctrine of natural rights and the derived doctrine, that the legislature has only "legislative power," of which it is

95. 6 Ind. 501 (1855).
96. 27 Vt. 328 (1854).
97. 15 Ill. 589 (1854).
98. 4 Gibbs (Mich.) 244 (1856). See also 3 Gibbs (Mich.) 330 (1854).

therefore for the court to prescribe the limits. The court rejects both arguments. The opinion runs:

> The whole sovereignty of the people is conferred upon the different departments of government; what the judiciary and executive have not would seem from necessity to have been granted to the other; and that other must possess all the powers of a sovereign state except such as are withheld by the state constitution and such as are conceded to the general government. In that grant there are many powers that are not strictly legislative and which are essential to administrative government. If this department is limited as a law-making power, what is the limitation upon the exercise of those powers strictly administrative? . . . It must be conceded there is none.

But let us consider more particularly the attitude revealed by the courts in these decisions toward due process of law. A good illustrative case anterior to the Wynehamer decision is the Massachusetts case of Fisher v. McGirr.[99] Said Shaw, C. J., in his decision:

> We have no doubt that it is competent for the legislature to declare the possession of certain articles of property, either absolutely or when held in particular places and under particular circumstances, to be unlawful because they would be injurious, dangerous, and noxious; and by due process of law, by proceedings *in rem,* to provide both for the abatement of the nuisance and the punishment of the offender, by the seizure and confiscation of the property, by the removal, sale, or destruction of the noxious article.

Still more in point, however, is the language of the opinions in State v. Paul[100] and State v. Keeran,[101] which the Rhode Island Supreme Court decided with the Wynehamer decision before it and indeed with particular animadversion to that decision. With reference to attorney's argument based upon the derived view of the law of the land clause, the court said:

> It is obvious that the objection confounds the power of the assembly to create and define an offense with the rights of the accused to trial by jury and due process of law . . . before he can be convicted of it.

Later the court enters protest against—

> the loose habit of taking constitutional clauses, which from their history and obvious purpose have a well defined meaning, away from all their natural connections, and by drawing remote inferences from them, of pressing them into the service of any constitutional objection which the ingenuity or fancy of the objector may contrive or suggest,—

a practice which has gone far, it thinks, to bring constitutional questions into "jest and ridicule." But surely, it continues,

> if any clause in the constitution has a definite meaning which should exclude all vagaries which render courts the tyrants of the constitution, this clause [law of the land] . . . can claim to have [it] both from its history and long received interpretation.

99. 1 Gray (Mass.) 1 (1854).
100. 5 R.I. 185 (1858).
101. *Id.* 497. See also 3 R.I. 64 (1854); also *id.* 289.

It is urged that it limits the legislature in regulating the vendability of property.

> Pushed to its necessary conclusions the argument goes to the extent, that once
> make out that anything real or personal is property, as everything in a general
> sense is, and legislation as to its use and vendability . . . must stop at the precise
> point at which it stood when the thing first came within the protection of this
> clause of the constitution.

A better reasoned or more conclusive refutation of the derived doctrine of due
process of law, both from the standpoint of logic and history, could not well be
asked for.

Thus the Wynehamer decision found no place in the constitutional law that
was generally recognized throughout the United States in the year 1856.
Neither had it been foreshadowed by decisions in similar cases in other states,
nor was it subsequently accepted in such cases. Also it met locally an immense
amount of hostile criticism, both lay and professional. Altogether it must be
considered an adversity, for the time being, to the derived doctrine of due
process of law. All that was needed apparently to dispose of that doctrine at
once and for all time was another such Pyrrhic victory: nor was such event long
impending.

Just as the Court of Appeals of New York had persuaded itself that it must
intervene to save the proprietors of spirituous liquors from the too harsh hand
of legislative wrath, so also the Supreme Court of the United States had
convinced itself that "the peace and harmony of the country" was to be
preserved only by its "settling by judicial decision" the question of slavery in
the territories adversely to the power of the national legislature. It came about,
therefore, that exactly a twelvemonth after the Wynehamer decision, Taney, C.
J., read his famous opinion in Scott v. Sanford,[102] pronouncing the Missouri
Compromise to have been void under the due process of law clause of the Fifth
Amendment of the United States Constitution. His language is as follows:

> An act of Congress which deprives a citizen of the United States of his liberty or
> property merely because he came himself or brought his property into a particular
> territory of the United States and who had committed no offense against the laws
> could hardly be dignified with the name of due process of law.

The extraordinary character of this pronouncement is shown by two circumstances: first, the fact that counsel at the bar did not allude in the remotest way
to any such restriction upon congressional power; and secondly, by the fact that
at this point the chief justice carries with him only two of his associates, Grier
and Wayne, both of whom present but short opinions accepting perfunctorily
the chief justice's line of argument. Daniel, Campbell, and Catron, JJ., also
held the Missouri Compromise to have been unconstitutional but upon far
different grounds, Catron availing himself of the doctrine of the equality of the
states, and Campbell and Daniel—and particularly the former—of Calhoun's

102. 19 How. (U.S.) 393 (1857).

doctrine of state sovereignty and the correlative doctrine that Congress is but the agent of the states in the exercise of its delegated powers. Furthermore, at no other point is Justice Curtis' dissent more convincing than in his refutation of this use of the term "due process of law." Already two years earlier Curtis, J., speaking for the Court in Murray v. Hoboken Land and Improvement Co.,[103] had ruled that legal process is not necessarily due process, and that the due process required by the Fifth Amendment means the processes of the common and statute law as these stood at the time of the adoption of the Constitution, that Congress in providing procedure for the enforcement of its acts must provide the procedure that is due. But no question of procedure was at issue in connection with the Missouri Compromise. How then could the Fifth Amendment be invoked? If the Missouri Compromise did indeed comprise one of a class of legislative enactments proscribed by the Fifth Amendment, what then, inquired Curtis, J., was to be said of the Ordinance of 1787, which Virginia and other states had ratified notwithstanding the presence of similar clauses within their constitutions? What again was to be said upon that hypothesis of the act of Virginia herself passed in 1778, which prohibited the further importation of slaves? What was to be said of numerous litigations in which this and analogous laws had been upheld and enforced by the courts of Maryland and Virginia against their own citizens who had puchased slaves abroad, and that without anyone's thinking to question the validity of such laws upon the ground that they were not law of the land or due process of law?[104] What was to be said of the Act of Congress of 1808 prohibiting the slave trade, and the assumption of the Constitution that Congress would have that power without its being specifically bestowed, but simply as an item of its power to regulate commerce? What, again, was to be said of the Embargo Act, if the scope of congressional authority to legislatate within the limits of powers granted it was restricted by the Fifth Amendment; and what, finally, was to be said of a recent decision of the Supreme Court itself upholding in principle at least the claim of power represented by the Embargo Act?[105] Such were some of the questions which Curtis, J., put, to which obviously the chief justice's easy assumption of the point to be proved afforded no answer at all.

103. 18 How. (U.S.) 272 (1855). See also Justice Curtis' opinion in Greene v. Briggs, 1 Curt. (U.S.) 311. See also Johnson, J., in Bank of Columbia v. Okely, 4 Wheat. (U.S.) 235 (1819): The words "law of the land" (of the Maryland constitution) "were intended to secure the individual from the arbitrary exercise of the powers of government, unrestrained by the established principles of private rights and distributive justice." The purport of his vague dictum has been much abused by late writers and judges: see, for example, Cooley, *Const. Lim.* 355, where it is praised as a "terse" and "accurate" statement. Bank of Columbia v. Okely involved only questions of procedure, and procedure is all that Johnson, J., had in mind, as is shown by his remark shortly afterward: "The forms of administering justice and the duties and powers of courts . . . must ever be subject to legislative will." 4 Wheat. (U.S.) 245.

104. Citing 5 Call (Va.) 425; 1 Leigh (Va.) 172; and 5 Harr. & J. (Md.) 107. See Murray v. McCarty, 2 Munf. (Va.) 393 (1811), applying and enforcing the act of 1792, similar in purport to that of 1778.

105. United States v. Marigold, 9 How. (U.S.) 560.

VII

With Chief Justice Taney's decision in the Dred Scott case the story of due process of law anterior to the Fourteenth Amendment comes practically to a close. Proceeding to gather up our results, we discover at once that the most conspicuous fact about our constitutional law as it stood on the eve of the Civil War was the practical approximation of the police power of the states to the sovereignty of the state legislatures within their respective constitutions, the purpose of which constitutions was universally held to be not to grant power, but to organize and limit powers which were otherwise plenary.[106] But while this was the general rule, due in part to the temporary eclipse of the judiciary and in part to the dominance of the notion of states rights, yet there survived a number of restrictive principles, now in a state of suspended animation, so to speak, but easily susceptible of resuscitation. And one of these was the doctrine of "due process of law," whose title to continued vitality may be put upon the following grounds: First, the availability imparted to the due process of law clause by the decision in Murray v. Hoboken Land and Improvement Co., as a constitutional buffer in connection with summary and administrative proceedings, a function hitherto subserved almost entirely by the trial by jury clause;[107] secondly, the steady extension, even among courts the most attached to the doctrine of legislative sovereignty, of the notion of "law of the land" and "due process of law" as equivalent to "general law" and as therefore inhibiting "special legislation";[108] thirdly, the equivalence established in Taylor v. Porter between "due process of law" and "due compensation" in questions of eminent domain; fourthly, the growing practice, for example, on the part of critics of the Dred Scott decision, to shift construction from the phrase "due process of law," to the terms "liberty" and "property" of the constitutional clause;[109] fifthly, the tendency of these terms, as shown in Ormond, J.'s opinion in the Dorsey case and in Hubbard, J.'s opinion in the Wynehamer case, to take on the progressively broader signification;[110] sixthly, the fact that the Massachusetts Supreme Court, owing to the formula by which power is vested by the Massachusetts constitution in the legislature to pass "all manner of wholesome and reasonable" laws, had never ceased to describe the police power, even when according it the broadest possible field of operation, as a power of "reasonable" legislation;[111] seventhly, the fact that the courts of New York had

106. See particularly Redfield, C. J., in Thorpe v. Rutland, etc. R.R. Co., 27 Vt. 140 (1854).

107. See the excellent old 1 *United States Digest* 562–64 (Boston 1847), by Metcalf and Perkins, Tit. "Constitutional Law," cap. "Right of Trial by Jury."

108. See particularly Coulter, J., in Ervine's Appeal, 16 Pa. St. 263 (1851); and Christiancy, J., in Sears v. Cottrell, 5 Mich. 251 (1858).

109. See the Republican Platform of 1860, para. 8.

110. See a remark of the court in Board of Excise v. Barrie, 34 N.Y. 657 (1866), on "inconsiderate dicta" in the Wynehamer decision.

111. See Massachusetts Constitution, pt. II, ch. 1, art. IV; Shaw, C. J., in Commonwealth v. Alger, 7 Cush. (Mass.) 53 (1851); State v. Gurney, 37 Me. 156 (1853). In this connection an

never surrendered the notion of legislative power as inherently limited;[112] eighthly, the fact that no court had *eo nomine* cast overboard the doctrine of vested rights;[113] ninthly, the fact that all courts generally described the police power, though without any apparent intention as yet of making such description a judicially enforceable limitation, in terms of its historical applications;[114] tenthly, and lastly, the fact that similarly the police power was often grounded upon the common-law maxim *sic utere tuo ut alienum non laedas,*[115] a definition which like the historical definition bore with it the possible implication that the police power was a peculiar kind of power, exercisable constitutionally only for peculiar ends.

But now in this enumeration we have included many, if not all, of the essential elements of the modern flexible doctrine of due process of law. True, the proper admixture of these elements had not as yet in 1860 been suggested, but that it would be in the course of time, with the legislatures pressing upon the courts from one side and private interests from the other, who could doubt?

---

utterance of the Massachusetts court with reference to police regulation of property rights has oftentimes been cited from the decision in Austin v. Murray, but without the least warrant, since the regulation referred to was by municipal by-law. The constitutional provision comes from the colonial charter of 1691.

112. See particularly Sill v. Corning, 15 N.Y. 297 (1857), and People v. Draper, *id.* 532.
113. See, for example, Miller, J., in Bartemeyer v. Iowa, 18 Wall. (U.S.) 129 (1874).
114. See Lincoln v. Smith, Goddard v. Jacksonville, above.
115. Thorpe v. Rutland, etc. R.R. Co., Commonwealth v. Alger, above, following 2 Kent, *Comm.* 340.

III.

THE EXERCISE OF
JUDICIAL REVIEW

6. Constitution v. Constitutional Theory: The Question of the States v. the Nation

THE relation of the states and the nation is a topic on which there is a good deal of discussion these days. One week last spring brought to my desk four pamphlets on the subject—all of them from an anti-nationalistic point of view, and most of them emanating from the sovereign state of Maryland. At the same time *The Times* newspaper carried several articles on the subject. One was a rebuke by the president of the present tendency to look toward the national government for everything. A day or two later another utterance from the same distinguished source called for the establishment of a "federal" bureau of recreation.

But, along with this ancient issue, whose infinite variety time has never yet been able to wither or custom to stale, goes another of even broader import.

Like other branches of learning, the constitutional interpretation pretends to a certain terminology or jargon of its own, but just how accurate this is, is indeed a question. And if it be inaccurate, this fact furnishes all the more reason why some attempt at defining terms should accompany a consideration of the question of the constitutional relationship of the states and the nation.

First, we have the term constitution, but even that is of ambiguous significance. In the formal sense the Constitution of the United States is the written instrument which was drafted at Philadelphia in 1787, plus the amendments which have been added since, in accordance with the forms laid down in the same instrument. In a material sense, however, the Constitution of the United States is much more than this. For what is the purpose of a constitution? Briefly, it is to lay down the general features of a system of government and to define to a greater or less extent the powers of such government, in relation to the rights of persons on the one hand, and on the other—in our system at any rate—in relation to certain other political entities which are incorporated in the system.

From 19 *APSR* 290 (1925). Reprinted by permission.

But now, if we keep this definition of purpose in mind, it at once becomes evident that the actual Constitution of the United States is much more than the formal written constitution. The former includes the latter—or much of it—but it also includes certain important statutes, for example, the Judiciary Act of 1789, as amended to date, the Presidential Succession Act of 1886, the Inter-State Commerce Act, or portions of it, and so forth. Also, it includes certain usages of government which have developed since the formal Constitution first went into effect, and some of which, indeed, have virtually repealed portions of the latter. In this connection the present role of the electoral colleges in the choice of president springs to the mind of everybody, but the rise of the committee system in Congress and the development of the president's cabinet have done scarcely less violence to the intention—or more accurately the expectation of the framers of the Constitution.

Lastly, the Constitution of the United States in its material sense includes a vast bulk of judicial decisions, particularly decisions of the national Supreme Court, which—at the behest of private interests for the most part—undertake to define certain terms of the formal Constitution. Nor can it be questioned that some of the terms which have furnished the basis of judicial decisions were inserted in the Constitution for the direct end of safeguarding private interests through the medium of the courts; but it is also clear that the scope of judicial supervision of political power in our system has been greatly enlarged by the assumption that private interests are legally entitled to the immunities arising from mere defect of power in this, that, or other instrument of government. It results, hence, that judicial interpretations of the Constitution are important, not only in the definition of the rights which are thereby recognized, but also for their effect upon the distribution of governmental power among the organs set up by the Constitution.

We are thus brought to a second term of interest to our science, constitutional law. This, too, is ambiguous—indeed doubly so, as we shall shortly perceive. In the first place, the term law is ambiguous—*multiguous,* if there be such a word. However, we may content ourselves with considering two definitions: (1) that law is a rule of action; (2) that it is a rule of judicial decision. The two ideas are not mutually exclusive, for a rule of judicial decision must still be a rule, unless we accept Professor Gray's apparent supposition that a court is incapable of apprehending a rule. On the other hand, there are rules which in fact determine constitutional procedure in our system, though they have never received judicial sanction, or have received it only incompletely. Indeed, it is demonstrable that in some instances the judicial theory of the Constitution has finally thrown up its hands in despair and surrendered to some rule of action of the political branches. Thus, if one will turn to the Insular Cases, he will find that at one time at least the Court entertained one theory on the question of whether the constitution follows the flag and that Congress followed a quite opposed theory, and he will find further that the Court at last surrendered its theory and adopted that of Congress. And it is much the same as to the question of the scope of Congress's powers in the appropriation of money for "the general welfare of the United States." The recent case of Massachusetts v. Mellon gives some indication that the Court has its own opinion on this matter, and that it is by no means the latitudinarian view which has always been acted upon by Congress; but the same case also shows the Court's persuasion that there are times when discretion is the better part of valor, and that the question of the validity of the Maternity Act was such an occasion. Neither has the Court ever ventured to traverse directly the doctrine that the power of removal is a branch of the executive power of the president, although it has made clear its opinion that this doctrine, viewed simply as a product of the human mind, is distinctly inferior to its own view that the power of removal is an incident of the power of appointment.

But the second ambiguity lurking in the term constitutional law is even more of a pitfall. It may be described as consisting of the indefiniteness of demarcation of constitutional law from constitutional theory. This indefiniteness furnished, it is hardly necessary to say, the very foundation of Marshall's work as expounder of the Constitution, and so it is not surprising that it is best illustrated in some of his opinions. Take, for instance, the case of McCulloch v. Maryland. In this case the Court ruled that a certain tax which the state of Maryland had levied on certain operations of a branch of the Bank of the United States located in Baltimore was void, as representing a claim on the part of the state of the constitutional power to control or even destroy an instrumentality of the United States government. The opinion is compounded of theories as to the nature of the power to tax, of the intrinsic limits of the state power, of the relation of the states to the national government under the Constitution, of the nature of the Constitution, and of the nature of its source. The Constitution, it is asserted, comes from the people of the United States and not the states, and is therefore to be generously construed from the point of view of making it a useful instrument of popular government. Therefore, the terms "necessary and proper," construed in this context, mean simply convenient, and the bank being a convenient fiscal instrument, is an agency of the United States government, beyond the reach of all state powers which might be wielded in a hostile fashion, among such powers being that of taxation, which is a power of destruction. And so on—what part of this argument is constitutional law, what part is constitutional theory?

Judging from the use which the Court itself has made at various times of the broader aspects of its own previous utterances, as well as from the practice of commentators, constitutional law should perhaps be defined as my-constitutional-doxy and constitutional theory as your-constitutional-doxy. But this flippant dismissal of the subject would end my paper right here and so must itself be dismissed. What is more important, I must utter a caution against a possible inclination to regard constitutional theory as a deduction from constitutional law. The truth is rather the exact reverse of this; and particularly is this so within that field of either, which deals with the relationship of the nation and the states. The relation of Constitution, constitutional law, and constitutional theory to one another—especially as they affect the problem just mentioned—may be shown diagrammatically—not that a diagram proves anything, except possibly the inability of the maker of it to express himself as well in some other way. You are, then, to conceive the Constitution in the formal sense as the nucleus of a set of ideas. Surrounding this and overlapping it to a greater or less extent, is constitutional law, in the formal sense too of a rule of decision. Outside this, finally, but interpenetrating it and underlying it is constitutional theory, which may be defined as the sum total of ideas of some historical standing as to what the Constitution is or ought to be. Some of these ideas do actually appear more or less clearly in the written instrument itself, as for example, that interpretation of the doctrine of the separation of powers which yields judicial review; others tend toward solidification in the less fluid mass of constitutional law; and still others remain in a more or less rarefied or gaseous state—the raw materials, nevertheless, from which national policy is wrought. But how wrought? In answering this question let us turn for a moment to the other phase of our subject—the relationship of the nation and the states.

Considered for its final result, the struggle which attended the adoption of the Constitution was less a struggle over whether it should be adopted than over the interpretation which should be put upon the act once it was accomplished. The friends of the Constitution were for the most part nationalists, and it was they who set the new government in operation. But the other point of view was early formulated in the Virginia and Kentucky Resolutions, which in time became a gloss upon the Constitution fully as authoritative as the written instrument itself; and in 1838 the United States Senate adopted by the vote of 31 to 13 a resolution offered by Calhoun which declared the Constitution to be a compact of sovereign states. Meantime, the other point of view had received reiterated statement from the Supreme Bench in the opinions of Chief Justice Marshall, whose greatest service perhaps was just this service of keeping the breath of life in the nationalistic tradition over a critical period. The Civil War, however, restored the idea of the national government as a territorial sovereign, though one of restricted powers. Then, two decades later, the development of industry on a national scale produced an alliance between the principle of nationalism and that of laissez faire, which operating through the commerce clause, shattered state control of business. But the commerce clause proved a two-edged sword, and the very precedents which relieved the railroads, for instance, from local regulation became the foundation of national regulation. The result has been a new turn of the kaleidoscope, a new combination of elements of constitutional theory, and some new constitutional law.

Of the issues between those who pose as the champions of nationalism today and those who take up the cudgels of states' rights, the most exigent and interesting one concerns the question of the allocation of the purposes of government in the United States. Both nationalists and states' righters are in general agreement that there are certain large purposes which any system of government should serve. The issue between them is of how these purposes are supposed to be served under the Constitution of the United States. The one party holds that the purposes for which the national government may constitutionally exercise its powers are relatively few, and that the ultimate objectives of good government are for the most part, under our system, reserved to the states, whose police power has been defined always as the power to promote the public health, safety, morals and general welfare. The other party answers, however, that while the powers of government are divided in the United States, its broader purposes may be served by each government within the field of its powers, and that the purposes which the police power of the states is designed to serve are by no means reserved exclusively to that power, that it was no thought of the framers of the Constitution in erecting a national government and assigning it certain powers to withdraw those powers from the service of the major objects of civilized society, that the preamble in the Constitution itself proves the contrary purpose. The one theory may be termed the theory of competitive federalism; the other, the theory of cooperative federalism.

Just at the present writing it would seem that the competitive theory has the better of it. In interpreting the commerce clause, the Supreme Court has shown itself ready to permit the national government to make vast inroads upon what had been thought to be reserved powers of the states, so long as its object is the promotion of commercial prosperity. On the other hand, as the recent child labor cases show, once the national government operating on the same clause undertakes a program of humanitarian legislation, then the reserved rights of the state become a very grave consideration indeed.

Yet this was not always so. More than a hundred years ago, a national judge, confronted with the states' rights argument of limited national purpose, answered it thus: "The power to regulate commerce is not to be confined to the adoption of measures exclusively beneficial to the commerce itself, or tending to its advantage; but under our system, as in all modern sovereignties, it is also to be considered as an instrument for other purposes of general policy and interest. . . . The situation of the United States in ordinary times might render legislative interferences relative to commerce less necessary, but the capacity and power of managing and directing it for the advancement of great national purposes seems an important ingredient of sovereignty." The judge then cited the constitutional clause interdicting a prohibition of the slave trade until 1808. This, said he, proved clearly the view of the framers of the Constitution "that under the power to regulate commerce, Congress would be authorized to abridge it in favor of the great principles of humanitarian justice."

Indeed, it was not so very many years ago that the Supreme Court itself, in sustaining the Mann White Slave Act, used the following language: "Our dual form of government has its perplexities, state and nation having different spheres of jurisdiction . . . but it must be kept in mind that we are one people, and the powers reserved to the states and those conferred on the nation are adapted to be exercised, whether independently or concurrently, to promote the general welfare material and moral.'' A better statement of the cooperative theory of the federal relationship could not be asked for.

So much for the national viewpoint; now for that of states' rights. It will be found underlying Chief Justice Taft's explanation, in the recent case of Bailey v. The Drexel Furniture Company, of the earlier decision in Hammer v. Dagenhart, in which the first Child Labor Act was held void. ''When Congress,'' says the chief justice, ''threatened to stop inter-state commerce in ordinary and necessary commodities, unobjectionable as subjects of transportation, and to deny the same to the people of a state in order to coerce them into compliance with Congress's regulation of state concerns, the court said this was not in fact a regulation of interstate commerce, but rather that of state concerns, and was invalid.'' ''State concerns,'' ''unobjectionable subjects of transportation'' —in other words. Congress may prevent child labor from injuring transportation, but not vice versa.

Let us now turn back to the other phase of the topic announced: Constitution v. constitutional theory. What I have been doing obviously is to seize the occasion to indoctrinate you with my favorite brand of constitutional theory on a certain current issue, while illustrating the relation of constitutional theory to the Constitution and to constitutional law. But at this point I am likely to be met with an objection which, in the very act of anticipating it, I shall endeavor to appease. This will be that the real stimulus to the development of constitutional law comes not from constitutional theory, but from considerations of public policy, themselves the outgrowth of social change, and that the relationship of constitutional theory to such considerations, like that of constitutional law, is a purely instrumental one. Indeed, the objector may speak more bluntly, and declare that the judges are often at least the partisans of identifiable economic interests, and that precedent and theory are only a camouflage in the shadow of which matters of choice take on the delusive appearance of inevitability.

No student would care to deny altogether the force of these views. A full explanation of the growth of American constitutional law must recognize that the relatively compact universe of constitutional theory is bathed in a vastly wider atmosphere of social and economic activity, athwart which are constantly blowing the winds of change, set loose no man knows how. Here is the very realm of the ''inarticulate major premise'' of which Justice Holmes has spoken. Nor is Justice Holmes's the voice in the wilderness that it was once. Nowadays almost everybody admits, however grudgingly, that the judges make law, and that not merely in the sense of adding to or subtracting from the supposititious intention of a more or less supposititious law-giver, but also in the sense of determining such additions and subtractions by their own preferences. Those, therefore, have a certain amount of truth on their side who would make legal history a side issue of judicial biography.

Yet granting all this, does constitutional theory—by which I mean, let me repeat in substance, those generalized, and often conflicting views of what the Constitution is or ought to be, which are often as old as the Constitution itself—does constitutional theory in this sense lose its significance? Certainly not altogether; and in one respect it takes on a new importance. I refer again to the matter of judicial legislation. The question nowadays is not so much whether the judges do make law, but rather the extent of such law-making, a question which arises from the extremely elusive character of judicial legislation. How is it that intelligent judges can deny to this day that they do make law? In the field of our constitutional law the answer is furnished in great part by the relationship which I have already pictured as existing between constitutional law and theory. Almost from the beginning, as we have seen, two theories have been going as to the relationship of the states and the national government under the Constitution. Each theory in turn has enjoyed its period of predominant influence with the Court, and each in consequence has back of it a respectable line of supporting precedents. It results that when the Court comes to deciding issues along the line which divides national and state power today, it finds itself in an extremely comfortable position. It has a free choice between two lines of precedents so that once its choice is made, it becomes assimilated to the one or the other of these lines, and every appearance of choice is thus automatically occulted. In the word of Montesquieu, "The judges are but the mouthpieces of the law."

In short, the existence of certain standardized, but conflicting views of the Constitution both confers upon the judges perfect freedom of decision where the issue before them is one that can be stated in the terms of such views, and at the same time sets up a defence against any attack based on conventional notions of judicial function, which it is extremely difficult to break down. When John Randolph declared of one of Marshall's decisions, "All wrong, all wrong, but no man in the United States can say wherein wrong," he was only expressing the sense of bafflement that many other critics of judicial decisions have felt.

The question, however, remains whether the average judge takes quite so sophisticated an attitude toward constitutional theory; and on that point I venture to express a strong doubt. The average Supreme Court judge, I believe, takes his constitutional theory very seriously. As Justice Holmes has observed from a long experience of judges, "They are apt to be naif, simple-minded men, with little of the spirit of Mephistopheles." To them such phrases as the separation of powers, check and balance, judicial independence, national supremacy, states' rights, freedom of contract, vested rights, police power, not only express important realities, the *are* realities—they are forms of thought with a vitality and validity of their own. Nor is it anything to the point that many of these ideas, when pressed to their logical extremes collide with others of them. The most ordinary function of a high court is to demark the limits of jurisdiction of conflicting principles of law. In the field of constitutional law the Court may well feel that its highest duty is so to adjust the claims of contradictory ideas as to prevent either from being crowded to the wall.

Nor is this the whole case for the importance of constitutional theory as a determinant of constitutional law, and so of the Constitution itself as a factor of every-day life. The further point I have in mind has been so well put by Sir Henry Maine, that I quote his words: "Nothing in law," says he, "springs entirely from a sense of convenience. There are always certain ideas existing antecedently on which the sense of convenience works, and of which it can do no more than form some new combination; and to find these ideas . . . is exactly the problem." Thus, in many instances, ideas inherited from the past furnish the mould of present policy, which takes shape and direction from them, and may in fact be entirely transformed by them. Take, for example, the Eighteenth Amendment. This makes prohibition a national policy; but in the very act of doing so, it subjects this policy to the general procedure of the Constitution, which is to say, of the Constitution as it has been interpreted to date. The final result may be to mitigate the original policy very decidedly. The enactment of a law is only the first step—often a comparatively unimportant step—in the *making* of a law; and one of the conditions to which the new law must accommodate itself is existing forms of thought on legal subjects.

These observations bring us into contact once more with the other phase of our subject. Two questions suggest themselves: first, whether it would not be a good thing if constitutional theory could be abolished; secondly what effect its abolition would have on the question of the relation of national and state power? Toward the end of the nineteenth century a school of German theologians, which had its followers in this country, announced it to be their program to get rid of what they called the incubus of the Pauline theology. Their augument was that while the authentic message of Christianity was as vital as ever, the harsh, stiff concepts of the Pauline teaching were unadjustable to modern needs and that, therefore, if Christianity was to survive, the screen which the Pauline theology obtruded between the modern believer and the pure faith must be kicked away. Might not a similar Puritanism be summoned to the defense of the Constitution and against the gloss of constitutional theory that so often encumbers its provisions?

It is certainly true that the maxims which the courts have built up to guide them in the construction of laws and constitutions owe far too much to their work of construction in other and quite different fields where the public interest was not involved. A maxim especially in point in this connection is that which says that the court must give effect to the will of the law-giver. This maxim comes straight from the law of wills. Naturally the intention which should govern the application of a will is that of its maker, although he is dead before the task of ascertaining his intention arises. But is there any reason why the intention of a law-maker, as distinct from that of the law itself should govern the law's interpretation? To be sure, the law-maker is dead the moment the statute is made; that particular law-maker—that is to say, that particular congeries, or consensus of individual wills—will never in all probability function again, legislatively or otherwise. Is there, however, any reason why weight should be given in the interpretation of the law to the fact that such a law-giver did for one single instant flash into existence and then with equal celerity pass into an unrecoverable oblivion?

Yet it is this maxim that the intention of the law-maker governs which has always been the principal, if not the sole viaduct, so to speak, between the Constitution and constitutional theory. Constitutional theories the most contradictory have from the first claimed the attention of the official interpreters of the Constitution on the score of representing the real honest-to-goodness intentions of the framers of the Constitution, or if not of its framers, then of those who adopted it. Fortunately, the Court has not always treated such arguments as relevant. Marshall in his opinion in Gibbons v. Ogden thought they should be heeded very rarely—though at other times his attitude is rather different. Not so many years ago the Court dismissed an appeal to the intention of the framers in these brusque words: "The reasons which may have caused the framers of the Constitution to repose the power to regulate inter-state commerce in Congress do not . . . affect or limit the extent of the power itself."

And is not this the position which the Court ought always to take in this year of grace, one hundred and thirty-five years after the framing of the Constitution? As a *document* the Constitution came from its framers, and its elaboration was an event of the greatest historical interest, but as a *law* the Constitution comes from and derives all its force from the people of the United States of this day and hour. In the words of the preamble, "We, the people of the United States, *do* ordain and establish this Constitution"—not *did* ordain and establish. The Constitution is thus always in contact with the source of its being—it is a living statute, to be interpreted in the light of living conditions. Resistance it offers to the too easy triumph of social forces, but it is only the resistance of its words when they have been fairly construed from a point of view which is sympathetic with the aspirations of the existing generation of American people, rather than that which is furnished by concern for theories as to what was intended by a generation long since dissolved into its native dust.

Finally, let me put the question, what would result from such a procedure to the notion that the Constitution excludes the national government from the main purposes of good government? It can be confidently answered that this notion would fall and dwindle by the wayside. Again, the preamble is in point; for where could a better statement be found of the wider objectives sought by good government the world over, "to promote justice, insure domestic tranquillity, provide for the common defence and the general welfare?" Nor is this to say that the preamble is a grant of power; it is simply a catalogue of the ultimate ends to be served by the powers granted in the Constitution itself. No gloss derived from speculative theories about the nature of the Union should have ever been permitted to obscure its clear import.

Furthermore, is it not laid down in numerous cases that the purpose for which a legislature exercises its powers is a question of policy which no court is entitled to decide? The attempt, therefore, to apportion the general purposes of government between the national government and the states runs counter to a once-settled rule of constitutional law. Nor should we forget that, unlike certain specific clauses of the written Constitution—the due process clause, for instance—the division of powers between the states and the nation which the Constitution sets up does not exist primarily for the protection of private interests but for public benefit—a matter also for legislatures and not for courts. Indeed, if we were to apply in the field of the relation of the national government and the states the full doctrine of political questions, judicial review must cease altogether in this field. This is so because a political question is one primarily over conflicting claims of sovereignty, with the result that when Congress has passed its act, the "political departments" having spoken, their verdict becomes *res adjudicata* and binding on the courts. No doubt, this jurisdiction is too well established to be challenged today; but at least it is questionable if it should be extended. What justifies itself by precedent should observe the limits set by precedent.

These considerations are no doubt irrelevant to the main argument and indeed are added only for good measure. The main argument may be summarized thus: For many practical purposes the *Constitution* is the judicial version of it—*constitutional law*. The latter in turn derives in no small part from speculative ideas about what the framers of the Constitution or the generation which adopted it intended it should mean—*constitutional theory*. Such ideas, nevertheless, whatever their historical basis—and that is frequently most precarious—have no application to the main business of constitutonal interpretation, which is to keep the Constitution adjusted to the advancing needs of the time. On the contrary, they frequently contribute to rendering the written instrument rigid and inflexible far beyond what is the reasonable consequence of its terms. The proper point of view from which to approach the task of interpreting the Constitution is that of regarding it as a living statute, palpitating with the purpose of the hour, reenacted with every waking breath of the American people, whose primitive right to determine their institutions is its sole claim to validity as a law and as the matrix of laws under our system.

As an illustration of the artificial difficulties created by reliance upon constitutional theory I have instanced the recently developed doctrine of the Court that the national government may use its powers only in the service of certain very restricted interests—a theory which clearly underlies the recent Child Labor cases. The doctrine is a solecism and flies in the very face of the preamble of the Constitution. But furthermore, constitutional theory, by the choice which it frequently offers of contradictory premises, enables the Court often to legislate without assuming the due responsibilities of legislators. Lastly, had time permitted, I might have run over some older precedents of constitutional law, and have pointed out how essential it is that they should be rectified and how the task of their rectification would be assisted if the Court would but brush aside obscuring theories and read the textual Constitution afresh. Thus, the foundation of constitutional tax exemption is almost entirely doctrinal. When the written Constitution relieves anybody from the ordinary duties of citizenship it is quite explicit on the point. But if there still must be an appeal to the framers of the Constitution let it be Marshall's appeal: ''The constitution [was] intended to endure for ages, and consequently to be adapted to the various crises of human affairs.''

7. Judicial Review in Action

JUDICIAL review is the power of a court to pass upon the validity of the acts of a legislature in relation to a "higher law" which is regarded as binding on both. In this article we are especially concerned with the power of the Supreme Court of the United States to pass upon the validity of acts of Congress and of state legislative acts and state constitutional provisions under the Constitution of the United States. It should be understood, nevertheless, that the courts of every state in the Union exercise a like power over state statutes in relation to the several state constitutions; while the obligation of state judges, under Article 6 of the Constitution, to give a preference to "the supreme law of the land" as there defined over all state laws, links up the national and state judiciaries into one system for the maintenance of the supremacy of the Constitution as a rule of judicial decision over all other evidences of law.

But besides these generally recognized branches of judicial review as it is organized in this country, there is one other not so well recognized. I refer to the fact that both national and state courts have at times ventured to review legislative acts in relation to an *unwritten* higher law. In point of fact, the earliest suggestion of judicial review of which the cases afford evidence was made without any reference to a written constitution. This was in Sir Edward Coke's famous dictum in Dr. Bonham's Case, pronounced in 1612,[1] in which it was asserted that an act of Parliament "contrary to common right and reason" would be "void." Although this doctrine never made much headway in England, and is in this country today regarded as obsolete, yet some of the most important doctrines of American constitutional law are traceable to this source.

From 74 *University of Pennsylvania Law Review* 639 (1926). Reprinted by permission. Copyright 1926 University of Pennsylvania Law Review.
1. 8 Co. 113b (1612).

Writers on this subject sometimes speak as if judicial review consisted solely in the judicial *disallowance* of statutes as "void" because not squaring with the Court's reading of the Constitution. This notion of judicial review is too narrow for two reasons. In the first place, the Court regards its own previous decisions sustaining acts of the legislature as constituting precedents just as truly as its decisions setting such acts aside. Indeed, the opportunity which the Court has had to furnish well reasoned arguments in behalf of the claims of government— and especially the national government—has been one of the principal sources of its influence upon our political life, as witness the case of Chief Justice Marshall.

In the second place, disallowance of a statute is not always complete— sometimes it is only partial. That is to say, it sometimes takes the form of a construction of the statute which rids it of its unconstitutional features, but also of much of its effectiveness. Whenever a statute is thus curtailed by construction in consequence of the Court's view of the requirements of the Constitution, we have, obviously, a true case of judicial review—a true case of the simultaneous construction of constitutional provision and of statute with a view to discovering the binding rule of law.[2]

Chiefly because of the fact that the common law comes from them, courts seem rarely to have been under the necessity of pronouncing a rule of the common law unconstitutional. There is no common law in any state in conflict with the constitution thereof; and so far as the nation as a whole is concerned, there is very little common law anyway. Nor do rules of state common law appear to have been set aside under the United States Constitution save in a very few instances.[3]

Nature and Limitation of Judicial Review

There is no such thing as a specifically delegated power of judicial review— judicial review is simply incidental to the power of courts to interpret the law, of which the Constitution is part, in connection with the decision of cases. In the words of a recent opinion: "From the authority to ascertain and determine the law in a given case, there necessarily results in cases of conflict, the duty to declare and enforce the rule of the supreme law and reject that of an inferior act of legislation which, transcending the Constitution is of no effect, and binding on no one. This is not the exercise of a substantive power to review and nullify acts of Congress, for no such substantive power exists. It is simply a necessary concomitant of the power to hear and dispose of a case or controversy properly before the Court, to the determination of which must be brought the test and measure of the law."[4]

---

2. See, e.g., United States v. E. C. Knight Co., 156 U.S. 1 (1895), and United States v. D. & H. Co., 213 U.S. 366 (1909).

3. Muhlker v. N.Y. & Harlem R.R. Co., 197 U.S. 54 (1904), would seem to be such a case.

4. Justice Sutherland in Adkins v. The Children's Hospital, 261 U.S. 525 (1923).

From the very nature of judicial review as an outgrowth of ordinary judicial function arise certain limitations upon its exercise. This, however, is not the only source of the limitations which the Court has come to observe when exercising the most exalted of its powers. Alongside what may be termed *intrinsic limitations* of judicial review, and often modifying them, are others which owe their existence to *cautionary considerations*—to the desire of the Court to avoid occasions of direct conflict with the political branches of the government, and especially with that branch which wields the physical forces of government, the president.

Neither of these factors of judicial review, it should be added, is an altogether constant one. The Court's theory of the nature of judicial power will itself be found to have undergone development, and to this development judicial review has responded. More changeable has been the other factor, varying in its force with the times and with the personalities of judges—and perhaps also with the personalities of presidents. Marshall, for example, was a bold and enterprising magistrate, constantly ready to put the pretensions of the Court to the test;[5] while his successor, on the contrary, was—save on one fatal occasion—a notably cautious man. And in recent years, judicial review has undergone great advances.

Among the rules which the Supreme Court has recognized as governing judicial review are the following:[6]

1. A decision disallowing a legislative act, either national or state, must be concurred in by a majority of the entire membership of the Bench. This is a cautionary rule—originally a concession to state pride—for other kinds of decisions are binding when concurred in by a majority of a quorum of the Court.[7]

2. The Court will pronounce on the constitutionality of legislative acts only in connection with "cases."[8] By the Constitution the judicial power of the United States extends to certain cases and controversies; by the principle of the separation of powers it extends only to such. A *case* in this sense, moreover, must be a real case—not a simulated or "moot" case. That is, it must involve a real contest of antagonistic interests, requiring for its solution a judicial pronouncement on opposed views of law. Such is the theory, the obvious advantage of which is its tendency to secure for the Court the benefits of full argument on the issues presented. Actually, the Court seems not to have lived

---

5. There was one occasion, however, when Marshall lost his nerve. This was when Justice Chase was impeached. He then proposed that congressional recall of judicial decisions should supersede the power of impeachment! 3 Beveridge, *The Life of John Marshall* 176–78 (1916–19). His conduct on the stand when testifying at Chase's trial was far from admirable. *Id.*, at 195–96.

6. On this general subject see Cooley, *Constitutional Limitations* ch. 7; 1 Willoughby, *On the Constitution* ch. 2; R. P. Reeder, *The Validity of Rate Regulations* 369–77.

7. See C. J. Marshall's announcement in connection with the first argument of Briscoe v. Com. Bank of Ky. and Miln v. N.Y., 8 Pet. 118, 120 (1834).

8. See Muskrat v. United States, 219 U.S. 346 (1911), and cases therein cited.

up to its theory always. The celebrated Income Tax Case of 1895[9] was originally a moot case, both the parties to which had substantially the same interest at heart in seeing the act before the Court set aside; and there have been other constitutional cases of the same nature both before and since then.[10]

In contrast to this, the Court at an early date refused to render an advisory opinion on certain legal questions which were laid before it by President Washington;[11] and it has subsequently extended its scruple to the rendition of "declaratory judgments" even in cases involving a real contest of opposed interests, such a judgment being final on the legal issue presented, although not followed by process of execution.[12]

It should be added that the growing practice in recent years of raising the question of the constitutionality of legislative acts by injunction proceedings against their enforcement has come to serve many of the purposes of a Declaratory Judgment Act in this field.[13]

3. Corollary of the rule against moot cases is the rule that nobody may attack the constitutionality of a legislative act in a case before the Court unless his rights are actually affected or clearly menaced by such legislative act; and also the rule, which is the converse of this, that the Court will pass on the constitutional question raised by such an attack only when it is necessary to do so in order to determine the rights of parties to a case before it.[14] The criticism visited upon the Court in connection with the famous Dred Scott decision was based in part on the supposition that the Court had gone out of its way to discuss Congress's powers in the territories in violation of this rule.[15] Yet the rule would not seem to forbid the Court from resting its determination of the constitutionality of an act on more than a single ground. This at least was not Chief Justice Marshall's understanding of it.[16]

The question arises as to how valuable "rights" have to be in order to invoke a decision of the Court on a constitutional point? In contrast with some of the state courts the Supreme Court seems generally to have discouraged taxpayers'

9. Pollock v. Farmers' Loan & Trust Co., 157 U.S. 429 (1894); 158 U.S. 601 (1894). When the attorney general, with singular maladroitness, joined in the action, the case ceased to be moot.

10. Brushaber v. U.P.R.R., 240 U.S. 1 (1916), was a moot case, at least at its inception. Hylton v. United States, 3 Dallas 171 (U.S. 1795), was a deliberately planned moot case, in which counsel on both sides were paid by the government. See 1 Warren, *The Supreme Court in the United States Hisory* 146–49. Fletcher v. Peck, 6 Cranch 37 (U.S. 1810), bears all the earmarks of having been a moot case (1 Warren 392–99); as does Buchanan v. Warley, 245 U.S. 60 (1917).

11. 1 Warren 108–11.

12. Gordon v. United States, 117 U.S. 697 (1885), was such a case. JJ. Miller and Field dissented from the holding that the Court had no jurisdiction.

13. See Ex parte Young, 209 U.S. 123 (1908).

14. Chicago & G.T. R'y Co. v. Wellman, 143 U.S. 339 (1892); and see generally the references in note 6, above.

15. See my *Doctrine of Judicial Review* 133–40 (1914); also 3 Warren, *The Supreme Court in United States History* 1–41.

16. Cf. his opinions in Brown v. Maryland, 12 Wheat. 419 (U.S. 1827), and in Cohens v. Virginia, 6 Wheat. 264 (U.S. 1821).

suits, as well as those in which the aggressive party had only the general
interest of seeing the Constitution enforced.[17]

4. Another maxim stated with great positiveness by the writers is that no
legislative act may be pronounced void by a court on the ground of its being in
conflict with natural justice, the social compact, fundamental principles, etc.
—in short, on any other than strictly constitutional grounds.[18] This is because
the supremacy of the Constitution—its claim to be considered higher law by the
courts—is today traced to its quality as an ordinance of the people rather
than—as orginally—as due in part to its content; to this expression of the will
of the sovereign people all other evidences thereof must give way.

This does not signify, however, that judicial review rests on a narrower basis
than it once did—it signifies, indeed, the exact contrary. Few American courts
ever did invoke extra-constitutional principles as grounds for the disallowance
of statutes; but today the utmost latitudinarian view of such principles ever
taken by any American court are today available, and freely available, to all
courts in the United States in the form of the modern conceptions of "liberty"
and "due process of law."[19] Furthermore, so far as the Supreme Court is
concerned, it is by no means strictly accurate to say that even today it will close
its ears to arguments based on extra-constitutional principles.[20]

5. Probably no maxim of judicial review is encountered in the decisions
more frequently than that which says that a statute may be declared unconstitutional only in "a clear case"; or as it is also phrased, that all legislative acts are
"presumed to be constitutional" until shown to be otherwise, and that all
"reasonable doubts" concerning their constitutionality will be resolved in their
favor.[21] Yet in the face of judicial reiteration and insistence on this point, the
maxim in question has been termed "a smoothly transmitted platitude," and
treated even with levity by recent writers.[22] What actually is its restrictive
force?

17. Cf., for instance, Wilson v. Shaw, 204 U.S. 24 (1907), and Frothingham v. Mellon, 262
U.S. 447 (1923).

18. Note 6, above. The principle originates in Justice Iredell's opinion in Calder v. Bull, 3
Dallas 386 (U.S. 1798), in answer to the contrary doctrine of Justice Chase's opinion in the same
case.

19. See the present writer's "The Basic Doctrine of American Constitutional Law," 12 *Mich. L.
Rev.* 247 (1914); and "Due Process of Law before the Civil War," 24 *Harv. L. Rev.* 366 and 460
(1911).

20. Cf. Dorr v. United States, 195 U.S. 138 (1904) and Gilbert v. Minnesota, 254 U.S. 325
(1920).

21. "The declaration [that an act of Congress is void] should never be made except in a clear
case. Every possible presumption is in favor of the validity of a statute and this continues until the
contrary is shown beyond a rational doubt"; Chief Justice Waite in the Sinking Fund Cases, 99
U.S. 700 (1878). "It is but a decent respect due to the . . . legislative body by which any law is
passed, to presume in favor of its validity until the violation of the Constitution is proved beyond
all reasonable doubt," Justice Washington in Ogden v. Saunders, 12 Wheat. 213 (U.S. 1827). See
also Chief Justice Marshall in Fletcher v. Peck (above, note 10). Compare, however, Justice
Chase's statement in Calder v. Bull (above, note 18) that there are certain powers which "it cannot
be presumed" the people have entrusted the legislature.

22. See W. F. Dodd, "Growth of Judicial Power," 24 *Pol. Sci. Q.* 193 (1909).

To begin with, what is meant by a "clear case" and "reasonable doubt"? In some circumstances the mere fact that clients, advised presumably by competent attorneys, have seen fit to prosecute a constitutional point into the highest Court of the land is sufficient to show some measure of doubt regarding the merits of the question. But the fact more insisted upon by the critics just referred to is the so-called "five to four decision" when it is adverse to an act of Congress or a state act. When four of the nine judges of the Supreme Court, supported it may be by a majority of the judges in the courts from which appeal was taken, find a statute constitutional, there is, it is urged, at least a "reasonable doubt" of its invalidity; so that, if the maxim under discussion were to be taken seriously, the acts must have been sustained.

An answer sometimes returned to this argument is that it misconceives the nature of the issue between the majority and the minority of the Court; that this is not really whether the act under review is unconstitutional, but whether there is reasonable doubt as to its unconstitutionality; and this question having been decided in the negative, the maxim is satisfied. Unfortunately, a study of dissenting opinions hardly sustains this contention—they usually show the dissenting judges to be quite as positive in their opinion of the constitutionality of the act before the Court as the majority are as to its unconstitutionality.

The real issue seems to be whether a judge should permit his evaluation of a legislative act to be determined by his knowledge of the attitude of his brethren, or whether he should form his opinion substantially independently of such considerations. The maxim evidently assumes that he should do the latter.

A remark of Sir George Jessel concerning an opinion handed down by him as Master of the Rolls in a certain perplexing case is apposite in this connection. Asked if he had no doubts as to the correctness of his decision, Sir George answered: "I may be wrong, but I have no *doubts*."[23] And we should also recall the old saying that "hard cases make bad law." A close decision is apt to indicate a hard case; so that it is not surprising that some bad constitutional law has been made in this way.

The maxim, therefore, that all reasonable doubts must be resolved in favor of the legislative act is to be regarded as addressed primarily to the conscience of the individual judge, just as an analogous maxim of the criminal law is addressed to the conscience of the individual juror. Its operation has consequently taken place for the most part beyond the power of any but divine scrutiny.

On the other hand, the notion that statutes ought to be presumed to be constitutional does seem to have become embodied in a tangible, even though not always observed, rule of judicial review, to wit, the maxim that of two possible constructions of the statute, one of which renders a statute constitutional and the other unconstitutional, the former is to be preferred as presum-

---

23. The anecdote is related by Lord Bryce in his *Essays in Contemporary Biography* {*sic; Studies in Contemporary Biography (1903)*}.

ably representing the legislature's intention. Overlooked in some instances in which it would have saved a statute from judicial condemnation,[24] this maxim has in other cases been enforced with such severity as to secure practically the full results of outright disallowance of the act before the Court.[25] Lastly, it should be noted that in an endeavor to meet certain devices of the state legislatures for escaping constitutional limitations, the Court has been forced in recent years to recognize a category of state legislative acts which are *"prima facie* void"—for which, in other words, the preliminary presumption of validity is avowedly dismissed.[26]

6. Another limitation on judicial review, which is partially cautionary, partially logical, grows out of the doctrine of "political questions." Originally this doctrine required that when the political departments—the president and Congress, or either—had decided such a question the Court must, in cases coming before it, accept their decision as binding on itself. So if the decision was one of opposed claims resting on opposed views of law, the doctrine clearly interfered with the maxim that the interpretation of the law rests finally with the courts. Originating in the field of international relations,[27] where the law involved was either the law of nations or a treaty, the doctrine was extended in the leading case of Luther v. Borden[28] to constitutional law, the Court holding in that case that it could not question a previous determination by the president and Congress that the then existing government of Rhode Island was "republican in form" within the requirement of article 4, section 4 of the Constitution.

In the strictly accurate sense of the term, then, a *political question* in the field of constitutional law is one growing out of conflicting claims to political authority. Earlier the Court would not decide such an issue even in connection with a case involving private rights—such as Luther v. Borden was—if the views of the political branches were ascertainable by it. Today the utmost that can be said is that it will not take jurisdiction of a case for the mere purpose of deciding such a question under the Constitution; and even this statement does not hold as to cases brought by a state in defense of its "quasi-sovereign" rights—whatever these may be.[29] And, of course, the Court has never hesitated in cases involving private rights to pass upon the validity of acts of Congress alleged to invade the sphere of state power and vice versa.

But there is also a broader meaning of the term "political questions" which

24. The Trade-Mark Cases, 100 U.S. 82 (1879); James v. Bowman, 190 U.S., 127 (1903); Howard v. Ill. Central R. Co., 207 U.S. 463 (1908).

25. See note 2, above.

26. Ex parte Young (above, note 13); also, International Harvester Co. v. Kentucky, 234 U.S. 199 (1914).

27. See my *President's Control of Foreign Relations* 10, 100–104, 163–67 (1917).

28. 7 How. 1 (U.S. 1849); off'd in Pac. T. & T. Co. v. Oregon, 223 U.S. 118 (1912).

29. Cf. Missouri v. Holland, 252 U.S. 416 (1920), and Massachusetts v. Mellon, 262 U.S. 447 (1923).

extends it to practically any exercise of governmental discretion. In this sense, whether Congress shall increase the tariff on sugar is a political question; also whether the president shall pardon one who has been convicted of an offense against the United States. Ordinarily, of course, such questions are not for the courts, being mere questions of policy. Yet this is not universally the case. The *purposes* for which certain governmental powers may be validly exercised came to be treated as a judicial question at an early date;[30] while recently the Supreme Court has laid claim to an entirely new range of power of this nature with respect to acts of Congress which appear to invade the historical jurisdiction of the states.[31]

The importance of the doctrine of political questions as a limitation of judicial review seems, in short, to be declining. As a limitation on the Court's pretensions to a supervisory role in relation to the president, on the other hand, it apparently retains its original vigor. One obvious reason for this is the cautionary consideration that executive action is not always subject to automatic correction by the simple device of disallowing it. The subject is one which will be dealt with more at length later on.

7. Being an outgrowth of the judicial power to ascertain the existing law, judicial disallowance of a statute does not repeal it, but treats it as void *ab initio* from want of conformance to a "higher law." There is an exception to this, however, in the case of state acts rendered void by the subsequent enactment of a conflicting act of Congress which is otherwise constitutional, or with a treaty made under the authority of the United States. In such a case the state act ceases to have operation only from the going into effect of the act of Congress or of the treaty, and may conceivably be brought into operation again by the repeal or abrogation of the latter.

But an act of Congress or a state act which is found by the Court to be contrary to the Constitution is as if it has never been. In the words of the Court: "An unconstitutional act is not a law. It confers no rights; it imposes no duties. . . . It is, in a legal contemplation, as inoperative as though it had never passed."[32] Such is the view that has usually been taken by the Supreme Court, although state courts have sometimes proceeded on a somewhat different principle.[33]

This question arises: Suppose some of the provisions of a statute to be constitutional and others to be unconstitutional—what becomes of the former when the latter fall under judicial condemnation? The answer depends upon that

---

30. The doctrine that the power of eminent domain may be exercised only for a "public purpose," that is, for a purpose deemed by the Court to be *public*, was stated by Kent in 1816, in Gardner v. Newburg, 2 Johns. Ch. 162 (N.Y. 1816).

31. Cf. McCray v. United States, 195 U.S. 27 (1904); and Bailey v. Drexel Furniture Co., 259 U.S. 20 (1922).

32. Norton v. Shelby C'ty, 118 U.S. 425 (1886).

33. Cf. Allison v. Corker, 67 N.J.L. 596, 52 Atl. 362 (1902); also United States v. Realty Co., 163 U.S. 427 (1896).

returned by the Court to another question: Would the legislature have enacted the constitutional provisions by themselves, divested of the unconstitutional provisions? If the Court's answer to this question is negative, then the whole statute falls to the ground; if affirmative, then the constitutional provisions still stand.[34]

It has become in recent years a rather common practice for legislatures, in enacting elaborate and complex measures, to declare the separate paragraphs thereof independent, and to direct that the holding of any paragraph or part of the statute invalid shall not affect the question of the validity of the rest. Such declarations are apparently regarded as binding by the Court.[35]

8. A further limitation on the exercise of the power of judicial review arises from the doctrine of precedent; but the real force of this limitation in the case of the Supreme Court of the United States is difficult to estimate. Logically the Court should, no doubt, regard its own past interpretations of any law whatsoever. But it the first place, unlike the House of Lords, the Supreme Court has never said that it considered itself absolutely bound by its own previous decisions, while, in the second place, its construction of certain acts of Congress—the Sherman Act is an especially glaring example—has been characterized by anything but hide-bound deference to the logic of decided cases.

That, therefore, the Court should claim equal freedom in relation to the Constitution—a law not amendable by ordinary legislative processes—is not strange. It has, to be sure, decided many cases by reference to the authority of past decisions, but this may have been because it still approved of the reasoning upon which these decisions rest. It has frequently shown itself astute to "distinguish" the case before it from analogous cases previously decided—a method of escape from the thraldom of *stare decisis* recognized by the doctrine itself. Lastly, it has on several occasions, with varying degrees of candor, overruled past decisions, and sometimes it has silently suppressed them.[36]

What, however, do we mean precisely by the word *decision* in this context? Only the finding by the Court that a certain statute was unconstitutional? Or the reading of the Constitution on which this finding was based? Or the line of

34. Cases cited in notes 9 and 24, above; also, Lemke v. Farmer's Grain Co., 258 U.S. 50 (1922).

35. See, e.g., Keller v. Potomac Electric Co., 261 U.S. 428 (1923).

36. Compare the following braces of cases: The Genesee Chief, 12 How. 443 (U.S. 1851), with The Thomas Jefferson, 10 Wheat. 428 (U.S. 1825); Leisy v. Hardin, 135 U.S. 100 (1890), with License Cases, 5 How. 504 (U.S. 1847); Wabash R'y Co. v. Illinois, 118 U.S. 557 (1886), with Peik v. Chicago & N.W. R'y Co., 94 U.S. 164 (1876); Pollock v. Farmers' L. & T. Co., 157 U.S. 429 (1895), with Springer v. United States, 102 U.S. 586 (1880); Lochner v. New York, 198 U.S. 45 (1905), with Bunting v. Oregon, 243 U.S. 426 (1917); Terral v. Burke Construction Co., 257 U.S. 529 (1922), with cases therein cited, the cases cited in note 31, above, with each other. See also C. J. Taft's remarks concerning the Lochner case in his dissenting opinion in Adkins v. Children's Hospital (above, note 4).

reasoning—*ratio decidendi*—by which this reading was justified, involving often a wide range of speculation in the realm of what was described in the previous chapter as constitutional theory? Sometimes, it would seem, we mean one thing and sometimes another. It was Chief Justice Marshall's practice to lay down the most sweeping principles in interpretation of the Constitution; and he not only carried the Court with him ordinarily, but he succeeded in this way in impressing the stamp of his mind upon our constitutional law permanently. On the other hand, the Court which followed him frequently found itself in difficulties when it came to the formulation of an "opinion of the Court," with the result that most of the opinions of this period are hardly more than historical curiosities today.

Practically speaking, that part of an opinion of the Court is *decision* which the Court subsequently treats as such. Nor does this deny the right of a critic to show if he can that any utterance thus invoked by the Court was originally gratuitous, that is, was *obiter dictum*.

At this point we encounter a question which is of much theoretical interest, and which at times has been of considerable practical importance, and may be again. This is the question, to what extent are Congress and the president bound by decisions of the Supreme Court interpretative of the Constitution?[37]

The doctrine of judicial review builds on an act of faith: the notion that the true meaning of the law is a revelation reserved for judges—which means in the constitutional field that the judicial version of the Constitution *is* the Constitution. And since both Congress and the president are bound by the Constitution, it follows that they are bound by the judicial version of it. Or to put the same theory in different terms—it is assumed that judicial interpretation of the Constitution is of such a nature that it does not alter the Constitution, while that of other organs of government may. Whence it follows that if the Constitution is to be supreme, the judicial version of it must be supreme.

But this theory is confronted by another, which asserts, in effect, that the supposed correctness of judicial interpretations of the law, and so of the Constitution, is only an assumption, which holds, moreover, only within the field of judicial power, namely, that of deciding "cases." In other words, the courts are not vested with any power of law interpretation as such, but only incidentally to the discharge of their primary function of adjudication. Indeed, when the law invoked is the Constitution, the very contrary is the fact. For in relation to the Constitution the three departments are "equal," and so are equally entitled to construe the Constitution within their respective fields.

The advantage of the first and older theory is that it assures us of one final authorized version of the Constitution. Its disadvantage is that which was pointed out by Lincoln, in his first Inaugural, when, with the Dred Scott decision in mind, he said:

37. See my *Doctrine of Judicial Review* on this question, at 20–26 and 66–68.

I do not forget the position assumed by some that constitutional questions are to be decided by the Supreme Court, nor do I deny that such decisions must be binding in any case upon the parties to a suit as to the object of that suit, while they are also entitled to a very high respect and consideration in all parallel cases by all other department of the government. . . . At the same time, the candid citizen must confess that if the policy of the Government upon vital questions affecting the whole people is to be irrevocably fixed by decisions of the Supreme Court the instant they are made in ordinary litigation between parties in personal actions, the people will have ceased to be their own rulers, having to that extent practically resigned their government into the hands of that eminent tribunal.''[38]

The second theory, of which Jefferson and Jackson, as well as Lincoln, were at various times exponents, avoid this difficulty, but invites to the opposite one of governmental and administrative anarchy. For if pursued to its logical consequences it would sustain any president in imitating Jackson when he said—or is *said* to have said—''Well, John Marshall has made his decision, now let him enforce it!''—and the decision went unenforced.[39] It would also sustain Congress in using any of its powers—its power, for instance, to enlarge the membership of the Court—in order to overcome an unpopular decision of the Court.

For the working compromise that practice has brought about between these two theories we must turn to the usages of the Constitution—to ''constitutional law'' in the broader sense. The following are the salient points relevant to this issue: (1) It is the duty of the president as chief executive to enforce the decisions of the Court, even when they are grounded on what he may consider mistaken views of the Constitution and the laws. (What his duty is with respect to an act of Congress which he thinks unconstitutional, in the absence of a decision of the Court to the contrary, is dealt with in another connection.) (2) Congress will not, at least in any but the gravest cases, ''swamp'' the Court in order to overcome an unwelcome decision. (3) Judges of the United States are not impeachable for holding mistaken views of the Constitution and laws, although it is possible that a pertinacious adherence to ''error'' might raise a different question. (4) Even in exercising their legislative powers, the president and Congress are prone nowadays to consult the decisions of the Court rather than the Constitution itself; nor does a distinction suggested by Lincoln between a settled course of decision and a sporadic holding—such as he

38. 6 Richardson, *Messages and Papers of the Presidents* 9–10 (1896–99).

39. This remark is credited to Jackson by Greeley, in his 1 *American Conflict* 106 (1866), with reference to Worcester v. Georgia, 6 Pet. 515 (U.S. 1832); but doubt is cast upon its authenticity by Mr. Warren, 2 *The Supreme Court in United States History* 205–26, *passim*. Taney is authority for the statement that ''General Jackson never expressed a doubt as to the duty and the obligation upon him in his executive character to carry into execution any Act of Congress regularly passed, whatever his own opinion might be of the constitutional question.'' *Id*. 224. This is a more dutiful attitude than that which has been displayed by some of Jackson's successors. Mr. Warren contends that no occasion ever arose for the president to bring force to bear in Worcester v. Georgia, inasmuch as the Court never issued a mandate in support of its decision.

believed the Dred Scott decision to be—seem to have been much heeded in this connection.[40]

All in all, therefore, the advantage remains decidedly with the early view which claims for the Supreme Court the *exclusive* power of interpreting the Constitution with *finality.* And yet the Court itself has repeatedly discarded outworn precedents. Why, then, should not a congressman sworn to support the Constitution be free to formulate, and to vote in accordance with, his own independent views thereof when considering the question of the validity of new proposals, particularly if he thinks them to be of serious moment? There could be no great disadvantage, and there might be great advantage, in forcing the Court to reconsider some of the positions it has taken up in the past and to say plainly whether it still adheres to them.

And, of course, whatever weight be assigned the Court's views as controlling the acts of government, it is only the Court's reasoning which can control opinion, and ordinarily the expession of it. While the Constitution, as some one has irreverently remarked, may be for all practical purposes, "the Supreme Court's last guess," it is always open to the critic to point out if he can just why and wherein the Constitution is something else. Thus he may try to show that a particular decision of the Court is not harmonious with the wording of the Constitution as construed according to certain accepted rules, or that it is not harmonious with the ascertainable intentions of the makers of the Constitution, or that it is not harmonious with the logic of past decisions or with the settled conduct of government to date, or again, that it is not harmonious with sound public policy. In short, the critic is free to find the Constitution wherever he wishes to look for it. Whether, however, he has uncovered the truth, in the pragmatist's sense of that which is destined to win out, or a mare's nest, time alone will determine.

Judicial Freedom in Constitutional Interpretation

The course of judicial review has also been influenced by the fact that the Constitution is a written instrument and, furthermore, a written instrument of a particular kind—a legal code.[41]

Underlying judicial interpretation of any code is always the idea which is expressed by Cooley for the Constitution in the claim that it is "an instrument complete in itself."[42] That is to say, the Constitution is furnished with an answer, for those who know how to read it, to every question of governmental

---

40. The attitude displayed by the president and Congress in 1909, in connection with the submission of the Sixteenth Amendment, is instructive in his connection.

41. See further the references given in note 6, above.

42. *Constitutional History of the United States as Seen in the Development of Constitutional Law* 30–31 (1899). Vinogradoff, Jellinek, and Ehrlich all comment on this judicial dogma of the logical completeness of the legal system. See the first mentioned writer's *Historical Jurisprudence,* Introduction 26–27 (1920–22).

power or of private rights against government which can possibly be addressed to it. It is a closed system.

And growing out of this idea is the further assumption that every clause of the Constitution is an available basis of private rights. As Marshall urged in Marbury v. Madison, if the Court may read any part of the Constitution—read it, that is, for the purpose of determining rights under it—why may it not read all parts? It results that the very terms in which governmental power is granted become the basis of judicially enforceable immunities against government. Whether this precise outcome of judicial review was always foreseen by its early advocates may be questionable;[43] but at least it was a development fully accordant with judicial traditions, and the curtailment which it receives from the concept of "political questions" is illogical, rather than otherwise.

It is not my purpose, however, to attempt to set down systematically the rules of documentary and statutory interpretation which the Court has from time to time adapted to interpretation of the Constitution. As we shall have ample reason to conclude, the effort would be largely a wasted one. I purpose instead to discuss the question whether such rules have operated in the long run to restrict the freedom of the Court in interpreting the Constitution, or to enlarge it—a question which at once raises the interesting problem of "judicial legislation."

In drawing a hard and fast line between the function of law-making and that of law-interpreting, and assigning the latter function to the judiciary, the American doctrine of separation of powers tacitly assumes that judicial interpretation leaves the law unaltered. This is the view of Montesquieu himself who speaks of the judges as "no more than the mouth that pronounces the words of the law, mere passive beings, incapable of moderating either its force or its rigor."[44]

On the other hand, even as early as the reign of Elizabeth, we find a certain Bishop Hoadley stating a very different view. "Whoever," he wrote, "hath an absolute authority to interpret any written or spoken laws, it is he who is truly the law-giver to all intents and purposes, and not the person who first wrote them." This sentense is regarded by an eminent American writer of recent times as stating the entire truth of the matter.[45] What are the merits of the question so far as relates to the Supreme Court's interpretation of the Constitution?

43. Compare Hamilton's own attitude in *Federalist* No. 33 with his argument for judicial review in No. 78.

44. 1 *The Spirit of the Laws* 170 (Pritchard's trans.). Marshall uses words of like purport in Osborn v. Bank of the United States, 9 Wheat. 738 (U.S. 1825).

45. John Chipman Gray, *The Nature and Sources of the Law* secs. 229, 276, 369. Professor Gray contended that "all the law is judge-made law," *id.* at 119. This position is based apparently on the assumption that it is impossible for a legislature to speak in terms so unmistakable as not to admit of interpretation. But if that is so, then it is impossible for a Court to lay down a decision in unmistakable terms; and so there is no law! Indeed, Professor Gray seems to have assumed that human communication by language was essentially impossible. As to rules not admiting of interpretation, see some words of Marshall, in Wayman v. Southard, 10 Wheat. 1 (U.S. 1825).

Let it be said at the outset that, speaking by and large, the version of the Constitution with which the Court has furnished us is a remarkably well-knit and coherent fabric, and one which offers, especially for the period before the Civil War, striking contrast with the wild inconsistencies of interpretation in which sections, parties, and individuals freely indulged themselves in those days. If anything, the Court has been *too* consistent; that is to say, it has been consistent on too narrow a basis. Far too often has it permitted itself to be governed by a picture of things as of the time when the Constitution was adopted, thus elbowing aside the truer conception of the Constitution as the source of a polity endowed with a life of its own.

Nor has the Court usually made law at the expense of the rules of logic. Champions of the idea that the judges ought to make law seem sometimes to think that courts are unduly hampered by logic, and that the law would be improved if the judges, taking courage of their convictions, would only thumb their noses at Aristotle.[46] This is sad nonsense. The judicial function is essentially a syllogistic one, and "freedom of judicial decision" is something far more important than freedom to argue badly from accepted premises. It is, in truth, freedom to choose, within limits, the premises themselves; and asserts itself, accordingly, not *after* but *before* the technical grounds of a decision are determined upon. The rules of formal logic are, therefore, its instrument, not its enemy.

That judicial interpretation cannot leave the law unaffected is proved by its very existence. The most ancient maxim of statutory interpretation is that the will of the makers of the statute should govern.[47] Yet were this clear for all situations, as undoubtedly it may be for many, there would be no necessity for interpretation. In theory, the law-maker had a definite intention respecting every case; in fact, he had no intention at all respecting most of the cases that get into court, and that is why they get there. And as regards the Constitution, this consideration has unusual force, first, because its makers deliberately left many questions to the hazards of interpretation; and secondly, because of the lapse of time since then—a period abounding in social and industrial developments which could not possibly have been foreseen in 1787. Nor should the testimony of the doctrine of *stare decisis* be altogether overlooked on this point. Why should a Court pay any attention to precedents if it did not regard them as modifying in some measure the statute which they interpret?

We now return to the questions suggested above: Has the Court's adaptation

46. The volume entitled *Science of Legal Method* in the Modern Legal Philosophy Series (1921) contains many such attacks on judicial adherence to logic, by continental writers. That bad logic, however, played a part in the development of constitutional law is obvious; but whether it was an indispensable means of arriving at some of the results reached is another question. Perhaps it was sometimes. The opinions in the Pollack Case (above, note 9), the Sugar Trust Case (above, note 2), and the first Child Labor Case, 247 U.S. 251 (1918), taken together, leave few of the rules of formal logic inviolate.

47. See Plucknett, *Statutes and Their Interpretation in the Thirteenth Century* (1924).

of the rules of documentary and statutory interpretation to its task of constitutional interpretation served to cramp its freedom in the latter field? Fortunately, we do not need to consider all these rules; at the outset the most fundamental one will suffice. This is the rule that the words of a statute or instrument should be given their "ordinary meaning."[48] In the case of the Constitution, however, the question at once arises, whether this is the ordinary meaning of 1789 or the present year of grace? The divergence is, naturally, at times a very broad one.

Previously to the Civil War the Court commonly invoked the shades of the men of 1789 as aids in interpretation. Subsequently it has gradually dropped this piety. On one occasion we even find it saying, with reference to the commerce clause, "the reasons which may have caused the framers of the Constitution to repose the power to regulate interstate commerce in Congress do not . . . affect or limit the extent of the power itself."[49] And long before the Civil War the Court, especially under Marshall, had imputed intentions to the framers which in fact removed the business of interpreting the Constitution far from the field of historical research.

In brief, the task of ascertaining the "ordinary meaning" of the words of the Constitution has produced two canons, of constitutional interpretation. One we may term *historical interpretation;* the other *adaptative interpretation.*[50]

Of the former no better statement could be asked than the following expression from Chief Justice Taney's opinion in the Dred Scott Case:[51] "As long as it [the Constitution] continues to exist in its present form, it speaks not only the same words, but with the same meaning and intent with which it spoke when it came from the hands of its framers and was voted on and adopted by the people of the United States. Any other rule of construction would abrogate the judicial character of this Court, and make it the mere reflex of the popular opinion or passion of the day."

With this passage compare a passage from Chief Justice Marshall's opinion in McCulloch v. Maryland:[52] "These words occur in a Constitution which was designed to endure for ages to come and consequently to be adapted to the various crises of human affairs." And again, the words of Chief Justice Waite in Pensacola Telegraph Company v. The Western Union Co.:[53] "The powers thus granted [by the Constitution to Congress] are not confirmed to the instrumentalities of Congress or the postal system known or in use when the Constitution was adopted, but they keep pace with the progress of the country and adapt themselves to the new developments of time and circumstances."

The moral of all this for judicial freedom of decision is fairly obvious. In all

48. C. J. Marshall, in Gibbons v. Ogden, 9 Wheat. 1 (U.S. 1824).
49. Addystone Pipe and Steel Co. v. United States, 175 U.S. 211 (1899).
50. The terms used by Vinogradoff are "historical" and "widening" interpretation. *Common Sense in Law* 134, 137 (1914).
51. Scott v. Sanford, 19 How. 393 (U.S. 1857).
52. 4 Wheat. 316 (U.S. 1819).
53. 96 U.S. 1 (1877).

cases in which two opposed canons of constitutional construction, leading to contrary results, compete for the Court's recognition, the Court is furnished from the outset with a double set of answers to choose between. It is true, however, that as between the two canons of construction just dealt with, the historical and the adaptative, its freedom of choice is today somewhat less broad than it once was, past decisions having delimited to some extent the fields within which they are respectively applicable.

Thus it will be generally found that words which refer to governing institutions, like "jury," "legislature," "election" have been given their strictly historical meaning,[54] while words defining the subject-matter of power or of rights like "commerce," "liberty," "property," have been deliberately moulded to the views of contemporary society.[55] Nor is the reason for this difference hard to discover. Not only are words of the former category apt to have the more definite, and so more easily ascertainable, historical denotation, but the Court may very warrantably feel that if the people wish to have their governmental institutions altered, they should go about the business in accordance with the forms laid down by the basic institution. Questions of power or of right, on the other hand, are apt to confront the Court with problems that are importunate for solution.

But this is far from disposing of the question of freedom of decision in relation to constitutional interpretation. For one thing, the Court has achieved some of its most striking results by actually switching from one canon of interpretation to the other.[56] Again, the Court's option between historical and adaptative interpretation is by no means the only option which the maxims of constitutional construction afford it. It has a similar choice between "exclusive" and "inclusive" interpretation;[57] and the contest between "loose" and "strict" construction is, of course, historical. Indeed, it is improbable that the Constitution has ever been brought into contact with a single rule of construc-

54. See Thompson v. Utah, 170 U.S. 343 (1895); Hawke v. Smith, 253 U.S. 221 (1920); Newberry v. United States, 256 U.S. 232 (1921). Historical interpretation often consists in assigning terms their common law signification. See United States v. Wilson, 7 Pet. 150 (U.S. 1833); also United States v. Wong Kim Ark, 169 U.S. 649 (1898), and cases there cited.

55. See notes 48, 52, and 53, above; also Allgeyer v. Louisiana, 165 U.S. 578 (1897); Truax v. Raich, 239 U.S. 33 (1915); Truax v. Corrigan, 257 U.S. 312 (1921).

56. Thus in early years the Court under Marshall assigned to the term "maritime jurisdiction" its fixed common law sense. But later this definition was found unsuitable to American conditions, and was abandoned by the Court speaking through Chief Justice Taney. And the construction of the "due process of law" has had a similar history, leading to even more remarkable consequences. See the first brace of cases in note 36, above; also Hurtado v. California, 110 U.S. 516 (1884).

57. Exclusive interpretation is grounded on the maxim *unius expressio, exclusio alterius*—the mention of one thing rules out all others of the same kind. Following this maxim in Marbury v. Madison, Marshall held that the enumeration in Article 3 of the cases in which the Supreme Court has original jurisdiction must be considered exclusive; otherwise, he asserted, "it would have no force." Yet in McCulloch v. Maryland he repelled the suggestion that because Congress is expressly authorized by the Constitution to enact penal laws in only three instances, it had no "implied" power to enact them for other cases also.

tion to the Court's manipulation of which there have not been exceptions,[58] and it goes without saying that the final judge of whether the rule or the exception shall be followed in any particular case is the Court itself.

Nor should the tendency of precedent to curtail the scope of judicial freedom of decision be too much insisted upon, least of all in the field of constitutional law. If precedent is a hurdle, it is also a screen. Once choice has been made between two lines of decisions, supporting perhaps two alternative rules of construction, the new decision becomes immediately assimilated to the line selected, with the result that every appearance of choice on the part of the Court becomes automatically occulted. Hence no doubt, the fervent denials by judges that courts make law; hence, too, the mask of fatality which has baffled critics of judge-made law from time immemorial.

To sum up: *Interpretation* consists of making clear the application of a rule of law in a situation as to which its application was not clear before. The only escape from the conclusion that this process involves a certain degree of law-making is the untenable notion that the judges enjoy a revelation of the authentic law. In the case of the Constitution of the United States its official interpreters are able to claim an unusual freedom of decision, both because of the generality of the language employed in that instrument, and also because of the variety and the contrariety in the rules of construction which have grown up about it. And if freedom of decision is sometimes hampered by precedent, it is sometimes assisted thereby, in consequence of the concealment which precedent can lend it.

The Purpose and Method of Constitutional Interpretation

Three questions remain, all closely related: First, what kind of considerations have governed the Court in its choice of the alternatives open to it in constitutional interpretation? Secondly, by which of the methods best known to formal logic—the "deductive" or the "inductive"—have such considerations usually been imported into constitutional law? Thirdly, what has been the final outcome of the method followed?

---

58. For instance, we are told that the Constitution contains no repetitious language. Calder v. Bull (above, note 18); Hurtado v. California (above, note 56). But strict adherence to this principle would today invalidate some of the most important branches of constitutional law, that, for example, dealing with railway rate legislation in relation to the Fourteenth Amendment. We learn that exceptions to a power serve to mark its limits. Brown v. Maryland (above, note 16). But we also learn that there are exceptions to exceptions. Cf. Cohens v. Virginia (above, note 16) and Hans v. Louisiana, 134 U.S. 1 (1889), in relation to the Eleventh Amendment. Again, we learn that an exception to a power should be narrowly construed. Hylton v. United States (above, note 10). Then we find the very exception alluded to broadly construed. The Pollock Case (above, note 9). Yet again, we are told by Chief Justice Marshall that "questions of power do not depend on the degree to which it may be exercised." Brown v. Maryland (above, note 16). But the abandonment of this principle in some of the most important provinces of constitutional law has within recent decades affected its fundamental transformation, particularly as it touches state power.

Writing with the common law in mind, Justice Holmes has said:

> The life of the law has not been logic: it has been experience.... The law embodies the story of a nation's development through many centuries, and it cannot be dealt with as if it contained only the axioms and corollaries of a book of mathematics.

And again:

> In substance the growth of the law is legislative. And this in a deeper sense than that what the courts declare to have always been the law is in fact new. It is legislative in its grounds. The very considerations which judges most rarely mention, and always with apology, are the secret root from which the law draws all the juices of life. I mean, of course, considerations of what is expedient for the community concerned. Every important principle which is developed by litigation is at fact and at bottom the result of more or less definitely understood views of public policy; most generally, to be sure, under our practice and traditions, the unconscious result of instinctive preferences and inarticulate convictions, but none the less traceable to views of public policy in the last analysis.[59]

Considerations of public policy also underlie American constitutional law, but whether they are *inarticulate* is another matter. Usually they purport to be highly articulate in such terms as "freedom of contract," "judicial independence," "freedom of commerce," "police power," and the like. Unfortunately, not only are such phrases often vague and jejeune, but the values which they connote are frequently more or less contradictory. So the queston arises whether the Court's employment of them may not conceal more than it reveals— whether, in other words, they may not serve, with or without the conscious intention of their users, as instruments for converting the unstated preferences and biases of individual judges into law.

The possibility must be admitted, and it is fairly plain that it has been occasionally realized. Yet, on the whole, the average Supreme Court justice seems to have taken his constitutional theory pretty seriously. Nor is it necessarily an argument to the contrary that in the more or less inchoate mass of ideas covered by this term are many which, when pressed to logical extremes, collide with one another. The most ordinary function of a high court is to mark off the fields of jurisdicton of conflicting principles of law. In the field of constitutional law the Court has evidently felt that one of its highest duties was so to adjust the claims of the conflicting principles which are thought to find embodiment in the Constitution as to prevent any of them from being crowded to the wall.

Instructive in this connection is a glance at the history of our constitutional law. It will be seen at once to fall into successive periods demarked from each other by the coming to ascendency on the bench of certain large generalized ideas of policy, which then continue to sway the bench often for years. Thence,

59. *The Common Law* 1, 35–36 (1881).

indeed, far more than from the doctrine of *stare decisis,* arises that substantial coherency which was noted earlier as characterizing the Court's version of the Constitution. Marshall deemed himself the apostle-elect of the nationalistic and individualistic creed of the framers of the Constitution. The Court under Taney represented the frontier reaction of the period of Jackson toward localism and notions of popular sovereignty, which also chanced to fall in well with the property interests of the slave-owning South. Then came a Court which felt the urge to repair the damage which had been wrought by the Civil War to the federal equilibrium; and after that a bench which thought all wisdom to be summed up in the teachings of the laissez faire political economists, the contemporary creed of the universities and of budding big business. In the past at least, before judicial ideas of public policy have been able to obtain solid foothold in American constitutional law, they have generally had to be accredited by some kind of political or social philosophy linking them with traditional American ideals of social order.

Nor is the attitude of the present Court essentially different from that of its predecessors. As heir of the past the Court is comfortably free to dispense with creative effort of the most striking sort. It is also, perhaps, a less "naif" bench than some that have gone before it; that is to say, is better aware of and more ready to confess both the opportunities and the responsibilities that fall to it in the way of law-making. Still this is all a matter of method rather than of fundamental purpose. The values safeguarded by the Court remain singularly the same they have always been; only their inter-relations have changed, the patterns which they make in the law having become, necessarily, more and more complex with the growing complexity of the social order itself.

2. And this brings us to the further question of the nature of the logical method pursued in judicial legislation. On this point some recently expressed views of Dean Pound are directly relevant.[60]

"Law begins," Dean Pound writes, "with definite detailed *rules* whereby a definite detailed consequence is attached to a definite detailed state of facts." Later with the increasing complexity of social organization, "other types of legal *precept* are required." Thus "the legal *principle*" makes its appearance, through a comparison of legal rules and the discovery of the distinctions between them. "For example, it is a rule that 'no state shall make anything but gold or silver coin a legal tender in the payment of debts.' It is a principle that whenever a power is given by a constitution, the grant carries with it by implication whatever is necessary to make the power effective." Nor is this the end of development. Presently legal *conceptions* appear, that is, "a generalized type of situation of fact is defined and established as a legal *institution.* . . . In constitutional law we have an example of a legal conception in the so-called

---

60. *The Supreme Court and the Minimum Wage* Introduction xvi–xx (1925). The italics are supplied by the present writer.

police power. The Constitution says nothing of such a power. It is a conception worked out by the courts.''

Then, ''in the maturity of the law still another type of legal precept grows up, namely, one establishing a *standard* to be applied to conduct.'' Thus ''in the everyday law of private relations'' we have the ''standard of due care which the common law imposes upon anyone who enters upon any course of action,'' while ''in constitutional law we have such a standard''—applicable to legislative and executive action—''in 'due process of law.' ''

Nor, Dean Pound continues, may we stop at this point. For in addition to legal precepts, there is also ''the traditional technique'' of the courts in ''developing and applying'' these, whereby they ''are eked out, extended, restricted, and adapted to the exigencies of the administration of justice.'' Furthermore, into every system of law enters ''a body of traditional or received ideals as to the nature of politically organized society and the purpose of the legal ordering of human relations, and hence as to what legal precepts should obtain . . . and how they should be applied.'' This element of our constitutional law has already been referred to under the designation of constitutional theory; and Dean Pound adds that it is an element which changes but slowly, though ''it does change with social, economic, and political development.''[61]

A passing word of comment is due Dean Pound's terminology. It is not to be supposed that he would insist upon its complete precision, or at any rate, its indispensability. Thus a ''principle,'' as he uses the term, would seem, in final analysis, to be only a more generalized ''rule,'' and a ''standard'' a more flexible one; and the line to be drawn between the content of any two of these terms must be often a very uncertain one. Nor is a legal ''conception,'' as he defines it, a thing apart; the very example he gives, the police power, can be phrased as the legal rule or principle that the state has power to promote the general welfare.

Of greater importance is the question raised as to the manner in which constitutional law has developed. While recognizing the controlling and durable

61. Worth quoting, too, is Dean Pound's application of these views to the question of judicial criticism. ''Critics of constitutional decisions,'' he asserts,

> seeing that something gets into those decisions continually which they cannot find in the texts, take the perfectly legitimate and, indeed, necessary resort of of the judiciary to this element of the law for ''usurpation.'' On the other hand those who defend the whole course of decision of the courts on the constitutionality of social legislation, and every item of it, ignore this element and assume that in all such decisions the courts have been applying rules of law analogous to the rule that Congress shall not pass an act of attainder or that a state shall not emit bills of credit. They assume that all such decisions have flowed inevitably, by a logical process, from the absolutely given content of constitutonal texts. The one view is no more mistaken than the other. It is no criticism of the courts to point out that they constantly resort to the third or ideal element of law, whether consciously or not. They must do so. Where they are sometimes open to criticism is that they give little or no consideration to this important and often controlling element in what they do, and hence speak dogmatically about matters very much open to dispute without adequate canvassing of the materials of their opinions. [*Id.*, xx]

influence of constitutional theory on the content of constitutional law, Dean Pound nevertheless strongly implies that the method of "growth" of the latter, like that usually attributed to the common law,[62] has been what the logicians call "inductive," that is to say, has been from the particular to the general, and has taken place in consequence of a comparison and summation of numerous particulars. Thus it seems a fair inference from his remarks that not only are the "rules" of constitutional law to be taken as corresponding to an older type of legal precept than its "principles," but also that the latter have frequently risen from judicial manipulation of the former, if in fact they could have arisen in any other way.

Such an account of the matter would, nevertheless, be quite erroneous, as regards most of the great leading principles, conceptions, and standards of our constitutional law. Instead of being due to the process of comparison and induction pictured by Dean Pound, they seem in almost every instance to be traceable to some general phrase or statement in the Constitution itself, approached from a selected rule of construction, or to repesent a direct transplantation from constitutional theory. They are, therefore, the outcome of *deduction,* in the sense of the spontaneous recognition by the Court of the presence in the situation before it of some antecedent principle or doctrine; or indeed, of *creation,* in a sense elsewhere suggested by Dean Pound himself, in the assertion that "except as an act of omnipotence creation does not mean the making of something out of nothing," but the reshaping of existing materials to new uses.[63]

Such certainly is the case with the Court's conception of "commerce," of "liberty," of "police power," of "necessary and proper," of "obligation of contract," of "due process of law." The issuance of every one of these as a citable legal principle can be assigned with fair accuracy to a specific judicial utterance in which it sprang from the forehead of the Court full grown.[64] Nor

62. The contrast which Ehrlich points out in his *Juristische Logik* between the development of the common law and law on the Continent, on the basis of the codified Roman law, is essentially that between the inductive and deductive methods. The following statement from Dicey, *Introduction to the Law of the Constitution,* illustrates the same contrast: "If it be allowable to apply the formulas of logic to questions of law, the difference . . . between the Constitution of Belgium and the English Constitution may be described by the statement that in Belgium individual rights are deductions drawn from the principles of the Constitution, whilst in England the so-called principles of the Constitution are inductions or generalizations based upon particular decisions pronounced by the Courts as to the rights of given individuals." *Id.,* 193 (7th ed. 1908). Tennyson's phrase about English liberty "broadening from precedent to precedent" expresses the same theory so far as the English Constitution is concerned. The accuracy of the theory is, nevertheless, open to grave doubt. It is to be suspected that it has owed much of its vogue to the Darwinian theory of the evolution of species by minute accretions and rests on just about as secure a foundation. Large speculative ideas have played a greater role in the development of British liberties than is generally admitted.

63. *Interpretations of Legal History* 127 (1923).

64. For "commerce," see Gibbons v. Ogden (above, note 48); for "liberty" Allgeyer v. Louisiana (above, note 55); for "police power," Charles River Bridge Co. v. Warren Bridge Co.,

have subsequent decisions generally enlarged the scope of these original conceptions; although they have sometimes pared them down, in accordance with what Dean Pound has termed "judicial technique."

And it is much the same even with what may be termed the intermediate precepts of constitutional law, those which have resulted from the Court's endeavors to adjust the broader conceptions and principles just mentioned to one another. That the Court has frequently derived needed principles of demarkation and differentiation from a consultation of precedents admits of no doubt. Still, it is true, that to a remarkable extent these have been drawn from the Court's own invention or from its borrowings from other branches of the law. That is to say, the subordinate principles of constitutional law are also, in no small measure, the product of adaptative creation, and of deduction in the sense just given. They spring from the covergence upon particular situations of already established conceptions, doctrines, principles; and denote, consequently, a logical progression from the more to the less general, not vice versa.[65]

But has not the Court itself sometimes said that it works by the "process of inclusion and exclusion" and by "pricking out lines" with successive decisions as the cases arise? It has; yet actually the fruitfulness of the method thus hinted in stateable principles of law—in the broader data of legal prophecy—is most especially open to doubt in the very field of constitutional decision with reference to which such assertions have been most frequent.

It was in 1877 that the Court, declining an invitation to be more explicit, said it would have to determine the meaning of the due process of law clause of the Fourteenth Amendment by "the judicial process of inclusion and exclusion."[66] Since then not far from a thousand cases have come before the Court involving the same clause. This of itself is eloquent of the persistent hazards attending prediction as to its meaning; and in fact the tests with which it confronts important categories of state legislation are probably less susceptible of practical statement today than ever before.

In this connection passing notice should be paid the *legal maxim*—the axiomatic statement of supposed elementary principles of justice. Some of these have played a considerable role in the development of our constitutional law. An illustration is the saying that "the legislature may not take the property

---

2 Pet. 420 (U.S. 1837); for "necessary and proper," McCulloch v. Maryland (above, note 52); for "obligation of contract," Fletcher v. Peck (above, note 10); for "due process of law," Hurtado v. California (above, note 56).

65. I am thinking particularly of the Court's application of the commerce clause as a restriction on state power. The "original package" doctrine is an instance of judicial inventiveness. The "unit" rule of taxation was transplanted from the law of taxation. The rule against taxation of gross receipts of concerns engaged in interstate commerce is a deduction through two stages from the general principle that a state cannot regulate interstate commerce. As an instance of "induction" may be mentioned the principle that transportation, or the immediate prospect of it, is a necessary ingredient of "commerce."

66. Justice Miller, in Davidson v. N.O., 96 U.S. 97 (1877).

of A and give it to B without A's consent"; another, the doctrine that no law should be given a retrospective interpretation at the expense of vested rights.[67] These and certain derivatives—for instance, the doctrine that taxation must be for a "public purpose"—were, before the Fourteenth Amendment was adopted, constitutional waifs, which since then have been gathered by the Court under the hospitable roof of the due process clause.[68] Yet even when axioms of this character tend to standardize the application of the clause, it is obvious that their recognition by the Court cannot be said to represent a triumph for judicial "inclusion and exclusion," but is only a fresh instance of transplantation and adaptative creation.

The fact is that the phrase "judicial process of inclusion and exclusion" is of far greater significance for the confession than for the promise which it imports. This is that the Court is really acting without there being any stateable rule of law at hand. And this, no doubt, is what Dean Pound has in mind in characterizing due process of law as a "standard." But even a *standard* implies stateable tests. Whether the modern doctrine of due process of law as "reasonable law" confronts the state legislature with stateable test is altogether doubtful. Mr. Justice Brandeis has said recently that the Constitution's present application of it makes of the Court a "super-legislature"[69]—a species of third house of every state legislature in the Union. Yet, it is, curiously, almost exactly the formula for judicial review which Coke suggested in 1612, before written constitutions had been thought of!

3. The final outcome of the Court's law-making in the constitutional field has been, therefore, to supersede, to a degree, the relatively predictable control of constitutional law with a discretionary superintendence of the Court—which answers our third question. Constitutional limitations in an important field of the law have been put in solution; but judicial review has, in consequence, been transferred to a broader basis than ever. By the same token, and in the same measure, the Court has resigned its *constituent* role for that of *legislation*—and this in face of the doctrine of the separation of powers on which judicial review rests! Nor can it be doubted that this result owes much to the Court's *a priori* and deductive method. In the presence of the complexities of modern industrial society, judicial review was forced to adopt *one* premise which would afford an eligible recourse when others proved too rigid. Confronted with the alternative of expanding or perishing, it chose the former.

To sum up: Judicial review arose out of the American doctrine to the separation of powers; and this doctrine still dictates the occasions of its exercise, to wit, in connection with the decision of cases. Yet too much might

67. See. e.g., Justice Chase's opinion in Calder v. Bull (above, note 18).
68. Compare Loan Association v. Topeka, 20 Wall. 655 (U.S. 1875), with Fallbrook Irrigation Co. v. Bradley, 164 U.S. 112 (1896).
69. Burns Baking Co. v. Bryan, 264 U.S. 504 (1924). Cf. Weaver v. Palmer Brothers Co., decided March 8th, last {270 U.S. 402 (1926)}.

easily be made of this fact, for the extended use of the injunction renders this limitation upon the availability of judicial review of much less moment than it once was. As to the implication of the doctrine of the separation of powers that interpretation of the law, and so of the Constitution, does not change it—that was never anything more than a pious fiction; while today, in consequence of the supersession of predictable rules in important fields of constitutional law by the vague standard which is connoted by the term "due process of law," judicial review has come to vest the Court with an almost undefined power of inhibitory guidance of state legislative policy. In brief, the entire history of judicial review is that of the progessive relaxation of the restraints which are implied in its doctrinal foundation.

On the other hand, the deference which constitutional usage today renders the doctrine of judicial review is, perhaps, more exacting than ever before, claiming as it does for the Court's reading of the Constitution finality not only as to *cases* but also as to *questions*. And this fact offers pre-eminent proof of the political conservatism of the American people; for the values which are safeguarded by judicial review remain essentially the same they have always been. It is from this cause that the general coherency of our constitutional law for the most part proceeds. The Court has seen the Constitution steadily and it has seen it whole. Indeed, the really important criticism to be made of the Court is that it has centered its attention too exclusively upon the document and the rights thought to be embodied therein, and has given but casual and incidental heed to the nature of the legal order thus implied and its relevancy to the times.[70]

70. See Pound, *Spirit of the Common Law* 203–4 (1921).

8. Reorganization of the Federal Judiciary

THE CHAIRMAN [SENATOR HENRY ASHURST]. The committee observes the presence of Professor Edward S. Corwin of Princeton University. . . .

Mr. CORWIN. I am going to speak about my reaction and reflections on the president's proposal. When I first saw the *New York Times* with the headlines announcing it I was a bit startled. On further reflection I became convinced that the president has grasped the realities of the situation. I have not read anything or found anything in the course of the various discussions that have taken place that has led me to change that opinion; rather I have been confirmed in it.

I think the realities of the situation are these: In the first place, the doctrines of constitutional law of the majority of the Court involve the entire program of the administration in a fog of doubt as to constitutionality; and second, that cloud of doubt can be dispelled within a reasonable time only by reestablishing that mode of reading the Constitution which adapts it to present needs in harmony with its intent as announced by its earliest expounders, that it should "endure for ages to come, and consequently be adapted to various crises in human affairs." Those are the words of Chief Justice Marshall. And also in harmony with the idea that the Constitution was intended for an "indefinite and expanding future."

The controlling majority of the Court has turned its back upon this point of view. Also, it has forgotten the principal maxim to which the Court adhered for nearly a hundred years, that all reasonable doubts are to be resolved in favor of challenged legislation.

Senator Beveridge, in his book on *The State of the Nation,* said:

> When five able and learned judges think one way, and four equally able and learned judges all on the same bench think the other way, and express their dissent

Reprinted from *Reorganization of the Federal Judiciary,* U.S. Congress, Senate, Committee on the Judiciary, 75th Cong., 1st sess., 1937, pt. 2, on S. 1392.

in powerful argument and sometimes with warm feeling, is it not obvious that the law in question is not a plain infraction of the written Constitution beyond any question?

There is no doubt but that many parts of the New Deal could have been sustained on the basis of doctrines which have been approved by the Court in the past, doctrines equally reputable—more reputable—than the doctrines by which it was overthrown. Modern principles of constitutional law confront the Court with great political questions. It is desirable that they should be decided by men whose social philosophy is modern; at least, by men who are willing to pursue a hands-off policy unless clearly agreed principles leave them no option but to interfere.

The present Court has not been content to do that. It has repeatedly, when it had a free choice, chosen the alternative which set it against the other branches of the government. And why? There is only one explanation that fits the situation. It has been endeavoring to elevate into constitutional law a particular economic bias of its own; the theory of political economy that government must keep its hands off of business and, particularly, must not interfere with the relations of employer and employee. The latter, it would have us believe, were placed by the Constitution beyond the reach of Government in this country, either state or national. You see the situation in Detroit resulting from that philosophy.

Now, I wish to speak briefly about the possibility of meeting the situation by amendment. That method is very hazardous. The Gallup poll revealed the fact that the child-labor amendment is favored by 76 percent of the voters, by a majority in every state, and by 83 percent of the voters of the state of New York, but it was recently defeated in that state. It has been pending for thirteen years and is still a long way from being ratified. No doubt the constitutional-convention method might prove more feasible, but one-twenty-fifth of the population in thirteen states can defeat an amendment. The people who talk about an amendment being the only square and honest way to meet the situation should answer this question: Suppose an amendment is clearly desired by a majority of the people, and still is defeated; what are they going to do about it? Do they have any plan in respect to that? Many of the amendments within recent years were the culmination of long-drawn-out periods of agitation reaching back as far as the Civil War. To rely solely on an amendment, to make that the sole reliance, would be extremely hazardous. If the president's proposal succeeds, the resisting power of those who are likely to resist amendments will be so weakened that it will not be as effective as it would be otherwise. They will be more apt to listen to reason, and it is possible that the extravagances of the campaign agaist the child-labor amendment, which involves the idea that the political branches are not to be trusted to use common sense, will be somewhat diminished.

What form is the amendment to take? Adding power to Congress? What powers are to be added? And what is to happen to the amendments, once they are within the Constitution? Are they to be exposed to the same type of interpretation as made them necessary in the first place? If so, how long will these amendements prove sufficient? If liberal principles and constitutional interpretations are reestablished, on the other hand, an amendment may not be necessary. Let us give the Constitution a chance to function.

Amendments sometimes prove disappointing. The Eleventh Amendment has not prevented the frustration of state administration by federal injunctions. In the St. Louis Stockyards case, Justice Brandeis mentioned one case of a public utility regulation which had been in suspension fifteen years, another thirteen and a half years, another seven years, another six years; although finally sustained by the Supreme Court, they had in the meantime been in suspension on account of injunctions. Theoretically, such an injunction cannot issue. Theoretically, an injuncton issues against a state officer only when he is exceeding his power.

The Sixteenth Amendment has proved somewhat a disappointment. Clarifying amendments have been suggested by some. What form are they to take? Here we have this principle of due process of law, in respect to depriving persons of life, liberty, or property. That was put into the Constitution in 1792, and was intended to apply to a man indicted by a grand jury. Is that to be stricken out entirely? How about the policy that the legislature may not delegate its power? That is not mentioned in the Constitution but it has been brought forward as an objection to enactments of Congress since a comparatively early date. But not until the "hot oil" cases was an act of Congress set aside on that ground. Is that policy to be set aside entirely, or is it to be left as it is, or is it to be qualified? It seems to me these are matters that are very difficult for the amendment process to handle, which, in fact, is a very unsatisfactory method of construing the Constitution. I believe the effect of these interpretations of the Constitution, when applied by an illiberal and interfering bench, is to frustrate the law and the intention of the Constitution.

Senator CONNALLY. When you say "law" do you mean statute law?

Mr. CORWIN. I mean statute law. I say that the result is to frustrate the law and the intention of the Constitution.

The president's proposal has centered attention on the Court, and rightly so. The present situation is not due to the inadequacy of the Constitution, but is due to interpretations of the Constitution by the Court which do not meet present-day needs.

In the second place, the president's proposal, or something equivalent to it, was required to correct a serious unbalance in the Constitution resulting from the undue extension of judicial review.

The Dred Scott case was the first case in which the Court began to apply constitutional tests not statable in plain language. The first Legal Tender decision was an example of the same sort of doctrine producing a situation which had to be met by somewhat special means. Within the last forty or fifty years the Court has in the exercise of judicial review dissolved every limitation upon the exercise of its power. I want to read in that connection a statement of Professor {Thomas Reed} Powell in 1932:

> Nine men in Washington have a pretty arbitrary power to annual any statute or ordinance or administrative order that is properly brought before them. The power is an arbitrary power, even though it may {not?} be arbitrarily exercised. It is arbitrary in the sense that in the last analysis it is exercised as five or more of the nine men think best.
>
> The Supreme Court can hardly be said to be controlled by the Constitution because so seldom does the Constitution clearly dictate a decision. It is not controlled by its own precedents, for it feels free to overrule them. It feels even more free to make distinctions that no sensible person would think of making except to avoid confession that a precedent is being disregarded. All this remains true even though in most of the cases it is also true that applicable precedents are either followed or are not there to be invoked. The Supreme Court does what it prefers to do when it prefers to do as nearly as possible what it has done before.

Of course, we have ample testimony from the bench itself as to the illimitable character of judicial review. We have the statement of Chief Justice Hughes in Elmira in 1908. "We live under the Constitution but the Constitution is what the judges say it is." And Senator Borah's statement in February 1930, in the debate on the approval of the nomination of Mr. Hughes for chief justice, that the Supreme Court had made itself "economic dictator of the United States." And Justice McReynolds' statement in the Nebbia case that the Court must pass on the wisdom {of} statutes; Justice Stone's statement in the A. A. A. case that the Court is subject only to its own sense of self-restraint, while the other branches of the government are subject to the courts; and so on and so forth. These might be multiplied.

You have only to look to the facts to see that these statements are justifiable. Compare, for example, the attitude of the Court toward the doctrine that the delegated powers of the United States are limited by the nondelegated powers, the reserved powers, of the states.

Are the delegated powers of the United States limited by the nondelegated powers? Not in 234 U.S.; not in the Shreveport case. However, in the Carter case and the N. R. A. case and the A. A. A. case, there the delegated powers of the United States are limited by the nondelegated powers of the United States.

Take this doctrine of "direct" versus "indirect" effects. That is the pivot on which the N. I. R. A. case and the Carter case turn. It comes from the Sugar Trust case, in which the Court said that any effects reaching interstate commerce from conditions surrounding production were "indirect," "however inevitable and whatever their extent"; and were therefore beyond the reach of Congress.

Now, that doctrine is revived in the N. I. R. A. case and in the Carter case.

In the meantime, Mr. Taft had written a book on the antitrust law, in which, in commenting on the Sugar Trust case and the Swift case, which followed ten years after, said the latter had virtually overruled the former. And when he became chief justice, Mr. Taft had occasion to pass on this question of the power of Congress over effects which reach interstate commerce from activities within the states, and in 258 and 259 and 262 U.S., he expressed himself as follows:

> This Court certainly will not substitute its judgment for that of Congress in such
> a matter unless subject to interstate commerce and its effect upon' it is clearly
> nonexistent.

That is 1923, and in 1934 we get a different doctrine; we go back to the Sugar Trust case. Little wonder, therefore, that Justice Holmes, in speaking of the Court's decision in constitutional cases, spoke of the Court's "sovereign prerogative of choice."

I might give you a little history of section 3224 of the Revised Statutes. That is most instructive of the way in which the Court has released itself from all legal limitations within recent years—all statable limitations. This section forbids any court of the United States to entertain any proceeding enjoining the collection of any tax of the United States. In Snyder v. Marks (109 U.S.), about 1887 or 1888, the Supreme Court said that that meant what it said, and left the suit against the collector of the taxes the sole remedy.

In the Pollock case, the Court continued to pay deference to the section, but permitted an evasion of it by taking jurisdiction of a suit brought by a stockholder against his company, his bank, which was enjoined from paying the tax.

Then in 240 U.S. in the Brushaber case, you get a similar device for evading the section.

In Dodge v. Brady, 240 U.S. the same volume, you get considered "arguendo" by Chief Justice White, the contention that this provision does not mean what it says, but merely forbids an injunction where there is no ground for an injunction in equity. This is considered "arguendo."

In 259 U.S., Hill v. Wallace, you find the Court granting a double-barreled injunction, an injunction against the payment of the tax by the company, and on the other hand an injunction accompaying that against the collector. And then finally in Miller v. Standard Nut Margarine Company, you have the Court making the statement that all that this section does is to forbid the issuance of an injunction on the sole contention that the tax law is unconstitutional. There must be some ground in equity, also. Well, of course, an injunction is an equity remedy. Nobody ever contended, I suppose, that an injunction could issue unless there was some ground in equity for it.

Justice Stone and one other justice dissented, contending that section 3224 meant what it said. But it was too late.

Well, that history is interesting, because it does show the tendency of judicial decisions in the last forty years by which the Court has put its power in the supervision of legislation beyond statable limits.

So it is my own belief that Mr. Roosevelt did a good thing to fall back upon the Constitution and to summon forth from the document itself an indisputable power in Congress, capable of correcting this unduly extended power of the Court.

It must be remembered that the framers of the Constitution were brought up on Locke and Blackstone, whose very definition of constitutional government was a government in which the legislative power is virtually supreme. Judicial review was at first confined to a pretty definite basis. But there were those who early came to see its possibilities, and when they did so they drew back from it.

Here is what Madison said—now, Madison in the Convention of 1787 had accepted the idea of judicial review. Then came this discussion between Yates of New York and Hamilton over the question whether this power existed or not. This was carried on in January and February of 1788 in the columns of New York newspapers. Hamilton stated his views in the *Federalist* 78 and *Federalist* 81, and of course Madison was a contributor to the *Federalist*. Madison was not convinced by Hamilton. In fact, he was frightened by what Hamilton said and by what Yates had said. So we find in the autumn of 1788 Madison writing to John Brown in Kentucky, who wanted him to propose a scheme for government there in Kentucky. What Madison said was this:

> In the State constitutions, and indeed in the Federal one also, no provision is made for the case of a disagreement in expounding them; and as the courts are generally the last in making the decision, it results to them by refusing or not refusing to execute a law, to stamp it with its final character. This makes the judiciary department paramount in fact to the legislature, which was never intended and can never be proper.

Here is what Abraham Baldwin, another member of the Convention, said in 1802 to the Senate in a debate on judicial review:

> If it had been intended to convey these distinguished powers, that would have been done in very conspicuous characters and not left to be obscurely explored by construction, not enlightened by the least recollection from anybody on a subject and on an occasion certainly of the most impressive kind and so little likely to have been forgotten.

Now, that is not the only testimony there is on this subject. There is a great deal of testimony on the other side to show that the framers did intend this thing. But you have great uncertainty, and you have a clear indication that some of the most important and influential members of the Convention, when they began to perceive the possible consequences of this idea, they began to recoil from it.

But there are also some lesser reasons for sympathizing with the president's proposal. In the first place, I think the suggestion of an enlarged Supreme Court is of itself a good thing. As matter of fact, I think that whole proposal, if it could have been divorced from any recollection of what has taken place in the last three years, would have been received most sympathetically by the whole country.

The attorney general made an excellent point the other day when he pointed out that the Supreme Court kept up with its docket because it clipped its pattern to suit its cloth. He showed them that a larger and larger percentage of certiorari cases are denied review every year. Well, now, what that means is this, that cases that are now thought deserving today of review will next year be thought not deserving of review, because the Court will feel it hasn't time to go into them.

The possibilities of an enlarged Court have not been properly explored. Down in New Jersey we have a chancellor and nine vice chancellors. The business is divided among them, and when a vice chancellor makes a decision, that is the chancellor's decision.

Similarly, the Supreme Court might be divided into sections. I am told that some branches of public law, the United States tax laws, for instance, are in a great deal of confusion. For example, I was told that you cannot get a review on the tax statutes until a divergence appears between different circuits. The result is that you get one version of the tax law in force for, say, a period of a year, when some other circuit challenges it, and perhaps the Supreme Court sustains the second view, and the result is you produce a great multitude of suits for the recovery of taxes.

I am also impressed by the fact that constitutional changes are not adequately argued. In the great constitutional cases of early years the Court spent days in hearing them argued. There is no opportunity given today to counsel to drive home his arguments and to pin the other counsel down.

Last year I happened to be associated to some extent with the Carter Coal case. The people who attacked that act devoted a great deal of attention to the historical phase of the thing, and their history was very spotted and of a very selective nature. Mr. Dickinson had a few minutes to spend on that subject. His criticisms should have been very effective, but they had to be made in ten or fifteen or twenty minutes. And what was the result? Mr. Wood got up in his answering period and said, "We stand on our brief." Mr. Dickinson had shown the brief was full of holes on that point, and what was needed was time to confront Mr. Wood with the statements he had made and which had been shown to be unjustified.

Mr. CORWIN. There was no time for that.

Senator CONNALLY. Mr. Dickinson said the brief was full of holes?

Mr. CORWIN. He certainly did.

Senator CONNALLY. Do you not suppose the judges could see that?

Mr. CORWIN. He had been spending weeks working that up. If the Court had had the time for it, it would have probably felt the same way about it.

Mr. Hughes says in his book on the Supreme Court that the Court has inflicted three self-wounds. One was the Dred Scott decision, another was the Legal Tender decision in 1870, and another was the Income Tax decision in 1895. The aged Chief Justice Taney, was at first opposed in the Dred Scott case to allow the constitutional question to be considered. In fact, an opinion had been already written for the Court by one of the justices deciding the case without any reference to the constitutional question. In 1870 it was Justice Greer's senility which produced confusion. In 1895 we had Justice Field's remarkable opinion, which was one of the last opinions he wrote, though he continued on the bench some years longer.

Elderly men look backward. The experience that elderly judges have had in life is inapplicable to changing conditions. There ought to be constant refreshment of knowledge of life and of new currents of thought available to the entire bench. The seventy-year age limit would appear to be reasonable. In the past, too large a proportion of the judges had already completed a career at the bar when appointed to the Court. I want to read what Justice Miller said about that kind of judge in 1874. Justice Miller was one of the ablest men who ever sat on the Court. He said:

> It is in vain to contend with judges who have been at the bar the advocates for 40 years of railroad companies, and all the forms of associated capital, when they are called upon to decide cases where such interests are in contest. All their training, all their feelings are from the start in favor of those who need no such influence.

I think that applies today as well as it did then. That is not to say that these judges are not upright and honorable men. They are. But, as somebody has said, the greatest pressure of all is the pressure of atmosphere, which would be intolerable except that it is inside of us as well as outside. The pressure a judge is subjected to from his own personal experience, his own education, his own training, is a pressure which is exceedingly difficult to withstand.

I do not believe that the president's proposal is satisfactory as a permanent solution. It does not guard against a recurrence of the situation which called it forth primarily. How should that problem be met? What the people demand of the Court is "a reasonable contemporaneity," in the words of the *New York Times.* How are we going to get that? I think a seventy-year age limit will help. I think a more regular system of appointments will help. Let us suppose we have a Court of fifteen. I have gone through the statistics on that subject, and I find if you have a Court of fifteen the Court could be kept approximately at that size by according each successive administration the appointment of four judges. Mr. Irving Dilliard pointed out in the November *Harper's* the fact that since the question of the constitutionality of minimum-wage legislation has been before the Court there have been seventeen judges on the Court, and ten of them believed the minimum wage was constitutional and seven believed it was unconstitutional, but those seven happened to have a majority on the Court at the critical moments. That is not a government of laws, but a government of chance. Whether a further reform is desirable, I am somewhat skeptical. The president's proposal is very moderate. It is the best thing that could have been proposed, as far as I can think, to maintain the general continuity of our Constitution undisturbed. The president's proposal tends to rescue the Constitution from a disabling and nullifying gloss.

I think that is all I have to say.

The CHAIRMAN. Members of the committee are now privileged to propound such questions to the witness as they see fit.

Senator NEELY. Professor Corwin, a member of the committee yesterday asked another witness in effect if he did not believe that there is sufficient authority in the Constitution to accomplish all purposes necessary for the progress and perpetuation of the republic, and that an amendment to the Constitution giving it more power would be vain. What do you think about that?

Mr. CORWIN. I am quite a conservative on that subject. I believe the Constitution is sufficient. I think it should be given a chance. As you no doubt remember, it has been said that "The law giver is not he who first spoke the law, but he who interpreted it." The law is not good unless it is properly interpreted. Chief Justice Hughes stated the fact, although he shocked the people, when he said it was what the judges say it is. The Constitution cannot speak. It has no tongue. As a matter of fact, these constitutional cases, nine-tenths of them, were decided on the basis of doctrines which were articulated with the Constitution by very few words. This is a Constitution of about 4,000 words, and of those 4,000 I suppose that 3,920 could be absolutely ignored, from the point of view of constitutional law.

Senator NEELY. Does your study of this question, which seems to have been very great, impel you to believe that the framers of the Constitution intended that the Supreme Court should declare acts of Congress unconstitutional?

Mr. CORWIN. It is very difficult to answer that question. When you go to Madison's notes you will find five or six gentlemen assuming that the Court would have that power. You have two or three gentlemen saying it would not have that power, and should not have that power. Mercer and Bedford expressed that view. Dickinson said he did not think it should have such power, but could think of no substitute.

When you go into the state conventions that ratified the Constitution, you find further expression of opinion. The people who wanted the Constitution were confronted with the argument that the states would be endangered in their rights, individual and state. They therefore scurried around and brought together all the limitations they could think of, one being the idea that the Supreme Court would have the power to check Congress. However, it is clear that they did not always take it so very seriously. Thus Hamilton discussed that question in the *Federalist* No. 34, as to who was going to construe the powers of Congress. He said the Congress would do so in the first place and their constituents in the last; if the Congress exceeded its power its acts would be unconstitutional, but he did not say the Supreme Court would have the power to say so. However, in *Federalist* No. 78 he took up the idea of judicial review and expounded it with great enthusiasm, but not in a way to convince Madison, who now took the opposite view.

In 1795 you have the fact that the Congress itself appropriated $1,000—$500 of which was to go to Hamilton and $500 to another man whose name I have forgotten—to argue before the Court the question of the constitutionality of the carriage tax. There you have Congress itself appropriating money to make possible an argument on a constitutional question. And yet as late as 1798 you find a judge of the Supreme Court expressing his doubt of this power. So you see it was a matter of opinion.

Senator KING. The question involved was whether it was a direct tax or an apportionment. There was no question over the fact of whether it exceeded or squared with the Constitution of the United States, but some believed it was an apportionment and others a direct tax.

Mr. CORWIN. Yes; the question was, What was the nature of the tax?

Senator KING. And, if I may be pardoned again?

Mr. CORWIN. Yes.

Senator KING. And did you know that the Federalist party did not believe that the federal government had a right to impose income taxes, and that was one of the differences between them?

Mr. CORWIN. I did not know any such thing.

Senator KING. I think you will find that if you read it. I am speaking of the Hilton case.

Mr. CORWIN. There wasn't any income tax involved. In his opinion in the Pollock case, Mr. Chief Justice Fuller, in his opinion, indicates that there were taxes on income derived from property back at the time of the framing of the Constitution. But he abandons that idea in his second opinion. As Mr. Seligman says in his book, there were no income taxes derived from property in 1787, and the only incomes taxes were on incomes from personal services.

The CHAIRMAN. Any further questions?

Senator NEELY. Professor Corwin, do you believe that the founding fathers ever intended to authorize, either expressly or by implication, five members of the Supreme Court of the United States to declare acts of the Congress null and void on the ground of unconstitutionality; particularly in a case in which the act had been supported by 48 lawyers in the Senate and 190 lawyers in the House, and the president, a distinguished lawyer, had by the affixing of his signature certified his faith in the constitutionality of the measure?

Mr. CORWIN. Well, nobody did propose it in the way the question is now put.

Senator NEELY. Do you believe that a constitution conferring such authority could have been adopted?

Mr. CORWIN. Well, that is a very speculative question. There is not sufficient data to answer; I cannot answer one way or the other. These people who say the framers intended it are talking nonsense; and the people who say they did not intend it are talking nonsense. There is evidence on both sides. Why not deal with the question as it stands in the year of grace 1937? As a matter of fact, the practice has stood since 1803. It is a fixed part of the Constitution now, and the Constitution is finally settled on any one point, if it is ever settled by long standing practice.

Senator NEELY. But the Supreme Court frequently reverses its practices.

Mr. CORWIN. Certainly. As the Supreme Court has extended this power, it has found more and more reason to reverse itself. The doctrine of stare decisis is practically nonexistent in constitutional law today. That is shown by Justice Brandeis' dissenting opinion in the case of Burnet v. Coronado Oil & Gas Company, as well as by other cases. The doctrine of stare decisis might just as well be dismissed from your mind as a feature of constitutional law. It has been dissolved.

The CHAIRMAN. Senator Austin has a question.

Senator AUSTIN. Yes; I want to ask the professor to clear up his answer relating to the cases that come up on certiorari. I wuld like to ask if it is not true that Congress itself is responsible for this right and obligation of the Court to select the cases that it will hear on applications for certiorari?

Mr. CORWIN. Right; the act of February 1925.

Senator AUSTIN. Yes. That was a jurisdictional act?

Mr. CORWIN. That is right.

Senator AUSTIN. Now, as a matter of practice, isn't it historically correct that the selection is not made on the basis of the wishes or inclination of the Court, but rather upon the basis of the determination of the question, whether there is involved an issue of public interest as against a mere issue of private interest?

Mr. CORWIN. I am not well acquainted with that point, Senator Austin. I should say that the issue now is whether the act of February 1925 is working well. It seems to me that the attorney general made an excellent point the other day on that. Here you find more and more cases coming into the Court on account of the increase in litigation all along the line, in which review on certiorari is asked for. But the Court keeps its docket to about two hundred cases, and the result is that a larger and larger proportion of cases are turned back without review.

Now, there is only one deduction you can draw from that, and that is that the cases which are received this year, five years hence will not be received; because the Constitution is bound to keep its docket within manageable dimensions.

Senator AUSTIN. Yes.

Mr. CORWIN. And then it will be able to say it is up with its docket.

Senator AUSTIN. That is what I understood you to testify, and it was about that answer that I was concerned.

Mr. CORWIN. Yes.

Senator AUSTIN. I might call to your attention the fact that the chief justice appeared before a subcommittee of the Judiciary Committee, this same committee, not long ago and testified regarding this subject. And in his testimony he said this, among other things:

> That is a very important exercise of authority, and there is nothing that we do to which we give greater attention with reference to the protection of the jurisdiction of the Court and its appropriate exercise.
>
> The principles are quite obvious. Cases should not go to the Supreme Court of the United States simply because of the amount of money involved, because of the character or prominence of the parties, or because of the counsel. The question before the Supreme Court is, manifestly, the importance of the question of law involved, the importance of an authoritative determination by the tribunal invested with that very important function. We consider these various applications with respect to that, not as to the parties, not as to the amount of money involved, not as to the counsel, but as to the law. The parties have the right of appeal to the circuit courts of appeal. That satisfies the rights of individual litigants. When it comes to a further review by the Supreme Court of the United States, the higher principle of importance to the public at large is involved.

I am not reading it all. But I read that because of your remark that you were not aware that the Court acted on that principle. I wanted to call that to your attention.

Mr. CORWIN. Yes; I have no doubt that is the principle they go on. But you have the fact, nevertheless, that a larger and larger proportion of these cases are turned back every year; and the docket is constant.

Senator AUSTIN. That is all, Mr. Chairman.

The CHAIRMAN. Senator Logan?

Senator LOGAN. Mr. Chairman, I would like to ask the witness—I note he has made some reference to the changing opinion as to the effect of the due process clause of the Constitution and some statutes, and the application and non-application of power. I would be very glad, individually, if the witness would make some reference to the opinions of the Court interpreting the commerce clause of the Constitution, as to whether the opinions have been a series of evolutions or retrogrations, or whatever they may have been; whether the attitude of the Court now is the same on the commerce clause as it was in the beginning of the government, for instance?

Mr. CORWIN. No; I think it is very different. I am sorry I did not bring down a book that I wrote last year on *The Commerce Power Versus States Rights*. I will be glad to send it, a copy of that book, as a part of my testimony. But I think I succeeded in showing there that down to about the year 1900 it was the accepted doctrine of the Supreme Court, announced again and again by the justices in authoritative decisions, that the power of Congress over interstate commerce is the same as the power over foreign commerce.

Beginning about 1901, in the case of Buttfield v. Stranahan, Mr. Chief

Justice White began insinuating in cases where it was not in point, the statement that there is a difference in these powers. And then you finally get the statement by Justice Sutherland in the Cleaners and Dyers case, a case which arose here in the District of Columbia, that it often happens that a word has different meanings in the same document, and cited in this connection the word "regulate" in the power of Congress to regulate commerce with foreign nations, between the several states, and with the Indian tribes. Well, of course, it does happen sometimes that a word in the course of a document of some dimension appears to bear two meanings, or even three or more meanings; but the presumption of the law is that the meaning is constant throughout. What Justice Sutherland stated was that in one short sentence the word "regulate" has two, and in fact three meanings. It has the power to govern, in the case of foreign commerce; and the power to regulate in a very mitigated sense as to interstate commerce; and has the power to govern again in the case of commerce with the Indian tribes. I think that is nonsense. That is a contribution to the science of hermeneutics, certainly, such a discovery as that.

The CHAIRMAN. Would you spell that word "hermeneutics" for the reporter?

Mr. CORWIN. Now, wait; is that fair?

Senator KING. The professor may not know it.

Mr. CORWIN. I think it is "h-e-r-m-e-n-e-u-t-i-c-s."

The CHAIRMAN. Right.

Mr. CORWIN. Will you permit me to send you a copy of my book?

Senator LOGAN. Yes.

The CHAIRMAN. Any objection to appending as a part of Professor Corwin's testimony the document he referred to—oh, it is a book?

Senator CONNALLY. It could be filed.

The CHAIRMAN. It may be; but not printed in the record.

Mr. CORWIN. I will send it to you, Senator Ashurst. And I will send Senator Logan a copy also, if I may.

Senator LOGAN. I will be very glad to get it.

The CHAIRMAN. I will be glad to accept it.

Senator KING. Having examined it, you need not send me one.

The CHAIRMAN. Senator Dieterich?

Senator DIETERICH. Professor Corwin?

Mr. CORWIN. Yes, sir.

Senator DIETERICH. I was somewhat interested in the statement you made in reference to the sufficiency of the Court to properly transact its business. I think you stated that not enough attention was given to the enlargement of the Court?

Mr. CORWIN. I say, I don't think enough attention has been given to the possibility of an enlarged Court, dividing it into sections or panels, much the same as the Interstate Commerce Commission.

Senator DIETERICH. Well, you do feel that the increased business of the Court jeopardizes a careful consideration of the questions that are brought before it?

Mr. CORWIN. I do; absolutely.

Senator DIETERICH. And regardless of whether this present measure is adopted, or some other measure is adopted, in order to increase that membership?

Mr. CORWIN. Exactly so.

Senator DIETERICH. And you feel that an increased membership in the Court would equip it better to transact the judicial business brought before it?

Mr. CORWIN. Yes; if the Court was divided into sections that would handle a certain type of decisions.

Senator DIETERICH. And you think some of the reasons why some of the opinions are disappointing to those who are learned in the law is the fact that, in order to accommodate themselves and to transact their business, they do not give sufficient time for the argument of serious constitutional questions?

Mr. CORWIN. Yes; I think there is not enough of the old common-law battle before the Court, where they get up and attack one another with questions and force answers.

Senator DIETERICH. I understand; and they do not make that thorough investigation that, if they had more time, they probably would make?

Mr. CORWIN. Yes; that is my feeling about it.

Senator DIETERICH. And in a parliamentary or constitutional government such as ours, where every liberty and every property right is regulated by law, it is essential that we have courts that are adequate to protect the citizens in those rights; is it not?

Mr. CORWIN. Certainly, sir.

Senator DIETERICH. Would you say the doctrine of stare decisis as stated by Madison is in effect a constitutional question?

Mr. CORWIN. I should think so.

Senator DIETERICH. The doctrine of stare decisis is an important doctrine governing the rights of the people.

Mr. CORWIN. The expectations were based on previous decisions of the Court.

Senator DIETERICH. Almost as much as though there had been a legislative enactment?

Mr. CORWIN. Yes.

Senator DIETERICH. And when the Court departed from that it necessarily disturbed many property holdings, did it not?

Mr. CORWIN. It depends on the kind of cases.

Senator DIETERICH. There were cases where such decisions disturbed valuable property holdings, were there not?

Mr. CORWIN. I think the Court was probably more conservative in adhering to stare decisis regarding such questions. For example, the question of tax exemption which was up before the Court the other day. I understand the decision reasserted that doctrine. I am not sure. I have not read it.

Senator CONNALLY. The Court said you could not tax the income of an engineer who was working for the city water works.

Mr. CORWIN. Yes.

Senator DIETERICH. When the Court announced a certain rule the business world naturally shaped itself in accordance with that rule, and when it announced a different rule it naturally caused some disturbance, did it not?

Mr. CORWIN. However, I will say, Senator Dieterich, that I think the Court has done well to abandon that doctrine of stare decisis. I do not think it is workable, under a strict interpretation. You can get a statutory interpretation corrected by legislative enactment, but you cannot get a correction of the Constitution except by a very difficult process. I do not say they have entirely abandoned it. I think there were some things to be said in favor of that doctrine, but I think we must recognize that in the Supreme Court we have a hybrid body, whose functions are partly political, just like the Privy Council in England. Before 1830 the Privy Council in England was a very good example of the present Supreme Court of the United States, to my mind.

Senator DIETERICH. The extension of judicial review means additional work for the Court, does it not?

Mr. CORWIN. Yes.

Senator DIETERICH. And is an additional reason why that Court should be sufficient in number to properly transact the business that comes before it.

Mr. CORWIN. Yes. I think constitutional questions are not today adequately argued, and especially as they often turn to a great extent on questions of fact.

Senator DIETERICH. And you think it is desirable to remedy that?

Mr. CORWIN. I think if you would divide the Court into panels you would save a great deal of the Court's time. About three-fifths of the Court's time is spent on nonconstitutional questions. Those could be disposed of with a great deal of economy of time if the Court would assign certain cases to section A, and other cases to section B, and so on, and then the whole Court could hear constitutional questions.

Senator DIETERICH. I was interested in what you said in reference to the effect of age. I assume it affects judges the same as other human beings.

Mr. CORWIN. Yes.

Senator DIETERICH. One of the early evidences of senility is the fact that the mind goes back to past transactions rather than later transactions.

Mr. CORWIN. I think so. I hope I am not reaching that stage.

Senator DIETERICH. There are some elderly people, we may say in the Senate, who will give more thought to the past than to the future.

Mr. CORWIN. I think that is the general characteristic of elderly people.

Senator DIETERICH. You do not think judges of the Supreme Court are exempt from that rule, do you?

Mr. CORWIN. The seventy-year rule, I understand, is applied to many industries and professions, and is quite generally applied to the executives of great corporations.

Senator DIETERICH. They may enforce it in the Senate.

Mr. CORWIN. That would be regrettable, of course.

Senator DIETERICH. I was interested in some other things you said about prejudice. The person who is prejudiced is usually the last one to be conscious of it, is he not?

Mr. CORWIN. The stronger the prejudice the less one is conscious of it.

Senator DIETERICH. Just one more question. You believe that an increase in the number of judges on the Supreme Court, with the condition of litigation existing at the present time, would be desirable?

Mr. CORWIN. I think so.

Senator BURKE. In reference to the statement you just made in answer to Senator Dieterich's question that you believe additional members on the Supreme Court are desirable in order to carry on the work of the Court, do you wish us to accept that statement which you make today or the statement which you are reported to have made as long ago as February 11, 1936, from which I read:

> One way to curb the Court would be to "pack it" with new members favorable to certain constitutional views; another way would be to require more than a majority vote on the Court in setting aside an act of Congress; still another way would be to deprive the Court of its appellate jurisdiction in constitutional cases. The first and third of these methods, it is generally admitted, would be within the power of Congress, but they are objectionable on other grounds.

This is the point to which I wish to particularly call your attention:

> The Court is already large enough, and cases involving constitutional questions have to be decided somewhere; and where more appropriately than in the Supreme Court? One should not forget the old warning not to throw out the baby with the bath.

Was that your view on February 11, of this year?

Mr. CORWIN. Last year; was it not?

Senator BURKE. Yes; February 11, 1936.

Mr. CORWIN. Yes.

Senator BURKE. But you now reverse that doctrine which you announced a little over a year ago and say that the Court is not large enough.

Mr. CORWIN. I had not had the facts before me that have been brought out as a result of this proposal.

Senator BURKE. Have you not been studying these matters all your life?

Mr. CORWIN. Not the question of federal jurisdiction.

Senator BURKE. Did you not understand that the subject of judicial review, almost as long as twenty-five years ago, has been a matter of study and discussion?

Mr. CORWIN. Yes; but I did not go into the question of jurisdiction or adequacy of the Court. I went into entirely different questions.

Senator BURKE. You want us to believe now that, while a little over a year ago you said the Supreme Court was large enough to properly and expeditiously handle its work, according to the statements in your printed book, we should place some reliance on your statement when you say the Court is not large enough. Is that a fact?

Mr. CORWIN. Yes.

Senator KING. You were an attorney in the Carter case and, therefore, were familiar with the proceedings in the Supreme Court, were you not?

Mr. CORWIN. I was not an attorney. I was a consultant in the case. I am not a member of the bar.

Senator KING. You are not a member of the bar?

Mr. CORWIN. No.

Senator KING. You gave me the impression that you participated in that case.

Mr. CORWIN. I did participate in the case as a consultant.

Senator KING. You were in the courtroom and complained because Mr. Dickinson did not have more time to reply.

Mr. CORWIN. Right.

Senator BURKE. Returning to your expressed opinion of a year ago, you say that to curb the Court by "packing" it with new members is generally admitted to be within the Constitution. I think we generally agree on that. But you say it is objectionable on other grounds. May I ask you what were the grounds that then appeared to you to be important when you said the proposition of appointing additional members to the Court was objectionable?

Mr. CORWIN. Objectionable from this point of view: That the Court is a hybrid body, in that it is a judicial body and also a political body. The question is what emphasis should be given to one or the other aspects of the Court. I think it is rather unfortunate, from the point of view of our standard ideas of a judicial body, that it should be subject to this power of Congress. But, on the other hand, considering the tremendous importance of the political functions of the Court, it was simply inevitable that it should be subject to political forces. That is due to a great extent to the Court itself. It is not due to this present Court. This present Court has not built up that theory of judicial review. It has extended it, but, after all, it was just following in the track that had been laid out by its predecessors.

Senator BURKE. Then you think there are serious objections to the proposal to add six members to the Court?

Mr. CORWIN. I think there are serious objections, but not to adding six members to the Court. What I say is that there are serious objections to the kind of situation that requires that type of remedy. My only criticism of the president's proposal is that it does not provide assurance against a recurrence of the situation which it is designed to meet, which I think should be and can be provided against by more regular replacement of judges.

Senator BURKE. I would like, if possible, to have a direct answer to this question. You certainly did feel in February 1936 that there were many serious objections to any proposal to add members to the Court under the circumstances that justified the use of the term "packing" the Court? You did feel that way a year ago, did you not?

Mr. CORWIN. I think I clearly stated that is correct.

Senator BURKE. It is all right once, but you do not want it again?

Mr. CORWIN. Unless the same situation arises. I think the only argument against the president's proposal, when you consider the whole situation, is the argument against it as a precedent. If that situation should recur I should say the precedent should be followed, but I should say we should take all possible measures against its recurrence. I think the one weak spot in the president's proposal is that it does not provide against a recurrence of the situation.

Senator AUSTIN. When you have no means of preventing a recurrence of the situation, then you destroy the argument of the president, do you not?

Senator BURKE. The ideal arrangement, from your standpoint, as I understood from your answer to some earlier questions asked by some other senator, would be to have those new members, fresh from the people, that were appointed on the Court, have them sit as a separate panel to judge all questions involving the constitutionality of acts of Congress?

Mr. CORWIN. I said that the justices of most recent appointment might constitute the constitutional section. I also suggested the whole Court's time could be saved by dividing the Court into panels for other questions, in order that the whole Court might as a whole hear constitutional questions. That would be a matter for consideration.

Senator BURKE. But, Professor Corwin, as a lifetime student of the Constitution and the function of the Court and all, does it not seem a very startling thing that you should even consider the possibility of urging seriously such a proposal, that we should now add six members to the Court and then take the most recently appointed members and set them up in a panel by themselves to pass on a certain type of cases that came before the Court?

Mr. CORWIN. Well, I don't know that that is more startling than that you should have the judges of oldest appointment.

Senator BURKE. All right; we will pass it.

Mr. CORWIN. Yes.

Senator BURKE. Just one or two other questions: On this matter of judicial review. I understand you to say now that it has been recognized since 1803, and we can very well forget it. I think that is an entirely laudable statement to make, and correct. But as to whether the framers of the Constitution did or did not intend to vest in the courts the powers to pass on acts of Congress, I am uncertain what your position is, and I don't want to go into it particularly further. As I understood you, you say that the evidence is not very complete, and you can build up a case on one side or the other side, or no one can say certainly what the framers of the Constitution intended.

You were not in any doubt twenty-five years ago, when you were much further away from such certainty, when you wrote your work on *The Doctrine of Judicial Review,* were you?

Mr. CORWIN. I said there that in the Constitutional Convention, and in the ratifying convention, you could get testimony of fifteen or sixteen people in favor of the proposition.

Senator BURKE. Well, let me read you what you said in your work published in 1914, just an excerpt or two: On page 17 of your book on *The Doctrine of Judicial Review:*

> In short, we are driven to the conclusion that judicial review was rested by the framers of the Constitution upon certain general principles which in their estimation made specific provision for it unnecessary, in the same way as, for example, certain other general principles made unnecessary specific provision for the President's power of removal.

And again on page 26 of the same volume:

> It is accordingly submitted that judicial review rests upon the following propositions and can rest upon no others: 1, that the Constitution binds the organs of government; 2, that it is law in the sense of being known to and enforceable by the courts; 3, that the function of interpreting the standing law appertains to the courts alone, so that their interpretations of the Constitution as part and parcel of such standing law are, in all cases coming within judicial cognizance, alone authoritative, while those of the other departments are mere expressions of opinion. That the framers of the Constitution of the United States accepted the first of these propositions goes without saying. Their acceptance of the second one is registered in the Constitution itself, though this needs to be shown. But it is their acceptance of the third one which is the matter of greatest significance, for at this point their view marks an entire breach, not only with English tradition, but, for the vast part, with American legal tradition as well, anterior to 1787.

After a careful reading of your book on *The Doctrine of Judicial Review,* which I found most interesting, I have formed the opinion that the author of the book at that time, whatever his view might be today, had no manner of doubt that it was the intention of the framers of the Constitution to vest in the courts this power. If I do you wrong in that, your earlier statement is probably sufficient for the record.

Mr. CORWIN. Yes. I think my earlier statement is true in his sense, that it was the belief at that time on the principles as then understood. But I might say, Senator Burke, that in 1924 I went over this whole question again, and wrote a paper which I have not published, but which will be published, and which I am going to make the basis of an address before the Boston Unversity on April 2, and in which I reconsider the question and I consider far more a matter of doubt than I did then. I think that this is a better-considered statement of the thing. I don't think I gave the weight that should have been given to the objections made by Dickinson and by Madison, and afterward by Charles Pinckney and by Baldwin. Now, you have there four people, all members of the Convention. You have Charles Pinckney, saying in 1799, that there was no intention to vest this power in the Court.

Judicial review is a matter of inference, which depends upon certain concepts, and unless those terms are retained you don't get the inference. In the first place, it is a question whether the Court would have any power to take account of the Constitution for itself. That was the question that Chief Justice Marshall dealt with in Marbury v. Madison. The bulk of his argument, you will remember, is on this question of the right to read the Constitution for himself, instead of through the eyes of Congress. His argument is, Why, otherwise, should a judge take an oath to support the Constitution? And he says, how immoral to impose the oath upon them to support the Constitution if they cannot read it for themselves. Of course that applies to members of Congress, as well. It means it is equally for members of Congress to read the Constitution for themselves, and for the Court under their oath to support the Constitution, to read that Constitution for themselves.

There is the first question, therefore, whether the judges would have any right to take account of the Constitution at all in the decision of the cases.

Now, the Constitution does not say it is the law, or the supreme law. The Constitution says that the Constitution and the laws of the United States made in pursuance thereof—and all treaties made, and so forth—shall be the supreme law of the land, and the judges in every state shall be bound thereby, anything in the constitution or laws of any state to the contrary notwithstanding. That is all it says. The supreme law is the Constitution plus the act of Congress made in pursuance thereof, and of course also the treaties. The Constitution does not say that the Constitution is the supreme law of the land.

But the next question arises then, and that is, What weight is to be attached to a decision made casually, as it were, an interpretation of the Constitution made casually in the course of a decision of a case? Does that bind the other branches of the Government? Mr. Marshall, it seems to me by his argument, virtually said no. And of course Jefferson denied it, and Jackson denied it, and Lincoln denied it, and Theodore Roosevelt denied it. And George Bancroft denies it, and George Ticknor Curtis also.

My analysis of the problem of judicial review which was written in 1914 was correct at the time, but it was incomplete in that I overlooked two very important questions.

Senator BURKE. I shall read your unpublished statement in 1924, and your revision of it in 1937; but you must pardon me if I recognize that when you made the statement you were ten years older, and weakening, apparently, in your faculties; and now there are still thirteen years added on to that, and I don't know that I should be able to pay as much attention to the latter statement as to the earlier ones, when you were more fresh from law school and in the condition, as you say, fresh on the bench of the Supreme Court?

Mr. CORWIN. Have you got anything there I wrote when I was six years old?

The CHAIRMAN. Any other questions?

Senator BURKE. One more, and that is all. In your statement this morning you referred, I believe once, or more often, to the words of the present Chief Justice Hughes when he said, "We are under a Constitution, but the Constitution is what the judges say it is."

I find that statement on the flyleaf of your book. *The Twilight of the Supreme Court,* published a couple of years ago; and later on in the volume at page 181, you use this statement:

> Even prior to this first appointment to the Supreme Court Bench, as the successor of Justice Brewer, Mr. Hughes had spoken the capable words quoted at the outset of this volume, "We are under a constitution, but the Constitution is what the judges say it is."

And when you say that this incisive statement describes with accuracy not only an achieved result but a still operating practice as well.

Do you consider, Professor Corwin, that the words which you quoted from Chief Justice Hughes, the limited number of words that you quoted, correctly portrayed the thought that was in his mind and that he was expressing at the time he used that statement, or fully met the expression at anytime since?

Mr. CORWIN. I think so.

Senator BURKE. Can you tell us the circumstances under which the words were used from which you have quoted, not only in your books, but here today?

Mr. CORWIN. He was talking about the necessity of a liberal interpretation of the Constitution.

Senator STEIWER. Senator, he made that statement as governor of New York, did he not?

Mr. CORWIN. As governor of New York.

Senator BURKE. If I may, without asking a question, let me read the statement that Chief Justice Hughes made, and that will speak for itself.

The CHAIRMAN. Very well.

Senator BURKE. This was made in 1907 or 1908, possibly in 1908, at Elmira, N.Y., when the then Governor Hughes was invited to address a meeting at Elmira. He had his address ready to deliver, but the prior speaker, a well-known utility lawyer, took occasion to attack severely a measure which Justice Hughes was greatly interested in trying to get through the legislature. So Governor Hughes discarded the speech that he had prepared, and spoke extemporaneously. And in the course of it he used this one paragraph which I will read from this quotation, and I call your particular attention to the fact that the words used by the witness this morning are not even a complete sentence, and is followed by another statement. This is what he said, and I am quoting now from the present Chief Justice Hughes in an extemporaneous statement delivered at a speech made at Elmira, N.Y., in the year 1907:

> I have the highest regard for the courts. My daily life has been spent in work founded upon respect for the courts. I regard him one of the worst enemies of the community which will talk lightly of the dignity of the bench. We are under a constitution, but the Constitution is what the judges say it is—

Comma—

> and the judiciary is the safeguard of our liberty and of our property under the Constitution. I don't want to see any direct assault upon the courts, nor do I want to see any indirect assault upon the courts. And I tell you, ladies and gentlemen, that no more insidious assault can be made upon the conscientiousness and esteem of the judiciary than to pursue it with these questions of administration—

And so on, on other matters.

Mr. CORWIN. I think that statements stands for itself. I don't think that statement is distorted by taking it from the context.

Senator HATCH. Practically all of the proposals contained in this bill have been accepted by the entire country, have they not, with the possible exception of the Supreme Court?

Mr. CORWIN. I think there are about four proposals. One is enlargement of the Court; another is in relation to the congestion of business in the lower federal courts; a third is the proposal that the attorney general shall be made a party to constitutional issues; and there is something about injunctions, I think.

Senator HATCH. And also with relation to the appointment of a proctor.

Mr. CORWIN. Yes. I think they all stand by themselves.

Senator HATCH. They have been generally accepted, have they not, in your opinion?

Mr. CORWIN. I think all of them have except the enlargement of the Court, but I think the discussion of that is so associated in the minds of the people with the big issue that it has not been thoroughly considered. Furthermore, I do not think the question has been raised as to the possibility of dividing the Court into panels, which is a necessary part of the proposal to make the Court more useful by enlarging it. If you are going to make the entire Court do all the business it does at present, than I think nine are better than fifteen; but if you are going to divide the Court into sections to handle particular types of business, the larger Court would be better. Some of the European courts are very large. I think some have about fifty members, divided into separate panels.

Senator HATCH. Have you thought how that could be done?

Mr. CORWIN. I think it could be done by legislation. Congress is the creative body. There is a myth that the Constitution created the Supreme Court, but it did not. It made that a duty of Congress.

Senator HATCH. You think the Congress has that power?

Mr. CORWIN. Yes.

Senator HATCH. And that it would be an improvement?

Mr. CORWIN. I think so.

Senator CONNALLY. Dr. Corwin, I believe you stated the men who made the Constitution had been grounded in the philosophy of Blackstone and Locke?

Mr. CORWIN. Yes.

Senator CONNALLY. Under which the parliamentary law was supreme?

Mr. CORWIN. Yes.

Senator CONNALLY. Did they adopt that system or did thy adopt a written constitution?

Mr. CORWIN. It does not make much difference about that.

Senator CONNALLY. It does make a good deal of difference, I think.

Mr. CORWIN. I do not know whether it does or not.

Senator CONNALLY. Let me ask you another question. Is it not a fact that they had been in contact with the British system, under which Parliament was supreme and the king's rule was supreme, so that they rebelled and set up a rigid constitutional system by which the powers of government were clearly set forth, and limitations placed upon both the legislative and executive branches of the government?

Mr. CORWIN. It is difficult to cover all those questons and see clearly through the haze of intervening events. The thirteen colonies had written constitutions but, generally speaking, a good deal of the material they have left shows that they regarded the legislative branch as supreme. Take Jefferson's Virginia Notes.

Senator CONNALLY. Are you speaking of the period after the Revolution?

Mr. CORWIN. Yes.

Senator CONNALLY. Under the Confederation?

Mr. CORWIN. That is right.

Senator CONNALLY. Not under the colonies?

Mr. CORWIN. Not under the colonies. Jefferson said the legislature could exercise any power whatsoever. He said the legislature could get its will as to any matter whatever by passing a law. His theory of legislative power was the political power, as that of Parliament. But through the process of judicial review the separation of these powers is made a principle of judicial decision, of judicial construction.

Senator CONNALLY. I think you are getting away from the question.

Mr. CORWIN. No; I am not getting away from the topic. The topic is whether the people of 1787 looked upon legislative power as supreme power.

Senator CONNALLY. I asked you if, when they went to make the Constitution, they adopted the political system of England by which Parliament could do anything it wanted to, or whether they departed from that and set up for the first time a written constitution.

Mr. CORWIN. Not the first time. There were thirteen written constitutions before that.

Senator CONNALLY. Well, the second time.

Mr. CORWIN. That is different.

Senator CONNALLY. Doesn't that have a good deal of importance? England has no dual system.

Mr. CORWIN. I know; but when you turn to the debates on the Constitution you will find it was considered that the Senate would be the chief protection of the states.

Senator CONNALLY. Just a short question. Did we adopt the British system or did we adopt a system of our own?

Mr. CORWIN. We adopted a system of our own.

Senator CONNALLY. And Blackstone and Locke did not control?

Mr. CORWIN. No. But these people did not get out of their minds everything they had been reading in Locke and Blackstone, including the idea that legislative power was the supreme power.

Senator CONNALLY. You said you did not regard this plan as a permanent solution, but it is a mere expedient.

Mr. CORWIN. As I have thought it out, I have come to the conclusion that it is a necessary expedient in the present situation.

Senator CONNALLY. It does not solve a situation that might exist fifty years from now?

Mr. CORWIN. I do not think I would support a plan that purported to do that. I think it is obvious that the president's plan does not provide against the recurrence of the present situation.

Senator CONNALLY. You are basing your support of this bill on the theory that the six judges would be the right kind of judges, are you not?

Mr. CORWIN. It is on the theory that they would not be quite so interfering as the present judges.

Senator CONNALLY. And if you did not think you were going to get tractable judges who would not interfere, you would not be in favor of appointing them, would you?

Mr. CORWIN. The fellow who used the expression "unpacking" the Court hit the nail on the head.

Senator CONNALLY. Who packed the Court in the first place? The president appointed and the Senate confirmed these men from time to time.

Mr. CORWIN. Ten of them were appointed by Mr. Taft and Mr. Harding.

Senator CONNALLY. Hoover appointed Cardozo, a very liberal man.

Mr. CORWIN. Yes. He did not want him very badly. There was a good deal of talk in the newspapers about somebody from Arizona, I believe, or New Mexico.

The CHAIRMAN. It was not Arizona, but New Mexico.

Senator CONNALLY. Regardless of what went before, he did appoint him?

Mr. CORWIN. Yes.

Senator KING. Was not the objection because New York already had one member?

Mr. CORWIN. I think so.

Senator KING. There was no objection per se to Cardozo?

Mr. CORWIN. The general thought was that Justice Cardozo, by reason of his character and outlook and knowledge, should be regarded as the successor of Justice Holmes. That was the way it was put in the newspapers. I think the opinion of the bar was quite favorable to him. He was certainly not objectionable to the bar.

Senator KING. I just wanted to know if you intended to convey the idea that there was serious opposition to Justice Cardozo.

Mr. CORWIN. Oh, no.

Senator KING. The objection was based solely upon the thought that New York was getting too large a proportion of the Supreme Court?

Mr. CORWIN. Yes.

Senator CONNALLY. Who packed the Court?

Mr. CORWIN. Every time a president appoints a justice, he packs the Court to that extent.

Senator CONNALLY. Was it packed when Cardozo was appointed? When and where was the packing done?

Mr. CORWIN. I say that manifestly the policies of the present Court on these constitutional questions are violations of the maxim that should govern judicial review that all reasonable doubt should be resolved in favor of the legislature. They have set up their own theory of economics.

Senator CONNALLY. Of course, I do not think that is an answer to my question, but I will ask you another.

Senator KING. I do not agree with that statement.

Senator CONNALLY. Neither do I. You say the present Court has a decided bias. Therefore you want to put six new judges on that are biased in the opposite direction? I do not care whether you answer yes or no, but is it not your theory that this plan is based on the proposition that the six new judges would be biased in an opposite direction from the members of the Court now?

Mr. CORWIN. Prospectively.

Senator CONNALLY. That is why you are for it?

Mr. CORWIN. That is one reason.

Senator CONNALLY. That is the main reason, is it not?

Mr. CORWIN. No, sir; that is not the main reason. I stated two reasons: First, because I thought it was necessary to secure a new type of constitutional interpretation.

Senator CONNALLY. That is one way of getting it.

Mr. CORWIN. It is the only way of getting it. Another reason was because I thought it was necessary to correct a serious imbalance in the Constitution; that the Court had extended its power beyond all limits, and it was necessary to find some other power capable of correcting it. That lies within the power of Congress.

Senator CONNALLY. All these decisions on constitutional questions date back to 1798, when the Court was young. How many acts of Congress have been held unconstitutional by the Supreme Court during the 147 years it has been in existence?

Mr. CORWIN. I might ask you—

Senator CONNALLY (interposing). You are not asking me; I am asking you.

Mr. CORWIN. I am answering you by asking you a question. How many men were killed when Lincoln was assassinated?

Senator CONNALLY. Now, will you answer my question as to how many acts of Congress have been held unconstitutional by the Supreme Court during the past 147 years?

Mr. CORWIN. Seventy-three, according to Mr. W. C. Gilbert.

Senator CONNALLY. Is it not true that, while there were seventy-three cases, there was a smaller number of acts, because some of them dealt with different portions of the acts? There were not seventy-three acts, but seventy-three cases.

Mr. CORWIN. Seventy-three legal decisions.

Senator CONNALLY. And fifty-five or fifty-six acts of Congress in the 147 years were declared unconstitutional.

Mr. CORWIN. Yes.

Senator CONNALLY. Now, how many acts of Congress have been passed in that time—do you know?

Mr. CORWIN. How many acts of Congress have been passed? Well, I suppose twenty thousand, or something like that.

Senator CONNALLY. About forty-five thousand; isn't it?

Mr. CORWIN. About forty-five thousand.

Senator CONNALLY. Or up to fifty thousand?

Mr. CORWIN. Yes.

Senator CONNALLY. Now, let me ask you one other thing about the Supreme Court—

Senator AUSTIN. Here is a statement of the exact figures.

Senator CONNALLY. The senator from Vermont comes to my aid there, and I thank him. This is not necessarily right up to the minute, Senator Austin?

Senator AUSTIN. Quite recent.

Senator CONNALLY. It is up to this date. Seventy-six cases in 147 years; and eighty-four different provisions of law in some respect invalidated. But in all, only sixty-four different acts of Congress construed, out of something like, as I understand it, fifty thousand acts of Congress that have been passed.

Now, you speak about dividing the Court so as to pass on more cases on certiorari. Now, isn't it true that the whole point is settled in that since the establishment of the circuit courts of appeal, you settle that problem by letting them perform that duty and settle most of these cases in the circuit courts of appeal and simply allow them to go to the Supreme Court because of high public importance? Is there any reason why every case from the circuit courts of appeal should have a second appeal to the Supreme Court, regardless of the question involved or the amount involved?

Mr. CORWIN. Well, I think it is highly desirable that you have one uniform construction of the statute throughout the whole country.

Senator CONNALLY. You do that now, don't you? That is the kind of case that may have a writ of certiorari now; that is one of the grounds for such a case, where two circuits differ as to the construction of a statute?

Mr. CORWIN. Yes; but the possibility is undesirable, isn't it, that the review should be delayed so long, because of the retroactive effect of the operation of the second decision if it is sustained by the Supreme Court?

Senator CONNALLY. Well, it seems to me that the fewer writs they grant, the less delay there would be in passing on them; than if they granted a great many writs.

Now, let me ask you this: Your theory is that if the Court is created of fifteen judges, you would then require them to sit in sections?

Mr. CORWIN. I would make that suggestion.

Senator CONNALLY. There is nothing in this bill to do that?

Mr. CORWIN. No.

Senator CONNALLY. The Court would want to do that on its own, wouldn't it?

Mr. CORWIN. I think Congress should do it.

Senator CONNALLY. Must we do it by an act?

Mr. CORWIN. I should think so.

Senator CONNALLY. Well, instead of having a Supreme Court of fifteen, you would then have three Supreme Courts of five each, wouldn't you?

Mr. CORWIN. No; you would have a section which would be a Supreme Court for a certain type of cases.

Senator CONNALLY. Exactly.

Mr. CORWIN. And section two for another type of cases.

Senator CONNALLY. Surely.

Mr. CORWIN. And section three for another type of cases; and one of those sections for constitutional cases, perhaps.

Senator CONNALLY. Perhaps.

Senator BURKE. Of the most recently appointed members?

Mr. CORWIN. The most recently appointed members would be desirable, to my mind, because these are political questions.

Senator CONNALLY. Without anything to offer, are you going to be satisfied with that?

Mr. CORWIN. Yes. Let us have a reasonable contemporaneity,

Senator CONNALLY. How is that?

Mr. CORWIN. Let us have a reasonable contemporaneity, as the *New York Times* put it a few weeks ago.

Senator KING. Did you use the word "packing" in the statement that was read, contemplating that their judgment would be packing; that is, that they would be all of one mind, along the line of thought you have attempted to elucidate?

Mr. CORWIN. I made the statement—I don't quite understand, Senator King; what is your question?

Senator KING. You used the word "packing" of the Court. You do that recognizing that they are to deal with this situation. You use the word in the ordinary sense, do you not; that is, to pack the Court with six men whose thoughts run along the line that yours do?

ı Mr. CORWIN. I made it in the sense—what I would expect, of course, would be that entirely competent people should be nominated and appointed to the bench; people whose knowledge of the law could not be challenged and whose general integrity was not open to challenge, but whose point of view is more recent.

Senator CONNALLY. Doctor, if these new judges are appointed, the system that you have been denouncing and talking about, that system will remain the same as it is. The Court will still have the same power of judicial review and still have this review on certiorari and passing on these cases; and you would still have a majority opinion in connection with this class of cases? It does not reach any of those things, does it?

Mr. CORWIN. No; it does not reach things of that kind.

Senator CONNALLY. And you still have that same thing?

Mr. CORWIN. Yes.

Senator CONNALLY. Now, the N. R. A. case you spoke about, in that N. R. A. case do you think that act was constitutional?

Mr. CORWIN. I think it would be. It would have been held constitutional by a better line of reasoning. In the line of reasoning by which it was overthrown, the Court had to go back to the Sugar Trust opinion and, as Mr. Taft said, that had been virtually reversed.

Senator CONNALLY. Well, nine judges of the Supreme Court concurred in the view that the act was unconstitutional. Even if you appoint six judges fresh from the country and the law schools, and with this new concept and this liberal outlook, you could not get that judgment reversed, could you? And yet you think it ought to be?

Mr. CORWIN. Well, of course—

Senator CONNALLY. Why not have ten, and put ten in the balance?

Mr. CORWIN. Well, the chief justice, in that connection, was rather ambiguous, as we discover when we come to Carter v. Carter Coal Company, where the decision, or opinion, whichever it is, in the N. I. R. A. case undergoes interpretation, and the Court tells what was done in its interpretation of it. You have the chief justice, who wrote the opinion, being adandoned by the majority of the Court.

What the opinion did really signify in the N. I. R. A. case is a matter for debate.

Senator CONNALLY. All right.

Mr. CORWIN. It is decidedly ambiguous.

Senator CONNALLY. Almost everything is subject to debate, and yet you want to require unanimity of the Court?

Mr. CORWIN. No; I don't want unanimity, and I don't think we will ever get it as long as the Supreme Court operates in these vague, indefinite fields of political and economic theory. Of course you won't get unanimity.

Senator CONNALLY. If there isn't some doubt about the question, it never gets to the Court, does it? Lawsuits are all controversial?

Mr. CORWIN. Right.

Senator CONNALLY. The more difficult question is, the more apt to a close division of the Court?

Mr. CORWIN. Yes; and why is it? Because of lack of concrete principle. If you have no concrete principle, then you have a choice, and in this field, in the whole field of constitutional law, important constitutional law, the Court is continually exercising choice. That is the thing we have to bear in mind. And this choice does not concern primarily any language of the Constitution, or decisions of the Court, but economic theories or prejudices or bias or point of view or outlook. That is the proposition; and that is the proposition upon which this proposal of the president is based.

Senator CONNALLY. Now, a while ago you spoke about the Court's action in a constitutional case not being binding on other agencies of the government and the present Congress?

Mr. CORWIN. Yes.

Senator CONNALLY. Now, what Mr. Jefferson referred to was this, wasn't it, that he said that the Court's action in a constitutional case was binding on the parties to the proceeding; but that when it came to him as president he had the right, in the exercise of his own function, to construe the Constitution himself. And that arose in the Callender case, in which a man by the name of Callender had been sentenced to the penitentiary for violation of the alien and sedition laws. The Court had convicted him, and Mrs. Jane Thomas wrote to Mr. Jefferson, appealing to him—

Senator KING. To grant a pardon?

Senator CONNALLY. About a pardon; not to pardon him. And Mr. Jefferson said that while the Court's action in its conviction is binding, and the construction of the law is binding; yet he said, "When I come to the exercise of my constitutional right of pardon or no pardon, I am not bound by the Court. I have a right to perform my constitutional duties as I see fit." Now, isn't that a fact? Isn't that how that arose?

Mr. CORWIN. Yes, sir. Here is what Jefferson said, "that to consider the judges as the ultimate arbiters of all constitutional questions would place us under the jurisdiction of an oligarchy."

Senator CONNALLY. That is something else.

Senator KING. You have not quoted the entire thing; you have just taken a few sentences from a long statement there, have you not?

Senator CONNALLY. That is on another matter, anyway.

Senator KING. I will get the statement.

Mr. CORWIN. That you will find in volume 15, pages 276 and 278.

Without regard to what that is, those men decided for themselves in such questions.

Senator CONNALLY. That is something else. But he said he had a right to construe his own action as to the pardon.

Now, when Congress comes to vote on the law, we have to pass on the constitutionality so far as our own vote is concerned, don't we?

Mr. CORWIN. I should think so.

Senator CONNALLY. That is not binding on the Court, any more than the Court is binding on us?

Mr. CORWIN. Surely.

Senator CONNALLY. All right. You also mentioned about the power of the Court to declare acts of Congress unconstitutional and you quoted from the Constitution which says, "This Constitution and the laws of the United States which shall be made in pursuance thereto"; didn't you?

Mr. CORWIN. In pursuance thereof.

Senator CONNALLY. In pursuance thereof; yes.

Mr. CORWIN. Yes, sir.

Senator CONNALLY. Well, who is going to say whether an act of Congress is in pursuance of the Constitution, if not the courts?

Mr. CORWIN. Well, that is a question. It is not inevitable that the Court should do it, but it has been considered since 1803 that the Court should do it.

Senator CONNALLY. It is a part of the Constitution now, whether it was orginally or not?

Mr. CORWIN. Read Justice Sutherland's statement in 261 U.S. that the Court has no substantive power to pass on the Constitution or on constitutional acts of Congress.

Senator CONNALLY. Oh, no; it has merely the power to—

Mr. CORWIN. Determine the law of the case.

Senator CONNALLY. Exactly. Now, when the Supreme Court declares a law unconstitutional, it doesn't come over there and say, "Well, let us look over the laws of the nation"?

Mr. CORWIN. Your objection to the proposal is that the president is trying to establish his theory of the Constitution; and yet you say he has the same right as the Court has to construe his functions under it.

Senator CONNALLY. I have not said that. But the Supreme Court does not go over there and say, ''Well, this Congress is getting a little fresh; let us look over the laws they have enacted and pick out the ones we think are unconstitutional''? They only ones they act on as to being constitutional are the ones in the suits?

Mr. CORWIN. Right.

Senator CONNALLY. And they have the same right where there is a conflict and the Court passes on it as a law between them, and that settles that particular matter.

Now, the effect of that decision will be to strike down a law of Congress, but it only can arise in a litigated case; and technically it is only binding on the parties to the suit, is it not? So the Court does not act as an arbiter like the president does?

Mr. CORWIN. Well, Webster—

Senator CONNALLY. That is, on certain acts of Congress.

Mr. CORWIN. Webster contends otherwise; and so did Stephen Douglas after the Dred Scott case.

Senator CONNALLY. But this bill does that as a part of the legislative machinery.

Mr. CORWIN. But Daniel Webster claimed the president had no right to veto on a constitutional ground, when the Supreme Court had held that the enactment was constitutional. That debate has been going on from the very beginning, as to what is the authority of a decision of the Court interpreting the Constitution.

Senator CONNALLY. Webster was just a man, after all?

Mr. CORWIN. Certainly; and so was Stephen Douglas just a man.

Senator CONNALLY. We haven't got anybody but men, or women, to put in. There are not any gods to put on these courts. They are all human beings.

Mr. CORWIN. But I was simply pointing out the fact, Senator, that this question of the authority of a constitutional pronouncement by the Court has always been a matter of debate.

Senator BURKE. Just one question, Mr. Chairman. Professor Corwin, you refer to this proposal as one to unpack a Court that is already packed. I direct your attention to the fact that President Wilson appointed Justice Brandeis and Justice McReynolds; President Coolidge appointed Justice Stone; President Hoover appointed Justice Cardozo, Justice Roberts, and Chief Justice Hughes. Will you tell us which one of these presidents and which Senate then sitting in conformation packed the Court?

Mr. CORWIN. What I meant there, Senator—I thought I made myself clear—was that whenever a president appoints a justice, he certainly ought to appoint him, and it is usual, I should say, to appoint him considering his general outlook. But certainly the debate in the Senate considers that. The debate on the nomination of Mr. Hughes for chief justice ran along several days, and the whole question was as to the outlook of the chief justice.

Senator BURKE. Very true.

Mr. CORWIN. It was based on—Mr. Borah summed the whole thing up when he said that the Court had made itself the economic dictator of the country. So they were considering Chief Justice Hughes, and they said to themselves, "Let us see what kind of decision this man is apt to make."

Senator CONNALLY. Very true, and with that limitation we have no criticism of that appointment. But on this matter, whereas you propose to undo what may have been done heretofore in that respect, never before was the question submitted to Congress to authorize the appointment of six men at one time to accomplish the purpose; and you would at least admit that this is the most extensive packing of the Court ever suggested, would you not?

Mr. CORWIN. In 1837 the Court was enlarged from seven to nine, and the discussion that had preceded that through several years indicated pretty clearly that one reason for it was the desire to break down the influence of John Marshall.

Senator DIETERICH. I was interested in the answer you made, I think to Senator Burke, in which you indicated that you think the six additional judges would be biased in the opposite direction. Do you mean that you feel the president, if this bill passes and he is authorized to increase the membership of that Court by the appointment of additional judges, would select biased or unbiased men?

Mr. CORWIN. I think he would endeavor to appoint men who are learned in the law, honorable men, who would act independently; and that he would consider, as I think he should, their general philosophy.

Senator DIETERICH. You do not answer my question.

Mr. CORWIN. What was your question?

Senator DIETERICH. My question was, are you in favor of selecting biased men in any direction on that Court, or unbiased men?

Mr. CORWIN. Well, I will tell you, Senator Dieterich, I think that is a matter of opinion.

Senator DIETERICH. It might be for some and it might not be for others. I am asking you if you base your entire testimony on the increase of the judiciary on the fact that men would be selected who would be prejudiced or biased on one side or the other of proposed legislation that might be enacted.

Mr. CORWIN. No; I do not think so.

Senator DIETERICH. Would you not be in favor of selecting unbiased men?

Mr. CORWIN. Why should I not?

Senator DIETERICH. Who would use their own unbiased judgment is passing on the constitutionality of acts of Congress.

Mr. CORWIN. Absolutely.

Senator DIETERICH. Did you mean to say that you would expect the president to select biased men?

Mr. CORWIN. No.

Senator DIETERICH. The fact is, he would not select such men.

Senator CONNALLY. Let him answer the question.

Senator HUGHES. You do not allow the professor to answer the question.

Mr. CORWIN. You gentlemen, if I may say so, are looking at this from the point of view of the conventional phraseology of the law. You regard the Supreme Court of the United States as being primarily a judicial body, but that Court is not primarily a judicial body. It is a hybrid body. It exercises political functions as well as judicial functions. It is only in relation to judicial functions that the question of bias is important. It is only in relation to judicial questions that lack of bias can be attributed to anybody. Justice Holmes appreciated that perfectly well. He was the most learned man in the history of the law of any of them. He therefore constantly deplored and deprecated the extent of judicial review, because he felt, and rightly felt, that the Court was thrusting its oar and sickle into a field in which bias or lack of bias became meaningless terms. When it came to a question of whether A should pay B some money, a controversy between two private persons, there was a legal rule for settling that question. Then the question of bias or lack of bias, of partiality or impartiality was pertinent. But when the question was whether we should pursue a certain legislative policy in the government, then bias or lack of bias means nothing at all.

Senator DIETERICH. Professor Corwin, you would not want a Court established, would you, that would just obey the will of the majority, even though the majority might be misled?

Mr. CORWIN. No.

Senator DIETERICH. You would not want a Court established whereby, probably by lack of education or misinformation, the people believed a condition to exist that did not exist, and they would pass a law that would seriously interfere with the liberties of a certain class—you would not want a Court established that because of a majority passed an act which would declare that constitutional?

Mr. CORWIN. No; but I want a Court that will maintain agreed constitutional values.

Senator DIETERICH. I understand. I was talking about the Court passing on constitutional questions. If the legislature should attempt to pass laws that would infringe upon the liberties of a certain class of citizens, the only recourse that class would have, being in the minority, would be to appeal to the Court, the only tribunal to protect the minority.

Mr. CORWIN. Yes; but the question is, "What were their rights?"

Senator DIETERICH. You would leave that to the Court, would you not?

Mr. CORWIN. What court?

Senator DIETERICH. The Supreme Court. In the state court you would probably leave it to the ordinary course of judicial procedure. What I wanted to understand more particularly, Professor Corwin, was your statement that the president would balance the Court by the appointment of judges. The president made a statement in which he indicated what he would do, did he not? He indicated that he would select high-class, qualified men, who would be fair and open-minded. That is all you would expect, it is not?

Mr. CORWIN. Certainly.

Senator DIETERICH. You would not want to subsidize that Supreme Court, would you?

Mr. CORWIN. Nevertheless, in the Senate of the United States, when a nomination came before it, the senators would say ''What is this man's history and general outlook?''

Senator DIETERICH. And you would have just as hard a time finding that out as we have in the investigation of other subjects, because the press would have prejudiced comments, and you would get all sorts of information about it, and when you got through you would have to go and ask some of his neighbors what kind of a fellow he was and whether he was ever convicted of crime or not.

Mr. CORWIN. I say the appointing power is under the obligation to consider what the outlook of that nominee is.

Senator DIETERICH. And you would want men who would have no prejudice against what they believe to be the will of the people, and who would be open-minded?

Mr. CORWIN. I have indicated my position. The president is not going to ask the Senate to confirm any nominee who is not an entirely competent man. I feel that he would appoint men who would have a different outlook on life from the present Court.

Senator DIETERICH. I want to ask you about your statement. As I recall it, that the Court is rather overcrowded and had to throw a lot of material away to keep from getting behind, and could not perform its work in the proper way and give it proper attention. If we had an increased number of judges, the judges now on the bench might get a different view of a good many things if they had more time.

Mr. CORWIN. I think that might be true.

The CHAIRMAN. We are honored this morning by the presence of Hon. Hatton Summers, a representative in Congress from the state of Texas and chairman of the Committee of the Judiciary of the House of Representatives, who will propound questions to the witness.

Mr. SUMNERS. Thank you very much, Mr. Chairman.

Professor Corwin, I am very much interested in your suggestion with regard to the division of the Supreme Court, after having increased the number of judges. I believe you say that may be done by act of Congress?

Mr. CORWIN. I think so.

Mr. SUMNERS. When Congress shall have passed an act to separate the Court into sections, should the sections having jurisdiction in regard to a particular class of matters speak the judgment of the entire Supreme Court?

Mr. CORWIN. I think so, as the vice chancellor in New Jersey does. They have one vice chancellor who speaks for the chancellor.

Mr. SUMNERS. I understand. I do not want to take too much time. You have answered my question.

Then, if you make a division of the Court and assign constitutional questions to five men, having divided the Court into three groups of five each, then those five would speak the judgment of the Supreme Court of the United States with regard to constitutional questions?

Mr. CORWIN. Yes.

Mr. SUMNERS. Do you believe that Congress can provide constitutionally that one-third of the Supreme Court may seek the judgment of the entire Court on constitutional questions?

Mr. CORWIN. I do not know about that. I am doubtful.

Mr. SUMNERS. You would not separate the Court unless they could do that, would you?

Mr. CORWIN. No. Of course, that is somewhat speculative. I do not know that I am wedded to that idea. It was only a suggestion I made.

Mr. SUMNERS. We will try to stay with that suggestion, if you will pardon me.

Mr. CORWIN. Yes.

Mr. SUMNERS. Suppose the Congress should designate the number on the Court that would pass on constitutional questions, and suppose the next Congress should decide they would try the old boys for awhile, what would happen?

Mr. CORWIN. I understand that an act of Congress would be subject to change by a succeeding Congress.

Mr. SUMNERS. May I ask you if you have thought about that? I will not take up any more time than necessary.

The CHAIRMAN. You may take all the time you desire.

Mr. SUMNERS. When the act of 1925 was passed, seeking to limit the powers of the Supreme Court, it was based upon the theory that the circuit courts of appeals would act as a court of last resort in adjudicating controversies among private persons, but those private persons had the right to come to the Supreme Court in certain cases. That would leave the Supreme Court free to adjudicate constitutional questions and other questions of great national import. I am asking you this question because it is important to Congress.

Do you not think, or do you think, that we should work toward a plan, as far as the volume of business would admit, of stopping at the circuit courts of appeals, making them the courts of last resort on all questions except such questions as are necessary for the Supreme Court to adjudicate as a court of last resort? I believe some members of the Congress would favor such a proposal. I would be glad to have you think that matter over. I think the whole Congress would be tremendously concerned in trying to find some solution of that.

Just one other question: I believe you hold to the view, as I understood the statement a moment ago, that the president has as much right to establish his idea on the Constitution as the Court. I was rather interested, if I may be excused, from wondering how he could do it, unless he would send to be judge some man, like a football captain would, send people in with instructions? How is he going to do that except through sending to the Court; wouldn't he be sending to the Court that man with such instruction? How else could he do it?

Mr. CORWIN. I don't think a fit appointee to the Court would be regarded in that light.

Mr. SUMNERS. Now, I don't want to press the question, but you say the president has as much right to judge his idea of the Constitution as the Court has. He cannot establish it by reason of any executive power, can he?

Mr. CORWIN. No; but through legislation, and so on.

Mr. SUMNERS. You mean he can establish his idea of the Constitution through this House and Senate?

Mr. CORWIN. That was Lincoln's position.

Mr. SUMNERS. I thought the Supreme Court had the last word about constitutional matters?

Mr. CORWIN. It has the last word in deciding cases under the Constitution.

Mr. SUMNERS. I thank you very much, Mr. Chairman.

Senator CONNALLY. I have two more questions: Doctor Corwin, you don't disbelieve entirely in the doctrine of judicial review on constitutional questions, do you?

Mr. CORWIN. No; I do not. I believe in it for one reason, I have a vested interest in it. I teach constitutional law.

Senator CONNALLY. In other words, you do believe in the power of the Supreme Court in proper cases to declare acts of Congress unconstitutional?

Mr. CORWIN. Yes; but I want to see that carried out, to the extent—

Senator CONNALLY. I understand.

The CHAIRMAN. Professor, please; your answer may be "yes" or "no."

Senator CONNALLY. He answered "yes," that he believed in the theory of the Supreme Court to declare acts of Congress unconstitutional.

Mr. CORWIN. That is part of our system.

Senator CONNALLY. Now, under our theory and system, suppose Congress passes a law regulating some matter, and a state legislature should undertake to come in, and they make a conflict. Who is going to decide which law is supreme and which shall govern, if we do not submit to the Supreme Court?

Mr. CORWIN. Well, of course that is made pretty clear by the Constitution, isn't it?

Senator CONNALLY. I know it.

The CHAIRMAN. Why can't you answer to that, "The Supreme Court?" Isn't that the answer?

Mr. CORWIN. It is; yes, sir.

Senator CONNALLY. And that would be the Supreme Court according to your theory?

Mr. CORWIN. Yes; I think the courts below should have judicial review over the state acts.

Senator AUSTIN. You referred to what you called a bias in the decisions of the judges?

Mr. CORWIN. Yes.

Senator AUSTIN. I ask you if you know, or whether you know that two days ago, March 15, the Supreme Court divided 7 to 2 in the case of Brush against the Commissioner of Internal Revenue, which it decided; that case involved these political and economic questions that are now pending; and that division had Justice Roberts and Justice Brandeis joining in a dissenting opinion, and that it had Justice Stone and Justice Cardozo joining a majority opinion? You take into consideration other cases of similar character, where these justices have apparently been labeled in your answers either liberal or conservative, and they have moved about in their attitude toward political and economic laws.

Mr. CORWIN. The Court decides a great many questions in which this bias that I attribute to a majority of the Court does not operate.

Senator AUSTIN. That is all.

Senator CONNALLY. You have no objection to bias if it is your way, do you? I mean, mental bias?

Mr. CORWIN. These questions just indicate that what I have said just runs off of your back like water off a duck's back. What I have been trying to bring home is the fact that the Supreme Court is a mixed body, which exercises political powers and judicial powers. In the exercise of the political power choice determines the questions, and choice is determined by a man's outlook on life.

The CHAIRMAN. I want to be corrected if I have drawn an erroneous impression from your statement, but I have drawn the very definite impression that you want unbiased men on the Court; am I right?

Mr. CORWIN. Certainly.

The CHAIRMAN. That is what I want to know.

Mr. CORWIN. If you are going to use the words "biased" and "unbiased" in this connection. I say we want unbiased men. And I am using the word "biased" in the ordinary sense. Now, when you ask me the question whether we want biased or unbiased men—

The CHAIRMAN. I said that I had drawn the impression from your statement tha you want unbiased men; is that correct?

Mr. CORWIN. In the exercise of judicial power; yes.

Senator KING. May I say that I have drawn the conclusion that you want men on the bench who have predelictions, social and socialistic and economic, the same as you possess?

Mr. CORWIN. Well, that is not a fair inference.

Senator KING. I think it is.

The CHAIRMAN. I suggest, then, that Senator King has not drawn correct impression from your testimony?

Mr. CORWIN. The correct impression of my testimony would be this, that I want judges who will keep their sickle out of the political field, if possible; and as far as possible stick to concrete principles. But actually the Court today has not done that.

Senator KING. What are the concrete principles that you would have them stick to, those that you announced or those who belong to the school of thought of which you are a member?

Mr. CORWIN. I should say it would be a concrete principle that trial by the jury should not be abolished; and there should not be any ex-post-facto laws. It is a concrete principle that if one law is made for people with red hair, and another for people with black hair, that such a law would be unconstitutional. That violates all sense of fairness and justice. I do not concede that there is any concrete principle on which the justices may base a decision that the legislature should not pass minimum-wage laws. I do not consider that it is a concrete principle that Congress may not give any attention to the effects upon interstate commerce which ensue from activities within the states, simply because the Court chooses to call such effects "indirect," "however material and whatever their extent." All those things are matters of debate, and Congress should be conceded the right to decide them.

The CHAIRMAN. You are a learned man, and it must be obvious to you that is discussing these questions, somehow we go off, all of us, in an ever-increasing parabola; the more we talk the farther apart we get. Parallel lines never meet, but as to parabola, however, the more it travels the farther apart its lines get.

Mr. CORWIN. I want judges who are unbiased in the determination of concrete principles.

The CHAIRMAN. You do want unbiased men on the Court?

Mr. CORWIN. I would like to have a Supreme Court—

The CHAIRMAN. Do you want unbiased men? Answer "yes" or "no," please.

Mr. CORWIN. I want unbiased men in the sense that I have said unbiased men. I am not asking for any miracle.

Senator CONNALLY. I think you did the witness an injustice.

The CHAIRMAN. I did not intend to.

Senator CONNALLY. He said the Court has two functions; one is political and one judicial. He wanted unbiased men on the judicial question, but not on the other.

Mr. CORWIN. I will put it this way: I want unbiased judges in the sense in which the history of the Court has established the possibility of having unbiased judges. I am not asking for any miracle.

Senator KING. You want judges that have the same predilections as to social and economic theories as you have propounded to your students, I presume, whereby those judges would be of the same thought as the exposition in your books?

Mr. CORWIN. Well, as a matter of fact, I don't teach social theory or economic theory, or anything of the sort.

Senator KING. Then how do you know about the dual functions of the Court, unless you have been teaching that to your classes and going into the books as to judicial functions and political functions? Now, what do you mean by a political function?

Mr. CORWIN. That has been my criticism of the Court, that it has extended its power beyond a statable limitation, and has projected itself into this political field.

Senator KING. Haven't you indicated that is one of the functions of the Court, to deal with judicial and political questions, because in the consideration of the law necessarily there is some political atmosphere in connection with that?

Mr. CORWIN. I have not even intimated that the Court should place itself to the extent it has in the field of political questions.

Senator KING. Let me ask you by a number of questions: Haven't you indicated today that you think that the Court has been invalidating most of the legislation since Mr. Roosevelt came to the White House; and hasn't your attitude today been that the Supreme Court, in dealing with the questions since Mr. Roosevelt came to the White House, has been against what you contemplate is a liberal point of view?

Mr. CORWIN. I have said that the Supreme Court has invalidated legislation by a choice of doctrine, which was no better than other doctrine that was available to it, whereby the legislation could have been sustained. And, that being the case, the Court has sinned against the fundamental maxim of judicial review; namely, all doubts will be resolved in favor of the legislature.

Senator KING. That is accepted by the courts, as announced by Mr. Justice Sutherland back in 1923.

Mr. CORWIN. They say it again—

Senator KING. Let me complete my question: And has not been disclaimed by any justice of the Supreme Court since that? That has been the function?

Mr. CORWIN. My contention is they have not done that.

Senator KING. You have stated a half a dozen times before in dealing with judicial review, that you wanted, as I understand it, to divide the Supreme Court into the three branches, and one of those branches was to pass upon constitutional questions. Now, supposing that those six, or supposing it is five, that they should decide three and two or three and three. What would the position be as to the constitutionality that is different from what we have there now, if there is such a division?

Mr. CORWIN. I don't care to discuss that question, Senator King, for the reason that I threw that out as a sort of happy suggestion that may not be a happy suggestion.

Senator KING. I should think it is a very unhappy one. May I say that it would be a dangerous proposal.

Mr. CORWIN. That may be. Perhaps it should be the whole Court that ought to consider the constitutional questions.

Senator KING. Don't you think people would lose confidence in the Court if you set up a little wing of the Court, of five or six new men, and concede to them, delegate to them such acts of Congress and leave it to them to determine what was constitutional and what was not?

Mr. CORWIN. I rather think you are right. I think the whole Court should do that.

Senator KING. Coming back to the question I was about to ask, since Mr. Roosevelt has been in the White House there have been passed more than thirty important legislative enactments dealing with our political and economic and social conditions. Would you be surprised to learn that only a few of them have been declared unconstitutional; that most of them which have been challenged have been held to be constitutional? You know that, did you not?

Mr. CORWIN. Oh, yes.

Senator KING. Take the case of Booth v. United States, in which there was a unanimous opinion upholding the act; the case of Lynch v. United States, in which the opinion was unanimous; the case of Panama Refining Company v. Ryan, in which the Court held that the act amounted to an unconstitutional delegation of legislative powers to the president, but immediately a new act to correct that objection was passed and the validity of that act has been sustained. In the Schechter Poultry Co. case there was a unanimous decision. Do you differ from that decision?

Mr. CORWIN. I am not particularly interested in the precise number of cases. I am interested in the principles on which the Court operated. I think some of the principles stated in the Schechter opinion were not well stated.

Senator KING. You do not agree with the unanimous vote of the Supreme Court in that case?

Mr. CORWIN. I personally did not sympathize with the N. I. R. A., because I thought it was too widespread, and I thought its enforcement extended beyond possible policing. When Mr. Johnson called for a sort of boycott, I told people I was off the N. I. R. A.

Senator KING. I think you showed good judgment.

Mr. CORWIN. But I could not sympathize with the doctrine laid down by the Court in overthrowing it. The opinion of the chief justice was quite ambiguous, but as interpreted by a majority of the Court in the Carter Coal case, I think it was highly objectionable.

Senator KING. Coming back to the N. I. R. A., do you disagree with the statement by Justice Cardozo that it was delegation "run riot" or "run mad"?

Mr. CORWIN. Yes; I do.

Senator KING. And you think Justice Cardozo became illiberal and reactionary, in your view?

Mr. CORWIN. I am not looking at it from the point of view of liberal or reactionary. I am looking at the question as it affects the functioning of government. I think, for instance, that the facts show, with reference to fascism in Europe, that it arose outside the ranks of government, and because of its inefficient functioning.

Senator KING. That is not germane to the subject, but is it not a fact that facism resoluted largely in abolition of the courts and a denial to an independent judiciary of the right to function?

Mr. CORWIN. Not at all. That was a part of the procedure that established it, but the fascist movement was due to the fact that government was so weak and ineffective that it could not do what was necessary to be done.

Senator KING. Are you acquainted with the Ebert Constitution that was adopted immediately after the war?

Mr. CORWIN. I have read it.

Senator KING. Do you know that it provided for an independent judiciary?

Mr. CORWIN. Yes.

Senator KING. And as soon as Hitler and his associates came into power they said, "We do not want any judicial body that may pass upon the constitutionality of our acts," and they threw that out of the window?

Mr. CORWIN. Nobody denies that. That was a part of fascism, but the fascist movement arose outside of that.

Senator KING. Then you do believe in a judicial system?

Mr. CORWIN. I certainly do.

Senator KING. You believe the fathers who wrote the Constitution sought to establish an independent judiciary?

Mr. CORWIN. I do.

Senator KING. Would you cripple it?

Mr. CORWIN. No.

Senator KING. Would you undermine it?

Mr. CORWIN. No.

Senator KING. Would you create in the minds of the people a disbelief in the integrity of the Courts?

Mr. CORWIN. No.

Senator KING. Ought we not accept a view announced by Mr. Justice Hughes, as read by Senator Burke a few moments ago, as to the maintenance of the Court and the duty of the people to respect the Court and its integrity and support its hands?

Mr. CORWIN. I do not think everything the Supreme Court has decided is entitled to respect because the Supreme Court said it.

Senator KING. That may be true.

Mr. CORWIN. Do you remember what Justice Brewer said?

Senator KING. I know that. You do not assume that every college professor is entitled to respect.

Mr. CORWIN. Certainly not. I encourage my students to contradict me, as you have.

Senator KING. You would not want six of your students to be appointed to the Court, with predilections they might have obtained by reason of your teaching?

Mr. CORWIN. I would not object to that. It would give me quite a reputation.

Senator KING. Now, coming back to these decisions which you say have done so much harm, or which I understood you to say. If you did not say that, I beg your pardon. I think you said they had done so much to destroy our judicial system and the functioning of the Court. I call your attention to these important cases that have been enacted under Mr. Roosevelt's administration and which have been affirmed, except the one which Justice Cardozo declared was delegation of power run mad.

Mr. CORWIN. I do not think the delegation of power there was nearly as great as in Mr. Wilson's time when he had a great army at his back.

Senator KING. Are we going to thresh out the questions incident to that?

Mr. CORWIN. I think what Mr. Justice Cardozo said may have been influenced by the fact that there were 674 codes. If there had been only one code, I doubt if he would have used that expression.

Senator KING. At any rate, as I understand you, you do not disagree with the decision of the Court in the N. R. A. case.

Mr. CORWIN. I do not disagree with the result. I am glad of it.

Senator KING. You think we should have continued it?

Mr. CORWIN. I think Congress should have repealed the statute.

Senator KING. Congress should never have passed it. I happen to have been one who voted against it.

Mr. CORWIN. I do not know that I agree with that.

Senator KING. I presume not, although you did not agree with the act.

Mr. CORWIN. It was too broad and sweeping.

Senator KING. Take the case of Peery v. United States, in regard to the gold measure. You know the decision of the Court in effect was an affirmation of the right of Congress to, what shall I say, increase or modify contracts in the sense that they recognized the change in the content of the gold dollar.

Mr. CORWIN. Yes.

Senator KING. And the Supreme Court on that important question sustained the administration.

Mr. CORWIN. Yes.

Senator KING. That was one of the most important questions that has been brought to the Court.

Mr. CORWIN. Right.

Senator KING. In Rickert Rice Mills v. Fontanet there was a unanimous decision.

Mr. CORWIN. That was an offshot of the A. A. A. case.

Senator KING. That was part of the policy.

Mr. CORWIN. That was settled in the A. A. A. case. The constitutional issue was settled in the A. A. A. case.

Senator KING. In the case of Curtiss-Wright Co. v. United States, my recollection is that was unanimous.

Mr. CORWIN. One dissent.

Senator KING. You would not charge that the Court was wrong in that case, would you, showing a biased or reactionary tendency?

Mr. CORWIN. I think the Court has from the very beginning sustained the broad view of national power in foreign fields.

Senator KING. We will not argue that. I would not agree with your interpretation. . . .

Senator KING. Coming back to the question propounded by the senator from Texas, I understood you to desire the inference to be drawn that our fathers, in framing the Constitution of the United States, accepted the view of Blackstone and not the view of Coke, that Parliament was omnipotent. You did not mean to convey that idea, did you?

Mr. CORWIN. No. I said that most of those men had been educated in Locke and Blackstone, and that their views of constitutional government were in the first instance taken from those sources, and their conception of it was one in which legislative power was normally supreme. However, the senator from Texas brought out—and it is a good point—that a written constitution was devised with the idea of putting certain limits on the power of the legislature. The question of judicial review was confined to pretty narrow limits to begin with, and it was probably due to that fact that we only had two acts of Congress declared void up in 1865.

Senator KING. You have gone over that very fully.

Mr. CORWIN. I want to say in answer to a remark of Senator Connally that judicial review has grown tremendously in recent years. Between 1920 and 1930 there were twenty-two cases of acts of Congress being overturned, according to Mr. Gilbert.

Senator KING. That would be due in part, would it not, to the great increase in population, and the great increase in our industrial development? For the first forty or fifty years the population was limited, largely along the Atlantic coast.

There were not the complex questions and problems in those days that have developed in more recent years, with the increase in population which has expanded toward the Pacific coast. You understand, do you not, there would naturally be an increase in legislation, and an increase in business, and, of course, an increase in the appeals to the courts.

Mr. CORWIN. Right. That is one of the causes for the increased judicial review, but when you go into these cases you find other very important factors.

Senator KING. I think you are exaggerating, if you will pardon me for saying so, the number of cases that have been subject to judicial review. It has just been mentioned that there were less than seventy and it got down to less than fifty, and most of those were unimportant.

Mr. CORWIN. You spoke about the statutes of first importance enacted during the Roosevelt period, and the number that had been declared void.

Senator KING. I am not going into that now. Coming back to the question, is it not a fact that there were efforts to establish an independent judiciary that would have authority to pass upon the validity of acts of Congress and other acts, except those enumerated?

Mr. CORWIN. The framers of the Constitution intended to establish the judiciary establishment that they established.

Senator KING. That is obvious.

Mr. CORWIN. I don't know; to a certain extent, they were not independent, because Congress has the creative power.

Senator KING. Coming back to that again, before the Constitution was drafted there was a recognized authority for the judicial department to declare acts invalid; was there not?

Mr. CORWIN. There were three or four sporadic cases.

Senator KING. Oh, no; there were eight clearly indicated, and I have the references here to historians who say that subsequent investigations show a very large number more.

Mr. CORWIN. Well, if you will read the note in my *Doctrine of Judicial Review,* you will find a good many of these cases discussed. There were about four cases, which were fairly clear. One was in progress while the Convention was going on.

Senator KING. There were over two decided when the Convention was in progress. On one of them, a brief was written and appended which had been directed by Mr. Iredell, who subsequently became justice of the Supreme Court of the United States.

Now, going back again on that, they recognized, the states themselves recognized the power of their courts before the Constitution was formed to pass upon the validity of constitutional enactments?

Mr. CORWIN. No; I refuse to assent to that. That is not so. Some courts had asserted it.

Senator KING. And isn't it a fact that more than a thousand of the acts of the colonial councils were carried to the Privy Council in Great Britain and the authority of those acts was tested and challenged?

Mr. CORWIN. That is just the bunk.

Senator KING. Oh, no.

Mr. CORWIN. You are referring to Mr. Russell's book.

Senator KING. Oh, no.

Mr. CORWIN. Yes.

Senator KING. I am not referring to Mr. Russell's book, but a number of books.

Mr. CORWIN. Yes; Mr. Russell's book. You asked me a question and I am going to answer it.

Senator KING. Let me ask you the question, and you can answer it. Isn't it a fact that many acts of colonial councils were carried to Great Britain and subject to review by the Privy Council? Answer that "yes" or "no," without a speech.

Mr. CORWIN. I am not going to answer.

Senator KING. Well, you cannot, I assume.

Mr. CORWIN. Without an explanation.

Senator KING. Were any carried over for review?

Mr. CORWIN. I know of one true judicial case, Winthrop v. Lechmer, that was carried from Connecticut to the Privy Council, and the act involved was declared to be void. That was the only genuine precedent.

Senator KING. I will put into the record evidence to the contrary, contrary to the statement of this learned professor on constitutional law.

(The matter referred to is as follows:)

STATEMENT RELATING TO QUESTION OF JUDICIAL REVIEW BY STATES PRIOR TO ADOPTION OF CONSTITUTION, AND ALSO RELATING TO REVIEW OF COLONIAL ACTS BY THE CROWN AND PRIVY COUNCIL OF ENGLAND

In the *American Doctrine of Judiciary Supremacy,* Professor C. G. Haines devotes a chapter of the discussion of cases and precedents before 1789 wherein the doctrine of judicial review of legislative acts was involved. In the chapter referred to he discusses the following cases: Case of Josiah Phillips, Virginia, 1778; Holmes v. Walton, New Jersey, 1780; Commonwealth v. Caton, Virginia, 1782; Rutgers v. Waddington, New York, 1784; Symsbury case, Connecticut, 1785; Trevett v. Weeden, Rhode Island, 1786; Bayard v. Singleton, North Carolina, 1787; and a Massachusetts precedent in 1788.

Professor Haines states that the list of cases referred to ". . . is not intended to be exhaustive—for historians are still finding data on new cases—but representative precedents are selected which were known and recognized as instances involving either directly or indirectly the issue of the validity of a legislative act as in conflict with natural law and natural rights or with fundamental law."

He also points out that "The account of early cases is not confined to definite legal precedents, for a number of cases are included in which no act was held invalid, but in which the judge discussed the issue of judicial review in the form of dicta. . . ."

Mr. Brinton Coxe, in *Judical Power and Unconstitutional Legislation*, refers to the cases commented upon by Mr. Haines.

Charles Warren, in *Congress, the Constitution, and the Supreme Court*, refers to the cases of Trevett v. Weeden, Holmes v. Walton, and Bayard v. Singleton, and states:

"In Pennsylvania itself, a committee of the Council of Censors, reporting in 1784 on breaches of the state constitution, had recorded many 'flagrant' and 'wanton' violations of the 'sacred rights of a citizen to trial by jury.' The legislatures of four other states, prior to the Federal Constitution, had sought to deprive citizens of the right to jury trial; and in each state a state court had decided the state statute to be invalid."

Mr. Warren states that another—

". . . case has been little referred to by historians; but it appears that inferior courts of New Hampshire, in 1787, held invalid a law of that state depriving citizens of jury trial; and the news of this decision reached New York and Philadelphia and was published in the daily papers while the Federal Convention was sitting, and just at the time when the New Hampshire Delegates arrived at the convention."

There can be little doubt but that these early cases were known to the framers of the Constitution. Madison undoubtedly referred to Trevett against Weeden when he declared during the course of the Constitutional Convention.

". . . In Rhode Island the judges who refused to execute an unconstitutional law were displaced and others substituted by the legislative who would be willing instruments of the wicked and arbitrary plans of their masters. . . ."

On June 6, 1787, Gerry said to the framers of the Constitution:

". . . In some of the states the judge had actually set aside laws as being against the Constitution. . . ."

Mr. Warren notes that the *Pennsylvania Packet,* a newspaper of wide circulation, informed its readers on several days in April and May 1787, that Varnum's famous argument in the case of "Trevett against Weeden on information and complaint for refusing paper bills in payment" of indebtedness could be purchased from book sellers; and also that the *Independent Gazeteer* [Philadelphia] in June 1787, published a "letter from a gentleman in Virginia to his friend in this city" in which it was stated:

". . . The majority of the House of Delegates in Rhode Island have lost all character and even shame itself. Yet you see there are honest men in that State. The judges behaved handsomely in the affair of the Tender Law."

Professor McLaughlin, in *Constitutional History of the United States,* referring to the preconvention period, states (p. 312):

"If we examine the decisions of the state courts passing upon the construction or the validity of state acts, we find a number of instances in which the principle we are here considering [judicial review] was applied or announced. . . . The early exercise of this power by state courts to declare such state acts void as they believed to be in conflict with the principles of state constitutions is especially impressive because no constitution contained the specific statement that it was law. Pronouncements of the principle which we are considering was made both before and after the Federal Constitution was adopted."

Mr. William M. Meigs, writing in the *American Law Review,* states:

"It is plain enough, too, from the history of the years about 1787, that the colonial doctrine was not forgotten, and there are several reported decisions in several different states close to that time asserting or enforcing the judicial power. . . . Again, these specific cases were beyond all question in the minds of members of the Convention, when they referred to such decisions by the courts and discussed in general the powers of the judiciary in regard to unconstitutional laws..." [40 *Am. Law Rev.* 650–51].

Professor McMaster, in his *History of the United States* (vol. 5, p. 395) informs us that—

"When the struggle for the rights of Englishmen took on the form of a struggle for independence, the same idea of the judicial control of the legislative power was taken up by the leaders and asserted more broadly still.... But it was not until the colonies had becomes states, with written constitutions of government, that the courts began the continuous practice of controlling legislation by deciding laws unconstitutional."

Professor McMaster further stated:

"The majority of the colonies for years before their quarrel with the mother country had seen their laws disallowed at pleasure by the King or Queen in council. They had, therefore, become used to the idea of the existence of a body that could set aside a law enacted by a legislature and approved by a governor. They were used to written charters and frames of government and were accustomed to appeal to them as the course of all authority under the King. When, therefore, in their quarrel with the mother country it became necessary to find some reason for resisting the stamp tax, the colonists appealed to a written document and declared the tax invalid because it violated the provisions of the Magna Carta."

Professor Hugh E. Willis, is his recent book on Constitutional Law, declares (pp. 75–76):

"One reason for the fact that the Supreme Court finally took this power to itself was the colonial practice. The colonial courts, and on appeal of the Privy Council of England, had the power to declare legislative acts void if in conflict with colonial charters. The colonists, consequently, acquired the habit of seeing colonial laws occasionally declared void by the courts. Hence, upon the adoption of state constitutions it was the natural thing for the state courts tacitly to assume the function of interpreting the new state constitutions; and judges in the states of New Jersey, New York, and Rhode Island rendered decisions declaring legislative acts unconstitutional because in violation of their constitutions; and this action was generally acquiesced in, though not without some opposition. This accustomed the people of the new country to the supremacy of the judiciary over the legislative branch of government."

Professor Dickerson, in his able discussion on the subject of judicial review in *American Colonial Governmen, 1696 to 1765,* states (p. 227):

"During the period from 1686 to 1765 nearly 400 different laws, from the continental American colonies alone were disallowed by the Crown...."

Professor Haines, in his *American Doctrine of Judicial Supremacy,* refers to the extent of judicial review in colonial times, and states (p. 49):

"The extent to which such an administrative review was exercised is shown by the fact that of 8,563 acts submitted by the colonies, 469, or 5.5 percent, were disallowed by orders in council."

In the *Review of American Colonial Legislation by the King in Council,* Elmer Beecher Russell observes:

"The power of review exercised by the Privy Council was analogous to that assumed by the Supreme Court of the United States after the formation of the new Government. The Privy Council, it is true, declared acts void upon grounds other than the contravention of a fundamental law; but it frequently did disallow laws because they conflicted with the colonial charters, or with acts of the British

Parliament, or the common law of England. Under its tutelage the colonists become accustomed to a limitation upon the power of their legislatures. In this sense the work of the Privy Council constituted at once a precedent and a preparation for the power of judicial annulment upon constitutional grounds now exercised by the state and federal courts in the United States...."

Professor Dickerson points out that—

"The Declaration of Independence lays the responsibility for the royal vetoes at the door of the King, but probably unjustly. Although every order in council for the disallowance of a law stated that it was done by 'the King in council,' the King had nothing to do with the matter personally. The phrase is only one of the numerous fictions of the British Government. The real work of considering colonial laws was done by the board of trade, and the final action was only recorded as done by the King in the presence of and with the advice of his Privy Council. Hence, 'disallowed by the King in Council' must be understood to mean by the board of trade on the advice of able legal opinion and finally ratified by the Privy Council. As will be shown later, this action corresponded very closely to that of a careful court of record, rather than to the hasty, arbitrary action of an irresponsible individual...."

Mr. Meigs, in the "American Doctrine of Judicial Power" (47 *Am. Law. Rev.* 689), declares:

"This system prevailed everywhere throughout the country for several generations—about a century and a half—and I think modern history would tell us in convincing tones that such a doctrine so grown would not be likely suddenly to die out and disappear from the face of our corner of earth, simply because we broke loose from Great Britain.... It certainly did not disappear, but soon began to dovetail with our new system...."

Mr. CORWIN. Would you let me answer the question on that? Would you let me answer it in detail?

Senator KING. You have answered it; you said, "No."

Mr. CORWIN. There was only one such case, and that was not known until about 1890.

Senator KING. I hope you are satisfied with that answer?

Mr. CORWIN. I am satisfied.

Senator KING. And every state in the Union except one in its constitution has set up a judicial system analogous to that in the federal government; that is to say, it has created a supreme court?

Mr. CORWIN. They have a judicial system, but the judges are usually elected for a short term of years.

Senator KING. But they have a judiciary?

Mr. CORWIN. Surely.

Senator KING. And the conferring of judicial power is substantially in the same manner as that in the Constitution of the United States?

Mr. CORWIN. Right.

Senator KING. And the state of New York—by the way, did you ever live in New York?

Mr. CORWIN. No.

Senator KING. The state of New York's courts declared more than three hundred laws unconstitutional through their highest court in a period of forty or fifty years.

Mr. CORWIN. Well, that is not true.

Senator KING. Is it not true?

Mr. CORWIN. I made a study of this subject, and I will send you a copy of my article on judicial review in New York.

Senator KING. I have made a study myself, and that is the evidence I have found.

Mr. CORWIN. What forty or fifty years are you referring to?

Senator KING. More, perhaps; from 1805 up to 1850 or 1860.

Mr. CORWIN. Well, I see you need to read my pamphlet, and I will send it to you.

Senator KING. But all of the state constitutions have substantially the same provision for judicial authority, do they not, as the federal Constitution? That is to say, the supreme court and such other courts as are set up shall have judicial powers?

Mr. CORWIN. This was not established, you know, in some of the states until a good while after—long after.

Senator KING. But that is in the state constitutions, is it not, every state constitution except Georgia, as I recall, has a provision that the judicial power is conferred upon the supreme court and such other courts as may be authorized and established. And the supreme court of the states declared acts unconstitutional, did they not; and has there been any great protest by the people of the various states because their state courts have declared acts unconstitutional?

Mr. CORWIN. Well, there were in the earlier days; yes.

Senator KING. And have they modified their state constitutions in that regard because the supreme courts of the various states have held acts to be unconstitutional?

Mr. CORWIN. No; but they have largely abandoned generally the need for such provision.

Senator KING. I am speaking about have they modified their constitutions in that respect?

Mr. CORWIN. They have modified their courts so they are more responsive to public opinion.

Senator KING. But they are the sole authority to determine the constitutionality of acts?

Mr. CORWIN. They are the sole authority to determine the constitutionality of acts in the decision of cases.

Mr. CORWIN. Exactly; because that is all that is brought to the court.

The CHAIRMAN. Anything further?

Senator CONNALLY. One question: Doctor, I have been very greatly interested in your testimony; I think you know a lot about these things. You refer to the fact that at the beginning of the adoption of the Constitution, with the exception of the case of Marbury v. Madison, there were no constitutional cases until the Dred Scott decision; isn't that right?

Mr. CORWIN. That is right.

Senator CONNALLY. Now, isn't it true in those days, they were denouncing and attacking the court? Jefferson and Madison and Jackson and the Democrats of that time were denouncing and abusing the Court because it would not declare acts of Congress unconstitutional?

Mr. CORWIN. No; that is wrong. The only thing they were denouncing the Court for was declaring such laws unconstitutional.

Senator CONNALLY. How about the Alien and Sedition laws?

Mr. CORWIN. That was prior to 1802.

Senator CONNALLY. I said from the beginning of the Constitution.

Mr. CORWIN. In 1798 and 1799 there was a good deal of criticism for not declaring them unconstitutional.

Senator CONNALLY. And did they not denounce the Court because they would not hold the National Bank Act unconstitutional?

Mr. CORWIN. Yes; I think perhaps so. I am not sure about that.

Senator CONNALLY. Don't you know that from reading the history of that time, that Jefferson and Madison and all of them were doing that?

Mr. CORWIN. They denounced the bank for that.

Senator CONNALLY. And they did not want to turn over to the federal government such powers, and thought the states should not pass so many powers over, because they would not declare the acts unconstitutional?

Mr. CORWIN. They could hardly blame the courts; it was for Congress to repeal them.

Senator KING. The proposal in your book entitled *Doctrine of Judicial Review* is that you discuss there the question as to whether the Constitution sanctions judicial review; and did you not state in that book:

> That the members of the Convention of 1787 thought the Constitution secured to the courts in the United States the right to pass on the validity of acts of Congress under it cannot be reasonably doubted.

Mr. CORWIN. I answered that question from Senator Burke.

Senator KING. You wrote that, did you not?

Mr. CORWIN. Yes.

Senator KING. Do you agree with the statement made by Professor Beard— and I think you have expressed a contrary view—when he stated that there were more than twenty-five of the members of the Constitutional Convention who had unequivocally expressed their acceptance of that view?

Mr. CORWIN. Well, I think that Professor Beard went a little afield for some of his evidence. That is, you don't have any evidence of that sort from the debates of the Constitutional Convention.

Senator KING. I have read them all, and I have read the various states' conventions, and I think that Dr. Beard was a little too modest. I want to read here a sentence or two from a more recent book, one by Professor McLaughlin and also Mr. Meigs. I will put those into the record; and also Professor Haines.

Mr. CORWIN. I have testimony here, too.

Senator KING. They have been giving testimony here for a long time previously.

Mr. CORWIN. Perhaps James Madison is a better witness than any of these people.

The CHAIRMAN. Professor Corwin, it is not often we have the privilege of these intellectual feasts with college professors, and while they talked to us when we were in college, we certainly enjoy the privilege of talking with them now.

Mr. CORWIN. You are enjoying it; you are the audience. Mr. King is giving the show and doesn't enjoy it.

Senator KING. I am enjoying it.

Mr. CORWIN. I don't claim to know everything, I am sure.

The CHAIRMAN. Well, you know, the word "Senators"—I have forgotten whether it is Greek or Latin—but it means knowledge, wisdom, know it all. So you must not be offended if we allocate to ourselves the privilege of pretending at least to know it all. The very words means wisdom, know it all.

Senator Burke has a question.

Senator BURKE. I wanted to quote from Professor Felix Frankfurter, who said, "Our scheme of government is ideal, but in it the professor should be on tap, but not on top."

Mr. CORWIN. I think I have been on tap.

The CHAIRMAN. Thank you.

Senator KING. Do you agree with what Professor Frankfurter and his associates stated in their book, that to add to the Supreme Court would only add to the confusion; that it was not necessary?

Mr. CORWIN. I think so, unless this idea of panels and sections is adopted.

Senator KING. One other question: Have you examined the record of the Supreme Court with respect to the cases that come up on writ or certiorari?

Mr. CORWIN. No.

Senator KING. I may say that I have made an examination of those, and is it not a fact that nearly all of those cases that come up on certiorari are unimportant cases relating to private rights; and the litigants have had their day in court, first the district court and then the circuit court of appeals, so that they had had two chances to determine the righteousness or unrighteousness of their claims?

Mr. CORWIN. Well, you can answer that better than I. You have gone into the subject.

Senator KING. I am not on the witness stand.

The CHAIRMAN. Did you desire to print something in the record?

Mr. CORWIN. Madison said in 1788 [reading]:

In the state constitutions, and indeed in the federal one also, no provision is made for the case of a disagreement in expounding them; and as the courts are generally the last in making the decision, it results to them by refusing or not refusing to execute a law, to stamp it with its final character. This makes the Judiciary Department paramount in fact to the legislature, which was never intended and can never be proper.

Senator KING. I ask permission to insert in the record at this point a number of statements by Mr. Madison and others, indicating their views of power of the judiciary to pass upon the constitutionality of acts of Congress.

The CHAIRMAN. If there be no objections, that will be the order.

(The matter referred to is here set forth in full, as follows:)

STATEMENTS MADE BY MADISON AND OTHERS SUPPORTING THE VIEW THAT THE SUPREME COURT IS EMPOWERED TO DECLARE LEGISLATIVE ACTS INVALID

Professor Beard, in his *Supreme Court and the Constitution,* lists nineteen members of the Convention as showing definitely that they recognized and approved the view that the Supreme Court is authorized to declare legislative acts unconstitutional, and others frankly approved it, or at least acquiesced in it, and six others who were favorable to it. These members are listed below, together with the reasons assigned by Professor Beard for placing them in this category:

John Blair, a member of the Virginia Court of Appeals which decided the case of Commonwealth v. Caton, in 1782, agreed with the rest of the judges "that the Court had power to declare any resolution or act of the legislature, or of either branch of it, to be unconstitutional and void; that 10 years later he was one of the three judges of the federal Circuit Court for the District of Pennsylvania who claimed that they could not perform certain duties imposed upon them by a law of Congress, because the duties were not judicial in nature and because under the law their acts would be subject to legislative or executive control. Blair, as a Member of the Senate, supported the Judiciary Act of 1789, which accorded to the Supreme Court the power to review and reverse or affirm the decisions of state courts denying the validity of federal statutes.

Dickinson wrote in advocacy of the Constitution in 1788:

"In the Senate the sovereignties of the several states will be equally represented; in the House the people of the whole Union will be equally represented; and in the President and the federal independent judges, so much concerned in the execution of the laws and in the determination of their constitutionality, the sovereignties of the several states and the people of the whole Union may be considered as conjointly represented."

This indicates, declared Professor Beard, that whatever Dickinson's personal preference may have been, he "evidently understood that the new instrument implicitly empowered the federal judiciary to determine the constitutionality of laws; and he presents this implication to the public as a commendable feature of the Constitution."

Ellsworth held that the federal judiciary would declare acts of Congress contrary to the Constitution null and void, and he so explained the Constitution in the Connecticut ratifying convention when he said:

"This Constitution defines the extent of the powers of the general Government. If the general legislature should at any time overleap their limits, the judicial department is a constitutional check. If the United States go beyond their powers, if they make a law which the Constitution does not authorize, it is void; and the judicial power, the national judges, who, to secure their impartiality, are to be made independent, will declare it to be void."

Professor Beard also points out that Ellsworth was later chairman of the Senate committee which prepared the Judiciary Act of 1789.

Elbridge Gerry expressed himself very clearly on this point in the Convention. When the proposition relative to a council of revision was first taken up by the Convention he expressed doubts "whether the judiciary ought to form a part of it, as they will have a sufficient check against encroachments on their own department by their exposition of the laws, which involved a power of deciding on their constitutionality."

He then brought squarely to the attention of the Convention the fact that the courts of the several states had passed on the validity of state laws, stating:

"In some states the judges had actually set aside laws as being against the constitution. This was done, too, with general approbation. It was quite foreign from the nature of the office to make them judges of the policy of public measures."

Alexander Hamilton's views on this questions are expressed in No. 78 of the *Federalist*, where he said:

"Some perplexity respecting the right of the courts to pronounce legislative acts void, because contrary to the Constitution, has arisen from an imagination that the doctrine would imply a superiority of the judiciary to the legislative power.... There is no position which depends on clearer principles than that every act of a delegated authority, contrary to the tenor of the commission under which it is exercised, is void. No legislative act, therefore, contrary to the Constitution, can be valid.... Whenever a particular statute contravenes the Constitution, it will be the duty of the judiciary tribunals to adhere to the latter and disregard the former."

Rufus King, in the discussion of the proposed council of revision took the same position as Gerry, observing "that the judicial ought not to join in the negative of a law because the judges will have the expounding of those laws when they come before them; and they will no doubt stop the operation of such as shall appear repugnant to the Constitution."

Madison expressed his views on the question of judicial review in the Constitutional Convention on July 23, 1787, when he said that "he considered the difference between a system founded on the legislatures only, and one founded on the people, to be the true difference between a league or treaty, and a constitution.... A law violating a treaty ratified by a preexisting law might be respected by the judges as a law, though an unwise and perfidious one. A law violating a constitution established by the people themselves would be considered by the judges as null and void."

Professor Beard sums up Madison's views on the subject of judicial review as follows:

"In cases of a political nature involving controversies between departments, each department enjoys a power of interpretation for itself [a doctrine which Marshall would not have denied]; in controversies of a judicial nature arising under the Constitution the Supreme Court is the tribunal of last resort; in cases of federal statutes which are held to be invalid by nullifying states the Supreme Court possesses the power to pass finally upon constitutionality." Luther Martin, during the debate on July 21, said:

"... And as to the constitutionality of laws, that point will come before the judges in their proper official character. In this character they have a negative on the laws. Join them with the executive in revision and they will have a double negative. It is necessary that the supreme judiciary should have the confidence of the people. This will soon be lost, if they are employed in the task of remonstrating against popular measures of the legislatures."

Mason favored associating the judges with the executive in revising laws. He recognized that the judges would have the power to declare unconstitutional statutes void, but he regarded this control as insufficient. In convention he said:

"They [the judges] could declare an unconstitutional law void. But with regard to every law, however unjust, oppressive, or pernicious, which did not come plainly under this description, they would be under the necessity as judges to give it a free course. He [Mason] wished the further use to be made of the judges of giving aid in preventing every improper law."

Gouveneur Morris declared, in the debate of July 21, that some check on the legislature was necessary; and he "concurred in thinking the public liberty in greater danger from legislative usurpation than from any other source."

Later, when Dickinson questioned the right of the judiciary to set aside laws, Morris said:

". . . He could not agree that the judiciary, which was a part of the executive, should be bound to say that a direct violation of the Constitution was law. A control over the legislature might have its inconveniences. But view the danger on the other side. . . . Encroachment of the popular branch of the Government ought to be guarded against."

His view was again expressed in the date on the repeal of the Judiciary Act of 1801, when he said:

". . . Did the people of America vest all power in the legislature? No; they had vested in the judges a check intended to be efficient—a check of the first necessity, to prevent an invasion of the Constitution by unconstitutional laws—a check which might prevent any faction from intimidating or annihilating the tribunals themselves."

William Paterson: Professor Beard declares that ". . . there is perhaps no finer statement of the doctrine of judicial control than that made by Paterson as Associate Justice of the Supreme Court in the case of Van Horne's Lessee v. Domance {*sic;* Dorrance}, decided in 1795." In the court {*sic;* course?} of his opinion, Justice Paterson said: "I take it to be a clear position that if a legislative act oppugns a constitutional principle the former must give way, and be rejected on the score of repugnance. I hold it to be a position equally clear and sound that, in such case, it will be the duty of the Court to adhere to the Constitution, and to declare the act null and void. The Constitution is the basis of legislative authority; it lies at the foundation of all law, and is a rule and commission by which both legislators and judges are to proceed. It is an important principle which, in the discussion of questions of the present kind, ought never to be lost sight of, that the judiciary in this country is not a subordinate, but coordinate branch of the government. . . ."

The case referred to is the case usually considered by historians as the first instance in which the federal courts held a state act void.

Beard says that Randolph seems not to have expressed himself in the Convention on the subject of judicial control, but he points out that the plan which he presented provided for establishing a council of revision composed of the executive and a convenient number of the judiciary, "with authority to examine every act of the national legislature before it shall operate", and he therefore must have been "convinced of the desirability of some efficient control over the legislative department." Professor Beard also point out that—

"Subsequently, as Attorney General, when it became his [Randolph's] duty to represent the Government in Hayburn's Case (2 Dall. 409) and he was moving from a mandamus to compel the circuit court for the district of Pennsylvania to execute a law under which the judges had declined to act on the ground of its unconstitutionality, Randolph accepted the view of the judges that they were not constitutionally bound to enforce a law which they deemed beyond the powers of Congress. . . . In a letter to Madison, August 12, 1792, Randolph said: 'The sum of my argument was an admission of the power to refuse to execute, but the unfitness of the occasion.' "

Add to these instances the fact that he approved the Judiciary Act of 1789, and it becomes apparent that Randolph was aware of, and approved of, the doctrine of judicial control over legislation.

Hugh Williamson, asserts Beard, certainly ". . . believed in judicial control over federal legislation; for in the debate on the proposition to insert a clause forbidding Congress to pass ex-post-facto laws, he said: 'Such a prohibitory clause is in the constitution of North Carolina and, though it has been violated, it has done good there and may do good here, because the judges can take hold of it.' It is obvious that the only way in which the judges can 'take hold of' ex-post-facto laws is by declaring them void."

James Wilson, declares Beard, expressed himself in favor of judicial control in the course of the debates on July 21 and August 23. The former occasion was when the proposition to associate the national judiciary with the executive in the revisionary power was before the Convention, and the latter occasion was when he spoke in favor of giving the national legislature a negative over state legislation. He thought that the ". . . judiciary ought to have an opportunity of remonstrating against projected encroachments on the people as well as on themselves. It had been said that the judges, as expositors of the laws, would have an opportunity of defending their constitutional rights. There was weight in this observation, but this power of the judges did not go far enough."

He also thought ". . . It will be better to prevent the passage of an improper law than to declare it void when passed. . . ."

In the debates in the ratifying convention in Pennsylvania he declared that the proposed constitution empowered the judges to declare unconstitutional enactments of Congress null and void.

In addition to the members of the Convention mentioned above, Professor Beard states that William Johnson, Robert Morris, and George Washington evidenced their approval of the doctrine in connection with the Judiciary Act of 1789. John {sic; Johnson?} and Morris were members of the first Senate and voted in favor of the act, and Washington, as President, approved it. Professor Beard asserts that there is direct or indirect evidence that Baldwin, Bassett, Wythe, Few, Read, and Strong, directly or indirectly, supported the doctrine of judicial control over legislation. He concludes:

"In view of these discussions, and the evidence adduced above, it cannot be assumed that the Convention was unaware that the judicial power might be held to embrace a very considerable control over legislation and that there was a high degree of probability (to say the least) that such control would be exercised in the ordinary course of events."

Professor Beard also point out that to the 23 members enumerated above should be added Bearley and Livingston, of New Jersey, who, through their connections with the early case of Holmes v. Walton, went on record as understanding and approving the doctrine of judicial review.

Furthermore, Professor Beard calls attention to the fact that on June 4 when King stated emphatically that the judges in the exposition of the laws would undoubtedly stop the operation of such as appeared repugnant to the Constitution, Bedford, McClurg, Pierce, and Yates were present at the Convention.

In "The Judicial Bulwark of the Constitution" (8 *Pol. Sci. Rev.* 167, et seq.), Frank E. Melvin states:

"Practically every name listed as favorable by Professor Beard can be verified and, indeed, at times, with additional and sometimes stronger evidence than he presents. . . . Perhaps really the chief fault to be found with [his] study is that it could so easily have been carried further and made more conclusive. . . ." Melvin contends that evidence is available to indicate . . . that of the 55 actual members of the Federal Convention some 32 to 40 of them, that is, two-thirds of the Convention, and including nearly every influential member, upheld or accepted the right of the courts to disregard as law any unconstitutional legislation; while 4 or 5 members apparently opposed it."

To the 25 whom Beard cites as favoring the doctrine, Melvin would add Rutledge, Gorham, Sherman, Chas. Pinckney, Gen. C. C. Pinckney, Davis, and probably Langdon, while—

". . . inference based on evidence of intelligent participation in the critical debates without opposing the assertions of judicial control made by the leading debaters in the Convention—evidence frequently supported by other proofs— would suggest that Dayton, Clymer, Broom, Fitzsummins, and probably McClug, Carroll, and Franklin were either adherents of the idea or at least friendly neutrals."

Melvin continues:

"There remain then some 10 members whose views have not yet been ascertained. Among these are Yates of New York, who left on July 10, Pierce of Georgia, absent after July 1, and Houston who probably left about July 26, also Ingersoll and Mifflin of Pennsylvania, Bount {*sic;* Blount}, and Alexander Martin of North Carolina, Houston of New Jersey, Jenifer of Maryland, and Gilman of New Hampshire. Yet even touching certain of these there are some indications as to their attitude. Thus though Gilman and Langdon arrived late, yet they heard the most important debates touching the judicial power and the vote of New Hampshire was regularly accordant with votes favoring that power. Gilman also voted thus in the First Congress as far as can be determined and though, like Gerry, he voted with the opposition on January 9, 1793, yet on the final passage of the amended Pension Act [January 10] he changed his vote. Both Blount of North Carolina and Pierce of Georgia were Members in Congress on March 20, and April 3, 1787, when they agreed to the circular letter which contributed so much toward the wider recognition of the judicial power, and they doubtless shared the views of the other four elected members of the Federal Convention then present, King, Madison, Jo_.nson, and Few who are commonly admitted to be favorable to judicial review. As to Houston of New Jersey there seems no strong reason why he should be singled out from the other members of the New Jersey delegation, with whom he voted, and with whom he must have shared any impression in favor of judicial revision incident to the Holmes v. Walton precedent. For the news of this case evidently reached Congress while Houston was attending in 1780, and besides as clerk of the superior court of New Jersey in 1781, he could hardly escape full knowledge of their significant decision, of the previous year. Although

Yates of New York left the Convention his notes echo the first discussions on judicial revision and if he were the author of the Brutus letters in the *New York Journal and Weekly Register,* it is clear that while he may not have favored judicial control yet he clearly recognized it as a feature of the Constitution. Doubtless equally interesting indications could be found touching the attitude of the five remaining members, Ingersoll, Mifflin, Jenifer, Alexander Martin of North Carolina, and Houston of Georgia, none of whom certainly attempted to dispute the opinion of the vast majority of the Convention, and all of whom apparently advocated the adoption of the Constitution by their States.

"If out of 55 members of the Convention but 5 remain without our having direct evidence or at least some specific clue as to their attitude, beyond the fact that they never openly opposed judicial control, and if, moreover, but a half dozen can be found to have seriously disbelieved in or even objected to the doctrine of judicial power, what reasonable doubt can there be that the common, and indeed the logical interpretation of their work, shows their real intention that the Constitution should find in the courts a bulwark against its infraction. Verily stronger confirmation of our chief contention could scarcely be desired than that afforded by the so-called opponents of the doctraine {*sic;* doctrine?} themselves as shown by Mercer, Dickinson, and Yates, that judicial control clearly was wrought into the fabric of the Constitution."

Mr. Charles Warren, in his *Congress, the Constitution, and the Supreme Court,* states:

"With such practical illustrations of state court actions and of the views of the Congress of the Confederation in their minds and before their very eyes in the newspapers, while they were sitting in Convention, the framers of the Constitution (several of whom were also members of Congress) had no doubt as to what powers their new federal courts were to, and should, exercise and possess; nor did they omit to express their views on the floor of the convention. Thus, Elbridge Gerry of Massachusetts spoke of the judges' exposition of the laws, which 'involved a power of deciding on the constitutionality', and he said: 'in some states, the judges had actually set aside laws as being against the Constitution. This was done too with general approbation.' Luther Martin of Maryland said: 'As to the constitutionality of laws, that point will come before the judges in their proper official character.' James Madison of Virginia said: 'A law violating a constitution established by the people themselves would be considered by the judges as null and void.' Gouverneur Morris and James Wilson of Pennsylvania, Caleb Stong of Massachusetts, George Mason of Virginia, Rufus King of Massachusetts, Hugh Williamson of North Carolina, and John Rutledge of South Carolina recognized and admitted the judges' power over Acts of Congress, and Roger Sherman of Connecticut referred to the power of state courts to set aside State statutes if violative of the Federal Constitution.

"To these 11 men, there should be added at least the following: William Livington, William Paterson, David Brearly, and Jonathan Dayton of New Jersey; William R. Davie of North Carolina; Abraham Baldwin of Georgia; John Blair, George Wythe and Edmund Randolph of Virginia; Alexander Hamilton of New York; Oliver Ellsworth of Connecticut; Thomas Fitzsimmons of Pennsylvania; Charles C. Pinckney of South Carolina—each of whom within a few years after the Convention, explicitly favored the judicial power. Only four members of the convention announced themselves as opposed."

Mr. Warren further states:

"It was clearly seen that the judges should not be allowed to concern themselves with the merits or demerits of a statute, for their functions only related to the legality and constitutionality of the statute; and his function could only properly be exercised in the decision of an actual law suit, after argument. Others were strongly opposed to the judges having any power in the making of a statute which might come later before them for judicial decision."

He points out that—

". . . There was a general admission by the members of the Convention that the Court would have power, eventually, to pass on the validity of the Acts of Congress; and therefore, many did not believe it right that the Court should have a double chance."

Mr. Corwin, in his work entitled *The Doctrine of Judicial Review* discusses the question as to whether the constitution sanctions judicial review, and it is his opinion that while there was no clause inserted in the Constitution for the specific purpose of bestowing this power on courts, the power rests upon certain general principles thought by its framers to have embodied in the Constitution. And he adds that—

". . . the members of the Convention of 1787 thought the Constitution secured to courts in the United States the right to pass on the validity of acts of Congress under it, cannot be reasonably doubted."

Mr. Corwin names 17 members of the Convention who entertained their view, and states:

"We are driven to the conclusion that judicial review was rested by the framers of the Constitution upon certain general principles which in their estimation made specific provision for it unnecessary, in the same way as, for example, certain other general principles made unnecessary specific provision for the President's power for removal."

During a discussion of the Constitution Strong stated:

"That the power of making ought to be kept distinct from that of expounding the laws, and that no maxim was better established."

Mr. Corwin further states that—

"The utterances of other members bear out the words . . . for in one form or another the notion of legislative power as inherently limited power is distinct from and exclusive from the power of interpreting the standing law was reiterated again and against and was never contradicted when the Convention adopted Article III of the Constitution vesting 'the judicial power of the United States in one court and such inferior courts as Congress shall from time to time establish,' it must be regarded as having expressed the intention of excluding Congress from the business of law interpreting altogether."

In an article entitled "Progress of Constitutional Theory," published in volume 30, *American Historical Review,* Mr. Corwin concludes (p. 536):

"Finally, from Madison, who from the first interested himself in every phase of the rising movement for constitutional reform both in his own state and the country at large, came the idea that the problem of providing adequate safeguards for private rights and adequate powers for a national government can be made a make-weight against the swollen prerogatives of the states legislatures. It remained for the Constitutional Convention, however, while it accepted Madison's main idea, to apply it through the agency of judicial review. Nor can it be doubted that this determination was assisted by a growing comprehension in the Convention of the doctrine of judicial review."

In *A Constitutional History of the United States,* published in 1936, Professor A. C. McLaughlin, after reviewing the decisions of the state courts, passing upon the construction or the validity of state acts, prior to the Constitutional Convention of 1787, and finding in these cases a trend of political thought toward the acceptance of the doctrine of judicial supremacy, declares that a careful examination of the debates in the Convention will convince the skeptic that the men of the Convention assumed that such power would be exercised by the courts.

Professor McLaughlin further stated:

"No one can understand the rise of judicial authority unless he understands the nature and course of revolutionary argument, the American inheritance of principles of individual rights, and the seriousness with which men, in the midst of political turmoil, went back to fundamental principles of political philosophy and strove to make them actual."

And he added:

"The assertion of independent judicial power to maintain the fundamental law and to preserve individual liberty, even against the encroachment of legislative bodies, appears to be the natural product of the ages, finding place and opportunity for expression in a new and free country where people were making their institutions."

Professor McLaughlin, in his work *The Court, the Constitution, and Parties,* states the doctrine of judicial review as follows:

"In theory any court may exercise the power of holding acts invalid; in doing so it assumes no special and peculiar role, for the duty of the court is to declare what the law is and, on the other hand, not to recognize and apply what is not law."

Mr. Curtis, in his *Constitutional History,* volume 2, page 13, edition of 1890, states that—

"...the right to find relief against an act of Congress which transcends its constitutional powers springs from and is regulated from the Constitution itself. It is a right that can be exercised only by resorting to a judicial remedy."

President Wilson said:

"Our courts are the balance wheel of our whole constitutional system; and ours is the only constitutional system so balanced and controlled."

STATEMENTS RELATING TO JUDICIAL REVIEW MADE IN THE RATIFYING CONVENTIONS OF THE STATES

Mr. Wilson, in the Pennsylvania state convention stated:

"I say under this Constitution, the legislature may be restrained and kept within its prescribed bounds by the interposition of the judicial department. I had occasion on a former day to state that the power of the Constitution was paramount to the power of the legislature acting under that Constitution; for it is possible that the Legislature, when acting in that capacity, may transgress the bounds assigned to it, and an act may pass in the usual mode notwithstanding that transgression; but when it comes to be discussed before the judges—when they consider its principles and find it to be incompatible with the superior power of the Constitution—it is their duty to pronounce it void. And judges independent and not obliged to look to every session for a continuance of their salaries, will behave with intrepidity and refuse to the act the sanction of judicial authority" (Elliot, vol. 2 p. 445).

Mr. Grayson, in the same convention, said:

"If Congress cannot make a law against the Constitution, I apprehend they cannot make a law to abridge it. The judges are to defend it. They can neither abridge nor extend it" (Elliot, vol. 3, p. 567).

John Marshall, also in the same convention, said:

"Has the Government of the United States power to make laws on every subject? Does he [referring to Patrick Henry] understand it so? Can they make laws affecting the mode of transferring property or contracts or claims between citizens of the same state? Can they go beyond the delegated powers? If they were to make a law not warranted by any of the powers enumerated, it would be considered by the judges an infringement of the Constitution which they are to guard. They would not consider such a law as coming under their jurisdiction. They would declare it void. . . . To what quarter will you look for protection from an infringement on the Constitution, if you will not give the power to the judiciary?'' (Elliot's *Debates,* vol. 3 pp. 553, 554.)

William R. Davie of North Carolina said:

''There is no rational way of enforcing the laws but by the instrumentality of the judiciary. . . . It appears to me that the judiciary ought to be competent to the decision of any question arising out of the Constitution itself.''

George Nicholas of Virginia said:

''Who is to determine the extent of such powers? I say the same power which, in all well-regulated communities, determined the extent of legislative powers. If they exceed these powers, the judiciary will declare it void or else the people will have a right to declare it void.''

Luther Martin of Maryland said:

''Whether, therefore, any laws of regulations of the Congress, any acts of the President or other officers, are contrary to, or not warranted by, the Constitution rests only with the judges, who are appointed by Congress to determine; by whose determination every state must be bound.''

The CHAIRMAN. Professor Corwin, we thank you for your contribution.

9. Standpoint in
Constitutional Law

At the Council of Nicea, we are told, Constantine the Great enthroned the Bible as "the infallible judge of truth," the final outcome of which act was the doctrine of papal infallibility. In this country we have enthroned the idea of "a government of laws and not of men," and the outcome—perhaps not *final*—has been government by allowance of the Supreme Court. For all that, the conception of a self-speaking, self-enforcing Constitution still has considerable vitality in certain quarters, as discussion of President Roosevelt's Court proposal has amply shown; and the obverse of this conception is that of the automatic nature of the judicial function when the possessors of judicial power are not subjected to *political* pressure, that alone of all forms of pressure being capable of diverting the judicial needle from the North Pole of constitutional truth. So in preparing this paper I have felt that I should not be chargeable with slaying the slain if I addressed the bulk of it to the above mentioned conceptions—the bulk of it although not all of it.

I

As it occurs in everyday usage the term "Constitution of the United States" refers to the document of 1787 plus the amendments which have since been added to it. But this, if I may employ an available French distinction, is only the *"formal"* sense of the term. In the *"material"* sense a constitution is a body of rules in accordance with which a government is organized and operates; and in this sense "the Constitution of the United States" comprises a vastly extended system of legislation, customs and adjudications, of which the

From 17 *Boston University Law Review* 513 (1937). Reprinted by permission.

This paper was read in the Gaspar G. Bacon Lectureship on the Constitution of the United States, at Boston University (1937).

constitutional document is, as it were, but the nucleus, and into which it tends ever to be absorbed.

Turning at the outset, however, to the document itself, we find that it serves three broad objectives: first, it supplies a framework of national government; secondly, it delegates certain powers to that government; and thirdly, it lays down certain restrictions both on these powers and on those of the states also, in the interest of private rights and of individual freedom of conduct. Actually for the purposes of this discussion the second and third of these objectives may be merged, inasmuch as it has been assumed from an early date that the individual citizen is entitled to challenge judicially an exercise of governmental power as being *ultra vires* even when no specific *limitation* in the interest of individual rights has been transgressed.[1] In this respect, in other words, the Constitution came early to approximate a corporate charter.

Illustrations of the way in which the governmental framework supplied by the document of 1787 has been supplemented, at times indeed supplanted, but {*sic;* by} later practice and legislation are numerous. The Judiciary Act passed by the first Congress to implement the meagre phraseology of Article III of the Constitution is one example of such legislation; the Presidential Succession Act of 1886 is another; the successive acts establishing the great executive departments are still others. Although of course enacted and repealable like ordinary statues, such measures, when evaluated for their content, are much more than that. Again adopting French terminology, we may term them "organic acts".

And with regard also to practice and usage we must be content with a brief citation of examples, beginning with the President's cabinet. Not merely is this institution totally unknown to the Constitution; it would be no extraordinary application of a certain type of constitutional interpretation to show that it is "unconstitutional." The Constitution says that the president may take the opinion of the heads of the executive department "in writing." Given an "exclusive construction" such as was applied by Chief Justice Marshall in Marbury v. Madison[2] to the delineation in Article III of the Supreme Court's original jurisdiction, this provision clearly rules out anything like a cabinet council of departmental heads; and indeed, it appears to have been the intention of the framers that the Senate should serve this purpose, or something akin to it. The expectation was defeated partly by the size of that body, but more immediately by its self-conscious insistence upon its legislative character. Everybody has heard the story of Washington's disgust with the upper house when, early in his first administration, he went to consult with it regarding some Indian treaties. It being moved that the treaties be "committed," the great man, "red-faced and angry," withdrew, declaring "he'd be damned" if

---

1. This assumption appears, for example, in McCulloch v. Maryland, 4 Wheat. 316 (1819). It is, of course, a logical corollary of the notion of the national government as one of delegated powers.
2. 1 Cr. 137 (1803).

he ever went there again. Yet even Washington had to have advisors, and so he
fell back on the heads of his departments, with the result that before quitting
office he had entirely altered his conception as to the primary qualification to be
demanded of officials. Whereas it had been his original idea that they should be
chosen to represent all sections of opinion, his final cabinet was selected in the
first instance for the party loyalty of its members. In the Myers Case,[3] decided
in 1926, we find Chief Justice Taft, a former president, characterizing the
members of the cabinet as the president's "alter ego's."

Even more striking is the transformation which the Electoral College, or
Colleges, have undergone. It was the belief in 1787 that these bodies would
comprise the leading men of the American community, who would exercise
their own individual judgments in the choice of a president. As Hamilton put
the idea in the *Federalist*, "the immediate election" of president would be
"made by men most capable of analyzing the qualities adapted to the station
and acting under circumstances favorable to deliberation and to a judicious
combination of all the reasons and inducements that were proper to govern the
choice."[4] As we know today, this beautiful theory prevailed just so long as
George Washington was willing to be president and there was consequently no
diversity of opinion calling for exercise of judgment. But our second president
was chosen in 1796 by a body of political marionettes, and such has continued
to be the nature of presidential electors to this day.[5] Writing in 1898, a former
president of the United States expressed the conviction that should an elector
fail to vote for the nominee of his party, "he would be the object of execration,
and in times of very high excitement might be the subject of a lynching."[6]

Then there is the question which was raised for the first time in 1841,
following the fatal bowl of cherries upon which "the Hero of Tippicanoe"
feasted not wisely but too well; to what, under the Constitution, did his
successor succeed? The pertinent words of the Constitution read as follows: "In
the case of the removal of the President from office, or of his death,
resignation, or inability to discharge the powers and duties of the said office,
the same shall devolve on the Vice-President. . . ." What is the antecedent here
of "the same"—the "office" of president, or its "powers and duties"? There
used to be a legend to the effect that while the Senate was debating this
momentous question shortly after Harrison's death, and whether they should
address Tyler as "president" or "acting president" a message arrived from that
gentleman signed, "John Tyler, President of the United States." Mr. Horwill
argues persuasively that the story is apochryphal, and that furthermore John
Tyler was not entitled to call himself president.[7] Despite which, practice has

3. 272 U.S. 52.
4. No. 67 (Lodge ed. 1888).
5. H. W. Horwill, *The Usages of the American Constitution* ch. 2 (1925).
6. *Id.* 38.
7. *Id.* ch. 3.

unquestionably settled it that whenever a vice president succeeds on account of the permanent disappearance of the president from the scene, it is to the "office" of president that he succeeds and not merely to its "powers and duties." Whether the same rule would hold in the case of a merely temporary "inability" on the part of the president is a different question, but the wording of the recently adopted "Lame Duck" Amendment strongly reinforces Mr. Horwill's argument as to such a contingency.

Finally, as was remarked above, the documentary Constitution is also supplemented—when not superseded—by an extended system of adjudications. These are comprised in what is termed "constitutional law," which is the product ultimately of the power of the Supreme Court to disallow such acts of Congress and state legislative acts as in its opinion contravene the Constitution. Here it is the former branch of this power of "judicial review," as it is today generally termed, in which we are chiefly interested. Whence comes it—from the Constitution itself, or from constitutional law or from usage?

So far as the Constitution is concerned, judicial review of acts of Congress is clearly a result of inference rather than of explicit grant, and while many drew this inference at the time of the Constitution's framing and adoption, others did not; while still others—including the important case of Madison—changed their minds about it.[8] And by the same token is constitutional law a somewhat precarious basis logically of the institution of which it is the child; albeit as a matter of history we must recognize that the "judicial bootstraps" have ever been a potent source of judicial prerogative. In short, it is judicial practice, ratified by popular acquiescence, which established judicial review of acts of Congress in the first place, and it is the same factors which account for the great extension of the institution in recent years.

II

Thus I am brought to the topic which I announced at the outset, as my principal one. I am going to show, first, how the constitutional document, viewed as *a bulwark of individual rights,* has been absorbed into constitutional law; and secondly, how constitutional law, in turn, is derived chiefly not from the constitutional document but from outside ideas and theories, with regard to which moreover the Court has from the first exercised a highly selective function.

Compared with the constitutional document, with its four thousand words,

8. "In the state constitutions, and indeed in the federal one also, no provision is made for the case of a disagreement in expounding them; and as the courts are generally the last in making the decision, it results to them by refusing or not refusing to execute a law, to stamp it with its final character. This makes the judiciary department paramount in fact to the legislature, which was never intended and can never be proper." 5 *Writings* 294 (Gaillard Hunt ed. 1900–1910). This was written in the autumn of 1788.

more or less, the bulk of material designated by the term "constitutional law" is simply immense. First and last the Supreme Court has handed down not far from thirty thousand opinions, occupying in the published *Reports* probably two hundred thousand pages large octavo; and of this total probably one fourth at least comprises cases involving constitutional points. Still more striking is the fact that by far the greater number of these have arisen out of four or five brief phrases of the Constitution, "necessary and proper," "regulate commerce," "obligation of contracts," "life, liberty and property without due process of law"—which phrase occurs both as a limitation on the national government and as a limitation on the states—; and out of two or three general doctrines, that for instance of "dual federalism"—of which more hereafter—and the doctrine that the legislature may not delegate its powers, which hails more immediately from John Locke's *Second Treatise on Civil Government* and more remotely from a text of Justinian's Digest which has no reference to legislative power.

How little of the constitutional document is really involved in the content of constitutional law was shown notably in 1929 when Professor W. W. Willoughby brought out the second edition of his famous work on the Constitution, the first edition of which had appeared nineteen years before. Of the sixty-five chapters of the earlier edition Willoughby was able to carry over more than forty into the new edition without substantial change or addition. Why? Because these chapters dealt with clauses of the Constitution the interpretation of which has given rise to few if any questions from the outset. On the other hand, when we turn to Congress's power over commerce we find that two chapters comprising 148 pages of the earlier edition have been superseded by eighteen chapters of 376 pages. And the contrast between the two editions as to their treatment of due process of law is even more remarkable. In the earlier work this subject was disposed of in a single chapter of eighteen pages, while in the second edition the same topic and the related topic of equal protection of the laws are treated in fifteen chapters of 276 pages. From these two buds of the original constitutional tree have sprung, and largely in the last fifty years, a whole forest of constitutional law and doctrine.

So returning to those outside ideas and theories to which I referred a moment since, I apply to these the term "constitutional theory"; and this I define as embracing that considerable accumulation of ideas and speculations, often mutually contradictory, regarding the nature and purposes of the Constitution which have in the past determined to greater or less extent its practical application and especially its judicial interpretation. I say "determined," and yet constitutional theory is by no means always a final term, but like constitutional law too is often simply instrumental of more ultimate ideas, points of view, values, or to speak more concretely, is translative of the social philosophies, outlooks and predilections of members of the Bench. I shall first illustrate these truths from the history of constitutional interpretation prior to the Civil War and then turn to more modern issues.

The foremost purpose of the Convention of 1787 was to establish an effective national government. In this connection the following entry in the official Journal of the Convention for July 17th is most instructive.

> It was moved and seconded to postpone the consideration of the second clause of the Sixth resolution reported from the Committee of the whole House in order to take up the following:
>
> "To make laws binding on the people of the United States in all cases which may concern the common interests of the Union; but not to interfere with the government of the individual states in any matters of internal police which respect the government of such states only, and wherein the general welfare of the United States is not concerned" which passed in the negative (Ayes—2; noes—8). It was moved and seconded to alter the second clause of the 6th resolution so as to read as follows, namely,
>
> "And moreover to legislate in all cases for the general interests of the Union, and also in those to which the states are separately incompetent, or in which the harmony of the United States may be interrupted by the exercise of individual legislation."
>
> Which passed in the affirmative (Ayes—6; Noes—4).
>
> It was moved and seconded to agree to the following resolution, namely,
>
> "Resolved that the legislative acts of the United States made by virtue and in pursuance of the articles of Union and all treaties made and ratified under the authority of the United States shall be the supreme law of the respective states as far as those acts of treaties shall relate to the said states, or their citizens and inhabitants—and that the judiciaries of all the several states shall be bound thereby in their decisions, anything in the respective laws of the individual states to the contrary notwithstanding."
>
> Which passed unanimously in the affirmative.[9]

Two things here emerge fairly clearly: first, that the legislative powers subsequently delegated the national government in more specific terms were intended by the framers to serve "the general interests of the Union" and those purposes "to which the States are separately incompetent"; secondly, that it was not intended that the supremacy which the Constitution accords national legislation made in pursuance of the Constitution should be qualified or limited by the powers of the states even with respect to "matters of internal police only." Whether these expectations of the framers have been realized, is a question worth bearing in mind.

As a good Federalist Chief Justice Marshall sought, naturally, to embody the point of view of his party—which in the main was that of the framers—in constitutional law. The Marshall creed may be summarized as follows: 1. The Constitution, being derived from the American people, is to be interpreted solely from the point of view of securing to them the fullest benefit of its

---

9. 2 Farrand, *Records* 21–22 (1911).

provisions, a fact emphasized by the "necessary and proper" clause. 2. State power as such is no ingredient of national power and sets no independent limit thereto, a fact made clear by the "supremacy" clause. 3. The chief role of the Supreme Court is that of ultimate organ of the national supremacy, and its construction of the Constitution and laws of the United States is binding on the states in all cases whatsoever. 4. The Constitution was intended to "endure for ages to come," and the Court's function of interpreting it involves accordingly the corollary responsibility of adapting it "to the various crises of human affairs."[10]

Marshall had the opportunity to develop his constitutional creed most systematically in the classic case of McCulloch v. Maryland,[11] decided in 1819. The question primarily at issue was the right of the state of Maryland to tax the operations of the Baltimore branch of the second Bank of the United States; which raised the further question of the power of Congress to create such an institution, it being admitted on all hands that the Constitution did not confer the power in definite terms.

Marshall sustained the bank as a valid agency under the "necessary and proper" clause of the more specific powers of the national government to lay taxes, borrow money, regulate the coinage, etc. "Let the end be legitimate," said he,

Let it be within the scope of the Constitution, and all means which are appropriate, which are plainly adapted to the end, which are not prohibited, but consist with the letter and spirit of the Constitution are constitutional.

Nor had Maryland the right to tax the operations of this or any other constitutional agency of the national government. If that did not result from the fact that "the power to tax involves the power to destroy," while the power to create includes the power to preserve, it was at any rate the consequence of the "supremacy" clause, it being

Of the very essence of supremacy to remove all obstacles to its action within its own sphere, and so to modify every power vested in subordinate governments as to exempt its own operations from their influence.

While Marshall's logic was impeccable, his history was inadequate, inasmuch as it stopped short of recognizing the important fact, that once the Constitution was adopted it became the supreme law of those elements of the American population who had opposed its adoption as well as of those who had urged it, and that the former were much the more numerous. Throughout the whole latter half of his chief justiceship Marshall was consciously waging an up-hill fight against states rights or—in his own phrase—against "the confederatization of the Union."

10. The present writer in *Twilight of the Supreme Court* 7 (1934).
11. Note 1, above.

Marshall died July, 1835, and a few months later the Court was enlarged from seven justices to nine, a measure which enabled the appointing power of the day to water down the little that remained of his influence on the bench. Within twenty-two months the Court received a new chief justice and five new associate justices, and a new set of constitutional dogmas which may be summed up as follows: 1. The Constitution is primarily a compact of the people of the states, and only secondarily a part of the law of each state, albeit an unchangeable part so long as the compact lasts; 2. The peculiar field of the national government is that of external relationship; the peculiar field of the states is that of internal government, and within the latter field the principle of national supremacy does not apply; 3. The Supreme Court is not, therefore, primarily the instrument of a supreme national power but rather it is an impartial umpire between two seats of *equal* power, the states and the national government; 4. The Constitution is static, speaking always "not only in the same words, but with the same meaning and intent" as when it came from its framers.[12]

The central idea here is, obviously, that of *federal equilibrium* or *dual federalism,* which signifies in practical effect that the distribution of powers between the national government and the states which exists at any particular moment ought to be treated as something permanent; and that the main reason for judicial review is to secure this permanency. The conception thus exalts the role of the Court even while it curtails the national legislative authority. The supremacy of the national government becomes, in truth, that of the Court.

Three outstanding cases of the Taney period were the famous Dred Scott case,[13] Kentucky v. Dennison,[14] and Ableman v. Booth.[15] In the first, several of the justices, going far beyond the logic of dual federalism, denied that Congress had any independent powers in the territories at all—its powers were those merely of trustee and steward for the co-proprietor states and their divergent interests. In the second case we find a unanimous Court asserting, on the eve of the Civil War, the proposition that "the federal government under the Constitution has no power to impose on a State official as such any duty whatever and compel him to perform it"—an assertion which at once challenges comparison with Marshall's statement in Cohens v. Virginia[16] that the national government may, when acting within its sphere, "legitimately control all individuals and governments within the American territory."

Lastly, in Ableman v. Booth the Court, in setting aside a judgment of the supreme court of Wisconsin which had claimed for the courts of that state the right to issue a writ of *habeas corpus* to a prisoner in the custody of the United

12. *Twilight of the Supreme Court* 11–12.
13. 19 How. 383 (1857).
14. 24 How. 66 (1861).
15. 21 How. 506 (1859).
16. 6 Wheat. 264 (1821).

States, set forth its theory of its own place in the federal system in the following arresting language:

This judicial power was justly regarded as indispensable, not merely to maintain the supremacy of the laws of the United States, but also to guard the states from any encroachment upon their reserved rights by the general government . . . So long . . . as this Constitution shall endure, this tribunal must exist with it, deciding in the peaceful form of judicial proceeding the angry and irritating controversies between sovereignties, which in other countries have been determined by the arbitrament of force.

III

The constitutional law of John Marshall gave embodiment, to the extent at least of its delineation of national power, to ascertainable intentions of the framers, and in that sense sprang very immediately from the constitutional document itself. Between the constitutional law of the Taney Court and the constitutional document intervened a states rights gloss, the classic expression of which is to be seen in the Virginia and Kentucky Resolutions of 1798–99. Still farther removed from the constitutional document is the constitutional law which the Court has spun for us since 1885. Now and then, to be sure, a phrase of the document itself affords a casual rafter, as it were, from which the Court, spider-like, has swung its web, but the fabric itself is of its own secretion and that of the contemporary bar.

In this latest period states rights v. national power is no longer a vital issue, though still capable of serving as a screen for vital issues. The great issue, the controlling issue, has been that of government v. business; and the point of view from which the Court has predominantly approached this issue has been that of the laissez-faire theory of political economy. Dominant political forces had determined that the American citizen should be a voter—that could not be helped; but "the mere force of numbers" *must not be permitted to project government into the field of business management; and especially must business management be allowed to dictate the terms of the employer-employee relationship,* this being the very essence of constitutional liberty in a capitalistic regime.

With the successive appointments of Chief Justice Fuller and of Justices Brewer, White and Peckham, in the late eighties and early nineties, the Court was brought to full awareness of the new problem confronting it; and these men found already on the bench a valiant and redoubtable ally in Justice Field. To be sure, Field knew little, and probably cared less, about the Manchester School of Political Economy and its doctrines; but he was of Puritan stock, a frontiersman, and a successful graduate from the school of hard knocks. To him the individualistic tenets of the Declaration of Independence were an evangel of eternal verities, and what they meant was that individual initiative was not to be curbed by the government so long as it did not take form in actual violence or the grosser species of fraud.

And how was this new philosophy articulated with the Constitution? So far as state power was concerned two clauses of the Constitution became of supreme importance, the "due process" clause of the recently adopted 14th Amendment and the "commerce" clause. Let us consider these in order.

All that "due process of law" meant originally was a fair trial for accused persons, and the question of its observance therefore never came up until someone had been arraigned for an alleged violation of law. Today the clause is chiefly important as a restriction upon the substantive content of legislation, and what it means is, in effect, the *approval of the Supreme Court*. The phraseology of judicial decisions is, of course, hardly so outspoken as this. What the Court says is, that legislation must not be "arbitrary" or "unreasonable"; but what this means inevitably, and all that it means, is that legislation must not be *unreasonable* to the Court's way of thinking.

Besides, the clause has two other dimensions—"liberty" and "property." In Munn v. Illinois,[17] decided in 1876, the Court laid down the doctrine that the police power of the states extended to the setting of "reasonable" returns for "businesses affected with a public interest." Furthermore, it was at least strongly implied that both the material terms of this proposition were for the legislature and not the Court to define. But the ink was hardly dry on Chief Justice Waite's opinion when the Court began to pare and qualify it, and in two decades it had become the accepted doctrine of the Court that it alone was authorized to say with finality whether a business was one "affected with a public interest" and whether a return imposed by public authority was "reasonable."

Even more illuminative, however, of the laissez-faire creed of the Court was what happened to the word "liberty" in the "due process" clause. The right which was originally guaranteed by this term was physical liberty, freedom from illegal detention, a right which the writ of *habeas corpus* exists to protect and violation of which is redressible by an action for false imprisonment. But in the Lochner Case,[18] decided in 1905, we find "liberty" to mean the right of males twenty-one years of age to work in a bake shop more than ten hours a day and sixty hours a week; while in the Coppage Case,[19] decided in 1915, it means the right of an employer to fire an employee from belonging to a labor union; and in the late District of Columbia Minimum Wage case,[20] decided in 1923, it means the right of women to work for less than a living wage.

And meanwhile the "commerce" clause was undergoing an interpretation which rendered it of scarcely secondary importance as an instrument of laissez-faire-ism. Before the Civil War, indeed, the Court had ratified with

17. 94 U.S. 113.
18. 198 U.S. 45.
19. 236 U.S. 1.
20. 261 U.S. 525; adhered to in Morehead v. New York, 298 U.S. 587 (June 1, 1936); overruled in West Coast Hotel Co. v. Parrish, decided March 29, 1937 {300 U.S. 379}.

some qualifications the theory, which had been advanced in Marshall's time and had been partially accepted by him, that while in form merely a grant of power to Congress, this clause is also a restraint on the states, forbidding them to do that which it authorizes Congress to do, although Congress has not exercised its power. Building on this beginning, the Court began about 1885 to press the "commerce" clause more and more into the service of the economic forces which were making even then for the nationalization of business. The taxing power of the states was first brought under judicial control in this way,[21] but in the Liquor Cases,[22] which were decided in the late 80's and early 90's the Court also projected the same doctrine sharply into the field of the local police power. In the cases referred to it was held that since liquor was "a legitimate article of commerce," a state could not forbid its entry from another state, a ruling which put the solution of the liquor question on a local basis out of the bounds of constitutional possibility and so led eventually to the 18th Amendment, in somewhat the same way as the Dred Scott decision had, in rendering a legislative solution of the slavery question constitutionally impossible, contributed to bring on the Civil War.

The theory of these cases and of others like them was that stated recently by Justice Cardozo in one of the New York Milk Cases,[23] where it was held that New York was not entitled to keep out milk from Vermont which had been purchased at a price lower than that decreed for milk in New York. He said:

> The Constitution was framed under the dominion of a political philosophy less parochial in range. It was framed upon the theory that the peoples of the several States must sink or swim together, and that in the long run prosperity and salvation are in union and not division.

But did this mean that Congress could govern the sale in New York of milk brought from Vermont? The decision setting the N.I.R.A. aside shortly after answered this question with a resounding *NO*.[24]

IV

And so we are brought to consider the articulation of the laissez-faire philosophy to that part of constitutional law which has to do with national power. In the history of the Supreme Court, two terms of Court have, until recently, stood out above all others for the significance of their results to American constitutional law, the February term of 1819, when McCulloch v. Maryland, Sturges v. Crowninshield,[25] and Dartmouth College v. Woodward,[26]

21. The great leading case is the State Freight Tax Case, 15 Wall. 232 (1873).
22. Bowman v. Chicago & N.W. Ry. Co., 125 U.S. 465 (1887); Leisy v. Hardin, 135 U.S. 100 (1890).
23. Baldwin v. Seelig, 294 U.S. 511 (1934).
24. Schechter Poultry Corp. v. United States, 295 U.S. 495 (1934).
25. 4 Wheat. 122.
26. 4 Wheat. 518.

were decided; and the October term of 1894 when the Sugar Trust Case,[27] the Income Tax Cases,[28] and In re Debs[29] were passed upon. Nor, indeed, would it be easy to conceive how three decisions could possibly have been more to the liking of business than the three decisions last mentioned. In the Sugar Trust Case, the recently enacted Sherman Anti-Trust Act was put to rest for a decade, during which period capital, fulfilling the Pauline injunction of "diligence in business, serving the Lord," made the most of its opportunities. In the Income Tax Case, the Court, undertaking to correct what it termed a "century of error," ruled that the wealth of the country was to be no longer subject to effective national taxation. At the same time, when the said wealth was menaced with physical violence, it was entitled, by the decision in the Debs Case, to have every resource of the national executive and judicial power brought to its protection.

Any one of these cases might easily furnish a text for instruction regarding the effect of laissez-faire-ism on our constitutional law, but I shall content myself with considering the subject in relation to Congressional power over interstate commerce. In the case of Hammer v. Dagenhart,[30] which along with the Sugar Trust Case just referred to, may be taken to mark the crystallization of the laissez-faire interpretation of Congress's power to regulate commerce among the states, it was held that an act of Congress which forbade the transportation from one State to another of products of concerns employing child labor was not a regulation of commerce among the states, but was an invasion of the reserved powers of the states. The doctrine of the case is resolvable into certain constituent propositions, the first of which is that Congress's power to *regulate* commerce does not include the power to prohibit it except for the benefit of commerce itself;[31] the disproof of which proposition, however, so far as *foreign* commerce is concerned appears on the very face of the Constitution. Otherwise, how explain the provision in Article I, section 9, that the slave trade was not to be prohibited until 1808? As a federal judge pointed out in the early case of The William,[32] which grew out of Jefferson's Embargo, this provision shows that "the national sovereignty" was thought by the framers to be authorized to abridge commerce "in favor of the great principles of humanity and justice," and for "other purposes of general policy and interest."

But, the answer is returned, the power to regulate *foreign* commerce is of greater scope than the power to regulate commerce among the states, and so the

27. 156 U.S. 1.
28. 157 U.S. 429; 158 U.S. 601.
29. 158 U.S. 564.
30. 247 U.S. 251.
31. See the present writer's *Commerce Power versus States Rights* ch. 4 (1936).
32. 282 Fed. Cas. (16,700) 614 (1808).

above proposition does not hold as to the latter.[33] Despite, however, the distinguished provenience of this idea, which appears to have originated with Madison in 1829, the Court had rejected it no fewer than ten times prior to 1904. That year Justice (later Chief Justice) White in deciding a case having nothing to do with the point, bundled the Madisonian thesis into his opinion,[34] and Hammer v. Dagenhart clearly presupposes it. And quite recently we find Justice Sutherland invoking in its behalf "the rules of statutory construction."[35] It is of course true, as Justice Sutherland contends, that a word which recurs in a document may not always retain the same meaning throughout the document, although the legal *presumption* is that it does. But that a word should have two quite different meanings in a single short sentence in which it occurs but once, as is the case with the word "regulate" in the "commerce" clause, is certainly a novelty to the science of hermenutics—if not indeed to that of linguistics!

Furthermore, laying the above results achieved by our laissez-faire Court in the field of national power over commerce alongside the results achieved by the same Court's application of the commerce clause as a restraint on state power—what do we discover? The answer is to be found in the fact that at the time of Hammer v. Dagenhart no state could exclude child labor products from sister states, these being, like liquor, "legitimate objects of commerce." In short, what we have in this field is a total defect of governmental power— Congress may not act because to do so would be to invade the powers of the states, and the states may not act because to do so would be to invade the powers of the Congress! So we have a governmental "no man's land"—the Utopia, the City of the Sun, the Elysian Fields of laissez-faire-ism, where injunctions spring up like ginger-bread to keep labor and the agents of government from troubling, and legislative power is pleasantly nonexistent.[36]

But while laissez-faire-ism has been the most important single influence determining the content of our constitutional law during the last fifty years, it has not been by any means the sole influence, nor has its influence been at all times a constant factor. Our constitutional law is a conglomerate and like our constitutional theory embraces different and often contradictory elements. First of all there are the doctrines of earlier Courts, which are frequently revived in contemporary crises. Then there have been wars and emergencies in the meeting of which certain national powers—that over the currency, for example— have undergone pronounced and permanent enlargement. Again, the Court is not at all times immune from the pressure of public opinion. Indeed, there have been periods when political liberalism has affected the bench directly through

---

33. *Commerce Power Versus States Rights* ch. 2.
34. Buttfield v. Stranahan, 192 U.S. 470.
35. Atlantic Cleaners and Dyers v. United States, 286 U.S. 427 (1932).
36. As Mr. Dooley once said to Mr. Hennessey: "Let thim as will write the laws of a counthry, if I may only write the injunctions"—or words to that effect.

the appointment to it of justices who were more or less sympathetic with the idea that economic forces need correction and supplementation on occasion from political forces. Finally, personal influences which are less easily classified have at times contributed to impart to the course of decision a different direction from that which laissez-faire-ism would have taken.

Not to mention the living, let us consider Justice Holmes and Chief Justice Taft in this connection. While neither of these men was at all of the reformer type, yet neither had served big business at the bar.[37] To the contrary, substantially the entire professional career of each was in the service of government; and the net result was that each sooner or later brought very positive support to the claims of political authority under the Constitution. Immensely learned in the law and the ways of courts from time immemorial, Justice Holmes felt that there were very definite limits to the conditions in which true judicial independence and impartiality can flourish, and that these limits were clearly transcended when courts were called upon to pass upon questions of great public moment without the aid of agreed standards. "It is a misfortune," he once asserted, with both our constitutional law and our common law in mind,

> If a judge reads his conscious or unconscious sympathy with one side or the other prematurely into the law, and forgets that what seem to him to be first principles are believed by half his countrymen to be wrong.... When twenty years ago a vague terror went over the earth and the word Socialism began to be heard, I thought and still think that fear was translated into doctrines that had no place in the Constitution, or the common law. Judges are apt to be naif, simple-minded men, and they need something of Mephistopheles.[38]

A friend of mine—an older man than myself—called upon the justice shortly after his retirement from the Court and asked him whether he had been guided by any one principle in the decision of constitutional cases. "Young man," said he, fixing my friend's eye sternly, "Young man, I discovered about 75 years ago that I wasn't God Almighty." And feeling himself not to be God Almighty, Justice Holmes became the mouthpiece of a new gospel of laissez-faire, namely of laissez-faire for legislative power, because legislative power represents, or under a democratic dispensation ought to represent, what he termed "the dominant power of society." And it was in a like spirit that he answered the Court's opinion in Hammer v. Dagenhart. Before the Constitution was adopted, he pointed out, the independent states could prohibit the entrance into their territory of any goods whatever from sister states, and by the Constitution that absolute power

---

37. Pertinent in this connection are some words written by Justice Samuel Miller in 1875: "It is in vain to contend with judges who have been at the bar the advocates for forty years of railroad companies, and all the forms of associated capital, when they are called upon to decide cases where such interests are in contest. All their training, all their feelings are from the start in favor of those who need no such influence." C. Fairman, "Justice Samuel Miller, a Study of a Judicial Statesman," 50 *Pol. Sci. Q.* 42–43 (1935).

38. *Collected Legal Papers* 295 (1920).

had been handed over to Congress. Why then, he asked in effect, should not Congress stipulate the terms on which people may engage in interstate commerce. In fact, it does stipulate the terms on which people may engage in foreign commerce.

Less sympathetic with legislative power as such than Justice Holmes, although he too dissented in the District of Columbia Minimum Wage Case,[39] Chief Justice Taft's views, when it came to the question of national power under the "commerce" clause, were those of a strong government man. As a young judge out in the Sixth Circuit Taft had seized the opportunity offered by the Addyston Pipe and Steel Case,[40] to undermine the decision in the Sugar Trust Case, and so persuasive was his opinion that it was adopted almost *in toto* by the Supreme Court in its disposition of the case on appeal. This occurred in 1899. Fifteen years later Mr. Taft, now Kent Professor of Law at Yale University, brought out a little book on *The Anti-Trust Act and the Supreme Court,* in which he declared that later decisions had "practically eliminated" the Sugar Trust decision[41] and in this relation he stressed particularly Justice Holmes's opinion in the Swift Case of 1906,[42] where it had been held that a course of business which is dominated by its interstate characteristics constitutes "a stream of commerce among the States," the local incidents of which—in this case local purchases and sales of cattle, followed by slaughter and preparation of meat products—may be governed by Congress by virtue of its power to protect interstate commerce against detriment from whatever source proceeding.

And building on the Swift Case, which he characterized as " a milestone in the interpretation of the commerce clause of the Constitution," Mr. Taft as chief justice elaborated a canon of constitutional construction capable of vesting Congress with almost indefinite control of large scale productive enterprises which seek an interstate market, as of course such enterprises invariably do. Thus dealing with Congress' power over effects which reach interstate commerce from intrastate operations, he laid down this doctrine:

> Whatever amounts to a more or less constant practice, and threatens to obstruct or unduly to burden the freedom of interstate commerce is within the regulatory power of Congress under the commerce clause, and it is primarily for Congress to consider and decide the fact of the danger and meet it. This Court will certainly not substitute its judgment for that of Congress in such a matter unless the relation of the subject to interstate commerce and its effects upon it are clearly non-existent.[43]

And it was in reliance upon this doctrine that Congress in 1933 enacted the N.I.R.A. which, among other things, attempted to govern hours of labor and

---

39. Note 20, above.
40. 175 U.S. 211.
41. *The Anti-Trust Act and the Supreme Court* 70 (1914).
42. 196 U.S. 375.
43. Stafford v. Wallace, 258 U.S. 495, at 521; Board of Trade v. Olsen, 262 U.S. 1, at 37. These cases were decided in 1922 and 1923.

wages in productive industry, on the theory, in part, that in the circumstances of the then existing emergency they affected commerce among the states. The act, however, was set aside by the Court in the Poultry Case[44] on the basis of the doctrine of the Sugar Trust Case, that any effect reaching commerce among the states from conditions surrounding production is "indirect" and *per se* beyond national power "however inevitable" such effect is, and "whatever its extent." And in the spring of 1936 the same doctrine was reiterated by the Court in setting aside the Guffey Coal Conservation Act of 1935,[45] although the trial court had found that as a matter of fact interstate commerce in soft coal had been repeatedly interrupted for long periods by disputes between owners and workers on questions of hours and wages.

In short, we see that as the Court confronted the problem of the constitutionality of the New Deal legislation in 1934, it had available to it two points of view; and we see also that it chose the laissez-faire point of view and the course of decision which had been projected from that approach—a course of decision which inevitably set it at variance with the politically responsible branches of the national government. Can there be any serious question that it might have chosen otherwise, or that it would have done so had it heeded Marshall's doctrine "that the Constitution was intended to endure for ages to come" and consequently to be "adapted to the various crises of human affairs;" or even the doctrine upon which Justice Holmes based so much of his constitutional jurisprudence, that all doubts must be resolved in favor of the legislature?

In point of fact, *it has since chosen otherwise*. For in sustaining the Wagner Act,[46] a new majority of the Court, headed by the present chief justice—whose career too, be it noted, has been largely a public career—declined further to weigh the question of "direct" versus "indirect" effects "in an intellectual vacuum" and invoked the Taft dictum quoted above.[47] Thus the distinction between "direct" and "indirect" effect ceases being one of kind, as Justice Sutherland so strenuously insisted it was, in the Carter Case,[48] and becomes one of degree only—ceases being one of *formula* and becomes one of *fact*. And the result is to throw down the barriers of dual federalism which have heretofore excluded Congress from the regulation of productive industry. We have been presented, overnight as it were, with a constitutional revolution, the purport of which seems to be that Congress is entitled, so far at least as dual federalism is concerned, to require in the form of law what labor is willing to strike for on a large enough scale.

---

44. Cited above, note 24.

45. Carter v. Carter Coal Co., 298 U.S. 238.

46. National Labor Relations Board v. Jones & Laughlin Steel Corp., and attendant cases, 57 S. Ct. 615, decided April 12th.

47. Only the first sentence of it, however. Possibly it was thought that the second sentence would reduce judicial review too much!

48. Cited in note 45, above.

Nor is this the entire story by any means. For the Wagner Act decisions also record a revolution in the conception of "liberty" in the sense of the Constitution. In the Coppage Case,[49] as was mentioned earlier, the Court had held that an employer's right to "hire and fire" was an element of such liberty, and embraced the right to force an employee to choose between his job and his labor union. In the Wagner Act Cases the Court ruled, on the other hand, that the right of employees which the act protects "to form, join, or assist labor organizations," and "to bargain collectively through representatives of their own choosing" "is a fundamental right," growing out of the fact that employees are helpless singly in dealing with an employer, and that "discrimination and coercion to prevent the free exercise" of this fundamental right "is a proper subject for condemnation by competent legislative authority." From a purely *negative* concept restrictive of legislative power liberty thus becomes a *positive* concept calling for legislative implementation and protection.

Finally, we can hardly withhold a passing glance from the temporal relation between the decisions in the Wagner Act Cases and the president's proposal to remake the Court. However one may regard the latter—whether he abhor it as an invasion of "judicial independence" or applaud it as a timely move to reconstitute the ultimate legislative authority of the country, with a view to bringing it into harmony with the politically responsible branches of the government—in either case, one can not be blind to the probable future significance of the simple fact that the president's proposal was dated February 5th, 1937, and that the Wagner Act decisions were handed down the *following* April 12th. It is unlikely that the Court will feel entitled in any near future again to discharge its tremendous function of judicial review of acts of Congress in—to use the chief justice's phrase—"an intellectual vacuum!"

It has been my purpose in this paper to delineate the relationship which has come to exist between the Constitution of the United States—the document of 1787 and its amendments—and a much more considerable constitutional apparatus. Particularly, however, has it been my purpose to indicate that in relation to constitutional law—the product, in other words, of the Supreme Court's efforts to apply the Constitution in the decision of cases—the constitutional document has become hardly more than a formal point of reference. For most of the Court's excursions in the constitutional sphere, the constitutional document is little more than a taking-off ground; the journey out and back occurs in a far different medium, of selected precedents, speculative views regarding the nature of the Constitution and the purposes designed to be served by it, and unstated judicial preferences. All of which signifies that in the constitutional field the Court is a *legislature;* and to the extent that the doctrine of the finality of its interpretations of the Constitution actually prevails, it is a *super-legislature*.

49. Cited in note 19, above.

On the other hand, the Constitution does not belong to the Supreme Court—it does not belong even to the American Bar Association. It is the people's law, and *they* in the long run are entitled to determine its meaning and application—*and the run should not be too long either!* Utilization of the Court for the interpretative process has, however, great technical advantages. It is, for instance, far preferable usually to recourse to the amending process.[50] At the same time, if the Court is to retain its power of judicial review, it must adjust that power to the underlying popular character of our political institutions, and hence must adopt a sympathetic attitude toward clearly established contemporary needs and opinion. The obstinate adherence of the Court in recent years to outmoded doctrines which were largely of its own fabrication, and the arrogance of certain of its opinions during this period,[51] showed the Court to be in the grip of a gravely erroneous conception of its place in our system, one which is fortunately contradicted by well established principles governing judicial review.

50. *Commerce Power versus States Rights* 262–65.
51. I am thinking particularly in this connection of Justice Sutherland's ill-tempered opinion in Jones v. S.E.C., 298 U.S. 1. The decision itself drew forth a strong protest from Justice Cardozo, speaking also for Justices Brandeis and Stone, as calculated to "give immunity to guilt." It should never be overlooked that an unsympathetic Court can do almost as much in the way of laming governmental policy by a hostile interpretation of statutes as by judicial disallowance.

APPRAISALS OF
JUDICIAL REVIEW

10. The Dred Scott Decision in the Light of Contemporary Legal Doctrines

HAVING had occasion recently to renew my acquaintance with the case of Scott v. Sandford,[1] I have become persuaded that the usual historical verdict with reference to it needs revision in three important particulars: first, as to the legal value of the pronouncement in that case of unconstitutionality with reference to the Missouri Compromise; secondly, as to the basis of that pronouncement; thirdly, as to the nature of the issue between Chief Justice Taney and Justice Curtis upon the question of citizenship that was raised by Dred Scott's attempt to sue in the federal courts.[2]

The main facts leading up to and attending this famous litigation may be summarized as follows.[3] Dred Scott, a slave belonging to an army officer named Emerson, was taken by his master from the home state, Missouri, first into the free state of Illinois and thence into that portion of the national territory from which, by the eighth section of the Missouri Compromise, slavery was "forever" excluded. Here master and slave remained two years before returning to Missouri, the latter in the meantime having married with his master's consent. In 1852 Dred sued his master for freedom in one of the lower state courts and won the action, but upon appeal the decision was reversed by the supreme court of the state, upon the ground that Dred's status at home was fixed by state law regardless of what it was abroad—a decision which plainly ran counter to the whole trend of decision by the same court for the previous

From 17 *American Historical Review* 52 (1911). Reprinted by permission.

In substance this paper was read before the American Historical Association at its last annual meeting, December 29, 1910.

1. 19 Howard 393–633 (cited below as "Rep").

2. See 2 James Ford Rhodes, *History of the United States* 251 et seq. (1907); 5 James Schouler, *History of the United States* 377 et seq. (1880–91); 2 Nicolay and Hay, *Abraham Lincoln* ch. 4 (1890); Theodore Clarke Smith, *Parties and Slavery* ch. 14 (1906).

3. The agreed statement of facts is to be found in Rep. 397–99.

generation. Thereupon the case remanded to the inferior court for retrial but Dred, having in the meantime upon the death of Emerson passed by bequest to Sandford, a citizen of New York, now decided to bring a totally new action in the United States circuit court for the Missouri district, under section II of the Act of 1789. In order to bring this action Dred had of course to aver his citizenship of Missouri, which averment was traversed by his adversary in what is known as a plea in abatement, which denied the jurisdiction of the court upon the ground that Dred was the descendant of African slaves and was born in slavery. The plea in abatement the circuit court overruled, but then proceeded to find the law on the merits of the case for the defendant Sandford; and from this decision Dred appealed to the United States Supreme Court.

Scott v. Sandford was first argued before the Supreme Court in the December term of 1855. From a letter of Justice Curtis we learn that in the view the Court took of the case, it would find it unnecessary to canvass the question of the constitutionality of the Missouri Compromise.[4] And indeed it was evidently of a mind to evade even the question of jurisdiction, as raised by the plea in abatement, had it not been for the fact, as it presently transpired, that Justice McLean, a candidate for the Republican presidential nomination, had determined to make political capital of the controversy by writing a dissenting opinion, reviewing at length the history of African slavery in the United States from the Free Soil point of view. McLean's intention naturally produced some uneasiness among his brethren and particularly such as came from slave states, three of whom now began demanding reargument of the questions raised in connection with the plea in abatement.[5] This demand being acceded to, the case came on for reargument in the December term of 1856, that is, after the presidential election was over. Yet even now it was originally the purpose of the Court to confine its attention to the question of law raised by the circuit court's decision, which rested upon the same ground as the state supreme court's earlier decision, and Justice Nelson was commissioned to write an opinion sustaining the circuit court.[6] Since the defeat of Fremont, however, and Buchanan's election, the advantage of position lay all with the pro-slavery membership of the Court. Some of the latter contingent, therefore, but chiefly Justice Wayne of Georgia, who had on another occasion displayed a rather naive view of the judicial function, now began bringing forward the notion

4. Curtis to Ticknor, April 8, 1856. 1 George Ticknor Curtis, *Life of Benjamin Robbins Curtis* 80 {*sic.; A Memoir of Benjamin Robbins Curtis?*}

5. Ashley of Ohio's positive testimony, on the basis of a report current at the time Scott v. Sandford was pending, supplies the explanation needed of the demand for reargument, since the final disposition of the case would be precisely the same whether the circuit court were held to have erred in taking jurisdiction or, having rightfully taken jurisdiction, to have properly decided the case on its merits. *Congressional Globe*, 40th Cong., 3d sess., App., at 211. See also McLean's opinion, Rep. 529–64, and Curtis's animadversions on the same, *id.* 620.

6. Rep. 529–64. The fact that Nelson was commissioned to write an opinion *sustaining* the lower court again shows that intrinsically the question of the lower court's jurisdiction was regarded as unimportant.

that, as expressed in Wayne's very frank opinion, "the peace and harmony of the country required the settlement . . . by judicial decision" of the "constitutional principles" involved in the case.[7] Yielding at last to this pressure, Chief Justice Taney consented to prepare "the opinion of the Court," as it is labelled, covering all issues that had been raised in argument before the Court in support of the defendant's contentions. What was to be the scope of the Court's decision was known to Alexander H. Stephens, as early as January, 1857,[8] and undoubtedly to Buchanan when he delivered his inaugural address. And to know what scope the decision was to take was equivalent practically to knowing its tenor, since it was extremely improbable that a majority of the Court could have allowed so broad a range to inquiry had they not been substantially assured beforehand of its outcome. When, therefore, Buchanan in his inaugural address bespoke the country's acquiesence in the verdict of the Court, "whatever it might be," his very solicitude betrayed that, as Lincoln inferred, he was talking from the card.

For obvious reasons, hostile criticism of the Dred Scott decision has always found its principal target in the chief justice's opinion, and the gravamen of such criticism has always been that the great part of it, particularly the portion dealing with the Missouri Compromise, was *obiter dictum*. I do not, however, concur with this criticism, for reasons which I shall now endeavor to make plain. And in the first place, it ought to be be clearly apprehended what difficulty attaches to a charge of this sort against a deliberate utterance of the Supreme Court of the United States, evidently intended by it to have the force and operation of law, and for the reason that the ultimate test of what *is* law for the United States is, and at the time of the Dred Scott decision was, the opinion of the Supreme Court. On the other hand, the Supreme Court is not theoretically an irresponsible body: by the very theory that makes it final judge of the laws and the Constitution it is subject to these; as by virtue of its character as court it is subject to the *lex curiae*, that is to say, is bound to make consistent application of the results of its own reasoning and to honor the precedents of its own creation. What the charge of *obiter dictum* amounts to therefore is this: first, that the action of the chief justice in passing upon the constitutionality of the eighth section of the Missouri Compromise was illogical, as being inconsistent with the earlier part of his opinion, the purport of which, it is alleged, was to remove from the Court's consideration the record of the case in the lower court and, with it any basis for a pronouncement upon the constitutional question; and secondly, that the action of the chief justice was also in disregard of precedent, which, it is contended, exacted that the Court should not pass upon issues other than those the decision of which was strictly necessary to the determination of the case before it, and particularly that it should not unneces-

7. Rep. 454–55.
8. See 2 Rhodes, *History of the United States* 253, and references.

sarily pronounce a legislative enactment unconstitutional. Let us consider these two points in order.

As already indicated, the primary question before the Court upon the reargument was what disposition to make of the plea in abatement which the circuit court had overruled, thereby taking jurisdiction of the case,[9] and upon this point a majority of the Court, including both Chief Justice Taney and Justice Curtis, ruled decisively both that the plea in abatement was before it and that the decision of the circuit court as to its jurisdiction was subject to review by the Supreme Court.[10] Evidently the charge of illogicality lies against only those judges of the above mentioned majority who, after overruling the plea in abatement and so pronouncing against the jurisdiction of the circuit court upon the grounds therein set forth, passed to consider the further record of the case, by which the constitutional issue was raised. But was such proceeding necessarily illogical? Upon this point obviously the pertinent thing is to consider Taney's own theory of what he was doing, which he states in substantially the following language at the conclusion of his argument on the question of the plaintiff's citizenship: but waiving, he says, the question as to whether the plea in abatement is before the Court on the writ of error, yet the question of jurisdiction still remains on the face of the bill of exceptions taken by the plaintiff in which he admits that he was born a slave but contends that he has since become free; for if he has not become free then certainly he cannot sue as a citizen.[11] In other words, the chief justice's theory was, not that he was canvassing the case on its merits, which he could have done with propriety only had he chosen to ignore the question of jurisdiction, but that he was fortifying his decision upon this matter of jurisdiction by reviewing the issues raised in the bill of exceptions, *as well as* those raised by the plea in abatement; in other words that he was canvassing the question of jurisdiction afresh.

The matter of the validity of the chief justice's mode of proceeding then comes down to this question: Is it allowable for a court to base a decision upon more than one ground and if it does so, does the auxiliary part of the decision become *obiter dictum?* Upon the general question of what constituted *dictum* we find the writer in the *American and English Encyclopedia of Law* indicating the existence of two views among common-law courts. By one of these views none of a judicial opinion is decision save only such part as was necessary to the determination of the rights of the parties to the action. By the other view, on the contrary, all of an opinion is decision which represents a deliberate application

9. *Supreme Court Reports,* Lawyer's ed., bk. 15, 694, 697.

10. This majority consisted of the chief justice and Justices Wayne, Daniel, Campbell, and Curtis. Grier considered it sufficient to canvass the question of the lower court's jurisdiction on the basis of the facts stated in the bill of exceptions. Nelson did not consider the question of jurisdiction. Catron and McLean did not deem the question of jurisdiction to be before the Court.

11. Rep. 427. Note also the chief justice's statement of the issue at the opening of his opinion, Rep. 400.

of the judicial mind to questions legitimately raised in argument.[12] On the precise question above stated the writer speaks as follows:

> Where the record presents two or more points, any one of which, if sustained, would determine the case, and the court decides them all, the decision upon any one of the points cannot be regarded as *obiter*. Nor can it be said that a case is not authority on a point because, though that point was properly presented and decided in the regular course of the consideration of the case, another point was found in the end which disposed of the whole matter. The decision on such a question is as much a part of the judgment of the court as is that on any other of the matters on which the case as a whole depends. The fact that the decision might have been placed upon a different ground existing in the case does not render a question expressly decided by the Court a dictum.[13]

True, this exact statement of the matter is of comparatively recent date, but it is supported by judicial utterances some of which antedate the Dred Scott decision and others of which, conspicuously one by Chief Justice Waite in Railroad Companies v. Schutte, plainly purport to set forth long standing and settled doctrine.[14] It is apparent moreover that this is the only doctrine tenable, for, were the opposite view taken, the law would remain unsettled precisely in proportion as the Court presumed to settle it, since with a decision resting upon more than a single ground it would be always open to those so disposed to challenge the validity of all but one of such grounds, and that one selected at whim. Thus granting—what indeed is evident—that Taney was under no necessity of canvassing both the question of Dred's citizenship and that of his servitude, yet since he did canvass both questions with equal deliberation, who is to say which part of his opinion was decision and which *obiter?*

However, it is urged that an exception must be made in the case of constitutional questions, which should be left undecided if possible. To quote Justice Curtis's protest against the Chief Justice's opinion: "a great question of constitutional law, deeply affecting the peace and welfare of the country, is not . . . a fit subject to be thus reached"; such is the argument.[15] So far however is this alleged exception from being justified by the history of the matter, that it would be far nearer the truth to say that, if constitutional cases comprise a class by themselves in this reference, they warrant an exceptionally broad view of the legal value of judicial opinion. Let us consider for example some of Chief Justice Marshall's decisions in this connection, but particularly his decision in Cohens v. Virginia.[16]

12. 9 *Encyc.* 452–53 "Dictum" (2d ed.): 26 *Encyc.* 168–69 "Stare Decisis." Cf. Carroll v. Carroll's Lessee, 16 How. 275, 287, and Alexander v. Worthington, 5 Md. 471, 487.
13. *Id.* 171. I am indebted for this reference to Elbert W. R. Ewing's *Legal and Historical Status of the Dred Scott Decision* (1909). I may add that this is the sum total of my indebtedness to the work mentioned.
14. 103 U.S. 118, cited with approval in Union Pacific R.R. Co. v. Mason City etc. R.R. Co., 199 U.S. 160 (1874).
15. Rep. 590.
16. 6 Wheat. 264 (1821).

In that case the plaintiff in error had been indicted and subjected to trial and penalty under a Virginia statute for selling tickets for a lottery which Congress had chartered for the District of Columbia. As in the Dred Scott case, the primary question before the Court was one of jurisdiction, though in this case the Supreme Court's own jurisdiction, which counsel for Virginia denied upon four grounds: first, that a state was defendant, contrary to the Eleventh Amendment; secondly, that no writ of error lay from a state court to the Supreme Court; thirdly, that if the act in question was meant to extend to Virginia it was unconstitutional; and fourthly, that it was not 'meant so to extend. Ultimately Marshall dismissed the case for want of jurisdiction upon the last ground, which involves no constitutional question, but before he did so he not only invited argument upon the other points, but in the greatest of his opinions he met and refuted every argument advanced by counsel for Virginia thereupon. Yet by the test set for Taney's opinion in the Dred Scott case, all the valuable part of this great decision is *obiter dictum,* and that of the most gratuitous kind, since its purport was not in support of but counter to the final disposition of the immediate issue before the Court.[17] And in truth Cohens v. Virginia was criticized by Jefferson[18] upon grounds quite similar to those taken by the critics of Chief Justice Taney's opinion in Scott v. Sandford, notwithstanding which, however, it has always been regarded as good law in all its parts and indeed was so treated and enforced, once and again, by the Court over which Taney himself presided.[19]

The fact of the matter is that the critics of Chief Justice Taney take their view of the proper scope of judicial decision from the common law rather than from American constitutional law. Altogether, the only feasible definition, historically, of *obiter dictum* in the field of American constitutional law would seem to be, a more or less casual utterance by a court or members thereof upon some point not deemed by the court itself to be strictly before it and not necessary to decide, as preliminary to the determination of the controversy before it. Such an utterance, for example, is that of Chief Justice Marshall at the close of his decision in Brown v. Maryland, where he says that he "supposes" that the principles he has just applied to a case arising in connection with foreign

17. The portion of Marshall's opinion in Cohens v. Virginia which comprises the leading decision on the point with which it deals runs as follows: "It is, then, the opinion of the Court, that the defendant who removes a judgment rendered against him by a state court into this Court, for the purposes of reexamining the question whether that judgment be in violation of the Constitution or laws of the United States, does not commence or prosecute a suit against the state." By the test set by the critics of C. J. Taney's opinion in Scott v. Sandford, however, the above quoted utterance is not decision; for its author continues thus: ". . . But should we in this be mistaken, the error does not affect the case now before the Court," the reason being that since Cohens was not a citizen of "another state," the Eleventh Amendment did not apply.

18. 15 *Writings* 297–98, 326, 389, 421, 444–52 (Mem. ed. 1903).

19. Rhode Island v. Massachusetts, 12 Pet. 744 (1838), and Prigg v. Pennsylvania, 16 Pet. 539 (1842). See also Taney's own opinion in United States v. Booth, 21 How. 506 (1858).

commerce would also apply in a case of commerce among the states.[20] This pronouncement is obviously an aside upon a point not argued before the Court and it is quite justifiably ignored by Chief Justice Taney in his opinion in the License cases,[21] whereas the rest of Marshall's opinion in Brown v. Maryland Taney treats as law, though the entire second portion of it, dealing with the commerce clause, was unnecessary, as the immediate issue before the court had already been disposed of under Article I, Section 10 of the Constitution.

Chief Justice Taney had therefore, it appears, an undeniable right to canvass the question of Scott's servitude in support of his decision that Scott was not a citizen of the United States, and he had the same right to canvass the question of the constitutionality of the Missouri Compromise in support of his decision that Scott was a slave. To all these points his attention was invited by arguments of counsel and to all of them he might cast it with propriety by a well-established view of the scope of judicial inquiry in such cases. If then the decision rendered by six of the nine judges on the bench, that the Missouri Compromise was unconstitutional, is to be stigmatized as unwarrantable, which is all that the court of history can do with it, it is not by pronouncing it to have been *obiter dictum* but by discrediting, from the standpoint of the history of constitutional law antedating the decision, the principles upon which it was rested.

Turning then to consider the constitutional decision directly, we find our task simplified to this extent: that the entire Court, majority and dissenting minority alike, are in unanimous agreement upon the proposition that, whatever the source of its power, whether Article IV, Section 3 of the Constitution or the right to acquire territory and therefore to govern it, Congress in governing territory is bound by the Constitution—a proposition to which the Court has always adhered, though there has been latterly some alteration of opinion as to what provisions of the Constitution control Congress in this connection. And this was the question that troubled the majority in the Dred Scott case. The Missouri Compromise was unconstitutional, that was certain; but just why— that was immensely uncertain. The extremest position of all was taken by Justice Campbell, whose doctrine was that the only power Congress had in the territories, in addition to its powers as the legislature of the United States, was the power to make rules and regulations of a conservatory character "for the preservation of the public domain, and its preparation for sale or disposition." From this it was held to follow that whatever the Constitution and laws of the states "validly determine to be property, it is the duty of the Federal Government, through the domain of jurisdiction merely Federal, to recognize to be property."[22] This of course is the extremest Calhounism, from which it came later to be deduced, with perfect logic, that it was the duty of the federal

20. 12 Wheat. 419, 449 (1827).
21. 5 How. 504, 574–78 (1847); see also J. McLean, *id.* 594.
22. Rep. 509–17; the quotations are at 514 and 515.

government, not only to admit slavery into the territory, but to protect it there. But, as Benton showed in his famous *Examination of the Dred Scott Case,* this particular phase of Calhounism was, at the date of the Dred Scott decision, less than ten years old.

And it is at this point that we come upon the second error I had in mind at the outset of this paper, an error traceable to Benton, but ever since repeated by historians of the Dred Scott decision, namely, the assumption that that decision rested exclusively upon Calhounist premises. Nothing however could be farther from the fact, for though Justice Daniel of Virginia seems to go almost as far as Campbell in representing the power of Congress in governing the territories as a mere proprietary power of supervision, yet even he rejects Campbell's notion that Congress was the mere trustee of the states; while Justices Catron of Tennessee, an old Jacksonian Democrat, Grier of Pennsylvania and of similar traditions, Wayne, a southern Whig, and the chief justice himself, could by no means consent thus to read the Constitution through the spectacles of the prophet of nullification. Upon what grounds then were these judges to rest their pronouncement of the unconstitutionality of the Missouri Compromise? Let us take up the case of Catron and then turn to that of the chief justice, who spoke upon this point for himself, for Grier and Wayne, and to a great extent, for Daniel.

Catron paid his respects to the Calhounist point of view in the following words: "It is due to myself to say, that it is asking much of a judge, who has for nearly twenty years been exercising jurisdiction, from the western Missouri line to the Rocky Mountains, and, on this understanding of the Constitution," namely that Congress has power really to govern the territories, "inflicting the extreme penalty of death for crimes committed where the direct legislation of Congress was the only rule, to agree that he had been all the while acting in mistake, and as an usurper." Setting out from this extremely personal point of view, Catron found that Congress possessed *sovereignty* over its territory, limited however in this case by the treaty with France, with which the anti-slavery article of the Missouri Compromise was, he held, incompatible, and always by the spirit of the Constitution, which stipulates for the citizens of each state the rights and privileges of citizens of the several states and demands that the citizens of all states be treated alike in the national territory. It is true that Catron draws the idea of the equality of the states to his support, but his concern is plainly for the rights of citizenship rather than the prerogatives of statehood.[23] And in this connection it is worth recalling that almost exactly thirty years before, as chief justice of Tennessee, Catron had rendered the decision in Van Zant v. Waddell,[24] which is the first decision in which the concept of class legislation is distinctly formulated as a constitutional limitation, and which is a landmark in the history of American constitutional law.

But the most strongly nationalistic, or more precisely *federalistic,* of all the

23. Rep. 522–27.
24. 2 Yerg (Tenn.) 260.

opinions upon the constitutional question was that of the chief justice, who again followed Marshall in tracing the power of Congress to govern territories to its power to acquire them. Upon what ground then was he to rest his condemnation of the Missouri Compromise? In one or two passages Taney speaks of Congress as "trustee," but it is as trustee of the "whole *people* of the Union" and for *all* its powers. The limitations upon the power of Congress must therefore, in this case as in all cases, be sought in the Constitution, "from which it derives its own existence, and by virtue alone it continues to exist and act as a government and sovereignty."[25] From this it follows that when Congress enters a territory of the United States it cannot "put off its character and assume discretionary or despotic powers which the Constitution had denied to it": it is still bound by the Constitution. Therefore Congress can make no law for the territories with respect to establishing a religion, nor deny trial by jury therein, nor compel anyone to be a witness against himself in a criminal proceeding. "And," the chief justice continues, "the rights of private property have been guarded with equal care." They "are united with the rights of person, and placed on the same ground by the fifth amendment to the Constitution, which provides that no person shall be deprived of life, liberty, and property, without due process of law. And an act of Congress which deprives a citizen of the United States of his liberty or property, merely because he came himself or brought his property into a particular Territory of the United States, and who had committed no offence against the laws, could hardly be dignified with the name of due process of law.[26]

Such then is the basis of the chief justice's decision: the "due process of law" clause of the Fifth Amendment. The striking feature of this objection to the prohibitory clause of the Missouri Compromise is its baffling irrelevancy. It is true that the Supreme Court had in 1855, in Murray v. the Hoboken Company,[27] laid down the doctrine that all legal process was not necessarily due process, that in providing procedure for the enforcement of its laws Congress was limited in its choice to the methods in vogue at the time of the adoption of the Constitution. But in the Dred Scott case no matter of procedure was involved, the antagonists of the law in question being opposed not to the *method* of its enforcement, but to its enforcement at all; not to the mode of its operation, but to its substance. If lack of due process therefore was chargeable in such a case, it was chargeable in the case of any enactment, penal or of other sort, no matter by what machinery it was designed to be carried out, if the general result of its enforcement would be to diminish someone's liberty or property for no fault of his own, save as determined by the law in question. In a word, legislation would be practically at an end.

Naturally, the amazing character of this doctrine did not escape the attention

25. Rep. 448–49. The italics are mine.
26. *Id*. 450.
27. 18 How. 272.

of Justice Curtis, who had been spokesman for the Court in the Hoboken case. If the Missouri Compromise did indeed comprise one of a class of enactments proscribed by the Fifth Amendment, what then, Justice Curtis inquired, was to be said of the Ordinance of 1787, which Virginia and other states had ratified notwithstanding the presence of similar clauses in their constitutions? What again was to be said upon that hypothesis of the act of Virginia herself, passed in 1778, which prohibited the further importation of slaves? What was to be said of numerous decisions in which this and analogous laws had been upheld and enforced by the courts of Maryland and Virginia, against their own citizens who had purchased slaves abroad, and that without anyone's thinking to question the validity of such laws upon the ground that they were not law of the land or due process of law? What was to be said of the act of Congress of 1808 prohibiting the slave trade and the assumption of the Constitution that Congress would have that power without its being specifically bestowed, but simply as an item of its power to regulate commerce? What finally, if the scope of congressional authority to legislate was thus limited by the Fifth Amendment, was to be said of the Embargo Act, which had borne with peculiar severity upon the people of New England states, but the constitutionality of which had been recently asserted by the court in argument in the roundest terms.[28]

The plain implication of this apparently crushing counter-argument of Justice Curtis is that the chief justice was, at this point, making up his constitutional law out of whole cloth. Was this implication quite fair? The answer is that it was not, as a brief examination of the legal history involved will show.[29] What Taney was attempting to do in the section of his opinion above quoted was to engraft the doctrine of "vested rights" upon the national Constitution as a limitation upon national power by casting round it the "due process of law" clause of the Fifth Amendment. But neither the doctrine of "vested rights" nor yet such use of "due process of law" was novel, and indeed the former was, in 1857, comparatively ancient. The doctrine of "vested rights" signified this: that property rights were sacred by the law of nature and the social compact, that any legislative enactment affecting such rights was always to be judged of from the point of view of their operation upon such rights, and that when an enactment affected such rights detrimentally without making compensation to the owner, it was to be viewed as inflicting upon such owner a penalty ex post facto and therefore as void. The foundation for the doctrine of "vested rights" was laid in 1795 by Justice Patterson in his charge to the jury in Van Horn v. Dorrance,[30] but more securely still by Justice Chase in his much cited dictum in Calder v. Bull,[31] in which he propounds what may be regarded as the leavening

28. Rep. 626–27; the Virginia cases cited are 5 Call 425 and 1 Leigh 172, and the Maryland case is 5 Harr. and J. 107. He might have added 2 Munf. (Va.) 393.
29. See the writer on "The Doctrine of Due Process of Law before the Civil War," 24 *Harv. L. Rev.* 366 *et seq.;* 460 *et seq.* (1911).
30. 2 Dallas 309 (1795).
31. 3 Dallas 386 (1798).

principle of American constitutional law, the doctrine, namely, that entirely independent of the written Constitution, legislative power is limited by its own nature, the principles of republican government, natural law, and social compact.

Reposing upon this foundation, as well as upon the principle of the separation of the powers of government, the doctrine of "vested rights" soon found wide acceptance, being infused by Marshall in 1810 into the "obligation of contracts" clause of the national Constitution[32] and receiving from Chancellor Kent in 1811 its classic formulation in Dash v. Van Kleeck.[33] Presently, however, principles hostile to the doctrine began to appear, particularly the doctrine of "popular sovereignty," which insisted in the first place upon tracing the sanctity of the written Constitution, not to a supposed relation to fundamental rights but to its character as the immediate enactment of the sovereign people, and in the second place upon the natural predominance of the legislature in government as comprising the immediate representatives of the people. From 1830 on, the doctrine of the "police power," that is, the power of the legislature to regulate all rights in the furtherance of its own view of the public interest, began to supersede the doctrine of "vested rights" as the controlling maxim of American constitutional law, receiving indeed from Taney himself, in his opinions in the Charles River Bridge case and License cases, a distinct impetus.[34] In this situation obviously the problem before those judges who wished to adhere to the older doctrine was to discover some phrase of the written Constitution capable of subserving the purposes of the doctrine of "vested rights." The discovery was made by the North Carolina supreme court, in 1832, in the case of Hoke v. Henderson,[35] in which the use made of the phrase "law of the land" of the North Carolina constitution affords an exact counterpart to Taney's use of "due process of law" in Scott v. Sandford. From North Carolina the notion spread to New York, where it was utilized by Justice Bronson in 1843 in Taylor v. Porter.[36] The immediate source of Taney's inspiration, however, was probably—though there is no hint of the matter in the briefs filed by Sandford's attorneys—the decision of the New York court of appeals in the case of Wynehamer v. the People, in which, in the interval between the first and second arguments of the Dred Scott case, an anti-liquor law was pronounced unconstitutional under the "due process of law" clause of the New York constitution, as comprising, with reference to existing stocks of liquor, an act of destruction which it was not within the power of government to perform, "even by the forms which belong to due process of law."[37]

32. Fletcher v. Peck, 6 Cr. 87 (1810).
33. 7 Johns. (N.Y.) 498.
34. 11 Pet. 420 (1837); 5 How. 504 (1846).
35. 2 Dev. 1, preceded by University of North Carolina v. Foy, 2 Hayw. 310 (1807). See also Webster's argument in the Dartmouth College case, 4 Wheat. 518, 575 *et seq.* (1819).
36. 4 Hill (N.Y.) 140, preceded by the matter of John and Cherry Sts., 19 Wend. 676, and followed by White v. White, 5 Barb. 474, Powers v. Bergen, 6 N.Y. 358, and Westervelt v. Gregg, 12 N.Y. 209 (1854).
37. 13 N.Y. 378, 420 (through Justice A. S. Johnson).

So much by way of justification of Chief Justice Taney. There is however another side to the matter. In the first place, as above hinted, Taney was performing in Scott v. Sandford what for him was a distinct *volte face* toward the doctrine of "vested rights." In the second place, he was availing himself of what at the time was decidedly the weaker tradition of the law. For not only had the doctrine of "vested rights," in 1857, generally gone by the board in its original form, but save in North Carolina and New York it had, in its new disguise, practically no hold anywhere. Essentially contemporaneous with the Wynehamer case were similar cases in an even dozen states. In all save one the law was upheld, and in that case it was overturned upon the basis of the doctrine of natural rights.[38] Furthermore, in only one court, that of Rhode Island, and that subsequently to the New York decision, was the "due process of law" or "law of the land" clause adduced as a limitation upon substantive legislation. Said the Rhode Island court on that occasion: "It is obvious that the objection confounds the power of the assembly to create and define an offense, with the rights of the accused to trial by jury and due process of law...before he can be convicted of it."[39]

This utterance may be taken, without hesitation, as decisive of the established interpretation of the "due process of law" clause in 1857. But all this is upon the assumption of a parity between Congress and the state legislature with reference to the doctrine of vested rights. In the third place, however, no such parity could, upon fundamental principles, have been justifiably conceived to exist at the date of Scott v. Sandford. The doctrine of "vested rights" rested upon the hypothesis of the recognition by the common law of certain fundamental rights which the people of the respective states possessed from the outset and which they could not be supposed to have parted with by mere implication in establishing the legislative branch of the government.[40] But these considerations were entirely irrelevant to the case of the legislative powers of Congress for two distinct, but equally powerful, reasons. In the first place it was a fundamental maxim in Taney's day that there was no such thing as a common law of the United States.[41] In the second place the power of Congress is not a loosely granted general power of legislation but a group of specifically granted powers. While, therefore, the federal courts from the very outset—though very sparingly in Taney's day—in cases which fell to their jurisdiction because of the character of the parties involved and in which therefore state law was to be enforced, repeatedly passed upon the validity of state laws under "general principles of constitutional law,"[42] the United States was

38. 24 *Harv. L. Rev.* 471-74.

39. St. v. Keeran, 5 R.I. 497; see also 5 R.I. 185, and 3 R.I. 64 and 289.

40. See J. Patterson in Van Horne v. Dorrance, cited above; also J. Story in Terrett v. Taylor, 9 Cr. 43 (1815), and in Wilkinson v. Leland, 2 Pet. 627 (1829).

41. The leading case on this point is that of Wheaton and Donaldson v. Peters and Grigg, 8 Pet. 591, 658 (1834).

42. See note 39, above; see also J. Miller in Loan Association v. Topeka, 20 Wall. 655 (1874), and in Davidson v. New Orleans, 96 U.S. 97 (1877).

always conceived strictly as a government of delegated powers, neither deriving competence from, nor yet finding limitation in, principles external to the Constitution. It was therefore always a fundamental principle of constitutional construction with Marshall that within the sphere of its delegated powers the national government was sovereign, not merely as against the rights of the states but also against the rights of individuals, a point of view which he sets forth with great explicitness in his opinion in Gibbons v. Ogden[43] with reference to the commercial power of Congress and which Justice Daniel reiterates, so far as the rights of persons are concerned, as late as 1850 in United States v. Marigold.[44] True, Taney does find the restriction which he is applying in the Constitution itself, namely, in the "due process of law" clause of the Fifth Amendment, but what this admission signifies is simply this: that his use of the clause in question can draw no valid support from the earlier history of the doctrine of "vested rights," which upon fundamental principles was applicable only as a limitation upon the legislative power of the states, and that therefore its only justification is to be found in what, in 1857, was a relatively novel doctrine peculiar to the courts of two states.

But though Taney's invocation of the "due process of law" clause of the Fifth Amendment had so little to warrant it in the constitutional law of the day, it has received subsequently not a few tokens of ratification. Particularly is it noteworthy that the Republican opponents of the Dred Scott decision, instead of utilizing Curtis's very effective dissent at this point, now pounced upon the same clause of the Constitution and by emphasizing the word "liberty" in it, instead of the word "property," based upon it the dogma that Congress could not *allow* slavery in the territories.[45] After the Civil War Taney's Republican successor, Chase, used the "due process of law" clause of the Fifth Amendment in his opinion in Hepburn v. Griswold in the same sense in which Taney used it in Scott v. Sandford, but only as a limitation upon the implied powers of Congress.[46] This doctrine was flatly rejected by the Supreme Court, speaking through Justice Strong, in Knox v. Lee[47] Yet a few years later, Justice Strong himself was elaborating the Taney-Chase point of view in his dissenting opinion in the Sinking Fund cases, and connecting it with Hoke v Henderson.[48]

43. 9 Wheat. 1, 196–97 (1824). The doctrine here stated is that the only limitations upon the power of Congress in the regulation of foreign and interstate commerce are the purely political limitations which arise form the responsibility of Congress to its constituents.

44. 9 How. 560 (1850).

45. See the Republican Platform of 1860, para. 8. At this point the Republicans followed McLean's opinion rather than Curtis's. Note the significance in this connection of the discussion as to whether slaves were recognized by the Constitution; and also of the discussion as to whether slavery was recognized by natural law.

46. 8 Wall. 603, 624 (1870); cf. J. Miller's cogent answer, *id.* 637–38. Also, cf. the chief justice's own decision in Veazie Bank v. Fenno in the same volume of reports, 533 *et seq.*

47. 12 Wall. 457, 551 (1871). C. J. Chase elaborates upon his earlier argument under the Fifth Amendment at 580–82; he quotes the old dictum in Calder v. Bull to support his position.

48. 99 U.S. 700, 737–39.

Of late years too the same doctrine has shown a disposition to crop up repeatedly, though it is uncertain whether it has ever attained the dignity of formal decision.[49] Meantime of course, since the middle nineties, when the Supreme Court began to regard itself as the last defense of the country against socialism, it has been applying steadily in modified form the North Carolina–New York doctrine in limitation of state legislative power under the Fourteenth Amendment.[50]

Turning finally to the consideration of our third main topic, namely the character of the issue between Chief Justice Taney and Justice Curtis upon the question of citizenship raised by Dred's attempt to sue in the federal courts, we find that it can be disposed of rather briefly. The usual view of the issue referred to is that it resolved itself into a dispute as to the relative weight to be given to the two conflicting sets of facts bearing upon the question whether Negroes were in any case capable of citizenship at the time of the adoption of the Constitution, a dispute in which it is generally agreed that Justice Curtis had the weight of evidence on his side. This account of the matter is inaccurate. A careful comparison of Chief Justice Taney's opinion with that of Justice Curtis reveals the fact that the fundamental issue between the two judges, though it is not very specifically joined, is not whether there may not have been Negro citizens of states in 1787 who upon the adoption of the Constitution became citizens of the United States, but from what source citizenship within the recognition of the Constitution was supposed to flow henceforth. Upon this point, Curtis's view was that citizenship within the recognition of the Constitution in the case of persons born within the United States was through the states, while Taney's view was that a "citizen of the United States," to use his frequent phrase, always, unless descended from those who became citizens at the time of the adoption of the Constitution, owed his character as such to some intervention of national authority—was, in short, a product of the government.[51] Curtis's theory, it can hardly be doubted, was that of the framers of the Constitution, wherefore Taney's pretense of carrying out not only the spirit but the very letter of the Constitution as it came from the framers, becomes at this point particularly hollow.[52] On the other hand, Taney's view is a very logical, and indeed inevitable, deduction from his whole body of doctrine with reference to the federal system. This doctrine, which came from the "Virginia

49. See the various justices in the Northern Securities Company case, 193 U.S. 197 (1904), 332, 362, 397–400. See also J. Harlan in Adair v. United States, 208 U.S. 161 (1908), 172–74; cf. J. McKenna, id. 180–90, and J. Holmes, 191.

50. See the writer on "The Supreme Court and the Fourteenth Amendment," 7 Mich. L. Rev. 642–72 (1909). See also Holden v. Hardy, 169 U.S. 366, and Lochner v. the People of the State of New York, 198 U.S. 45 (1905).

51. Taney states his position on this point at 404–6 and 417–18 of the Report, and Curtis states his at 581.

52. Taney translates the "citizens of each state" clause of the Constitution as "citizens of the United States," but the derivation of this clause form the Articles of Confederation forbids any such notion. See also Federalist No. 42.

School'' after its disappointment at the failure of the Virginia and Kentucky Resolutions to establish the primacy of the states in the federal system, was the theory of the dual nature of that system: the states independent and sovereign within their sphere and the national government within its. This theory Taney had voiced from the beginning of his judicial career, so that, at this point at least, he was acting consistently with his past. Also, without a doubt, the doctrine in question was pretty well established by 1857, both in judicial decision and in political thinking.[53]

To summarize: I conclude, first, that the Dred Scott decision was not *obiter dictum* within any definition of *obiter dictum* obtainable from a fair review of the practice of the Supreme Court, particularly under Marshall, in constitutional cases; secondly, that it was not based by the majority of those entering into it upon Calhounist premises; and thirdly, that Justice Curtis's supposed refutation of Taney's argument upon the question of Dred Scott's title to a *prima facie* citizenship within the recognition of the Constitution is a fiction. None of these results, however, goes far to relieve that decision of its discreditable character as a judicial utterance. When, as in this case, the student finds six judges arriving at precisely the same result by three distinct processes of reasoning, he is naturally disposed to surmise that the result may possibly have induced the processes rather than that the processes compelled the result, though of course such surmise is not necessarily sound; but when he discovers further that the processes themselves were most deficient in that regard for history and precedent in which judicial reasoning is supposed to abound, his surmise becomes suspicion; and finally when he finds that beyond reasoning defectively upon the matter before them, the same judges deliberately gloss over material distinctions (as for example, in this case, the distinction between sojourn and domicile) and ignore precedents that they have themselves created (as for example, in this case, the decisions regarding the operation of state decisions upon questions of comity) his suspicion becomes conviction. The Dred Scott decision cannot be, with accuracy, written down as usurpation, but it can and must be written down as a gross abuse of trust by the body which rendered it. The results from that abuse of trust were moreover momentous. During neither the Civil War nor the period of Reconstruction did the Supreme Court play anything like its due role of supervision, with the result that during the one period the military powers of the president underwent undue expansion, and during the other the legislative powers of Congress. The Court itself was conscious of its weakness, yet notwithstanding its prudent disposition to remain in the background, at no time since Jefferson's first administration has its independence been in greater jeopardy than in the decade between 1860 and 1870; so slow and laborious was its task of recuperating its shattered reputation.

53. For a statement of this doctrine, see Taney's opinion in the United States v. Booth, cited above, note 19. It should be noted in passing that this elucidation of the real issue between Taney and Curtis on the citizenship question throws additional light on the close relation existing in Taney's mind between the question of Dred's servitude and that of his citizenship.

11. Game Protection and
the Constitution

THE Agricultural Department Appropriation Act of March 4, 1913, contains these provisions:

> All wild geese, wild swans, brant, wild ducks, snipe, plover, woodcock, rail, wild pigeons, and all other migratory game and insectivorous birds which in their northern and southern migrations pass through or do not remain permanently the entire year within the borders of any state or territory, shall hereafter be deemed to be within the custody and protection of the government of the United States, and shall not be destroyed or taken contrary to regulations hereinafter provided therefore.
>
> The Department of Agriculture is hereby authorized and directed to adopt suitable regulations to give effect to the previous paragraph by prescribing and fixing closed seasons, having due regard to the zones of temperature, breeding habits, and times and line of migratory flight, thereby enabling the department to select and designate suitable districts for different portions of the country, and it shall be unlawful to shoot or by any device kill or seize and capture migratory birds within the protection of this law during said closed seasons, and any person who shall violate any of the provisions or regulations of this law for the protection of migratory birds shall be guilty of a misdemeanor and shall be fined not more than $100 or imprisoned not more than ninety days, or both, in the discretion of the court.[1]

Such are the provisions, in essential part, of the so-called Weeks-McLean Migratory Bird Act. In pursuance of the authority thus vested in it the Department of Agriculture promptly drew up "suitable regulations" which were approved by the president. At once, however, the validity of the act itself was drawn into question on the constitutional ground, and within the last two years two state supreme courts and two lower federal courts have pronounced against it in opinions more or less elaborate, while one lower federal court has

From 14 *Michigan Law Review* 613 (1916). Reprinted by permission.

1. 37 United States Statutes at Large, at 847.

sustained it without opinion.[2] Quite recently the Supreme Court of the United States, to which the question of constitutionality had been appealed, has asked for a re-argument of the matter, presumably on account of the division of opinion among its members on a matter recognized to be one of gravity. Altogether, the question as to whether Congress had the power to pass the Act of March 4, 1913, seems an immediately pertinent one.

As to the vast importance of birds in protecting grain, fruit, and trees from insect enemies, whose annual toll upon the wealth of the people of the United States even now amounts into the hundreds of millions of dollars, there is no dispute. Nor would any but the most brutish fail to lament the loss of beauty which the disappearance of many of the diminishing species of our feathered neighbors would mean to life. Again, it is not denied that the states are generally incompetent, either by joint action or singly, to protect bird life in the United States. But do these facts touch the constitutional question? In one of the cases referred to the argument was made in behalf of the act that "Where the state is clearly incompetent to save itself, the national government has the right to aid",[3] but the Court answered with the words of Mr. Justice Brewer in Kansas v. Colorado, as follows:

> But the proposition that there are legislative powers affecting the nation as a whole which belong to, although not expressed in the grant of powers, is in direct conflict with the doctrine that this is a government of enumerated powers. That this is such a government clearly appears from the Constitution, . . . for otherwise there would be an instrument granting certain specified things made operative to grant other and distinct things. This natural construction of the original body of the Constitution is made absolutely certain by the Tenth Amendment. This amendment, which was seemingly adopted with prescience of just such contention as the present, disclosed the wide-spread fear that the National Government might, under the pressure of a supposed general welfare, attempt to exercise powers which have not been granted. With equal determination the framers contended that no such assumption should ever find justification in the organic act, and that if in the future further powers seemed necessary they should be granted by the people in the manner they had provided for amending that act. . . . Its principal purpose was not the distribution of power between the United States and the states, but a reservation to the people of all powers not granted.[4]

That this passage embraces an established canon of constitutional construction, no student of constitutional law would care to deny; yet the canon in question has certain important limitations. And whether it is relevant to the present case may perhaps be doubted.

But before I come to this phase of the question, there are some other matters

---

2. United States v. Shauver, 214 Fed. 154 (May 25–July 9, 1914); United States v. McCullagh, 221 Fed. 288 (March 20, 1915); State v. Sawyer, 113 Me. 458, 94 Atl. 886 (July 21, 1915); State v. McCullagh, 96 Kans. 786, 153 Pac. 557 (Dec. 11, 1915). The decision rendered without opinion was in the United States District Court for South Dakota, 17 West Pub. Co.'s Docket, 1476.

3. United States v. Shauver, 214 Fed. 154, 157.

4. Kansas v. Colorado, 206 U.S. 46, 89–90 (1907).

to be touched upon; and first I wish to call attention to two features of the decisions above referred to, which in the light of the history of our constitutional law are of the greatest significance.

The first of these features is furnished by the fact that no one of the four courts pronouncing the act of Congress void made anything of the delegation of powers authorized by that act to the Department of Agriculture. This is undoubtedly to be explained by the United States Supreme Court's decision in United States v. Grimaud,[5] in which a similarly broad delegation of power to the same department was sustained, partly on the basis of an equivocal distinction between the making of administrative rules and legislation proper and partly on the basis of the more intelligible principle that in order to exercise this power beneficially Congress must often delegate it. True, the penalties for the violation of authorized administrative regulations must be set by Congress itself,[6] but this condition being complied with the Court will today almost invariably sustain such regulations where they have "clear legislative basis."[7]

And even more significant is the second feature I refer to, namely, the recognition explicitly or implicitly accorded in all these opinions that if Congress had the power to pass the Act of March 4, 1913, such act would be supreme over any conflicting state statutes or constitutional provisions. Thus, in all these cases, the doctrine is asserted, on the authority of Geer v. Connecticut,[8] that the legislative power of the state extends to the protection of the wild game within the state, both because of "the common ownership of" such game "and the trust for the benefit of its people which the state exercises in relation thereto," and because of "the duty of the state to preserve for its people a valuable food supply." Yet at the same time, the enquiry was extended to the question whether the national government possesses power capable of reaching the same subject matter in the manner of the act under review. And in United States v. McCullagh, the Court, (Justice Pollock), quotes the following passage from Mr. Justice Matthew's opinion in Smith v. Alabama:

> The grant of power to Congress in the Constitution to regulate commerce with foreign nations and among the several states, it is conceded, is paramount over all legislative powers, which, in consequence of not having been granted to Congress, are reserved to the states. It follows that any legislation of a state, although in pursuance of an acknowledged power reserved to it, which conflicts with the actual exercise of the power of Congress over the subject of commerce, must give way before the supremacy of the national authority.[9]

And this passage the learned judge follows up with the following words from Mr. Justice Van Devanter's more recent opinion in the Second Employer's Liability Cases:

5. 220 U.S. 506 (1911). See also Buttfield v. Stranahan, 192 U.S. 470 (1904).
6. United States v. Eaton, 144 U.S. 677 (1892).
7. United States v. George, 228 U.S. 14, 22.
8. 161 U.S. 519 (1896).
9. 124 U.S. 465, 473 (1888).

True, prior to the present act the laws of the several states were regarded as determinative of the liability of employers engaged in interstate commerce for injuries received by their employees while engaged in such commerce. But that was because Congress, although empowered to regulate that subject, had not acted thereon, and because the subject is one which falls within the police powers of the states in the absence of action by Congress.[10]

But, of course, the supremacy of acts of Congress regulating interstate commerce over conflicting state laws arises from Art. VI, Par. 2, of the Constitution, which secures a like supremacy to all exertions of national power over state power exercised in conflict therewith.

In other words, these decisions, though not entirely devoid of contradiction at this point, do on the whole attest that the judiciary of this country is gradually pulling itself loose from the bog into which the so long dominant doctrine of states' rights years ago landed it—in other words, is getting rid of the solecism that state power, to all exertions of which in the recognized forms of lawmaking national power is by the Constitution itself pronounced invariably paramount, may yet in some strange way or other comprise a separate limitation on national power.[11] More than one hundred and twenty years ago James Madison himself pointed out that "interference with the powers of the states was no constitutional criterion of the powers of Congress"; that "if the power was not given Congress it could not exercise it," but that if it was given "they might exercise it, although it should interfere with the laws and even the constitutions of the states."[12] The same principle underlay and determined Marshall's great decisions in McCulloch v. Maryland,[13] Cohens v. Virginia,[14] and Gibbons v. Ogden.[15] It has been reiterated by the present Court frequently within the last two or three years.

Had, then, Congress any constitutional power to enact the measure under discussion? That is the question before us, and the only question. Two clauses of the Constitution have been suggested as justifying this legislation, the commerce clause, and Art. IV, sec. 3, par. 2, of the Constitution, whereby Congress is authorized to "make all needful rules and regulations respecting the territory and other property belonging to the United States." Let us consider these in order.

Speaking to the argument based in behalf of the act on the commerce clause one of the opinions above cited says:

> The natural flight of wild fowl from one point to another does not constitute "commerce," unless that word be expanded beyond any significance hitherto given it.

10. 223 U.S. 1, 54–55 (1912).
11. See in general my *National Supremacy* (1913) on this question.
12. 2 Annals of Congress, col. 1891.
13. 4 Wheat. 316 (1819).
14. 6 Wheat. 264 (1821).
15. 9 Wheat. 1 (1824).

> Whatever other element may be spared from a definition of the term it has not heretofore applied to processes or occurrences not directed or affected by human intelligence.[16]

This is no doubt true, yet it does not necessarily conclude the question, even if the statute under discussion be regarded as a measure designed to safeguard an act of interstate commerce, such act being the flight of birds. There have before this been cases in which previously unaccepted definitions of the term "commerce" have confronted the Court and have been accepted by it. Take, for instance, the doctrine that the transportation of persons from one state to another is "commerce among the states." In Gibbons v. Ogden,[17] notwithstanding the definition of "commerce," there laid down as "intercourse," the Court hesitated to rule decisively that the carriage of persons fell within the concept; yet today this is established law. Consider, again, the much more recent case of Hoke v. United States,[18] in which the Court holds, by necessary inference at least, not merely the carriage of persons, but the passage of persons from one state to another, to fall within the power granted Congress. Consider, again, the extension of the same term in the familiar Pensacola Telegraph Co. case[19] to the transmission of intelligence. Perhaps we may conclude that the term "commerce" has not yet received its ultimate and finished definition. Perhaps we may claim reasonable ground for the expectation that "commerce," which has frequently been said to connote "the movement of persons and things," may refer to the literal movement of the latter as well as of the former, in addition to their carriage.

But a second difficulty in the way of an appeal to the commerce clause is found by some of the courts above mentioned in the decision in Geer v. Connecticut. In this case it was held that the state as common proprietor of the game within its boundaries might, in the exercise of the prerogatives of proprietor, require those whom it allowed to reduce such game to their possession to withhold the same from interstate commerce; and from this it was concluded by Justice Pollock that the state may "absolutely forbid" the game within its borders from "coming under the protection and control of the Commerce Clause of the National Constitution."[20]

Now, whether this conclusion is warranted by anything that was actually said in Geer v. Connecticut, I should hardly venture to say, inasmuch as no act of Congress was there involved and the only question before the Court concerned the scope of the state's power in the *absence* of congressional action. What I will venture to say is that, whether so warranted or not, the conclusion is erroneous, and for the reason indicated by the words quoted by Justice Pollock

16. State v. McCullagh, 96 Kans. 786, 788–89, 153 Pac. 557, 558. To same effect is State v. Sawyer, 113 Me. 458, 462, 94 Atl. 886, 888.
17. 9 Wheat. 1 (1824).
18. 227 U.S. 308 (1913). See also Covington Bridge Co. v. Kentucky, 154 U.S. 204 (1899).
19. 96 U.S. 1 (1878).
20. United States v. McCullagh, 221 Fed. 288, 292.

himself from Smith v. Alabama, and again for the reason stated by Madison, that "the powers of the States are no constitutional criterion of the power of Congress." Besides, the wild game of the state is not the only thing within the state with reference to which the state government stands in a relation of quasi-proprietorship; it has a similar relation to the atmosphere, the forests, and the water within its boundaries, and has a standing in court to protect these irrespective of the assent or dissent of the private owners immediately concerned.[21] Yet it is amply established that the state's control of the waters within its boundaries must always yield in the last analysis to the superior power of Congress in control of commerce and navigation among the states, a determination which again illustrates the general principle.[22]

Suppose, therefore, we concede the proprietorship of the state in its wild game to the fullest extent, what then is the legal character of the migration of game from state to another, considered in their aspect of successive proprietors of such game? Obviously, it is that of transfer of property across state lines from one legal person to another, *that is,* "commerce." True, the transfer is not by contract between the legal persons involved, but rather by the operation of a kind of legal prescription; yet it is none the less a legal transfer, and it is "among states." Nor is it a merely casual occurrence, as for instance, where a dog might elect to change masters, but it is a regularly recurrent, seasonal, and predictable process, which, even though not susceptible of "regulation" in many senses of the word, certainly ought to be capable of being protected by the government of the larger community which is benefitted by it.

Suppose, however, we dismiss the word "commerce" from consideration, contenting ourselves with the earliest definition ever fastened upon it by judicial decision, to wit, as including "navigation";[23] and then let us turn our attention to the other dimension of Congress' power in this field, the phrase "to regulate."

In United States v. The Rio Grande Irrigation Co., the question at issue was the validity of the Act of Congress of September 19, 1890, prohibiting the creation of obstructions to navigation in the navigable waters in the United States. Sustaining the act, the Court said:

> The unquestioned rule of the common law was that every riparian owner was entitled to the continual natural flow of the stream. . . . It is also true that as to every stream within its dominion the state may change this common law rule. . . . Yet two limitations must be recognized; first, that in the absence of specific authorization from Congress, a state cannot by its legislation destroy the right of the United States as the owner of lands bordering on a stream to the continued flow of its waters, . . . second, that it is limited by the superior power of the general government to secure the uninterrupted navigability of all navigable

21. Kansas v. Colorado, 185 U.S. 125 (1907); Georgia v. Tennessee Copper Co., 206 U.S. 230 (1907); Hudson Water Co. v. McCarter, 209 U.S. 349 (1908). See also the arguments of counsel in the last case.
22. See United States v. Rio Grande Irrigation Co., 174 U.S. 690 (1899), quoted from below.
23. The reference is to Gibbons v. Ogden.

streams within the limits of the United States. In other words, the jurisdiction of the general government over interstate commerce and its natural highways vests in that government the right to take all needed measures to preserve the navigability of the navigable water courses of the country, against even state action. It is true there have been frequent decisions recognizing the power of the state in the absence of Congressional legislation, to assume control of even navigable waters within its limits to the extent of creating dams, bridges, (etc.). . . . The power of the state to thus legislate for the interests of its own citizens is conceded, and until in some way Congress asserts its superior power and the necessity of preserving the general interests of the people of all the states, it is assumed that state action . . . is not subject to challenge. . . . Evidently Congress, perceiving that the time had come when the growing interests of commerce required that the navigable waters of the United States should be subjected to the direct control of the national government, . . . enacted the statute in question.[24]

Here are two propositions; first, that Congress' power to regulate commerce includes the power to maintain and preserve the navigability of the navigable streams of the United States: second, that this power overrides conflicting state authority over such streams. The basis of the latter proposition is already sufficiently obvious, and it demands, I trust, no further elaboration. But a recent application of the doctrine stated in the first proposition is most relevant to our question. I refer to the Act of March 1, 1911, creating a National Forest Reservation Commission with authority to establish the so-called White Mountain and Appalachian Reserve.[25] Said Senator Newlands, of Nevada, sponsor for the measure in the Senate: "This bill establishes and applies a constitutional principle of vast importance, which is that the regulation of the flow of rivers by the protection of the water-sheds from denudation and erosion and the preservation of forests as sources of water supply is a proper function of the National Government under its power to maintain the navigability of streams."[26] That Senator Newlands' assumption that a close relation exists between the preservation of the forests and the maintenance of water-supply is supported by the weight of scientific authority will not, I suppose, be questioned. Yet it may very well be questioned whether there is any more intimate relation in fact between the preservation of the navigability of streams and that of the forests at their head-waters than there is between the preservation of forests and that of the bird life of the country.

In other words, and to expand the argument at this point, I submit the following propositions: first, that the power of Congress to regulate commerce includes the power to preserve the navigability of the navigable streams of the country; second, that to this end Congress may pass all laws necessary and proper; third, that a law is "necessary and proper" in the constitutional sense when a real relation exists between it and the constitutional end to be achieved;

24. 174 U.S. 690, 702–3, 708 (1899).
25. 37 U.S. Statutes at Large, 961–63.
26. 46 Cong. Record, pt. 3, at 2589.

fourth, that such a relation is a matter of fact; fifth, that it is a fact, supported by scientific observation, that a real relation exists between the preservation of forests at the headwaters of streams and that of the streams themselves; sixth, that it is a fact, supported by scientific observation, that a real relation exists between the preservation of the bird life of the country and that of the forests; seventh, that, therefore, it is a fact that a real relation exists between the Act of March 4, 1913, and the maintenance of the navigability of the navigable streams of the country.

And thus much for the commerce clause as a basis for the Migratory Bird Act. We now turn to Art. IV, Sec. 3, par. 2: "The Congress shall have the power to . . . make all needful rules and regulations respecting the territory or other property of the United States."[27] In this connection the language of the opening section of the statute is interesting:

> All wild geese, wild swans, . . . and all other migratory game and insectivorous birds which in their northern and southern migrations pass through or do not remain permanently the entire year within the borders of any state of territory *shall hereafter be deemed to be within the custody and protection of the government of the United States.*

The act may then be regarded as an effort by the national government to assert formal ownership over the migratory birds of the country. Is there any constitutional warrant for the authority thus asserted?

It is, of course, today settled doctrine that the national government may exercise the power of eminent domain whenever it is necessary for it to do so in the exercise of any of its enumerated powers,[28] but that principle is not available in the present instance, since the only "enumerated" power of Congress to which this assumed exercise of the power of eminent domain—so to consider it for the moment—is related as a means is the power to regulate commerce, and that phase of the question we have already discussed.

We come then, to the question whether the government of the United States is one of merely enumerated powers. As we have seen, the Court has sometimes said that such is the case; and so far as it was the intention of the Court to deny the validity of that canon of constitutional construction whereby powers are claimed for the national government solely because of actual inadequacy of the state governments, or so far as it was its intention to assert the principle that the national government is one of *granted* powers, there can be no question of the soundness of its position. Taken literally, however, the proposition that the government of the United States is one of *enumerated powers only* runs counter to the facts.

Thus, in the first place, the government of the United States has its

---

27. Curiously enough, two of the judges in the cases under review speak of this paragraph of the Constitution as the "general welfare" clause. The general welfare clause is to be found in Art. I, sec. 8, par. 1.

28. Kohl v. United States, 91 U.S. 367 (1876), is the leading case.

"necessary and proper" powers, which, so far from being enumerated, are of practically unlimited range, provided only that they be "conducive to" some end within the power of Congress to achieve.[29] Again, the government has what have been called "resultant" powers, powers which ensue from its possession of certain other powers, considered singly or in groups, as for example its power to issue legal tender notes which, as was shown in Julliard v. Greenman,[30] flows from a number of the enumerated powers considered *ensemble;* or its power to carry the mails which ensues from its power "to establish post-offices and post-roads." Finally, it has certain powers from the fact, pointed out by Mr. Justice Bradley in Knox v. Lee,[31] that "It is a national government, and the *only* government in this country that has the character of nationality."

That is to say, the United States is a political community and as such has community interests which the national government, in virtue of its quality as such, may constitutionally assert and protect. Thus, it is by virtue of its national agency that the national government may acquire territory.[32] Again, it is by virtue of its national agency that it may exclude aliens from the United States.[33] Again, it is by virtue of its national agency that it may declare and uphold what has been graphically designated "a national peace."[34] Why, then, the question emerges, may it not, in virtue of the same agency, recognize and assert a national ownership over the wild game of the country?

Let us in this connection turn again to Geer v. Connecticut. Here we find it distinctly recognized that wild game is a thing in which community ownership may exist. However, it will be objected that this was at the common law, and that, while there is a common law of the states, there is no common law of the United States. To this assertion there are several pertinent answers, the first being that in a number of fields, for example that of commercial law and that of international law, there *is* a common law of the United States which the national Courts have repeatedly recognized and enforced.[35] But more to the point at this instant is the query, *Why* the common law rule just referred to? and the answer to this question is, that the rule under discussion recognizes and protects a community interest. The real source, in other words, of the community

29. See McCulloch v. Maryland, 14 Wheat. 416 (1819); also Legal Tender Cases, 12 Wall. 457, 539 (1871).

30. 110 U.S. 421 (1884).

31. 12 Wall. 457 (1871).

32. American Insurance Co. v. Canter, 1 Pet. 511 (1828); Church of Jesus Christ v. United States, 136 U.S. 1 (1890).

33. Chae Chan Ping v. United States, 130 U.S. 581 (1889); Fong Yue Ting v. United States, 149 U.S. 698 (1893).

34. In re Neagle, 135 U.S. 1 (1890).

35. See for instance Swift v. Tyson, 16 Pet. 1 (1843), and The Paquete Habana, 175 U.S. 677 (1900). I am not insisting upon the identity of this law with the old English common law, but merely upon the fact that there is at points a community law of the United States that does not come from Congress.

ownership in *ferae naturae* is the public interest involved.[36] But now, is it not obvious that there is a national interest in migratory birds of precisely the same sort as that which confers upon the state a qualified ownership of the game within its boundaries? And if this is so, is not this interest of the same character as that of the state? And does not the Constitution, which is always to be interpreted in the light of the common law,[37] recognize this interest and create a government capable of protecting it?

Moreover, the question is approachable from another angle. Thus it will be observed that the Act of March 4, 1913, draws a line between "migratory" birds and those which "remain permanently" within the state. Our attention is consequently directed to that phase of the common law rule with reference to community ownership in *ferae naturae* which relates especially to migratory things. Actually, in origin this phase of the rule would seem to be a rule for the determination of the relative rights of *adjoining nations*[38] in the control of such things. It is thus a rule of international law, of which, therefore, the Act of Congress may be considered declaratory. A parallel case would be where a great island should arise from the sea partly within the marine belt of the United States. The right of the national government not only to exclude all foreign intruders therefrom but to assert complete domestic jurisdiction over it would probably not be challenged. In short, when attention is given to the prerogatives of the national government, in its quality as the organ of a member of the family of nations and as the guardian of the community interests of the United States, it would seem that the quasi-ownership that has hitherto been attributed to the states in migratory game has subsisted by the mere allowance of the national government, and that the true significance of the Act of March 4, 1913, is merely that this allowance has now been withdrawn.

However, there is one more phase of the general question demanding consideration in connection with Art. IV. Sec. 3, par. 4. Under this paragraph of the Constitution Congress is the custodian of the public lands of the United States, among which are millions of acres of valuable forest lands. Now no one, I suppose, would deny that Congress, in order to protect the timber on these lands, may enact fitting penalties against its theft, provide for the pursuit of the offenders throughout the United States, and visit penalties upon their accomplices wherever they may be found within the national jurisdiction. In fact, in one way or another Congress has done just these things; nor has its right to do so ever been impeached so far as I am aware.

But now, *why* may Congress so act? Clearly, it is not by virtue of its powers under Art. IV, which are powers of merely local application. The answer to the

---

36. See Geer v. Connecticut, *passim*.

37. See Mr. Justice Gray in United States v. Wong Kim Ark, 169 U.S. 649 (1898), and cases there cited.

38. See McReady v. Virginia, 94 U.S. 391 (1877), and Manchester v. Massachusetts, 139 U.S. 240 (1891).

question is to be found in the necessary and proper clause of Art. I, Sec. 8, which enables Congress in its capacity as national legislature to make all laws necessary and proper for carrying into execution any of the powers of the national government. By virtue of this clause, as Marshall pointed out for a parallel case in Cohens v. Virginia,[39] Congress may give legislation intended to discharge its local functions nation-wide operation if it be necessary and proper for it to do so, and the only question that can arise with reference to legislation designed so to operate is whether it is incidental to such local functions. Such being the case, however, let the question be posed whether the Migratory Bird Act, with its nation-wide operation, is not a necessary and proper measure for the protection of the forest reserves of the United States? Can there really be any dispute on that heading?

In short, the Act of March 4, 1913, far from being the unwarrantable usurpation of power that the decisions which we have passed in review would make it out to be, is constitutionally justifiable on a number of grounds. But it is most advantageously and most correctly viewed as part and parcel of the great movement for the conservation of national resources, for the conservation of the navigable streams of the country, of its forests, of its wild life; for the elimination of the natural enemies of community prosperity. Putting its powers at the disposal of this great movement Congress has enacted several notable pieces of legislation, of which the Migratory Bird Act is one. Looked at either as a deliberate assertion by the national legislature of the nation's proprietorship of the migratory game of the country or as an act "necessary and proper" in a rational chain of causation for the preservation of the navigability of the streams of the country and its timber reserves, this act is valid.

39. 6 Wheat. 264, 423–30 (1821).

12. The Child Labor Decision

Is the Supreme Court entitled to define the purposes for which Congress may exercise its taxing powers, and if so, why not of all its powers? These are the fundamental questions raised by the recent decision of the Court in Bailey v. The Drexel Furniture Company, setting aside Title XII of the Revenue Act of 1921, which purported to levy a special tax amounting to 10 percent of their net profits on certain classes of concerns employing child labor. The following words of Chief Justice Taft's opinion for the Court indicate the principal grounds of the decision:

> Taxes are imposed in the discretion of the legislature on proper subjects with the primary motive of obtaining revenue from them and with the incidental motive of discouraging them by making their continuance onerous. They do not lose their character as taxes because of the incidental motive. But there comes a time in the extension of the penalizing features of the so-called tax when it loses its character as such and becomes a mere penalty with the characterization of regulation and punishment. Such is the case of the law before us.

One might pause to point out that there is something of a contradiction between an incidental motive of discouraging and a primary motive of raising revenue from the thing discouraged. Passing that by, however, these words reveal clearly the initial difficulty in the way of the decision. In attempting to define the taxing power of Congress by an alleged "primary" purpose the Court is forced to attempt to penetrate Congress's motives in enacting specific tax measures, and furthermore to classify these motives, as it does in this case, into "primary" and "incidental." It had hitherto been supposed that the Court could not do this. Thus in McCray v. United States (195 U.S.), in which the congressional tax on yellow oleomargarine was attacked as destructive of the

From *The New Republic*, July 12, 1922, pp. 177–79. Reprinted by permission. Copyright 1922 by The New Republic.

subject matter and, therefore, obviously a measure of regulation rather than of taxation, the Court, speaking through the late chief justice, answered:

> It is, however, argued, if a lawful power may be exerted for an unlawful purpose, and thus, by abusing the power, it may be made to accomplish a result not intended by the Constitution, all limitation of power must disappear, and the grave function lodged in the judiciary, to confine all the departments within the authority conferred by the Constitution, will be of no avail. This, when reduced to its last analysis, comes to this: that, because a particular department of the government may exert its lawful powers with the object or motive of reaching an end not justified, therefore, it becomes the duty of the judiciary to restrain the exercise of a lawful power wherever it seems to the judical mind that such lawful power has been abused. But this reduces itself to the contention that, under our constitutional system, the abuse by one department of the government of its lawful powers, is to be corrected by the abuse of its powers by another department.

Chief Justice Taft would appear to answer that the special levy on the profits of employers of child labor offered a clearer case of abuse of power than did the tax on oleomargarine. But this answer clearly does not touch the main proposition laid down in the McCray case as to the intrinsic limitations on the Court's own power; and, furthermore, its substantial accuracy is open to challenge. The regulatory purpose of the later tax was, Mr. Taft urges, "palpable" and apparent "on the very face of its provisions." But if the regulatory purpose of the oleomargarine tax was not also matter of common knowledge, at least that of the tax on state bank issues which was sustained shortly after the Civil War in the case of Veazie v. Fenno (8 Wall.) was. Indeed, the Court itself took cognizance of it—as Mr. Taft's own references to the case show—yet they sustained the law involved *as a tax,* going at length into the question whether it was a "direct" tax within the meaning of the Constitution and exonerating it from that charge.

But I submit further that a special tax on the profits of concerns employing child labor, viewed simply as a revenue-raising measure, is by no means an extravagance. That special profits accrue to such concerns directly from their occupying a degraded plane of competition is certainly a widely held belief and a well-warranted one; why then should not the government regard such profits as a proper source of revenue? That certain features of the tax on employers of child labor disclosed an expectation in Congress that the tax would have some effect on child labor employment and recognition that this effect ought to be kept in proper channels, may be conceded, but the concession does not vindicate the Court's conclusion as to the "primary motive" of the act. "On the face of it" what the act did was to impose a levy to be collected annually through the Treasury Department and to be measured by profits which were directly attributable, at least in part, to the occasion of the levy. And what is this but to describe an excise?

It is, therefore, abundantly clear that in undertaking to determine the relative weight of the motives which governed Congress in the enactment of the tax on employers of child labor, the Court essayed a somewhat delicate task, and one, be it emphasized, which it has hitherto declined to attempt. In short, the Court has set up a new canon of constitutional law, and one which it must experience great difficulty in manipulating. The stigmata of ulterior purpose can be easily avoided in future cases, and the Court will be driven back on its own unaided intuitions. When this happens it will find itself confronted with an embarrassing dilemma: either it must enter more and more upon the hazardous business of legislative psychoanalysis; or repenting of its somewhat hasty claim to greater insight than its predecessors, it must abandon its abortive doctrine. *Parturient montes, nascetur ridiculus mus.*

But the question of its enforceability aside, let us consider for a moment the intrinsic validity of Chief Justice Taft's assertion that "taxes are imposed . . . with the primary motive of raising revenue," viewed as a principle of constitutional law. The late Professor Maitand once remarked upon "the importance of commonplaces" in determining the content of constitutions, and Mr. Taft's assertion perhaps illustrates the observation. Nevertheless, it is to be feared that in this case the endeavor of the Court to elevate everyday wisdom into constitutional law has led it to attribute to popular ideas a precision they are far from possessing. No doubt, it is generally held that the *ordinary* purpose of tax laws is the raising of revenue; but to pass from this fact to the deduction that the *primary* purpose of revenue raising is an invariable ingredient of the idea of "tax" which must be satisfied in every specific instance of taxation is to move somewhat briskly. The American people know something of their legislative history in this respect. They are fully aware that almost every customs revenue act which has been passed since the beginning of the government has enacted whole schedules which were designed not for the purpose of raising revenue at all but for the purpose of excluding goods from the country. And yet are such duties any less "duties"—and so "taxes"—within the sense of the Constitution? If so, why are they subject to the requirement that they be "uniform throughout the United States?"

The peculiar danger, however, of the regulatory feature of the Child Labor tax, Chief Justice Taft further argues, is that it reaches matters not otherwise subject to national power, but falling under the control of the police powers of the states. This type of measure carried far enough, he says, would "completely wipe out the sovereignty of the states." What, however, is "the sovereignty of the states," within the Constitution? Mr. Taft refers only to the Tenth Amendment, which recognizes certain powers as being reserved to the states; but only on condition of their not having been delegated to the United States; and when they conflict with powers delegated to the United States the latter, by Article VI of the Constitution, have the right of way. It results that the powers of the national government are, generally speaking, to be defined quite indifferently to the existence of other powers in the states with which they may come into conflict in attempting to control the same subject matter.

This was the view of Madison, uttered in the earliest years of the Constitution: "Interference with the powers of the States," said he, "is no constitutional criterion of the power of Congress"; it is the view of the Court itself in the Minnesota rate cases (230 U.S.) and the cases following in the wake of these. That it was the view of Chief Justice Marshall needs hardly to be stated; his fundamental canon of constitutional construction was that, while the national government was one of the enumerated powers, within the field of the powers granted it was a sovereign government.

Nor does the passage which Chief Justice Taft quotes from Marshall's opinion in McCulloch v. Maryland militate at all against this view: "Should Congress," it runs, "under the pretext of executing its powers, pass laws for the accomplishment of objects not entrusted to the government, it would become the painful duty of this tribunal, should a case requiring such a decision come before it, to say that such an act was not the law of the land." The implication which Chief Justice Taft seemingly would read into these words is that, in respect of the choice of purposes for which it may exercise its powers, the national government is not a sovereign government; that its powers were given it for limited objects, and that the Court must hold it to these objects. Never was a quotation more entirely misapplied. As the words themselves show, Marshall was here speaking not of Congress's substantive powers but of the instrumental powers conferred upon it by the "necessary and proper" clause. Naturally, instrumental powers must be kept instrumental—that is precisely their difference from substantive powers, which are sovereign powers and carry with them sovereign discretion in their use. That Marshall had no idea that the Court might censor the purposes for which the substantive powers of government, and least of all the taxing power, might be exercised, is proved by this very case of McCulloch v. Maryland. The question at issue was whether Maryland had the right to tax the operations of the Bank of the United States. Counsel for the state urged that the state ought to be trusted to exercise its power reasonably and considerately, which argument Marshall answered with his famous maxim, that "the power to tax involves the power to destroy." In other words, concede the state the power to raise revenue from the bank and it would be free to use the same power to drive the bank from the state. It is submitted that this line of reasoning is fatally at variance with the doctrine of Bailey v. The Drexel Furniture Company.

To sum up: The logic of the decision of this case, overriding previous decisions, makes the Court the supervisor of the purposes for which Congress may exercise its constitutional powers. It thus cancels out the third dimension, so to speak, of the sovereignty of the national government within the field of its granted powers. At one stroke a new canon of constitutional interpretation is created and an out-of-date one revived: legislative motive becomes a test of legislative action; and any effort on the part of Congress to bring within its control matters heretofore falling to the states alone, raises the question of valid motive. The notion of the cooperation of the national government and the states in the furtherance of the general welfare, which was voiced a few years ago in Hoke v. United States (227 U.S.) has apparently dropped out of view. The one thing to be said for the new doctrine is that it will probably prove so unworkable in practice that it will not long survive.

Meantime we may fairly retort upon the Court the question which it has put Congress: What was its "primary" motive? It is only a surmise, of course, but perhaps not too wild a one, that the Court has been influenced by the talk of a breakdown of local self-government within recent years, and especially in consequence of national prohibition. The reflection is prompted that if the Court will cast its eye back over the last thirty years, it will have reason to conclude that it must itself shoulder some of the responsibility or credit for national prohibition, since it was another happy idea which, overruling the precedents of half a century, in the case of Leisy v. Hardin (135 U.S.), started the agitation, which culminated in the eighteenth amendment. Judicial adventures in saving the country have not always worked out quite as they were planned to.

But a more important lesson, too, is suggested by this decision and the broadening discussion affecting the whole doctrine of judical review to which it has given rise. The Supreme Court is, first of all, a court of justice and justice is a matter which touches individuals much more immediately than it does governments. The Constitution contains many provisions designed to safeguard individual justice—for instance, those of the Fifth and Sixth Amendments, and those of the first section of the Fourteenth Amendment—and the enforcement of these provisions the individual is entitled to claim directly from the Court. Of other provisions and principles of the Constitution, however, and especially of those which are designed to distribute power within the structure of government erected by the Constitution, the individual is only the indirect beneficiary. Yet even within this field the Court has a clear mandate from the Constitution to intervene to secure the supremacy of the Constitution itself and of the national laws, against conflicting state legislation. On the other hand, when we view the question of judicial review from the side of national power, a different principle is recognized both in the *Federalist* and in Marshall's decisions. This, in the words of the latter, was that "the wisdom and discretion of Congress, their identity with the people, and the influence which their constituents possess at election" were "the sole restraints" upon which the people had relied to secure them from abuse of its powers by the national government. "They are," he adds, "the restraints on which the people must often rely solely in all representative governments.'' Surely these words are still applicable. In the light of them, Bailey v. The Drexel Furniture Company must be written down as a piece of grandmotherly meddling, certainly wrong in principle, even though it do {*sic.,* does?} not prove actually mischievous in the final result.

13. Moratorium over Minnesota

UNDER the style of Home Building and Loan Association v. Blaisdell,[1] the good old melodrama "When the Mortgage Came Due" was reenacted in the Supreme Court last month, the chief justice taking the role of *deus ex machina* and Justice Sutherland being cast as villain.

In April of last year the Minnesota legislature passed an act which, declaring the existence of an emergency, provides that the time within which existing mortgages may be redeemed in that state shall be extended. The extensions are to be for such periods as a proper court may deem reasonable, but in no case are they to run beyond May 1, 1935, when the act itself comes to an end. The issue in the Blaisdell case was the validity of this act in relation to the "obligation of contracts" clause of the United States Constitution. The act was sustained by a vote of five justices to four, Chief Justice Hughes speaking for the Court and Justice Sutherland for the minority. The actual issue between the two sides appears on first consideration to have been a rather narrow one, but under closer examination it broadens into a quarrel of real significance, especially for issues that will be apt to arise out of the New Deal.

Let us first note the points as to which there was agreement on both sides. These were, first, that the obligation of a contract comes from the law under which it is made; secondly, that the essential attributes of the sovereign power which is vested in a state legislature comprise a part of the law of each state and hence of each contract; thirdly, that it is an essential attribute of the said legislative power to provide for emergencies—that is to say for *some* emergencies.

For it is at this point precisely that the split comes. The majority holds that

From 82 *University of Pennsylvania Law Review* 311 (1934). Reprinted by permission. Copyright 1934 University of Pennsylvania Law Review.

1. U.S.L.W. January 9, 1934, at 381.

the present financial and industrial depression falls within the conception of "emergency" which the legislative power of the state is empowered to meet by the type of measure which was before the Court; and the minority denies this. Why the difference? Surprisingly enough, there seems to be no quarrel at all between majority and minority as to the *seriousness* of the emergency which the Minnesota act is designed to alleviate. The minority does not, any more than the majority, traverse the recitation of facts in the preamble of the Minnesota act, to the effect that property values have fallen radically, that credit is almost unobtainable, that unemployment is general; that debtors are consequently unable in large number either to meet their obligations or to refund them, and so on. Nor is there any disposition on the part of the minority, any more than that of the majority, to challenge the ability of the state legislature, whose members "come from every community of the state and from all the walks of life" and are "familiar with conditions generally in every calling, occupation, profession and business of the state," to make a finding with respect to economic conditions which is entitled to the serious consideration of the Court.

No; the position of Justice Sutherland and his adherents is simply this, that the "obligation of contracts" clause was made exactly to prevent this type of legislation in this type of emergency; and it has to be added that, so far as historical investigation is to be relied upon in such a matter he is unquestionably right. The Revolution was also followed by a period of severe depression, in which debtors found themselves in serious plight; and in meeting this situation the legislatures in most of the states resorted to measures to some of which the Minnesota statute bears a strong family resemblance. And it was undoubtedly the discontent of creditors with such measures that dictated the "obligation of contracts" clause and secured its acceptance by the Convention which framed the Constitution on almost its last day, when everybody was in a hurry to get home. Furthermore, when the state legislatures again got busy following the great panic of 1837, the Supreme Court interposed its veto on certain statutes very like the Minnesota statute, in the name of the "obligation of the contracts" clause.[2]

How, then, does the Court meet this position? Unfortunately the chief justice, who ordinarily wields a very capable dialectic, appears to be a trifle shy of his own argument with the result that it is not quite so clear-cut at all points as that of his adversary. In general, however, his answer to Justice Sutherland amounts to this: the Constitution was made for a changing society, and consequently to be adapted to the needs thereof; and social changes since 1789 make the type of emergency with which the Minnesota statute deals a matter of public concern. The entire passage, however, which these two statements sum up is so relevant

2. Bronson v. Kinzie, 1 How. 311 (U.S. 1843); McCracken v. Hayward, 2 How. 608 (U.S. 1844).

to constitutional issues likely to come before the Court in the near future that it should be quoted:

> It is manifest from this review of our decisions that there has been a growing appreciation of public needs and of the necessity of finding ground for a rational compromise between individual rights and public welfare.
>
> The statement and consequent contraction of the public domain, the pressure of a constantly increasing density of population, the inter-relation of the activities of our people and the complexity of our economic interests, have inevitably led to an increased use of the organization of society in order to protect the very bases of individual opportunity. Where, in earlier days, it was thought that only the concerns of individuals or of classes were involved, and that those of the state itself were touched only remotely, it has later been found that the fundamental interests of the state are directly affected; and that the question is no longer merely that of one party to a contract as against another, but of the use of reasonable means to safeguard the economic structure upon which the good of all depends.
>
> It is no answer to say that this public need was not apprehended a century ago, or to insist that what the provision of the Constitution meant to the vision of that day it must mean to the vision of our time. If by the statement that what the Constitution meant at the time of its adoption it means today, it is intended to say that the great clauses of the Constitution must be confined to the interpretation which the framers, with the conditions and outlook of their time, would have placed upon them, the statement carries its own refutation.
>
> It was to guard against such a narrow conception that Chief Justice Marshall uttered the memorable warning—"We must never forget that it is a constitution we are expounding" (McCulloch v. Maryland, 4 Wheat. 316, 407)—"a constitution intended to endure for ages to come, and, consequently, to be adapted to the various crises of human affairs." *Id.* at 415.
>
> When we are dealing with the words of the Constitution, said this Court in Missouri v. Holland, 252 U.S. 416, 433, "we must realize that they have called into life a being the development of which could not have been foreseen completely by the most gifted of its begetters. . . . The case before us must be considered in the light of our whole experience and not merely in that of what was said a hundred years ago."[3]

In other words, the emergency met by the Minnesota statute is *not* the same type of emergency which the Convention of 1787 had in mind, and for the simple but irresistible reason that the *social environment has essentially changed since then*. But, Justice Sutherland urges in refutation, the Constitution must be construed according to "the intention of its founders." The answer is twofold: First, that the Constitution's founders could never have had an intention as to something—social conditions of 1933, to wit—which they could not have imagined or foreseen; secondly, that their broader intention was that the Constitution should, as Marshall phrased it, "be adapted to the various crises of human affairs," this being the condition of its survival.

It follows that the Court's work of construing the Constitution can never take the form solely of an historical inquiry into the supposed intention of the

---

3. Above, note 1, at 387.

framers regarding something as to which they could not possibly have had any intention—at least, without pretending to divine omniscience. It must also involve recognition of the facts of present everyday living. To such facts the Constitution simply *must be* and *will be* adapted sooner or later, and the only question is one of method. But having gradually appropriated the vast indefinate powers, which it today possesses over the Constitution, the Court has at the same time appropriated a commensurate responsibility to see to it that its reading of the Constitution shall avoid social catastrophe. Justice Sutherland himself admits that the Court has this responsibility with regard to the common law; and constitutional law is just as much judge-made as the common law. In it the Court has hold of a live wire and can let go thereof only if and when the current of its own power is cut off.

But Justice Sutherland objects: "A provision of the Constitution, . . . does not admit of two distinctly opposite interpretations. It does not mean one thing at one time and an entirely different thing at another time."[4]

The fact of the matter is, however, that the Constitution must mean different things at different times if it is to mean what is sensible, applicable, feasible. Indeed, Justice Sutherland himself mentions two instances in which the meaning of the Constitution has clearly undergone alteration. Thus, he admits that "it is not probable" that founders of the Constitution had any other purpose in mind for the "obligation of contracts" clause than the protection of creditors; but that in the Dartmouth College Case[5] it was given "a wider application" —which is putting it mildly. He also writes, in a footnote to his opinion, of the "commerce clause":

> When that was adopted its application was necessarily confined to the regula-tion of the primitive methods of transportation then employed; but railroads, automobiles and aircraft automatically were brought within the scope and subject to the terms of the commerce clause the moment these new means of transporta-tion came into existence, just as they were at once brought within the meaning of the word "carrier," as defined by the dictionaries.[6]

And what would Justice Sutherland have to say regarding the "due process" clause, and that construction of it which today underlies the judicial review of state legislation?

We return to the chief justice's opinion. Early in it occurs the following passage: "Emergency does not create power. Emergency does not increase granted power or remove or diminish the restrictions imposed upon power

---

4. *Id.* at 388.

5. 4 Wheat. 518 (U.S. 1819).

6. Above, note 1, at 389. Justice Sutherland seems to be implying here that the Constitution construes itself. Why, then, should we not do away with judicial review? Note also his distinction—a purely verbal one—between the *meaning* and the *application* of the Constitution. This idea of self-interpreting law is, of course, an old one. Constantine, at the Council of Nicea, enthroned the Bible as "the infallible judge of truth"—with the eventual result of making the papacy its final interpreter.

granted or reserved." Yet in face of this declaration the ensuing decision goes on to hold, as we have seen, that Minnesota had the power to enact the statute under review because of an emergency, although otherwise it would not have had the power to do so! One is reminded of a curious opinion of Chief Justice White's a few years ago in which he demonstrated (?) that the Sixteenth Amendment could not have been intended to bestow on Congress any power of income taxation which it previously had not had since, forsooth, its power was already "plenary"![7] Surely our judges ought to relinquish the idea that the judicial robe invests them with Humpty-Dumpty's facile prerogative over words.[8]

On the other hand, the Court's reliance on the emergency concept in this case and its insistence on the temporary character of the Minnesota statue do not imply that it will not be prepared eventually to sustain the N. I. R. A. as a permanent measure. The emergency concept has before this provided the Court a dignified, unhurried retreat to newer positions after older ones had proved untenable.[9] Besides, who could be certain that the emergency would not recur if the measures taken to remedy it were withdrawn or stricken down? There are emergencies and emergencies. An earthquake, a riot, a war, a housing shortage can perhaps be authenticated by a court without a too great strain on the normal judicial function; but what of a nation-wide depression—and just how depressed does it have to be? The emergency concept is important as illustrating the inherent ability of governmental power under the Constitution to expand to meet new necessities. But it does not signify that the only necessities which may be met by power thus expanded must be merely temporary. Whether they turn out to be temporary or otherwise will be determined by forces external to constitutional law.

Has the decision in the Blaisdell case any very broad significance, particularly for the New Deal? It is not unreasonable to think so. What can be ventured, at least, is that the two opinions present two points of view from which widely divergent lines of constitutional law may be imaginably projected. Justice Sutherland is the unconvinced, unconvincible, rugged individualist. It is amusing, the unction with which, in quoted passages, he harps on such themes as "individual distress . . . should be alleviated only by industry and frugality, not by relaxation of law" (just how frugal and industrious a family the Blaisdells are is unfortunately a topic not dealt with in either opinion); "debtors instead of seeking to meet their obligations by painful effort, by industry and economy,

7. Brushaber v. Union Pacific R.R., 240 U.S. 1, 36 Sup. Ct. 236 (1916).

8. "When *I* use a word," Humpty Dumpty said, in a rather scornful tone, "it means just what I choose it to mean—neither more nor less."

"The question is," said Alice, "whether you *can* make words mean so many different things."

"The question is," said Humpty Dumpty, "which is to be master—that's all." {Lewis Carroll, *Through the Looking Glass*}

9. Hepburn v. Griswold, 8 Wall. 603 (U.S. 1869); Knox v. Lee, 12 Wall. 457 (U.S. 1870); Julliard v. Greenman, 110 U.S. 421, 4 Sup. Ct. 122 (1884).

began to rest their hopes entirely upon legislative interference''; ''virtue and justice,'' ''general prudence and industry,'' ''high standards of business morale.'' Then he adds this highly untechnocratic homily on his own account:

> The present exigency is nothing new. From the beginning of our existence as a nation, periods of depression, of industrial failure, of financial distress, of unpaid and unpayable indebtedness, have alternated with years of plenty. The vital lesson that expenditure beyond income begets poverty, that public or private extravagance, financed by promises to pay, either must end in complete or partial repudiation or the promises be fulfilled by self-denial and painful effort, though constantly taught by bitter experience, seems never to be learned.[10]

Finally, he produces this shot from his locker: ''If the provisions of the Constitution be not upheld when they pinch as well as when they comfort, they may as well be abandoned.''[11] Here speaks the stern unflinching spirit of a truly Spartan jurisprudence: it craves a Constitution that pinches—the other fellow!

The outlook of the chief justice's opinion is very different, as we have seen. One sentence in it deserves repetition: ''Where, in earlier days, it was thought that only the concerns of individuals or of classes were involved, and that those of the state itself were touched only remotely, it has later been found that the fundamental interests of the state are directly affected; and that the question is no longer merely that of one party to a contract against another, but of the use of reasonable means to safeguard the economic structure upon which the good of all depends.''[12] This, and the invocation of Marshall's canon of adaptative construction, make the chief justice's opinion something whose future should be worth watching.

In brief, the issue between the chief justice and Justice Sutherland is purely on of *approach* to the constitutional problem before the Court. The latter treats the Minnesota statute *as if* it had been enacted contemporaneously with the Constitution; while the former treats the Constitution as contemporary with the Minnesota statute, that is, with today. It may be added that most constitutional issues *are* determined by the Court's *approach* to them, and that the Court is usually a perfectly free agent in choosing its approach.

10. Above, note 1, 393.
11. *Id.* at 395, as corrected at 401.
12. *Id.* at 387.

14. The Schechter Case—
Landmark, or What?

CHAMPIONS of the Supreme Court's decision in the Poultry Case (Schechter v. United States)[1] thank God that "the Constitution still stands" but others have asked if the decision does not mean rather that the Constitution stands *still*.[2] Certainly no question concerning a constitutional decision could be of greater moment. The Court has long since absorbed, for most purposes, the function of amending the Constitution. If it has now gone abruptly on strike the country may presently find itself in an exceedingly embarrassing position.

The founder of our constitutional law was under no misapprehension on this point. Even in asserting that the Court had the power and duty to pronounce "void" any act of Congress found by it to transcend the powers of that body, Marshall also declared that the Constitution was "intended to endure for ages to come, and consequently to be adapted to the various *crises* of human affairs,"[3] and he proceeded forthwith to make such an adaptation in the case then pending before the Court. That is to say, the Court's "guardianship" of the Constitution was recognized as involving a certain responsibility to "the undefined and expanding future" for which the framers of the instrument had intended it.[4] By the same sign, President Roosevelt's complaint that the Court had in the Poultry Case "reverted to the horse and buggy days,"[5] calls for a certain amount of clarifying explanation if it is to be justified. If the president had in mind "the horse and buggy days" of 1789, or even of a generation later, his words cast an unwarrantable aspersion on the statesmanship which established the Constitution, and the statesmanship which initially interpreted and

From 13 *New York University Law Quarterly Review* 151 (1936). Reprinted by permission.

1. Decided May 27, 1935.
2. See Professor W. L. Whittlesey in the *Survey-Graphic*, July, 1935, at 325.
3. McCulloch v. Maryland, 17 U.S. (4 Wheat.) 316, 413 (1819).
4. Hurtado v. People of California, 110 U.S. 516, 530–31, 4 Sup. Ct. 111, 118–19 (1884).
5. *New York Times*, June 1, 1935, at 1.

applied it. If, on the other hand, he had in mind "the horse and buggy days" of 1889 or thereabouts, his utterance appears in a different light, as will be made plain in due course.

There are those, to be sure, who take the position that the Court did wisely to put the question "squarely up to the people" whether the national government should exercise such powers as those which the decision in the Poultry Case denies it. This seems to be the position, for instance, of Senator Borah, as also it is of the distinguished professor of constitutional law at Columbia University. The latter has recently written:

> It seems unmistakable, then, that, despite all efforts to circumvent the plain prescriptions of the Constitution as expounded by the Supreme Court, no fundamental change in our economic system, no far-reaching alteration in the relations of government to business, can be brought about without changing the Constitution. And this is as it should be. We should not rush or drift into such important changes upon the high tide of an emergency. The common man should understand what is up.[6]

"Plain prescriptions of the Constitution *as expounded by the Supreme Court*"— a delightful example of what the dictionary terms *contradictio in adjecto,* which no doubt Dean McBain concocted with his tongue in his cheek. That, however, is by the way. Our real concern with the learned Dean's reflections is centered upon his contention that "the common man should understand what is up." Again one suspects an essay at drollery. Did "the common man" understand "what was up" in the Poultry Case? If so, "the common man" had the advantage over many puzzled members of the legal profession. And does "the common man" understand what has been up all the time the Supreme Court has been manipulating the commerce clause of the Constitution? If so, the many volumes which have been written to elucidate the subject would seem to have been time largely wasted, and the scriptural phrase "out of the mouths of babes and sucklings" receives confirmation in an unexpected quarter. And would "the common man" know what was up if an amendment was proposed to give Congress the powers denied it in the Poultry Case? To say the least, it seems doubtful.

On the other hand, that the decision in the Schechter Case did reflect the understanding of "the common man," in the sense of his *lack* of understanding, and consequent inability to choose, regarding the larger relationships of government and business today, is no doubt true. This was perceived at once by Sir Josiah Stamp, who was visiting this country at the time the decision was handed down. Thus he reports:

> I found also that the popular reaction to the Supreme Court decision on its constitutional side was paradoxical. It is appreciated that the economic life of the country should be looked at as far as possible as a whole, to secure the maximum advantage; it is also realized that economic forces do not lie state-confined. The

6. *Id.* July 7, 1935, sec. 7, at 18.

boundaries of the states are singularly artificial; they are generally neither rivers nor mountains, but imaginary lines on a map, which cannot permanently prevail against underlying economic forces. It must, therefore, be made possible for Washington to act on an embracing and comprehensive scale in economic affairs, yet the idea of a transfer of state rights to the Federal Government meets with every kind of psychological resistance . . . in such matters the average mind in the states is as old in its outlook as the Constitution itself.[7]

In short, the decision did not clarify—it did not lend that light and leading which have sometimes been urged as the best justification of the Court's constitutional prerogative—if anything, it left popular muddlement worse confounded. One implication of Sir Josiah's words should, however, be corrected. It is not true that the outlook of the Constitution is as "old" as that of the average mind in the matters mentioned by him—*old,* that is, in the sense of obsolete and no longer practicable. If we may attribute to the Constitution the outlook of its framers, that was *mercantilist* rather than laissez faire, and contemplated not a little activity on the part of government in the field of business enterprise, as Hamilton's *Report on Manufactures* goes to show. The forces of laissez faire were slower in assembling; nor has laissez faire ever prevailed to this day when it has been a question of government's *aiding* business.

I

The salient facts of the Poultry Case were as follows: Here defendant company, wholesale poultry dealers in New York City, were charged with having violated the Live Poultry Code set up by President Roosevelt under the N. I. R. A., first, with respect to minimum wage and maximum hour requirements, and secondly, by according preferential treatment to favored customers. It was conceded that most of the poultry handled by the company reached it, via commission men, from outside the state and hence through the channels of interstate commerce. It was conceded, too, that the only authority which Congress could claim over such a business must arise in its power to "regulate commerce among the several states," and its resultant power to foster and protect such commerce. The Court exonerated the defendants, first, on the ground that the Live Poultry Code represented an unconstitutional delegation of legislative power by Congress—a phase of the case with which this article is not concerned; and, secondly, on the ground that defendants' business was not subject to Congress anyway, being (1) neither interstate commerce in itself, nor (2) closely enough connected therewith to bring its conduct in the particulars above mentioned with Congress's regulatory and protective power. Before, however, taking up either of these two aspects of the Court's application of the

7. *Id.* July 14, 1935, sec. 3, at 6.

commerce clause, we must give a moment's passing attention to a preliminary
feature of the chief justice's opinion.

> "We are told," the chief justice recites, "that the provision of the statute
> authorizing the adoption of codes must be viewed in the light of the grave
> national crisis with which Congress was confronted." He then continues: "Un-
> doubtedly, the conditions to which power is addressed are always to be considered
> when the exercise of power is challenged. Extraordinary conditions may call for
> extraordinary remedies. But the argument necessarily stops short of an attempt to
> justify action which lies outside the sphere of constitutional authority. Extraordi-
> nary conditions do not create or enlarge constitutional power. The Constitution
> established a national government with powers deemed to be adequate, as they
> have proved to be both in war and peace, but these powers of the national
> government are limited by the constitutional grants. Those who act under these
> grants are not at liberty to transcend the imposed limits because they believe that
> more or different power is necessary. Such assertions of extraconstitutional
> authority were anticipated and precluded by the explicit terms of the Tenth
> Amendment—"The powers not delegated to the United States by the Constitu-
> tion, nor prohibited by it to the states, are reserved to the states respectively, or
> to the people."[8]

Just what meaning these carefully balanced phrases cancel down to is not
entirely clear. Certainly, if "extraordinary conditions may call for extraordinary
remedies" and this has to be considered "when the exercise of power is
challenged," then to people unacquainted with legalistic jargon, or not disposed to be unduly impressed thereby, it would seem that "extraordinary
conditions" *do* "enlarge constitutional power." Assuming, however, that it is
the chief justice's design to pronounce "a death sentence" upon the emergency
concept which has hitherto had some place in our constitutional law,[9] then it
must be admitted that much is to be said in modern unsettled conditions, for
such a procedure—*provided* the necessary corollary thereof be recognized,
namely, an enlarged interpretation of the *normal* powers of government.
Unfortunately, nowhere in his opinion does the chief justice evince the least
recognition of such a corollary. Instead he adopts the Pollyanna attitude—we've
always pulled through and we always shall, whatever version of the powers of
the national government is daily promulgated by the Court.[10]

We are thus brought to the Court's construction of the commerce clause.
That it was unnecessary for the Court to pass upon this aspect of the case is of

---

8. Schechter Poultry Corp. v. United States, 55 Sup. Ct. 837, 842 (1935).

9. See Corwin, *Twilight of the Supreme Court* 134–35 (1934).

10. To some extent at least, the emergency concept is an outgrowth of the idea that, while
economic power is *normal*, a part of the order of nature, *political* power is *artificial* and
exceptional, and is therefore justifiably applied to restrain economic power only in conditions of
stress and for the purpose only of removing such conditions as speedily as possible. In other words,
governmental power stands in about the same relation to economic power that the regime of martial
law, as described Ex parte Milligan, 71 U.S. (4 Wall.) 2 (1866), which was cited by the chief
justice at this point, does to the regime of civil law.

course evident. The case had been already disposed of so far as defendants' interest was concerned, by the holding that the Live Poultry Code represented an exercise of power which, even though Congress had been held to possess it, could not have been constitutionally delegated. In other words, "the law of the case" had been already sufficiently ascertained to determine its outcome for the parties to it; and "the authority to ascertain and determine the law in a given case" is, as the Court itself has said, the sole source of its power of judicial review.[11] In thus straying beyond the strict precincts of its judicial duty, the Court, no doubt unwittingly, lent countenance to the theory, which its present champions have vociferously seized upon and greatly magnified, that it has a specific function of guardianship of the Constitution, so that anyone, be he even president of the United States, who criticizes its exercise of this supposed function thereby writes himself down an enemy of the Constitution. The same position was taken in 1857 by defenders of the Court's comparable performance in the Dred Scott Case.[12]

The first question passed upon by the Court in relation to the commerce clause is whether defendants were engaged in "commerce among the several states," and this question is answered, "No." Once the poultry they dealt in reached them, says the chief justice, "interstate transactions in relation" to it "then ended." Continuing, the opinion reads:[13]

> Defendants held the poultry at their slaughterhouse markets for slaughter and local sale to retail dealers and butchers who in turn sold directly to consumers. Neither the slaughtering nor the sales by defendants were transactions in interstate commerce. . . .[14]

> The undisputed facts thus afford no warrant for the argument that the poultry handled by defendants at their slaughterhouse markets was in a "current" or "flow" of interstate commerce, and was thus subject to congressional regulation. The mere fact that there may be a constant flow of commodities into a state does not mean that the flow continues after the property has arrived and has become commingled with the mass of property within the state and is there held solely for

11. See Justice Sutherland's language in Adkins v. Children's Hospital (Minimum Wage Case), 261 U.S. 525, 544, 43 Sup. Ct. 394, 396 (1923):

> From the authority to ascertain and determine the law in a given case, there necessarily results, in case of a conflict, the duty to declare and enforce the rule of the supreme law and reject that of an inferior act of legislation which, transcending the Constitution, is of no effect and binding on no one. This is not the exercise of a substantive power to review and nullify acts of Congress, for no such substantive power exists. It is simply a necessary concomitant of the power to hear and dispose of a case or controversy properly before the Court, to the determination of which must be brought the test and measure of the law.

12. Dred Scott v. Sandford, 60 U.S. (19 How.) 393 (1857).
13. Schechter Poultry Corp. v. United States, 55 Sup. Ct. 837, 849 (1935).
14. Citing Brown v. Houston, 114 U.S. 622, 632, 633, 5 Sup. Ct. 1091, 1096 (1885); Public Utilities Comm. v. Landon, 249 U.S. 236, 245, 39 Sup. Ct. 268, 269 (1919); Ind. Assn. v. United States, 268 U.S. 64, 78, 79, 45 Sup. Ct. 403, 406, 407 (1925); Atl. Coast Line R. Co. v. Standard Oil Co., 275 U.S. 257, 267, 48 Sup. Ct. 107, 110 (1927).

local disposition and use. So far as the poultry herein questioned is concerned, the flow in interstate commerce had ceased. The poultry had come to a permanent rest within the state. It was not held, used, or sold by defendants in relation to any further transactions in interstate commerce and was not destined for transportation to other states. Hence, decisions which deal with a stream of interstate commerce— where goods come to rest within a state temporarily and are later to go forward in interstate commerce—and with the regulations of transactions involved in that practical continuity of movement, are not applicable here.

For a reason which will soon appear, this feature of the decision is of minor importance. Nevertheless, one or two comments upon it are in point for the light they shed upon the major problem before the Court under the commerce clause. The earliest case cited by the chief justice in support of his assertion that the Schechters' business did not comprise "transactions in interstate commerce" is Brown v. Houston,[15] decided in 1885. Here the Court held that a barge-load of coal from Pennsylvania which had arrived at New Orleans and was being held in the river before that town "for sale or disposal" had become a part of the mass of property in Louisiana, and as such was subject, *"in the absence of Congressional action,"* to the local taxing power.[16] The chief justice overlooks the qualifying phrase underscored above and the oversight is material, for the phrase evidently implies that Congress would have been free to treat the coal as still in interstate commerce or at least as so closely connected therewith as to be within its regulatory power. And the cases are numerous in which the protection of the commerce clause has been held to continue until goods brought from without a state reached a purchaser who intended to consume them.[17] And where the protection of the clause reaches, the power which it confers must reach also, the former being indeed only a deduction from the latter.

But the N.I.R.A. was not confined to transactions *"in"* interstate commerce; it also purported to govern transactions *"affecting"* such commerce; and it is from this feature of the Act that the major constitutional issue of the case touching Congress's powers arose. As the chief justice's opinion concedes,[18] "The power of Congress extends, not only to the regulation of transactions which are part of interstate commerce, but to the protection of that commerce from injury. It matters not that the injury may be due to the conduct of those engaged in intrastate operations."[19]

He then proceeds to illustrate this proposition as follows:[20]

Thus, Congress may protect the safety of those employed in interstate transpor-

15. 114 U.S. 622, 5 Sup. Ct. 1091 (1885).
16. *Id.* at 633, 5 Sup. Ct. at 1096 (italics inserted). There are also expressions to the same effect, *id.* at 630, 631, 632, 634, 5 Sup. Ct. at 1095, 1096, 1097.
17. See especially the cases stemming from Robbins v. Shelby Taxing District, 120 U.S. 489, 7 Sup. Ct. 592 (1887); and Leisy v. Hardin, 135 U.S. 100, 10 Sup. Ct. 681 (1890).
18. Schechter Poultry Corp. v. United States, 55 Sup. Ct. 837, 849 (1935).
19. Citing So. Ry. Co. v. United States, 222 U.S. 20, 27, 32 Sup. Ct. 2, 4 (1911).
20. Schechter Poultry Corp. v. United States, 55 Sup. Ct. 837, 849 (1935).

tation, "no matter what may be the source of the dangers which threaten it." . . .[21] We said in . . . (Second Employers' Liability Cases) . . .[22] that it is the "effect upon interstate commerce," not "the source of the injury," which is "the criterion of congressional power." We have held that, in dealing with common carriers engaged in both interstate and intrastate commerce, the dominant authority of Congress necessarily embraces the right to control their intrastate operations in all matters having such a close and substantial relation to interstate traffic that the control is essential or appropriate to secure the freedom of that traffic from interference or unjust discrimination and to promote the efficiency of the interstate service. . . .[23] And combinations and conspiracies to restrain interstate commerce, or to monopolize any part of it, are none the less within the reach of the Anti-Trust Act . . . —because the conspirators seek to attain their end by means of intrastate activities.

But, the chief justice continues:[24]

In determining how far the federal government may go in controlling intrastate transactions upon the ground that they "affect" interstate commerce, *there is a necessary and well-established distinction between direct and indirect effects. The precise line can be drawn only as individual cases arise, but the distinction is clear in principle.*

Applying, then, this distinction to the instant case, he says:

This is not a prosecution for a conspiracy to restrain or monopolize interstate commerce in violation of the Anti-Trust Act. Defendants have been convicted, not upon direct charges of injury to interstate commerce or of interference with persons engaged in that commerce, but of violations of certain provisions of the Live Poultry Code and of conspiracy to commit these violations. Interstate commerce is brought in only upon the charge that violations of these provisions— as to hours and wages of employees and local sales—*"affected"* interstate commerce.[25]

The initial question with respect to this holding is whether it should be treated as growing out of the peculiar facts of the Schechter Case, and hence as limited to those facts, or whether it was meant by the Court to have a much wider application—whether, indeed, the Court intended to lay down doctrine which would be equally applicable to congressional regulation of wages and hours in the great manufacturing and extractive industries, such as steel, oil and coal, and so on. To this interesting question no certain answer can be returned until the Court has spoken further, and then, perhaps, no answer will be necessary. Nevertheless, I am reluctantly inclined to agree with Mr. Jouett Shouse's new Super-Supreme Court that the wider interpretation of the holding

---

21. S. Ry Co. v. United States, 222 U.S. 20, 27, 32 Sup. Ct. 2, 4 (1911).

22. Citing Mondou v. N.Y., N.H. & H. R. Co., 223 U.S. 1, 51, 32 Sup. Ct. 169, 175 (1911).

23. Citing Houston, E. & W.T. R. Co. v. United States (The Shreveport Case), 234 U.S. 342, 351, 352, 34 Sup. Ct. 833, 836 (1914); Railroad Comm. of Wisconsin v. Chicago B. & O. R. Co., 257 U.S. 563, 588, 42 Sup. Ct. 232, 237 (1922).

24. Schechter Poultry Corp. v. United States, 55 Sup. Ct. 837, 850 (1935) (italics inserted).

25. *Id.* at 850.

is probably the correct one—at any rate, the one intended by a majority of the *present* Court.

Certain circumstances in connection with the case do, no doubt, support the narrower theory of its meaning, but only equivocally when they are scrutinized. Thus if the chief justice's dismissal of cases involving the "stream of commerce" concepts had occurred in connection with his distinction between "direct" and "indirect" effects upon interstate commerce, it would have furnished basis for the contention that, had defendants' business been merged with such a stream, the effects here classified as "indirect" might have been classified as "direct." But in fact the dismissal occurs in support of the proposition that defendants were not engaged in interstate commerce, and so no such conclusion can be drawn. Again the chief justice says that "the precise line can be drawn" between "direct" and "indirect" effects "only as the individual cases arise." What is thus suggested is that the Court looks forward to converting the distinction in question into a sort of due process clause protective of state power. But even so, the question remains as to what value the Court expects to assign its holding in the Schechter Case in the plotting of this line. Finally, while appearing to accept the chief justice's opinion, Justices Cardozo and Stone nevertheless dissociate themselves from it by filing a supplementary opinion.

The principal reason for favoring the more sweeping construction of the decision is furnished by the chief justice's emphasis upon the supposed necessity of maintaining the states in their powers over their "local concerns," especially when this is taken in connection with the fact that *the Court has always characterized production as "local."* Thus he says:

> If the commerce clause were construed to reach all enterprises and transactions which would be said to have an indirect effect upon interstate commerce, the federal authority would embrace practically all the activities of the people, and the authority of the state over its domestic concerns would exist only by sufferance of the federal government. Indeed, on such a theory, even the development of the state's commercial facilities would be subject to federal control.[26]

And again:

> The distinction between direct and indirect effects of intrastate transactions upon interstate commerce must be recognized as a fundamental one, essential to the maintenance of our constitutional system.
>
> Otherwise, as we have said, there would be virtually no limit to the federal power, and for all practical purposes we should have a completely centralized government.

Significant too are his summary of the government's defense of the N.I.R.A. and his answer to this. He reduces the former to two main contentions:[27]

26. *Id.*
27. *Id.* at 851.

Thus, the government argues that hours and wages affect prices; that slaughter-house men sell at a small margin above operating costs; that labor represents 50 to 60 per cent of these costs; that a slaughterhouse operator paying lower wages or reducing his cost by exacting long hours of work translates his saving into lower prices; that this results in demands for a cheaper grade of goods; and that the cutting of prices brings about a demoralization of the price structure. . . . The government also makes the point that efforts to enact state legislation establishing high labor standards have been impeded by the belief that, unless similar action is taken generally, commerce will be diverted from the states adopting such standards, and that this fear of diversion has led to demands for federal legislation on the subject of wages and hours.

To the former contention he returns the following answer:[28]

Similar conditions may be adduced in relation to other businesses. The argument of the government proves too much. If the federal government may determine the wages and hours of employees in the internal commerce of a state, because of . . . their indirect effect upon interstate commerce, it would seem that a similar control might be exerted over other elements of cost, also affecting prices, such as the number of employees, rents, advertising, methods of doing business, etc. All the processes of production and distribution that enter into cost could likewise be controlled. If the cost of doing an intrastate business is in itself the permitted object of federal control, the extent of the regulation or cost would be a question of discretion and not of power.

and his answer to the second argument is to like effect:[29]

The apparent implication is that the federal authority under the commerce clause should be deemed to extend to the establishment of rules to govern wages and hours in intrastate trade and industry generally throughout the country, thus overriding the authority of the states to deal with domestic problems arising from labor conditions in their internal commerce.

It is not the province of the Court to consider the economic advantages or disadvantages of such a centralized system. It is sufficient to say that the Federal Constitution does not provide for it. Our growth and development have called for wide use of the commerce power of the federal government in its control over the expanded activities of interstate commerce and in protecting that commerce from burdens, interferences, and conspiracies to restrain and monopolize it. But the authority of the federal government may not be pushed to such an extreme as to destroy the distinction, which the commerce clause itself establishes, between commerce "among the several states" and the internal concerns of the state. The same answer must be made to the contention that is based upon the serious economic situation which led to the passage of the Recovery Act—the fall in prices, the decline in wages and employment, and the curtailment of the market for commodities.

Giving this language its proper weight, it appears to boil down to the proposition that *any effect which may reach "commerce among the several States" from conditions surrounding production must be deemed "indirect"* and per se *beyond the corrective power of the national government under the*

28. *Id.*
29. *Id.*

commerce clause. And by the same token, it seems allowable to generalize the Court's further holding that defendants' practices in connection with their local sales had only an "indirect" effect upon interstate commerce and so were beyond national power.

Once again, however, it is necessary to note that in lending assent to language of such indefinite scope the Court ignored the requirements of the litigation before it. The Schechters were not engaged in "industry generally throughout the country"; they were engaged in production or manufacture only to the extent of dressing poultry for the local market. Their primary business was that of supplying retailers with poultry, that is, making what the Court holds to be "local sales." So, had the case been decided simply on the basis of the commerce clause, it would not have been necessary for the Court to use the sweeping expressions just quoted.

Nor is it without interest to point out that at this same sitting the Court, in deciding the Rathbun Case,[30] was compelled to disavow much of its ambitious opinion in the Myers Case of 1926,[31] regarding the president's removal power. This it did by quoting Chief Justice Marshall's statement in Cohens v. Virginia, "that general expressions, in every opinion, are to be taken in connection with the case in which those expressions are used."[32] It is not difficult to image the chief justice's opinion in the Poultry Case being subjected at some future time to the same sort of deflation.

II

What is to be said of this decision from the point of view of constitutional law? More definitely, what is to be said as to the soundness of the "principle" by which the chief justice's opinion for the Court endeavors to articulate it to the established structure of constitutional law as shown in previous cases? This "principle" is, as we have seen, that "there is a necessary and well-established distinction between direct and indirect effects" on interstate commerce arising from intrastate activities, and that Congress's power extends *only* to the former. First, is this "principle," as here applied, soundly grounded in the cases? Secondly, is there available from the cases an alternative principle which affords a more workable test of national power in relation to the actual organization of business today? To these questions we now address ourselves.

What we confront in the distinction between "direct" and "indirect" effects is, very evidently, a *formula,* a *verbal device,* such as constitutional law— indeed, all judge-made law—abounds in. Whence came this formula, what had been its judicial history prior to the Schechter Case? The former of these queries may be answered with complete assurance: the formula in question

---

30. Rathbun v. United States, 55 Sup. Ct. 869 (1935).
31. Myers v. United States, 272 U.S. 52, 47 Sup. Ct. 21 (1926).
32. 19 U.S. (6 Wheat.) 264, 399 (1821).

was *first* enunciated by the Court in a different, though adjoining field of constitutional law, than that in which we now face it, and as a test not of *national* but *state* legislative power in relation to the commerce clause. Its purpose was to supply a category for those acts which a state *might not* constitutionally pass, even in the absence of Congressional legislation, because of their "direct" effect upon "commerce among the several States," and likewise a category for those acts which, in the similar absence of Congressional legislation, a state *might* constitutionally pass although such acts affected "commerce among the several states" "incidentally" or "indirectly."

Nor do we have to search far for the law and doctrine bearing on this phase of our inquiry, for by a fortunate coincidence this was brought together by the chief justice (then Justice Hughes) more than twenty years ago in his famous opinion in the Minnesota Rate Cases.[33] From discussing a long line of cases illustrative of the doctrine that "the states cannot under any guise impose direct burdens upon interstate commerce," Justice Hughes next proceeds to point out that "there necessarily remains to the states, until Congress acts, a wide range for the permissible exercise of power appropriate to their territorial jurisdiction although interstate commerce may be affected. . . ." The opinion then continues:[34]

> . . . it is competent for a state to govern its internal commerce, to provide local improvements, to create and regulate local facilities, to adopt protective measures of a reasonable character in the interest of the health, safety, morals, and welfare of its people, although interstate commerce may incidentally or indirectly be involved. Our system of government is a practical adjustment by which the national authority as conferred by the Constitution is maintained in its full scope without unnecessary loss of local efficiency. Where the subject is peculiarly one of local concern, and from its nature belongs to the class with which the state appropriately deals in making reasonable provision for local needs, it cannot be regarded as left to the unrestrained will of individuals because Congress has not acted, although it may have such a relation to interstate commerce as to be within the reach of the federal power. In such case, Congress must be the judge of the necessity of federal action. Its paramount authority always enables it to intervene at its discretion for the complete and effective government of that which has been committed to its care, and, for this purpose and to this extent, in response to a conviction of national need, to displace local laws by substituting laws of its own. The successful working of our constitutional system has thus been made possible.

This passage is extracted from a discussion which extends through several pages and in which are cited many cases from the period of Marshall down. What is shown, in brief, is that the distinction between "direct" and "indirect" effects upon interstate commerce was originally laid down by the Court in order to *liberate* the states from a too rigorous application of its other doctrine that Congress's power over interstate commerce is "exclusive," and not in order to *restrict* Congress's powers in any way whatsoever. Quite to the

33. Simpson v. Shepard, 230 U.S. 352, 33 Sup. Ct. 729 (1913).
34. *Id*. at 402, 33 Sup. Ct. at 741.

contrary in fact. For it is the very purpose of the term "indirect" in these cases to designate effects upon interstate commerce from which, when they proceed from state legislation, relief must be found, if at all, not in the Constitution but in action by Congress. Two years later, in fact, in the Shreveport Case,[35] the Court, speaking again by Justice Hughes, found that Congress had, by the Act of 1887, provided a mode of relief from local rates which "discriminated" against interstate commerce, although such rates had been set in the first instance in exercise by a state of its admitted power to regulate its purely internal commerce.

And if "indirect" state interferences with interstate commerce may be disallowed by Congress, why are not "indirect" interferences by private persons subject to the same hazard? In the words of the Court in the Debs Case:[36] "If a state, with its recognized powers of sovereignty, is impotent to obstruct interstate commerce, can it be that any mere voluntary association of individuals within the limits of that state has a power which the state itself does not possess?" The question is evidently intended to answer itself.[37]

The distinction between "direct" and "indirect" effects upon interstate commerce was first erected into a limitation upon the national commercial power in the notorious Sugar Trust Case of 1895.[38] There a Court, dominated by the current laissez-fairism, which manifested its influence in other spheres of constitutional interpretation at the time, held that the Sherman Anti-Trust Act could not constitutionally reach a manufacturing concern which, it was admitted, controlled 98 percent of the sugar refined in the United States. To the government's argument that production necessarily contemplated sale of the product, and in this instance its sale throughout the Union, the Court opposed the following ideology: (1) Congress's power over "commerce" in the primary sense of traffic was virtually stricken out of the Constitution, on the ground that commerce in this sense "served manufacture to fulfill its function." (2) The "commerce among the several states" which Congress is given power to regulate was confined to transportation among the states, and this power was held not to operate until goods actually started from one state to another (3) In relation to "commerce among the several states" *as thus conceived,* the effect of a manufacturing monopoly was held to be "indirect" and beyond congressional power.

> "Contracts," said Chief Justice Fuller for the Court, combinations, or conspiracies to control domestic enterprise in manufacture, agriculture, mining, production in all its forms, or to raise or lower prices or wages, might unquestionably tend to restrain external as well as domestic trade, *but the restraint would be an indirect result, however inevitable, and whatever its extent,* and such result would

35. Houston, E. & W. T. R. Co. v. United States, 234 U.S. 342, 34 Sup. Ct. 833 (1914).
36. In re Debs, 158 U.S. 564, 581, 15 Sup. Ct. 900, 905 (1895).
37. The passage is quoted with approval in Addyston Pipe and Steel Co. v. United States, 175 U.S. 211, 230, 20 Sup. Ct. 96, 103 (1899).
38. United States v. Knight Co., 156 U.S. 1, 15 Sup. Ct. 249 (1895).

not necessarily determine the object of the contract, combination, or conspiracy. . . . Slight reflection will show that, if the national power extends to all contracts and combinations in manufacture, agriculture, mining, and other productive industries, whose ultimate result may affect external commerce, comparatively little of business operations and affairs would be left for state control.[39]

"Indirect result, *however inevitable and whatever its extent*"—thus the Court describes private interferences with "commerce among the several States" which Congress is helpless to prevent or control because otherwise the states would be in *theory* left with little control over that which *in fact* they cannot effectively control at all! But in what sense can a result *"however inevitable and whatever its extent"* be termed *"indirect"?* The answer is to be found, as above indicated, in the Court's mental image of the interstate commerce process as a *physical movement merely* of goods from one state to another. Upon "commerce" thus narrowly conceived, the impact of conditions attending manufacture and production may very well be termed "indirect," since it would be *first* felt by "commerce" in the primary sense of *buying and selling*, a function by hypothesis of manufacture and production. And it is on the same quaint model that the Court's decision in the Poultry Case was built in the year of grace 1935! The model itself hails in the first instance from the famous Log Case[40] of fifty years ago. What our nostalgic guardians of the Constitution seem really to have reverted to is the age of logs, skids and oxen!

But the thing which perhaps more than anything else makes this sudden revival of the Sugar Trust Case astonishing, is that its authority had been long since largely discredited as to the matter concerning which it was originally pronounced, namely the interpretation and application of the Sherman Act. Precisely a decade later, almost to the day, the Court handed down its decision in Swift & Co. v. United States,[41] which sets up an entirely new point of departure in this field of the Court's jurisprudence. In the language of Chief Justice Taft, speaking for the Court in 1923:[42]

> That case [the Swift Case] was a milestone in the interpretation of the commerce clause of the Constitution. It recognized the great changes and development in the business of this vast country and drew again the dividing line between interstate and intrastate commerce where the Constitution intended it to be. It refused to permit local incidents of great interstate movement, which taken alone were intrastate, to characterize the movement as such. The Swift Case merely fitted the commerce clause to the real and practical essence of modern business growth.

This was said in Chicago Board of Trade v. Olsen, in which the Court sustained the power of Congress to regulate sales of grain for future delivery.

39. *Id.* at 16, 15 Sup. Ct. at 255 (italics inserted).
40. Coe v. Errol, 116 U.S. 517, 6 Sup. Ct. 475 (1886).
41. 196 U.S. 375, 25 Sup. Ct. 276 (1905).
42. Board of Trade of Chicago v. Olsen, 262 U.S. 1, 35, 43 Sup. Ct. 470, 476 (1923).

The basis of the decision is succinctly stated in the headnotes of the case as follows:[43]

> Congress having reasonably found that sales of grain for future delivery (most of which transactions do not result in actual delivery but are settled by off-setting with like contracts), are susceptible to speculation, manipulation and control, affecting cash prices and consignments of grain in such wise as to cause a direct burden on and interference with interstate commerce therein, rendering regulation imperative for the protection of such commerce and the national public interest therein,—had power to provide in the Grain Futures Act . . . for placing grain boards of trade under federal supervision and regulation . . . as a condition to dealing by their members in contracts for *future delivery.*

Of foremost importance here for our present discussion, naturally, is the conception of "commerce" which is involved. This is clearly envisaged as comprising primarily *dealing, trading, business.* Such dealing is accompanied to be sure, in its interstate phases, by actual movements of commodities, which, as it were, authenticate its essentially interstate character. Physical obstruction, however, to a physical movement of goods is far in the background of the Court's mind, if indeed it is thought of. The act before it is sustained as being designed to protect a *business* against the "obstruction" which results from the effect of certain practices in that business upon the *price* of the commodity dealt in.

Speaking to this last point, Chief Justice Taft says:[44]

> The question of price dominates trade between the States. Sales of an article which affect the country-wide price of the article directly affect the country-wide commerce in it. By reason and authority, therefore, in determining the validity of this act, we are prevented from questioning the conclusion of Congress that manipulation of the market for futures on the Chicago Board of Trade may, and from time to time does, directly burden and obstruct commerce between the states in grain, that it recurs and is a constantly possible danger.

But it may be objected that even in the Olsen Case the Court uses the term "direct" to characterize the effects upon interstate commerce which the act there sustained reaches. This is true: but the answer is two-fold. In the first place, the *commerce* with reference to which such effects are termed "direct" is commerce in the sense of *trade, traffic, business;* whereas the commerce which by the Sugar Trust Case Congress was entitled to protect from "direct" effects was *transportation* only. In the second place—and what is more important—the Court's designation of the effects reached by the Grain Futures Act as "direct" *was based primarily on a finding of Congress itself* that such

43. *Id.* at 2 (headnote) (italics inserted).
44. *Id.* at 40, 43 Sup. Ct. at 478. See also some illuminating comment on the same point in the admirable address of Assistant Attorney General (then Assistant Secretary of Commerce) John Dickinson, at the annual banquet, June 1, 1935, of the George Washington Law Association, entitled "The Nation and the States." Department of Commerce Release, June 1, 1935.

was their nature. To quote again from Chief Justice Taft's opinion, which in turn quotes from his earlier opinion in Stafford v. Wallace:[45]

"Whatever amounts to a more or less constant practice, and threatens to obstruct or unduly to burden the freedom of interstate commerce is within the regulatory power of Congress under the commerce clause, and it is primarily for Congress to consider and decide the fact of the danger and meet it. *This court will certainly not substitute its judgment for that of Congress in such a matter unless the relation of the subject to interstate commerce and its effect upon it are clearly non-existent.*"[46]

It is apparent that the distinction between "direct" and "indirect" effects upon interstate commerce is employed in the Sugar Trust and Poultry Cases, on the one hand, and in Chicago Board of Trade v. Olsen, on the other hand, in two very different senses. In the former cases the distinction is treated as embodying an absolute principle dividing the field of the national commercial power from a field of inviolable state sovereignty, or something closely akin to such a principle. In the Olsen Case, as in Stafford v. Wallace, the distinction is treated as *one of fact,* and hence as one to be applied *in the light of* fact. The question is, does a particular business practice, carried on locally and so falling indubitably within the normal jurisdiction of the state, nevertheless affect interstate commerce "*unduly.*" If so, then Congress may regulate it to the extent of eliminating this effect; and the question is primarily one for Congress to determine; nor will the Court disturb Congress's determinations of this question unless they are clearly contrary to fact. This, it is submitted, is the doctrine of the Olsen Case so far as the distinction between "direct" and "indirect" effects is concerned.

So I repeat, the Court's application here of the distinction between "direct" and "indirect" effects upon interstate commerce represents an attempt to revive a precedent forty years old, and one which subsequent adjudication had almost completely discredited. But this miraculous evocation of the one-time dead is not made by name. The only cases which the chief justice *cites* in direct support of his pivotal principle are cases in which the Sherman Act was invoked against labor combinations. As to them the opinion reads:[47]

The distinction between direct and indirect effects has been clearly recognized in the application of the Anti-Trust Act. Where a combination or conspiracy is formed, with the intent to restrain interstate commerce or to monopolize any part of it, the violation of the statute is clear.... But, where that intent is absent, and the objectives are limited to intrastate activities, the fact that there may be an indirect effect upon interstate commerce does not subject the parties to the federal

45. 258 U.S. 495, 521, 42 Sup. Ct. 397, 403 (1922).
46. Board of Trade of Chicago v. Olsen, 262 U.S. 1, 37, 43 Sup. Ct. 470, 477 (1923) (italics inserted).
47. Schechter Poultry Corp. v. United States, 55 Sup. Ct. 837, 850 (1935).

statue, notwithstanding its broad provisions. This principle has frequently been applied in litigation growing out of labor disputes.[48]

But may these cases be legitimately appealed to in the present instance? In the chief justice's own words, they "related to the application of the federal statue and not to its constitutional validity." Are the two questions so closely identical as he seems to assume? On first consideration certainly, there appears to be little warrant for making a requirement of proof of a defendant's *intention* to violate a statute the test and measure of the *power* of Congress to enact such a statute. To put the matter otherwise, a court might well hesitate to impute to a defendant the *intent* to "restrain" commerce in doing a certain act, without its following that Congress could not prohibit such act as a restraint upon commerce. *Nor is Congress's power to regulate commerce solely a power to prevent restraints upon it.* Congress may itself restrain commerce for the general good.

And it is at this point that Justice Cardozo's supplementary opinion becomes of interest. The following passage from it is the pertinent one:[49]

> There is a view of causation that would obliterate the distinction between what is national and what is local in the activities of commerce. Motion at the outer rim is communicated perceptibly, though minutely, to recording instruments at the centre. A society such as ours "is an elastic medium which transmits all tremors throughout its territory; the only question is of their size. . . ."[50]
> The law is not indifferent to considerations of degree. Activities local in their immediacy do not become interstate and national because of distant repercussions. What is near and what is distant may at times be uncertain. . . . There is no penumbra of uncertainty obscuring judgment here. To find immediacy or directness here is to find it almost everywhere. If centripetal forces are to be isolated to the exclusion of the forces that oppose and counteract them, there will be an end to our federal system.

Yet even this language represents, it seems to me, a considerable departure from the doctrine of the Olsen Case, though that case is cited in support of it. The conventional gesture of deference to the finding of fact which the enactment of a statute is presumed to imply is omitted, and this despite the emphasis of the government's argument in the Poultry Case upon factual data. And is it sufficient to say that a certain "*view* of causation . . . would obliterate the distinction between what is national and what is local in the activities of commerce" without further effort to meet the contention that this distinction no longer corresponds with the actual conduct of "the activities of commerce" in this country? In a word, the conceptualism, the determination to resist the

48. Citing United Mine Workers v. Coronado Coal Co., 259 U.S. 344, 410, 411, 42 Sup. Ct. 570, 583 (1922); United Leather Workers' Union v. Herkert, 265 U.S. 457, 464–67, 44 Sup. Ct. 623, 624–26 (1924); Ind. Assn. v. United States, 268 U.S. 64, 82, 45 Sup. Ct. 403, 407 (1925); Coronado Coal Co. v. United Mine Workers, 268 U.S. 295, 310, 45 Sup. Ct. 551, 556 (1925); Levering & Garrigues v. Morrin, 289 U.S. 103, 107, 53 Sup. Ct. 549, 550 (1933).

49. Schechter Poultry Corp. v. United States, 55 Sup. Ct. 837, 853 (1935).

50. Quoted from Judge Learned Hand's opinion in the court below.

inrush of fact with the besom of formula, which pervades the chief justice's opinion for the Court, is not altogether absent from Justice Cardozo's opinion, though the difference may be sufficient to admit in time an opening wedge against this decision.

We now turn to the more fundamental aspect of the chief justice's opinion.

III

The distinction between "direct" and "indirect" effects upon interstate commerce was characterized on an earlier page of this article as a "*device*", and further scrutiny of the chief justice's opinion justifies the appellation. The distinction is, it is true, proffered as one which is well-grounded in previous cases, and hence as part and parcel of the accepted body of American constitutional law whereby the Court is obligated when it does not choose to cast aside the shackles of *stare decisis*. This contention we have just concluded examining. But underlying this argument for the distinction in question is another, namely, that its maintenance as a limitation upon Congress's powers over interstate commerce is essential unless the states are to lose control over their "internal concerns." In other words, the distinction, valid in itself, is further validated as being the logical outgrowth and indispensable instrument of an underlying purpose of the Constitution.

To quote again a passage from the opinion which was given earlier:[51] "If the commerce clause were construed to reach all enterprises and transactions which could be said to have an indirect effect upon interstate commerce, the federal authority would embrace practically all the activities of the people, and the authority of the state over its domestic concerns would exist only by sufferance of the federal government." And again: ". . . the authority of the federal government may not be pushed to such an extreme as to destroy the distinction, which the commerce clause itself establishes, between commerce 'among the several states' and the internal concerns of the state."

What these words of the chief justice set forth is much less a problem of constitutional *law* than of constitutional *theory.* It is a problem, that is to say, which grows out of the idea that the Constitution overlays certain fundamental values and certain antecedent institutions, the maintenance of which must always afford a prior claim upon the consciences of its official expositors and always condition their manipulation of its terms. The chief justice does, to be sure, cite the commerce clause itself as recognizing in "the internal concerns of the state" a limit to the power of Congress over "commerce among the several states," but the claim would be difficult to sustain merely on the basis of the commerce clause alone. The chief justice's case for his contention has to be sought farther afield.

Writing in *Federalist* 39, Madison contended that when considered "in

51. Schechter Poultry Corp. v. United States, 55 Sup. Ct. 837, 850, 851 (1935).

relation to the extent of its powers," the government proposed by the Constitution could not "be deemed a *national* one; since its jurisdiction extends to certain enumerated objects only, and leaves to the several states a *residuary and inviolable sovereignty* over all other objects."[52] He then continued:

> It is true that in controversies relating to the boundary between the two jurisdictions, the tribunal which is ultimately to decide, is to be established under the general government. But this does not change the principle of the case. The decision is to be impartially made, according to the rules of the Constitution; and all the usual and most effectual precautions are taken to secure this impartiality. Some such tribunal is clearly essential to prevent an appeal to the sword and a dissolution of the compact; and that it ought to be established under the general rather than under the local governments, . . . is a position not likely to be combatted.[53]

Here then is the original fountain-head of the doctrine of the Schechter Case. Two ideas appear quite clearly: (1) That the states retain under the Constitution an "inviolable sovereignty"; (2) that it is the duty of the Supreme Court to protect this sovereignty against invasion by the national government. And from these ideas ensues a *third*, that the Court must not construe any of the powers of the national government in such a way as to project them into the "inviolable sovereignty" of the states. In other words, *this "inviolable sovereignty" comprises of itself a limitation upon the powers of the national government.* A fourth idea is less clear, but seems, nonetheless, to be implied, to wit, that the "inviolable sovereignty" of the states is coextensive with their "residuary" powers—in other words, with those powers which the states still retain under the Constitution.

It is worthy of note that this doctrine of Madison's was formulated before the Tenth Amendment was yet a part of the Constitution. Does, then, the Tenth Amendment make the "reserved powers of the states" a limitation on national power? The words of the Amendment are as follows: "The powers not delegated by this Constitution to the United States, nor prohibited by it to the states, are reserved to the states respectively, or to the people." It is difficult to see how these words can be construed into recognition of an "inviolable sovereignty" in the states. They clearly recognize the character of the national government as one of delegated powers; but they imply logically that definition of the reserved powers of the states must wait upon the prior definition of national power. What is more, the Tenth Amendment is only *one* provision of the Constitution bearing on the relation of national to state power.

When the first twelve amendments were offered to the Constitution, of which ten were eventually ratified, it was generally understood to be their purpose to clarify rather than to alter the Constitution, then so recently adopted. A part of this Constitution however was the "supremacy" clause, which reads as follows: "This Constitution and the laws of the United States which are made

52. *The Federalist* 238 (Lodge ed. 1888) (latter italics inserted).
53. *Id.*

in pursuance thereof, and all treaties made or which shall be made, under the authority of the United States, shall be the supreme law of the land; and the judges in every state shall be bound thereby, anything in the Constitution or laws of any state to the contrary notwithstanding.'' Here again, as in the Tenth Amendment, it is recognized that not all the powers of government have been delegated to the national government, but that certain powers are still retained by the states. It is also foreseen—no inordinate act of prevision surely—that the states would at times use their conceded powers in a way to conflict with the exercise by the national government of its conceded powers, and the unqualified provision is made that in all such cases the laws of the national government shall prevail.[54]

What is more, for nearly a half century following its adoption the Court's construction of the Constitution hewed strictly to the clear line demarked by this language, and afforded no inkling of a suggestion that the Tenth Amendment derogated in any way from its literal force and effect. For present purposes it is sufficient to consider in this connection Marshall's opinion in Gibbons v. Ogden,[55] where the commerce clause was construed by the Court for the first time.

Here a monopoly which the state of New York had conferred upon certain persons to navigate steam-boats upon the waters of that state was held to be void because conflicting with an act of Congress which conferred the right to engage in the coasting-trade upon vessels licensed under the act. "Commerce" was broadly defined to comprise all "commercial intercourse," and hence navigation as well as traffic, while "commerce among the several states" was described as that commerce which "concerns more states than one." And the power of Congress to "regulate" such commerce was the power to *govern* it. This power penetrated state lines at will, and was vested in Congress "as absolutely as it would be in a single government." The only matters it did not reach were those "which are completely within a particular state, which do not affect other states, and with which it is not necessary to interfere for the purpose of executing some of the general powers of the government." And the sole restraint upon its exercise was, as in the case of declaring war, the responsibility of Congress to their constituents.[56]

At the same time, Marshall also described the reserved powers of the states in sweeping language. Referring to inspection laws, he said:[57]

54. Note Mr. Justice Holmes' language in Missouri v. Holland, 252 U.S. 416, 432, 40 Sup. Ct. 382, 383 (1920): ''. . . as we have said, the question raised is the general one whether the treaty and statute are void as an interference with the rights reserved to the states. To answer this question it is not enough to refer to the Tenth Amendment . . . because by Article 2, section 2, . . . the power to make treaties made under the authority of the United States . . . {is} declared the supreme law of the land.''

55. 22 U.S. (9 Wheat.) 1 (1824).

56. *Id.* at 194–97; and see further Corwin, *Twilight of the Supreme Court* at 10–15, 188.

57. *Id.* at 203.

They form a portion of that immense mass of legislation, which embraces everything within the territory of a state, not surrendered to the general government; all which can be most advantageously exercised by the states themselves. Inspection laws, quarantine laws, health laws of every description, as well as laws for regulating the internal commerce of a state, and those which respect turnpike-roads, ferries, etc., are component parts of this mass.

The opinion then continues:[58]

No direct general power over these objects is granted to Congress; and consequently, they remain subject to state legislation. If the legislative power of the Union can reach them, it must be for national purposes; it must be where the power is expressly given for a special purpose, or is clearly incidental to some power which is expressly given. . . . In our complex system, presenting the rare and difficult scheme of one general government, whose action extends over the whole, but which possesses only certain enumerated powers; and of numerous state governments, which retain and exercise all powers not delegated to the Union, contests respecting power must arise. Were it even otherwise, the measures taken by the respective governments to execute their acknowledged powers, would often be of the same description, and might, sometimes, interfere.

Proceeding from this basis, Marshall freely conceded the argument made for Ogden that New York might have created the monopoly which Gibbons was contesting, by virtue of its power to regulate its "domestic trade and police." But that fact, he promptly added, did not suffice to save the monopoly, since it conflicted with a constitutional act of Congress regulatory of "commerce among the several states."[59] His language at this point bears so directly on the problem immediately before us that it should be quoted at length:[60]

In argument . . . it has been contended that if a law, passed by a state in the exercise of its acknowledged sovereignty, comes into conflict with a law passed by Congress in pursuance of the constitution, they affect the subject, and each other, like equal opposing powers. But [he answers] the framers of the constitution foresaw this state of things, and provided for it, by declaring the supremacy not only of itself, but of the laws made in pursuance of it. The nullity of any act, inconsistent with the Constitution is produced by the declaration that the Constitution is the supreme law. The appropriate application of that part of the clause which confers the same supremacy on laws and treaties, is to such acts of the state legislatures as do not transcend their powers, but, though enacted in the execution of acknowledged state powers, interfere with, or are contrary to the laws of Congress made in pursuance of the Constitution, or some treaty made under the authority of the United States. In every such case, the act of Congress, or the treaty, is [the] supreme [law]; and the law of the state, though enacted in the exercise of powers not controverted, must yield to it.

It is evident, therefore, that so far as the decision in the Schechter Case turns upon the idea that "the internal concerns of the state" comprise matters which Congress may not reach by legislation otherwise within its power to enact, it

58. *Id.*
59. *Id.* at 209–10.
60. *Id.* at 210.

receives no support from either the literal reading of the supremacy clause, nor yet from Chief Justice Marshall's application of that clause. Not less evident is it that such an idea, pursued to its logical consequences, must, in view of the indefinite scope of "the internal concerns of the state", have stifled national power in its very cradle. The fact is that the idea in question received from the Court *only the most intermittent recognition and enforcement.*

Madison's doctrine became the doctrine of the Court two years following Marshall's death in the case of City of New York v. Miln.[61] The question at issue was the validity of a New York statue laying certain requirements upon masters of vessels arriving in the port of New York with passengers aboard, The Court found that there was no collision between this act and the relevant act of Congress. It then proceeded, however:[62]

> But we do not place our opinion on this ground. We choose rather to plant ourselves on what we consider impregnable positions. They are these: That a state has the same undeniable and unlimited jurisdiction over all persons and things, within its territorial limits, as any foreign nation; where that jurisdiction is not surrendered or restrained by the Constitution of the United States. That, by virtue of this, it is not only the right, but the bounden and solemn duty of a state, to advance the safety, happiness and prosperity of its people, and to provide for its general welfare, by any and every act of legislation, which it may deem to be conducive to these ends; where the power over the particular subject, or the manner of its exercise is not surrendered or restrained, in the manner just stated. That all those powers which relate to merely municipal legislation, or what may, perhaps, more properly be called *internal police,* are not thus surrendered or restrained; and that, consequently, in relation to these, the authority of a state is complete, unqualified, and exclusive.

Justice Story presented a dissenting opinion. "I admit," said he, "in the most unhesitating manner, that the states have a right to pass health laws and quarantine laws, and other police laws, not contravening the laws of Congress rightfully passed under their constitutional authority. . . . It was said by this Court in the case of Brown v. The State of Maryland . . . that even the acknowledged power of taxation by a state, cannot be so exercised as to interfere with any regulation of commerce by Congress." And he later added this interesting bit of evidence:

> In this opinion I have the consolation to know that I had the entire concurrence, . . . of that great constitutional jurist, the late Mr. Chief Justice Marshall. Having heard the former arguments, his deliberate opinion was, that the act of New York was unconstitutional; and that the present case fell directly within the principles established in the case of Gibbons v. Ogden, . . . and Brown v. The State of Maryland.[63]

The Court's opinion in the Miln Case, it seems clear, adopts the theory that the power of the state over its *purely internal affairs* lies outside the operation

---

61. 36 U.S. (11 Pet.) 102 (1837).
62. *Id.* at 130 (italics inserted).
63. *Id.* at 156, 161.

of the principle of national supremacy and hence comprises an independent limitation upon national power. Later *dicta* of individual justices from this time on till after the Civil War assert the same principle, or close approximations thereto. The underlying thought is that voiced as late as 1898 by Judge Cooley in his *Principles of Constitutional Law*, in the following words: "In strictness there can be no such thing as a conflict between state and nation. The laws of both operate within the same territory, but if in any particular case their provisions are in conflict, one or the other is void." And to the same effect is the following passage from Professor McLaughlin's *Constitutional History of the United States*, which was published only a few months prior to the decision in the Schechter Case: "Neither government was to be inferior to the other or in ordinary operation to come into contact with the other."[64] In other words, the supremacy clause is really nugatory except as asserting the supremacy of the Constitution itself; for when the powers of the two governments are properly construed in relation to each other they meet each other as equal, opposing powers—a view which was directly combatted by Marshall in Gibbons v. Ogden, as we saw above.

But to what extent has this doctrine actually influenced judicial definition of the national legislative power? One notable achievement must be conceded it at once—it lies at the basis of the doctrine of the constitutional exemption of "state instrumentalities" from national taxation. This was first established in Collector v. Day,[65] decided in 1870, as to the official income of a state judge. The following language from Justice Nelson's opinion for the Court is directly on the point in which we are here interested:

> The general government, and the states, although both exist within the same territorial limits, are separate and distinct sovereignties, acting separately and independently of each other, within their respective spheres. The former, in its appropriate sphere, is supreme; but the states within the limits of their powers not granted, or, in the language of the Tenth Amendment, "reserved", are as independent of the general government as that government within its sphere is independent of the states. . . .
>
> The supremacy of the general government, therefore, so much relied on in the argument of the counsel for the plaintiff in error, in respect to the question before us, cannot be maintained. The two governments are upon an equality. . . .
>
> We do not say the mere circumstance of the establishment of the judicial department, and the appointment of officers to administer the laws, being among the reserved powers of the state, disables the general government from levying the tax, as that depends upon the express power to lay and collect taxes but it shows that it is an original inherent power never parted with, and in respect to

---

64. McLaughlin, *Constitutional History of the United States* 194 (1935); cf. Marshall's words: "These states are constituent parts of the United States. They are members of one great empire—for some purposes sovereign, for some purposes subordinate" 19 U.S. (6 Wheat.) 264, 414 (1821).

65. 78 U.S. (11 Wall.) 113 (1871).

which the supremacy of that government does not exist, and is of no importance in determining the question.[66]

Other cases in which the Court has treated the "reserved" powers of the states as a limiting principle in the definition of national power have been few and unimportant *until recent years*. No one would today, I presume, challenge Chief Justice Marshall's assertion that "In war we are one people. In making peace we are one people."[67] Nor would anyone be apt, in view of Missouri v. Holland,[68] to place great reliance upon—to employ Justice Holmes' depreciatory language in that case—"some invisible radiation from the general terms of the Tenth Amendment."[69] Nor would anyone since the recent case of University of Illinois v. United States[70] be able to appeal with much confidence to the "reserved" powers of the states as against a national regulation of foreign commerce. Petitioner in that case, a state institution, relying upon Collector v. Day and supporting precedents, challenged the right of the national government to collect a customs duty upon some scientific apparatus imported from abroad. The Court, speaking by Chief Justice Hughes, unanimously denied the petition.

"It is," said the chief justice, "an essential attribute of the power that it is exclusive and plenary. As an exclusive power, its exercise may not be limited, qualified, or impeded to any extent by state action. . . . The principle invoked by the petitioner, of the immunity of state instrumentalities from federal taxation, has its inherent limitations. . . . In international relations and with respect to foreign intercourse, the people of the United States act through a single government with unified and adequate national power."[71]

It is in the field of the interstate commerce power that the most persistent effort has been made to set up, on one basis or another, state power as a limitation on national power. Let us review briefly some of the *verbal devices* or *formulas* which have been proposed to this end.

(1) Writing in 1829, Madison asserted that, although conferred in the same words as the power over foreign commerce, Congress's power over "commerce among the several states," "was intended as a negative and preventive provision against injustice among the states themselves, rather than a power to be used for the positive purposes of the general government, in which, alone, however, the remedial power could be lodged."[72] In other words, while "the

---

66. *Id.* at 124–27, *passim*. The exemption of state instrumentalities from non-discriminatory national taxation appears to be today in a rather precarious situation. See Burnet v. Coronado Oil & Gas Co., 285 U.S. 393, 52 Sup. Ct. 443 (1932) (a 5-to-4 decision).

67. Cohens v. Virginia, 19 U.S. (6 Wheat.) 264, 413 (1821).

68. 252 U.S. 416, 40 Sup. Ct. 382 (1920); cf. Prevost v. Greneaux, 60 U.S. (19 How.) 1 (1856); Bell v. Vicksburg, 64 U.S. (23 How.) 443 (1859).

69. *Id.* at 434, 40 Sup. Ct. at 383.

70. 289 U.S. 48, 53 Sup. Ct. 509 (1933).

71. *Id.* at 56–59, 53 Sup. Ct. at 509–10, *passim*.

72. Madison, *Letters and Other Writings* 14–15 (1903). Monroe expressed a similar view in 1822. 2 Richardson, *Messages and Papers of the Presidents* 161 (1896).

general government'' could prevent the states from regulating interstate commerce, it could not regulate that commerce itself—the very quintessence of laissez-fairism, certainly. Five years earlier Chief Justice Marshall had characterized Congress's power over the right to engage in interstate and foreign commerce as ''absolute,'' while Justice Johnson, in his concurring opinion had asserted it to be ''the power to regulate commerce which previously existed in the states,'' which was power ''to limit and restrain it at pleasure.''[73] The Madisonian doctrine naturally commended itself to the defenders of slavery, who feared a congressional ban upon the interstate slave trade; but when proffered the Court many years later by counsel who were attacking the Sherman Act, Justice Peckham, speaking for the Court, dismissed it with little ceremony. ''The reasons,'' said he, ''which may have caused the framers of the Constitution to repose the power to regulate interstate commerce . . . do not, however, affect or limit the power itself.''[74] Indeed, the history of congressional legislation since 1887 offers monumental proof that no doctrine *of such scope* has ever succeeded in establishing itself as a barrier to the national commercial power.

(2) A second suggested *device* for limiting the national power over interstate commerce is a modification of the above. It comprises the theory that, while by no means an entirely negative power, yet the power of Congress to regulate ''commerce among the several states'' is considerably less extensive than its power to regulate foreign commerce. Indeed the latter power is conceded to be ''plenary,'' being a phase of the national government's ''plenary'' authority in the field of foreign relations. Furthermore, it acts *externally* and so, it is contended, does not come into collision with the power of the states over their *internal* concerns. The interstate commerce power, on the other hand, always acts *vis-à-vis* the power of the states over their internal concerns, and hence must be curbed if this power is not to be overridden.

But the truth is that congressional regulation of foreign commerce *can* and frequently *does* interfere with the internal concerns of a state. Among such internal concerns, by the Child Labor, the Sugar Trust, and the Poultry Cases, are manufactures, the effect of the protective tariff upon which is notorious. And a further illustration is suggested by the Miln Case, discussed above. Here the power which the Court had most sharply in mind to safeguard against invasion by the national power over foreign commerce was the power of the state to protect itself against the introduction into its midst of undesirables from abroad, a protective function which ruling cases today attribute to the national government exclusively.[75] Moreover, it is only within recent years that the

    73. Gibbons v. Ogden, 22 U.S. (9 Wheat.) 1, 212, 227 (1824).
    74. Addyston Pipe & Steel Co. v. United States, 175 U.S. 211, 228, 20 Sup. Ct. 96, 102 (1899).
    75. See especially Henderson v. Mayor of New York, 92 U.S. 259 (1875).

Court ever voiced acceptance of the notion that Congress's power over foreign commerce is less extensive than its power over interstate commerce. Indeed, the idea has been repudiated in controlling opinions of the Court again and again, and may even today, perhaps, be set down as a whimsy of that arch-exponent of dual federalism, Chief Justice White.[76] It is true that in the recent case of University of Illinois v. United States, which was just referred to, we find Chief Justice Hughes asserting that "the principle of duality in our system of government does not touch the authority of Congress in the regulation of foreign commerce,"[77] which is perhaps meant to imply that it does touch Congress's power over interstate commerce. But inference is not decision and the point was not involved in the case.

(3) The idea was also early suggested that the power to *regulate* commerce presupposes the continuance of the thing to be regulated, and hence is not the power to *prohibit* it. It was on this ground in fact that the constitutionality of Jefferson's Embargo, which was a sweeping, though temporary, prohibition upon foreign commerce, was challenged. Again we may say that no doctrine *of such scope* has ever secured footing either in national legislative policy or in judicial decision. Even in the case of Hammer v. Dagenhart,[78] to which we shall give further attention in a moment, the Court admits that there are cases in which regulation may properly take the form of prohibition, while as Justice Holmes there points out in his dissenting opinion, any regulation whatsoever of commerce necessarily infers a power to prohibit it, it being the very nature of regulation to lay down terms on which the activity regulated will be permitted and for noncompliance with which it will not be permitted.[79]

(4) A highly important *device*—especially since the decision in Hammer v. Dagenhart in 1918—for converting state power into a restrictive principle on the national commercial power is the theory that this power is a subtraction which was made in 1789 from the total powers of government *for the sole purpose of promoting the commercial interests of the country*. From this it follows that while Congress may in "proper cases" prohibit commerce among the states, the said proper cases are confined to those in which the prohibition of a *branch* of such commerce will work to the benefit of such commerce when considered as a *whole*. And along with this theory goes the converse doctrine or *device*, (5) that all the other concerns of good government, the public health, safety, morals, social justice, and the general welfare (*except commercial*

76. See Thurlow v. Massachusetts, 46 U.S. (5 How.) 504, 578 (1847); Brown v. Houston, 114 U.S. 622, 630, 5 Sup. Ct. 1091 (1885); Bowman v. Chi. & N. R. Co., 125 U.S. 465, 482, 8 Sup. Ct. 689, 697 (1888); Crutcher v. Kentucky, 141 U.S. 47, 57, 11 Sup. Ct. 851, 854 (1891); Pitts. & So. Coal Co. v. Bates, 156 U.S. 577, 587, 15 Sup. Ct. 415, 418 (1895); cf. Buttfield v. Stranahan, 192 U.S. 470, 492, 24 Sup. Ct. 349, 353 (1904); Weber v. Freed, 239 U.S. 325, 36 Sup. Ct. 131 (1915).

77. 289 U.S. 48, 57, 53 Sup. Ct. 509 (1933).

78. 247 U.S. 251, 38 Sup. Ct. 529 (1918).

79. *Id.* at 277–78, 38 Sup. Ct. at 533.

welfare), are reserved to the states exclusively, constituting indeed the field of the so-called "police power."[80]

The difficulty in the way of squaring this two-fold formula with the Preamble of the Constitution is obvious at a glance. For while the Preamble is not, strictly speaking, a part of the Constitution, and so is not a grant of power; still it states, and in the language of the framers themselves, the objectives of the Constitution, and hence, presumably, the objectives of the powers created by it, in terms which are broadly descriptive of *all* the purposes of good government the world over. Nor did this theory meet with judicial acceptance when it was originally advanced, in 1808, against the Jeffersonian Embargo. Said Judge Davis, of the Massachusetts District Court, on that occasion, ". . . the power to regulate commerce is not to be confined to the adoption of measures, exclusively beneficial to commerce itself, or tending to its advancement; but, in our national system, as in all modern sovereignties, it is also to be considered as an instrument for other purposes of general policy and interest."[81] Citing then the clause of Article I, Section 9 of the Constitution, interdicting a ban on the African slave trade until 1808, the judge continued: those who framed the Constitution perceived that ". . . under the power of regulating commerce, Congress would be authorized to abridge it, in favor of the great principles of humanity and justice."[82]

Nearly a hundred years later the Supreme Court was proffered the same theory, in the famous Lottery Case of 1903;[83] but rejected it, sustaining the power of Congress to prohibit the transportation of lottery tickets from one state to another on broad grounds of national welfare, as well as of commercial benefit. Nor did the proponents of the theory make better headway with it in their attack ten years later on the "White Slave" Act of 1910. Said Justice McKenna, speaking for the Court:[84]

> Our dual form of government has its perplexities, state and nation having different spheres of jurisdiction, . . . but it must be kept in mind that we are one people; and the powers reserved to the states and those conferred on the nation are adapted to be exercised, whether independently or concurrently, to promote the general welfare, material and moral.

Nevertheless, five years later the Court held void an act forbidding the transportation of child-made goods from one state to another, as being *not* a regulation of commerce, but an interference with the powers reserved to the states.[85] And why was not this prohibition a regulation of commerce? The answer is given by Chief Justice Taft in his opinion in the second Child Labor

80. On this paragraph see Corwin, *Twilight of the Supreme Court* at 19–42, *passim;* Corwin, "Congress's Power to Prohibit Commerce," 18 *Corn. L. Q.* 477, 481–83 (1933).

81. United States v. The William, Fed. Cas. No. 16,700, at 621 (Mass. 1808).

82. *Id.*

83. Champion v. Ames, 188 U.S. 321, 23 Sup. Ct. 321 (1903).

84. Hoke v. United States, 227 U.S. 308, 322, 33 Sup. Ct. 281, 284 (1913).

85. Hammer v. Dagenhart, 247 U.S. 251, 38 Sup. Ct. 529 (1918).

Case in the following words: "... when Congress threatened to stop interstate commerce in ordinary and necessary commodities, *unobjectionable as subjects of transportation,* and to deny the same to the people of a state in order to coerce them into compliance with Congress's regulation of state concerns, the Court said that this was not in fact regulation of interstate commerce, but rather that of state concerns and was invalid."[86] In other words, goods produced by child labor not being harmful to interstate *transportation*—the primary significance of commerce as *tariff* is ignored—Congress had no legitimate concern with the matter; it is only the local police power which may deal with the child labor.

Two other suggestions for preventing invasion by the national commercial power of the accustomed field of state legislation may be disposed of more briefly: (6) Following the decision in Hammer v. Dagenhart the argument was offered the Court that even when Congress was otherwise entitled to prohibit transportation of an article of commerce, it might do so only in aid of the state police power; but the Court rejected the suggestion in the following words:[87]

> Congress may exercise this authority [over interstate commerce] in aid of the policy of the state, if it sees fit to do so. It is equally clear that the policy of Congress acting independently of the states may induce legislation without reference to the particular policy or law of any given state.... The control of Congress over interstate commerce is not to be limited by state laws.

(7) The other *device* just alluded to is really a complexus of devices, which comprises the ideology derived from the Log Case,[88] that commerce is primarily *transportation;* that Congress's power over transportation between states does not begin until the last stage of the journey begins; and that, therefore, Congress may not validly give any attention to what takes place prior to such movement of goods or persons. This *device* undoubtedly lent important support to the decision in Hammer v. Dagenhart. It is, however, contradicted by both earlier and later cases in which state laws were invalidated on the ground that they interfered with interstate commerce in the sense of *dealing* or *traffic;*[89] and it is also contradicted by the Court's later decision in Brooks v. United States,[90] upholding the Federal Motor Theft Act of 1919, the major purpose of which is acknowledged by the Court to be protection to owners of

---

86. Bailey v. Drexel Furn. Co., 259 U.S. 20, 39, 42 Sup. Ct. 449, 451 (1922) (italics inserted). The limitation here placed on the national taxing power, though taking the form of a definition of the word "tax," clearly represents a triumph of the Madisonian theory. It is, however, purely auxiliary to the limitation imposed in the first Child Labor Case upon Congress's power over interstate commerce and would fall with that doctrine. Moreover, the recent decision of the Court in Magnano Co. v. Hamilton, 292 U.S. 40, 54 Sup. Ct. 599 (1934), seems to leave it doubtful whether the decision in the Bailey Case, above, states a rule to which the Court proposes to adhere.

87. United States v. Hill, 248 U.S. 420, 425, 39 Sup. Ct. 143, 145 (1919).

88. Coe v. Errol, 116 U.S. 517, 6 Sup. Ct. 475 (1886).

89. See Dahnke-Walker Milling Co. v. Bondurant, 257 U.S. 282, 42 Sup. Ct. 106 (1921); Lemke v. Farmers' Grain Co., 258 U.S. 50, 42 Sup. Ct. 244 (1922).

90. 267 U.S. 432, 45 Sup. Ct. 345 (1925).

motor vehicles, that is to say, to interests in the state of the origin of the act of transportation which is penalized. Nor is this to mention the line of decisions, culminating in the Olsen Case, which also involve "commerce" in the primary sense of *traffic*.

Returning now to the Court's opinion in the Schechter Case, we note its tacit avoidance of all the above *devices*. It will be pertinent to refer in this connection briefly to (4), (5), and (7). The last was not invoked for the obvious reason that the offenses for which the Schechters were being prosecuted occurred, according to the Court's holding, not prior to an act of interstate transportation, or commerce, but after such act was completed. *Devices* (4) and (5) were not invoked for the reason that the government's argument in behalf of the N.I.R.A., that measure was justified not on the *humanitarian* grounds which sufficed to condemn the Child Labor Act, but on the ground that its controlling purpose was *the restoration of interstate commerce*, which the act aimed to bring about by increasing the national purchasing power. And not finding these devices available to its purpose, the Court fell back upon the Sugar Trust Case, from which it extracted the distinction between "direct" and "indirect" effects upon interstate commerce—*device* number (8).

IV

The chief justice's opinion in the Schechter Case represents an effort to fan into effective flame once more the dying embers of the Madisonian conception of an inviolable 'state sovereignty," incapable of penetration by national power, and hence constituting an independent barrier in delimitation of that power. Is such an effort likely to prove of enduring value in determining what powers the national government should exercise in the presence of modern conditions, especially in the presence of the national organization of commercial activities? This question could no doubt be more advantageously answered if we knew just what content the Schechter holding assigned the conception. But even according the term the most modest connotation permitted by any allowable interpretation of the holding, its workability in modern conditions is still open to challenge.

Let us in this connection consult once again Mr. Justice Hughes' famous opinion in the Minnesota Rate Cases. There the proposition was foreshadowed, which two years later became the basis of the Court's decision in the Shreveport Case, that Congress's power in the regulation of interstate railway rates was paramount over the states' uncontroverted power to regulate local rates, and capable therefore of curtailing and overriding the latter to any extent necessary to render effective the former. In support of this conclusion Mr. Justice Hughes offered the following highly concrete picture of the actual relationship at that date of the conduct of interstate transportation with that of local transportation:[91]

> The interblending of operations in the conduct of interstate and local business by interstate carriers is strongly pressed upon our attention. It is urged that the same right of way, terminals, rails, bridges, and stations are provided for both classes of traffic; that the proportion of each sort of business varies from year to year, and, indeed, from day to day; that no division of the plant, no apportionment of it between interstate and local traffic, can be made today, which will hold tomorrow; that terminals, facilities, and connections in one state aid the carrier's entire business, and are an element of value with respect to the whole property and the business in other states; that securities are issued against the entire line of the carrier and cannot be divided by states. . . . The force of these contentions is emphasized in these cases, and in others of like nature, by the extreme difficulty and intricacy of the calculations which must be made in the effort to establish a segregation of intrastate business for the purpose of determining the return to which the carrier is properly entitled therefrom.
>
> But these considerations are for the practical judgment of Congress in determining the extent of the regulation necessary under existing conditions of transportation to conserve and promote the interests of interstate commerce.

Suppose now the chief justice had approached the Schechter Case from the point of view suggested by this realistic mode of reasoning rather than from the point of view of the dogmatic conceptualism of the Sugar Trust Case—what kind of opinion would he have written? At any rate, it is not difficult to imagine one that he might have written. His point of departure would have been the primary idea of "commerce" as *buying, selling, traffic*— "commercial activities," in short. He would have urged the achieved economic solidarity of the country, quoting no doubt from recent opinions of the Court the statement, "Primitive conditions have passed; business is now transacted on a national scale."[92] He would have pointed to our nationalized system of credit, our nationalized system of transportation, our nationalized system of distribution. He would have urged that all large scale production has in contemplation the interstate market, that indeed a large percentage of carriers' loadings are of goods destined for other states. He would have noted how often it occurs that the article which reaches the consumer is the finished result of successive productive activities carried on in several states; that the consumer is, in other words, the *terminus ad quem* toward which sets a process neglectful of state lines and dominated by its interstate characterisitcs. Quoting then his own words in the Appalachian Coals Case, decided two years since, "realities must dominate the judgment,"[93] he would have continued: governmental regulation of an economy which is integrated to this degree must obviously be centered in

---

91. Simpson v. Shepard, 230 U.S. 352, 432, 33 Sup. Ct. 729, 753 (1913).

92. Farmers' L. & T. Co. v. Minnesota, 280 U.S. 204, 211, 50 Sup. Ct. 98, 100 (1930); Burnet v. Brooks, 288 U.S. 378, 402, 53 Sup. Ct. 457, 464 (1933).

93. Appalachian Coals v. United States, 288 U.S. 344, 360, 53 Sup. Ct. 471, 474 (1933).

a single government, not only if it is to be effective, but if indeed it is not to be positively mischievous.[94] In other words, *the choice is between national regulation and no regulation*. And in connection with the latter possibility he would not have failed to remark that there is a Gresham's law of business methods, as well as of currencies, that disreputable methods drive out good, and that the fittest who survive are frequently the least fit. Thus, turning to the case at hand, he would have pointed out that the defendants were charged with diverting the stream of interstate commerce in poultry toward themselves, and that this was in fact the necessary and *calculated* tendency of their acts; that by violating the law (''chiselling''), they were enabled to undersell their competitors, to increase their own sales, and hence to go into the interstate market for an increasing number of fowl. But such being the case, the chief justice would have queried, what becomes of the distinction between ''direct'' and ''indirect'' effects on interstate commerce? Indeed, it would have been appropriate, had he quoted at this point, the following evaluation of this distinction from a recent, though dissenting opinion.[95]

> . . . the traditional test . . . seems . . . too mechanical, too uncertain in its application, and too remote from actualities, to be of value. In thus making use of the expressions, ''direct'' and ''indirect interference'' with commerce, we are doing little more than using labels to describe a result rather than any trustworthy formula by which it is reached.

And his dismissal of the argument invoking in defendants' behalf the power of the states over their ''internal concerns'' would have been similarly factual and curt. A diversion of interstate commerce is not an ''internal concern'' of the state where it occurs, it is not—in Marshall's own words—one, ''which does not affect other states.'' And again quoting himself, he would have added: ''Within its sphere as recognized by the Constitution, the nation is supreme. The question is simply of the federal power as granted, where there is authorized exercise of that power, there is no reserved power to nullify it—a principle obviously essential to our national integrity, yet continually calling for new applications.''[96]

And so much for the opinion which the chief justice *might* have written the Poultry Case, but did not. A further question remains, which we may proceed to answer on our own account: just how effective, in point of fact, *is* the Court's present application of the commerce clause in protecting ''the internal concerns of a state''? Let us, in answer to this question, lay the actual decision in the Poultry Case alongside the decision three months earlier in the case of Baldwin v Seelig.[97] Here it was held that the New York Milk Control Act, in

94. See the address referred to above, note 44.
95. Justice Stone, in Di Santo v. Pennsylvania, 273 U.S. 34, 44, 47 Sup. Ct. 267, 271 (1927).
96. Address before New York State Bar Association, January 14, 1916, 39 *Report of New York Bar Association* 266, 275.
97. 55 Sup. Ct. 497 (1935).

attempting to prohibit the sale within the state of milk purchased outside it at less than stipulated prices, violated the commerce clause. Invoking "our national solidarity" Justice Cardozo, speaking for the Court, said:[98]

> The Constitution was framed under the dominion of a political philosophy less parochial in range. It was framed upon the theory that the peoples of the several states must sink or swim together, and that in the long run prosperity and salvation are in union and not division.

Adding together these two holdings rendered within a few weeks of each other, their net result seems to be that neither Congress nor a state may "for economic advantage" regulate the local sale of goods brought into the state from another state: Congress is prevented from so doing by the Court's solicitude for the *power* (!) of the states over their "internal concerns" and the states are disabled by its solicitude for Congress's *power* (!) over interstate commerce. Common sense suggests that possibly both solicitudes have been somewhat overworked. Why should not the state of New York govern local sales to the extent necessary to make its control over its "internal concerns" really effective, until Congress—the authority to which, after all, the Constitution gives the power to regulate "commerce among the several states"—decrees otherwise? And why should Congress's power be held to be limited by a power which no state can alone exercise effectively?[99]

To sum up: The grave concern expressed by the chief justice for the reserved powers of the states, and the prominent place which this occupies in his opinion, both strongly suggest that the governing intention of the decision, at least in the minds of a majority of the *present* Court, is to exclude the national government from the regulation of labor conditions in the field of the productive industries. In this respect business management is still to range uncontrolled save by the states, which is to say, very little at all. But the decision, however interpreted, reveals notable weaknesses. It was not required for the determination of the case, the argumentative basis supplied it by the chief justice is unnecessarily broad, and the doctrine of which this basis is compounded is gravely defective. The pivotal distinction between "direct" and "indirect" effects upon interstate commerce was originally employed in a sense almost diametrically opposed to that given it in this case. The only previous decision in which it was applied in the present sense, *adversely* to national power, is one which, prior to the Schechter Case, had come to be regarded as having been substantially overruled by later cases. The distinction is, moreover, as thus

---

98. *Id.* at 500.

99. "If neither Congress nor the state legislatures have such power, then we are brought to the somewhat extraordinary position that there is no authority, state or national, which can legislate upon the subject or prohibit such contracts. This cannot be the case." Addyston Pipe & Steel Co. v. United States, 175 U.S. 211, 231, 20 Sup. Ct. 96, 104 (1899). See also Corwin, *Twilight of the Supreme Court* at 34–35, and accompanying notes. The above evaluation of the effect of the Seelig and Schechter holdings taken together receives support from United States v. Seven Oaks Dairy Co., 10 F. Supp. 995, 1004 (Mass. 1935).

employed, artificial in the highest degree, although not inconceivably it might hereafter be adapted to a more realistic type of decision. Also, this distinction is merely one of a long series of devices which have been brought forward from time to time to blunt the principle of national supremacy, but none of which the Court has ever applied with any degree of consistency.

Finally, the decision is ambiguous, albeit insufficiently so. Squinting in two directions, it inclines in the wrong direction. A more astringent opinion, or one less sympathetic toward the actual task of government, has rarely if ever issued from the Court. This is truly unfortunate. The present Court is confronted with a need as great as that which faced Marshall, and materials are available to it in rich measure from the varied resources of our constitutional law wherewith to meet this need. Surely it is to be hoped that impending decisions will reveal a spirit more constructive and generous.[100]

100. When President Roosevelt said that doubts as to the constitutionality of the Guffey Coal Bill were "reasonable," he did not err as to *fact* but only as to *tact*. He should have said that doubts as to its *unconstitutionality* were reasonable, as indeed they were and still are.

15. The Court Sees a New Light

AMERICAN constitutional law has first and last undergone a number of revolutions, but none so radical, so swift, so altogether dramatic as that witnessed by the term of Court just ended. I have in mind only the results so far recorded in actual decisions; when the logical possibilities for the future of these holdings are considered, the impression left is, of course, still more striking.

A year ago minimum-wage legislation, even for women, still rested under the ban of the Court, the national government was for the most part without authority over the employer-employee relation in the industrial field, and social security was at best highly suspect on constitutional grounds. Today the truth contradicts each one of these statements. More than that, the *tone* of the Court has altered vastly in a twelvemonth. Last spring, following the slaughter of the AAA and "the little NIRA," the chief justice jauntily proclaimed in his American Law Institute address, "I have to announce that the Supreme Court still functions," and at about the same time six of the nine justices joined in the case of Jones v. the SEC in an opinion which sets an all-time high for judicial arrogance. These lapses from good sense and good taste would not today be repeated.

The Court first gave arresting notice of its change of mind when, on March 29, it sustained a minimum-wage statute of the state of Washington, and at the same time explicitly overruled its decision of 1923 in Adkins v. the Children's Hospital, which it had reaffirmed so recently as June, 1936. The new Court was the outcome of the defection of Mr. Justice Roberts from the Sutherland-VanDevanter-McReynolds-Butler combination, and the chief justice was its spokesman. While his opinion cites "the economic conditions which have

From *The New Republic*, August 4, 1937, pp. 354–57. Reprinted by permission. Copyright 1937 by The New Republic.

supervened'' since the Adkins case was decided, it also quotes with warm approval the views of the dissenters in that case. "We think," the opinion reads, "that the views thus expressed are sound and that the decision in the Adkins case was a departure from the true application of the principles governing the regulation by the state of employer and employee." But the decision more than recovers lost ground, since much of its reasoning goes to establish the constitutionality of minimum-wage legislation for all workers. Thus the Court pointed out that it was no objection to the act before it that it did not cover the entire field of possible legislation. It also cited the history of hour legislation, which underwent a like expansion. In the chief justice's words, "Liberty in each of its phases has its history and connotation. But the liberty safeguarded is liberty in a social organization which requires the protection of law against the evils which menace the health, safety, morals and welfare of the people." In the face of these words it becomes impossible to contend that difference in sex sets up an absolute barrier to governmental regulation of wages.

A fortnight later the new Court, again speaking through the chief justice, sustained the application of the Wagner National Labor Relations Act to certain industrial establishments which were found to be extensively engaged in interstate commerce. The Act forbids ''any unfair labor practice affecting interstate commerce'' and lists among these ''the denial by employers of the right of their employees to organize and the refusal by employers to accept the procedure of collective bargaining.'' Dealing first with the ''due process'' aspect of the case, the chief justice characterizes ''the right of employees to self-organization and to select representatives of their own choosing for collective bargaining or other mutual protection without restraint or coercion by their employer'' as ''a fundamental right,'' interference with which ''is a proper subject for condemnation by competent legislative authority.'' The chief justice then continues:

> Long ago we stated the reason for labor organizations. We said that they were organized out of the necessities of the situation; that a single employee was helpless in dealing with an employer; that he was dependent ordinarily on his daily wage for the maintenance of himself and his family; and that if the employer refused to pay him the wages that he thought fair, he was nevertheless unable to leave the employ and resist arbitrary and unfair treatment; that union was essential to give laborers opportunity to deal on an equality with their employers.

Thus ''liberty'' is recognized as something that may be infringed by other forces as well as by those of government; indeed, something that may require the positive intervention of government against those other forces. This recognition marks a development of profound significance in our constitutional history.

But the principal difficulty of these cases arose from the contention of the defendant companies that Congress could not, without unconstitutionally invading the reserved powers of the states, govern the relationship between industrial employers and employees. So, indeed, it has been asserted by the Court itself less than a year previous in the Carter case, in which the Guffey Coal Conservation Act was set aside. Said Mr. Justice Sutherland on that occasion:

> Much stress is put upon the evils which come from the struggle between employers and employees over the matter of wages, working conditions, the right of collective bargaining, etc., and the resulting strikes, curtailment and irregularity of production and effect on prices; and it is insisted that interstate commerce is *greatly* affected thereby. But, in addition to what has just been said, the conclusive answer is that the evils are all local evils over which the federal government has no legislative control. The relation of employer and employee is a local relation. At common law, it is one of the domestic relations. The wages are paid for the doing of local work. The employees are not engaged in or about commerce but exclusively in producing a commodity. And the controversies and evils, which it is the object of the act to regulate and minimize, are local controversies and evils affecting local work undertaken to accomplish that local result. Such effect as they may have upon commerce, however extensive it may be, is secondary and indirect. An increase in the greatness of the effect adds to its importance. It does not alter its character.

Furthermore, it is at least highly probable that in speaking thus, Mr. Justice Sutherland voiced what was the opinion of the entire Court at that date. Otherwise the effort of Mr. Justice Cardozo, speaking also for Justices Brandeis and Stone, to separate the price-fixing provisions of the Guffey Act from the hours-and-wages provisions would appear to have been gratuitous, while the chief justice's words, in his separate opinion, would be meaningless: "If the people desire to give Congress the power to regulate industries within the states and the relation of employers and employees in those industries, they are at liberty to declare their will in the appropriate manner, but it is not for the Court to amend the Constitution by judicial decision."

Fortunately the chief justice was mistaken. If it was a part of the Constitution in May 18, 1936, that Congress could not regulate the employer-employee relation in industry, then the Constitution was in that respect amended by the Court on April 12 last. Setting out from Mr. Chief Justice Taft's dictum in Stafford v. Wallace, decided in 1922, that "whatever amounts to more or less constant practice, and threatens to obstruct or unduly to burden the freedom of interstate commerce, is within the regulatory power of Congress under the commerce clause, and it is primarily for Congress to consider and decide the fact of the danger and meet it," the Court rejects the contention that the power thus recognized has reference only to the protection of the instruments of interstate commerce. "The agency," says the chief justice, "is not superior to the commerce which uses it. . . . The close and intimate effect which brings the subject within the reach of federal power may be due to activities in relation to productive industry, although this industry when separately viewed is local." Nor will it do to say that such effect is "indirect." Considering defendant's "farflung activities," the effect of strife between it and its employees "would be immediate and it might be catastrophic. We are asked to shut our eyes to the plainest facts of our national life and to deal with the question of direct and indirect effects in an intellectual vacuum. . . .

> When industries organize themselves on a national scale, making their relation to interstate commerce the dominant factor in their activities, how can it be maintained that their industrial labor relations constitute a forbidden field into which Congress may not enter when it is necessary to protect interstate commerce from the paralyzing consequences of industrial war? We have often said that interstate commerce itself is a practical conception. It is equally true that interferences with that commerce must be appraised by a judgment that does not ignore actual experience.

So the test of formula by which the Guffey Act was set aside, a formula derived from the old sugar-trust case of 1895, of evil memory, is replaced by one of fact, and this is speedily shown to be an extremely flexible test. In the Jones-Laughlin case, from the opinion in which the above quotations are taken, the defendant company was the fourth largest producer of steel in the United States, embracing nineteen subsidiaries, owning and operating ore, coal and limestone properties, steamship lines, railroads and manufactories scattered among several states and employing more than a half-million men. But the results reached by the Court in applying the Wagner Act to this immense enterprise were held equally applicable to a manufacturer of trailers located in Detroit but selling more than 80 percent of his products in other states, and to a manufacturer of clothing located in Richmond, Virginia, but selling more than 82 percent of his product in other states.

Let the employees of a concern, a considerable proportion of whose trade and activities extend beyond state lines, be ready and willing to strike resolutely for their "fundamental rights," and Congress can govern the employer-employee relation of such a concern with the purpose and effect of backing up such "fundamental rights"—that is the new constitutional law yielded by the Wagner Act cases, although not all of it. For by the same token Congress should have power also to protect the "fundamental rights" of employers against interruptions that would effect interstate commerce detrimentally. Undoubtedly the protective power of Congress over interstate commerce extends to the employer goose as well as to the employee gander.

Of less interest historically although certainly not practically were the brace of cases in which the new Court sustained, on May 24, the Social Security Act of 1935 as to its substantive provisions, and the companion case in which the Unemployment Compensation Act of Alabama was upheld. Salient features of Mr. Justice Cardozo's opinion for the Court in the former were emphasis on the lessons of the depression of 1929 and of experience with unemployment and old-age relief since then, and the notice taken of the inability of the states to deal separately with the problem of social security, both because of the national scope of the problem and because states compete with one another to attract investors.

Proceeding from this dual basis the Court upholds the power of the national government to tax employers on their employment rolls, such a tax being classified as an "excise"; also its power to spend money in support of unemployment insurance and to provide old-age pensions, expenditures of such nature being for "the general welfare of the United States" within the sense of the taxing clause of the Constitution; also, its power to cooperate with the states in a joint program of unemployment relief and old-age security, and to that end to offer financial inducements to the states to cooperate in such a program.

To the claim that the state of Alabama had been "coerced" by the provision in the act of Congress which accords a 90-percent credit against the federal tax to employers contributing under a satisfactory state law to unemployment compensation, Mr. Justice Cardozo answered: "From all that appears she is satisfied with her choice, and would be sorely disappointed if it were now to be annulled.... The petitioners' contention... confuses motive with coercion.... But to hold that motive or temptation is equivalent to coercion is to plunge the law in endless difficulties." That is to say, there is no constitutional reason why the national government should not supply motives for action by a state. Nor were the terms which Congress had stipulated for a satisfactory state unemployment act an intrusion upon state power, inasmuch as they were designed to protect the national Treasury and were related to activities fairly within the scope of national fiscal power and policy—a test, it may be remarked in passing, which would have saved the AAA.

And Mr. Justice Stone is similarly dexterous in meeting objections to the Alabama Unemployment Compensation Act. Answering the complaint that the tax levied by the act yielded no benefits to those who paid it, he says: "The only benefit to which the taxpayer is constitutionally entitled is that derived from his enjoyment of the privilege of living in a civilized society, established and safeguarded by the devotion of taxes to a public purpose." And answering the objection that the act involved an unconstitutional abdication of power by Alabama to the national government, he says:

> The United States and the state of Alabama are not alien governments. They coexist within the same territory. Unemployment within it is their common concern. Together the two statutes now before us embody a cooperative legislative effort by state and national governments, for carrying out a public purpose common to both, which neither could fully achieve without the cooperation of the other. The Constitution does not prohibit such cooperation.

Thus while the keynote of the Wagner Act cases is increased power for the national government over industry and the employer-employee relation therein, that of the Social Security Act cases is national and state cooperation in the field of social insurance. Together these decisions spell a new, a revitalized federal system. To be sure, many questions still remain unanswered—very important questions of statutory interpretation as regards the Wagner Act, several minor questions of constitutionality as regards the Social Security Act. But guaranteed the continuance of the mood which finds expression in the opinions here reviewed, these questions too should find solution satisfactory to the administration.

The question arises, of course, whether the Court's remarkable reversal in attitude, just recorded, is to be set down to the credit of the president's Court proposal. To some extent perhaps, but certainly not altogether. The lesson of the November election could have been lost only on members of the bench with a messianic complex of some sort; and the CIO "sit-down strikes" must also have had a profound effect in the demonstration which they afforded that the country is not to be governed by the simple expedient of tossing acts of Congress out of the window.

On the other hand, the confirmation which these decisions lend to the major premise of the president's argument for his proposal, of the essentially political nature of the Court's function today in the constitutional field, is impressive. Nor is the contention which is now forthcoming from certain opponents of the idea of reconstituting the Court entirely conclusive. Why, they ask in effect, follow up a successful shotgun wedding by shooting the bridegroom? Why indeed; but what of taking precautions to make it reasonably probable that the bridegroom will now turn to and support the family?

16. Statesmanship on the Supreme Court

Liberty is something which can be threatened by economic as well as
political power; and ... the latter may interpose ... against the former.

"We are very quiet there," Justice Holmes once wrote, referring
to the Supreme Court, "but it is the quiet of a storm centre, as we all know."
To remain at the center of a storm one has to keep moving, and there have been
times, as for instance in the early days of the New Deal, when the Court was
not as spry as it should have been, with the result that it lost a few plumes.
Within the last three years, however, it seems to have again caught up with the
tumultuous procession of which it is so essential a part—to be once more at the
center of the storm and prepared to serve it as a stabilizing rather than a
retarding agency. "The recent revolution in our constitutional law" has already
become more or less of a commonplace; therefore understanding of its nature
and probable import for the future is likely to have escaped attention.

We start from certain elementary propositions. One is that the Constitution is
the supreme law of the land and that all other laws have to conform to its
requirements; another is that all laws involve the courts sooner or later in their
enforcement; still another is that the courts enforce the laws, and hence the
Constitution, as they understand them; and yet another is that no law will be
enforced by the courts which they, following the lead of the Supreme Court,
deem to be in conflict with the Constitution. Also, it is agreed that the national
government is a government of "enumerated powers," which means practically
that Congress may legislate effectively only on matters which a majority of the
Supreme Court regard as falling within the "enumerated powers." Furthermore,
Congress may not pass laws even on such matters and get judicial support for
the legislation if it violates the Court's reading of certain prohibitions of the
Constitution—for instance the one which says that "no person shall be
deprived of life, liberty, or property without due process of law."

At this point, however, we leave the area of agreed principles and enter the

Reprinted from *The American Scholar,* Volume 9, Number 2, Spring, 1940. Copyright © 1940 by
the United Chapters of Phi Beta Kappa. By permission of the publishers.

field in which the "revolution" in our constitutional law has occurred. "The Congress," says the Constitution, "shall have power . . . to regulate commerce . . . among the states." But what is "commerce"? At the time the Constitution was adopted the term was sometimes used as virtually synonymous with business and as including even manufacturing. Yet a hundred years later it had come to be confined in some of the Court's decisions to transportation merely. And when is commerce "commerce among the states"? Does this phrase imply that in regulating commerce Congress must be careful not to regulate acts, like production, which take place exclusively within particular states; or may Congress on the other hand regulate commerce among the states, entirely regardless of the repercussions of its laws on intra-state affairs? And what is meant by "regulating" commerce in the sense of the Constitution? Must Congress' regulations be designed primarily to favor the development of "commerce among the states" or may they even prohibit such commerce in the furtherance of other interests, such as the repression of child labor?

Then there is that clause of the Constitution which says that "The Congress shall have power . . . to lay and collect taxes . . . to provide for the . . . general welfare of the United States." It is agreed, of course, that Congress may spend the proceeds from the taxes which it is entitled to lay and collect; the point in dispute is the meaning of the term "general welfare of the United States." Is "the general welfare of the United States" provided for when Congress hands over funds to the states to aid them in carrying out projects—vocational education, for example—which the national government could not otherwise promote; and is "the general welfare" provided for when Congress votes money primarily for private benefit, as in old age assistance or unemployment compensation?

Now it is evident that every one of the questions posed in the preceding paragraphs is capable of being answered unfavorably to national power and is equally capable of being answered favorably to national power. In fact, every such question has been answered in these contradictory ways at different times by very respectable authorities, including frequently the Court itself. So, when the New Deal first appeared on the political horizon, the Supreme Court had available to it a double set of answers to each of these questions—answers from which, without departing from its judicial role in the least, it could choose. And the "revolution" in our constitutional law consists simply in this: that whereas the Court between 1934 and 1936 chose its answers, in passing upon the constitutionality of New Deal legislation, largely from those which are unfavorable to national power, it has since, when confronted with similar questions, chosen them largely from those which are favorable to national power. In a word, the "revolution" is a revolution in the point of view of the Court itself. How is this to be accounted for?

The decisions of the Court in 1935 and 1936 setting aside the NIRA, the AAA and the Guffey Coal Act were the result of inertia in the precise sense of the tendency of a body to continue in the same direction unless and until it is interfered with by some outside force. For nearly a half-century prior to the Poultry Case, in which the NIRA was thrown out, our constitutional law—that is, the Court—had pursued, not without some interruptions and unevennesses, one general trend in cases touching the relation of government to business. This was the trend which is termed laissez-faireism, the practical purport of which was that government—state as well as national—should not interfere with the employer-employee relationship; and especially that the national government ought not to interfere with the employer-employee relationship in *productive industry*. But following these decisions three things happened, the accumulated effect of which on the Court was precisely that of an outside force and one of increasing momentum. These were: first, Mr. Roosevelt's overwhelming re-election; second, the CIO strikes in Detroit—giving the lie direct to the idea that great industry could be effectively governed by the states; and third, the president's Court proposal. The relative influence of these developments in shocking the Court out of its inertia and in persuading it to reconsider its position in our system of popular government it is, of course, impossible to determine, if it were worth while to do so. The essential thing is that the Court did reconsider its position, thus putting itself in line with the rest of the government—back in the center of the tornado.

The two groups of holdings which signalize the Court's new point of view, which comprise indeed the essential core of the "revolution" in our constitutional law, were those sustaining the Wagner Labor Act and those sustaining the Social Security Act. The former invoke those answers respecting Congress' power over commerce that are favorable to national power; the latter those answers respecting Congress' power in taxing and spending for "the general welfare" that are similarly favorable. But there is a larger implication of these holdings which must be taken account of in evaluating the recent "constitutional revolution." Simply put, this is that state lines no longer count greatly in determining the extent of Congress' powers over business activities and social and economic conditions which themselves ignore state lines. That is to say, in the field of business, governmental power marches abreast with economic and industrial organization.

There are, of course, those who complain that this means the end of states' rights, and indeed of individual liberty; but the complaint is justifiable only from the point of view of the laissez-faire conception of these. As to states' rights, the truth is that the states were no longer capable of exercising the powers which this conception attributed to them. Furthermore, such legislation as the Social Security Act, far from diminishing the usefulness of the states, has stimulated them to new tasks, to new usefulness—has endowed them with a new lease on life.

And it is much the same as to liberty. What is "liberty," and what is it "liberty" from? Laissez-faireism defined "liberty" as, above everything else, freedom of contract—that is, the freedom of employers to dictate the terms of employment; and the thing which it particularly feared was governmental interference with this. The Wagner Act, however, was sustained by the Court as a measure designed to protect "a fundamental right" of labor, the right of collective bargaining, against the superior bargaining power of employers. Liberty, in other words, is something which can be threatened by economic power as well as by political power; and when it is so threatened the latter may interpose in its favor against the former.

Further than this, recent decisions show the Court thoroughly alive to the importance of "liberty" in that enlarged sense which embraces freedom of speech, press and assembly, and alert to protect unpopular minorities from the encroachment of local tyrannies, state and municipal, upon the enjoyment of this liberty. Likewise, as in the Scottsboro cases, in which it came to the defense of the helpless victims of race prejudice, the Court has shown itself the champion of "due process of law" in the sense of a fair trial as against the mere forms thereof.

Projecting these results into the future we may arrive at some understanding of what the Court's position in our system of government is likely to be in the days to come. Its importance as defender of the "federal equilibrium" will be greatly diminished—it will no longer play states' rights against national power and vice versa as it often did throughout the half-century between 1887 and 1937. It will no longer be the make-weight, that it was during that period, of economic power against political power. It will not, in brief, play the role that it has done at times in the past in the shaping of governmental policy in the broader sense of that phrase. On the other hand, released from suspicion of political or partisan entanglement, it will be free as it has not been in many years to support the humane values of free thought, free utterance and fair play. The recent "revolution" in our constitutional law turns out, therefore, to be a superior act of statesmanship on the part of the Court itself—one than which there is no greater to its credit.

17. John Marshall, Revolutionist
Malgré Lui

In the final chapter but one of his biography of Marshall, Beveridge characterizes the aging Marshall as "the supreme conservative." Yet when Marshall first emerged on the national scene it was as a revolutionist in the fullest sense, and 106 years after his death, it was Marshall's version of the Constitution which supplied the constitutional basis for the most profound revolution in the history of our constitutional law. In this paper I shall deal briefly with the intervening story—the story, to wit, of the evolution of the federal concept in the thinking of the Supreme Court. But first some personal facts about Marshall himself.[1]

John Marshall was born September 24, 1755, on what was then the western frontier of the British province of Virginia. His father, Thomas Marshall, was a man of no pretensions to birth or learning, but of great energy of spirit and strong good sense. To him the chief justice was wont to attribute all his success in life, and it is evident that between father and son not only a powerful natural affection existed, but a remarkable congeniality.

With the outbreak of the Revolution, the two Marshalls set about training their frontier neighbors in the manual of arms. At about the time that his cousin, Thomas Jefferson, his elder by twelve years, was drafting the Declaration of Independence, young John was enlisting in the Continental line. First as lieutenant, later as captain, he fought at Brandywine, Germantown, Monmouth, and Stoney Point, and underwent with customary cheerfulness the rigors of Valley Forge.

Referring to this period many years later, he wrote: "I was confirmed in the habit of considering America as my country and Congress as my government."

From 104 *University of Pennsylvania Law Review* 9 (1955). Reprinted by permission. Copyright 1955 University of Pennsylvania Law Review.

1. See Corwin, *John Marshall and the Constitution* 25–52 (1919).

Another factor which contributed to his early nationalist bent was the influence of the revered Washington.

His regiment's term of enlistment having run out, John, in 1780, attended, for about one month, a course of lectures on law by the famed Chancellor Wythe at the College of William and Mary—the only institutional education he ever received. His self-instruction in the law had, however, begun some years earlier with his reading of the first American edition of Blackstone's *Commentaries* (1772), to which his father was a subscriber.

Marshall began legal practice in 1783 in the new state capital at Richmond and married the same year. His advancement, both professional and political, was rapid once it got under way. Meantime his political creed was taking shape. As a member of the Virginia Assembly, off and on from 1782, Marshall came to form a poor opinion of state legislatures. It seemed to him that generally they had an exaggerated conception of their own powers and that the selfish desires and narrow outlook of the farmer-debtor class usually controlled their proceedings. They refused to meet the obligations of their states under the Articles of Confederation, set at naught certain provisions of the Treaty of Peace, interfered freely with judicial decisions at the behest of litigating interests, put difficulties in the way of commerce among the sister states, voted cheap money laws, and played ducks and drakes generally with private contracts.

And for once his unloved and unloving cousin Jefferson agreed with him. In his *Notes on Virginia,* written in 1781, Jefferson assailed the Virginia Constitution of 1776 for having produced a concentration of power in the legislative assembly which answered to "precisely the definition of despotic government." Nor did it make any difference, he continued, that such powers were vested in a numerous body "chosen by ourselves"; "one hundred and seventy-three despots" were "as oppressive as one"; and "and *elective despotism* was not the government we fought for, but one which should not only be founded on free principles, but in which the powers of government should be so divided and balanced among several bodies of magistracy, as that no one could transcend their legal limits, without being effectually checked and restrained by the others."[2]

The remedy for the shortsightedness and irresponsibility of the state legislatures was ultimately supplied by a second revolution, that which culminated in the adoption of the Constitution; and to this revolution, too, Marshall lent a helping hand in its later stages. It was owing mainly to Marshall that the Virginia legislature submitted the Constitution to the ratifying convention of that state without hampering instructions. On the floor of the convention itself, Marshall gave his greatest attention to the judiciary article as it appeared in the

2. 3 *Writings of Thomas Jefferson* 223–24 (Ford ed. 1894).

proposed Constitution, espousing the idea of judicial review. If, said he, Congress "make a law not warranted by any of the powers enumerated, it would be considered by the judges as an infringement of the Constitution which they are to guard. They would not consider such a law as coming within their jurisdiction. They would declare it void."[3]

In 1799 Marshall made his once celebrated defense of President Adams' action in handing over to the British authorities, in conformity with the Jay Treaty, one Jonathon Robbins, who was allegedly a fugitive from justice. This was one speech on the floors of Congress which demonstrably made votes. Meantime, in 1797, Marshall had been one of the famous XYZ mission to France. He successively refused appointment as associate justice of the Supreme Court and as secretary of war, but in 1800 accepted the post of secretary of state. On January 22, 1801, while still holding that office, he was nominated to be chief justice and received the Senate's hesitant approval on January 27. The story of this crucial moment in his life and in the history of American constitutional law is related by Marshall in the *Autobiographical Sketch* which he prepared for Story in 1827:

> On the resignation of Chief Justice Ellsworth I recommended Judge Patteson [*sic*] as his successor. The President objected to him, and assigned as his ground of objection that the feelings of Judge Cushing would be wounded by passing him and selecting a junior member of the bench. I never heard him assign any other objection to Judge Patteson. . . . The President himself mentioned Mr. Jay, and he was nominated to the senate. When I waited on the President with Mr. Jay's letter declining the appointment he said thoughtfully "Who shall I nominate now?" I replied that I could not tell, as I supposed that his objection to Judge Patteson remained. He said in a decided tone "I shall not nominate him." After a moment's hesitation he said "I believe I must nominate you." I had never before heard myself named for the office and had not even thought of it. I was pleased as well as surprised, and bowed in silence. . . . I was unfeignedly gratified at the appointment, and have had much reason to be so.[4]

Marshall's assumption of the chief justiceship marks the beginning of his career as the "supreme conservative." Henceforth all his abilities would be directed to advancing through the Court the principles which underlay the Constitution, as he understood them, and these abilities were of a high order. Even Justice Holmes, while demurring to Senator Lodge's estimate of Marshall as "a nation-maker, a state-builder," conceded him, a bit condescendingly to be sure, "a strong intellect, a good style, personal ascendancy in his court, courage, justice and the convictions of his party."[5] Two things Holmes omitted: a profound conviction of calling and a singular ability, in the words of a

---

3. 1 Beveridge, *The Life of John Marshall* 452 (1944).
4. Marshall, *Autobiographical Sketch* 29–30 (Adams ed. 1937).
5. Lerner, *The Mind and Faith of Justice Holmes* 384 (1943).

contemporary, to "put his own ideas into the heads of others without their knowing it"—the residue, one may surmise, of his youthful experience as nurse-maid to a whole squadron of younger brothers and sisters.

The chief canons of Marshall's interpretation of the Constitution were the juristic weapons by which that interpretation became law of the land. For the purposes of this paper, they may be briefly summarized as follows:

1. The finality of the Court's interpretation of the law, and hence of the Constitution, which was the backbone of the doctrine of judicial review, as set forth particularly in Marbury v. Madison[6] in relation to acts of Congress, and in Cohens v. Virginia[7] in relation to state laws and constitutional provisions.

2. The popular origin of the Constitution, and its continuous vitality. The Constitution was "designed to endure for ages to come and hence to be adapted to the various crises of human affairs." The terms in which it grants power to the national government must, therefore, be liberally construed. The *locus classicus* of these doctrines is Marshall's decision in 1819 in McCulloch v. Maryland.[8]

3. The principle of national supremacy, which amounted to neither more nor less than a literal application of Article VI, paragraph 2 of the Constitution: "This Constitution and the laws of the United States which shall be made in pursuance thereof and the treaties made or which shall be made under the authority of the United States, shall be the supreme law of the land, and the judges in every state shall be bound thereby, anything in the Constitution or laws of any state to the contrary notwithstanding." This language, Marshall held, ruled out *ab initio* any idea that the coexistence of the states and their powers imposed limits on national power. The *locus classicus* of this doctrine is the following passage from his great opinion in Gibbons v. Ogden[9] where the scope of Congress' power to regulate commerce afforded the immediate issue:

> We are now arrived at the inquiry—what is this power? It is the power to regulate; that is, to prescribe the rule by which commerce is to be governed. This power, like all others vested in congress, is complete in itself, may be exercised to its utmost extent, and acknowledges no limitations, other than are prescribed in the constitution. These are expressed in plain terms, and do not affect the questions which arise in this case, or which have been discussed at the bar. If, as has always been understood, the sovereignty of congress, though limited to specified objects, is plenary as to those objects, the power over commerce with foreign nations, and among the several states, is vested in congress as absolutely as it would be in a single government, having in its constitution the same restrictions on the exercise of the power as are found in the constitution of the United States. The wisdom and the discretion of congress, their identity with the people, and the influence which their constituents possess at elections, are, in

6. 5 U.S. (1 Cranch) 137 (1803).
7. 19 U.S. (6 Wheat.) 264 (1821).
8. 17 U.S. (4 Wheat.) 316 (1819).
9. 22 U.S. (9 Wheat.) 1 (1824).

this, as in many other instances, as that, for example, of declaring war, the sole restraints on which they have relied to secure them from its abuse. They are the restraints on which the people must often rely solely, in all representative governments.[10]

Even, however, before Marshall had ascended the bench, the groundwork had been laid for a radically different conception of the union, viz. that of a union of sovereign states, whose reserved powers, recognized in Amendment X, stood on a footing of equality with the delegated powers of the general government. The first adumbration of such a conception appears in *Federalist 39,* the author of which was James Madison, and it was further elaborated and extended in the Virginia and Kentucky Resolutions of 1798 and 1799. It is hardly surprising, therefore, that as Marshall proceeded to develop his nationalizing principles, "the sleeping spirit of Virginia, if indeed it may ever be said to sleep," was aroused to protest.

Approaching Marshall's opinion in McCulloch v. Maryland from the angle of his quasi-parental concern for "the balance between the states and the national government," Madison declared its central vice to be that it treated the powers of the latter as "sovereign powers," a view which must inevitably "convert a limited into an unlimited government," for, he continued, "in the great system of political economy, having for its general object the national welfare, everything is related immediately or remotely to every other thing; and, consequently, a power over any one thing, if not limited by some obvious and precise affinity, may amount to a power over every other." "The very existence," he urged, "of the local sovereignties" was "a control on the pleas for a constructive amplification of the powers of the general government."[11]

Two more drastic critics were friends of Jefferson and constantly stimulated by him. One of these was John Tyler of Caroline, who pronounced Marshall's doctrines to be utterly destructive of the division of powers between the two centers of government; the other was Spencer Roane, Chief Judge of the Virginia Court of Appeals, who denied that the national government derived any "constructive powers" from the supremacy clause.[12] The designated constitutional agencies for the application of this clause, he argued, were the state judiciaries—"the judges in every state," to wit. In combatting this heresy Marshall composed one of his most powerful opinions, that in Cohens v. Virginia.[13]

And many coarser voices joined in the hue and cry, and not without effect. Hardly any session of Congress convened after 1821, but witnessed some effort

---

10. *Id.* at 196–97. See also *Id.* at 210–11.

11. 3 *Letters and Other Writings of James Madison* 143–47 (1865). For a more elaborate statement of the same position, see Hugh Swinton Legaré's review in 1829 of the first volume of Kent's *Commentaries.* 2 *Writings of Hugh Swinton Legaré* 102, 123–33 (M. Legaré ed. 1845).

12. Taylor's and Roane's quarrel with Marshall may be traced sufficiently in the entries in the index to Beveridge's biography of Marshall. 4 Beveridge, *The Life of John Marshall* at 657, 662.

13. See also Martin v. Hunter's Lessee, 14 U.S. (1 Wheat.) 304 (1816).

to curtail the powers of the Court, and the support accorded some of these in Congress reached sizeable proportions. Marshall became increasingly aware that he was fighting a losing fight.

> To men who think as you and I do,'' he wrote Story, toward the end of 1834, "the present is gloomy enough; and the future presents no cheering prospect. In the South . . . those who support the Executive do not support the government. They sustain the personal power of the President, but labor incessantly to impair the legitimate powers of the government. Those who oppose the rash and violent measures of the Executive . . . are generally the bitter enemies of Constitutional Government. Many of them are the avowed advocates of a league; and those who do not go the whole length, go a great part of the way. What can we hope for in such circumstances?''[14]

Marshall died July 5, 1935. A few months later Justice Henry Baldwin published his *View of the Constitution,* in which he paid tribute to his late chief justice's qualities as expounder of the Constitution. "No commentator," he wrote, "ever followed the text more faithfully, or ever made a commentary more accordant with its strict intention and language. . . . He never brought into action the powers of his mighty mind to find some meaning in plain words . . . above the comprehension of ordinary minds. . . . He knew the framers of the Constitution, who were his compatriots''; he was himself the historian of its framing, wherefore, as its expositor, "he knew its objects, its intentions." Yet in the face of these admissions, Baldwin rejects Marshall's theory of the origin of the Constitution and the corollary doctrine of liberal construction. "The history and spirit of the times," he wrote, "admonish us that new versions of the Constitution will be promulgated to meet the varying course of political events or aspirations of power.''[15]

Baldwin's prophecy was speedily justified by the event. Within twenty-two months following Marshall's demise, the Court, having been enlarged by Congress from seven to nine justices with the intention of watering down the still persisting Marshallian virus, received five new justices and a new chief justice. Volume 11 of Peters Reports reflects the juristic result of its transformation. Here occur three cases involving state laws, all of which, by Story's testimony, the late chief justice had stigmatized as unconstitutional. In 11 Peters all three are sustained. For present purposes the most significant of these cases was New York v. Miln,[16] in which it was alleged that the state, in imposing certain requirements upon captains of vessels entering New York harbor with aliens aboard, had violated applicable congressional legislation. Speaking for the Court, Justice Barbour said:

> There is, then, no collision between the law in question, and the acts of congress just commented on. . . . But we do not place our opinion on this ground.

14. Corwin, *John Marshall and the Constitution* 195.
15. *Id.* at 225–26.
16. 36 U.S. (11 Pet.) 102 (1837).

We choose rather to plant ourselves on what we consider impregnable positions. They are these: That a state has the same undeniable and unlimited jurisdiction over all persons and things, within its territorial limits, as any foreign nation; where that jurisdiction is not surrendered or restrained by the constitution of the United States. That, by virtue of this it is not only the right, but the bounden and solemn duty of a state, to advance the safety, happiness and prosperity of its people, and to provide for its general welfare, by any and every act of legislation, which it may deem to be conducive to these ends; where the power over the particular subject, or the manner of its exercise is not surrendered or restrained, in the manner just stated. That all those powers which relate to merely municipal legislation, or what may, perhaps, more properly be called *internal police,* are not thus surrendered or restrained; and that, consequently, in relation to these, the authority of a state is complete, unqualified and exclusive.[17]

Although Justice Wayne subsequently alleged that he had never assented to Barbour's "impregnable positions," and strongly hinted that they had been smuggled into the Court's opinion after it had been approved by the other justices, there can be no doubt that by the time of the decision of the License Cases,[18] ten years later, Barbour's dictum had, to all intents and purposes, become settled doctrine of the Court. What is more, Chief Justice Taney's opinion in these same cases projects on the basis of it a new conception of the Court's role in the Constitution, one which he later reiterates and enlarges in his opinion in Ableman v. Booth,[19] decided in 1858. Here the Supreme Court, which Marshall had regarded as primarily an organ for the maintenance of national supremacy, is depicted as an arbiter standing outside of and above both the general government and the states, with power to settle "with the calmness and deliberation of judicial inquiry" all controversies as to their respective powers—controversies which "in other countries have been determined by the arbitrament of force."[20] Ironically enough, two years later, the Civil War broke.

We move now into a new cycle of American constitutional law. The Civil War had settled the most urgent and dangerous issue of the federal relationship. A new problem had meantime arisen—that of the relation of government, and especially of the national government, to private enterprise. The problem was formulated in the first instance in the terminology of the laissez-faire conception of governmental function.

The bare facts of life, and especially the country's dependence upon the uncurbed energies of its pioneers for the conquest and appropriation of a vast wilderness, rendered American soil fertile ground for the laissez-faire ideology. Thus President Van Buren, in his special message to Congress of September 4, 1837, wrote:

17. *Id*. at 139.
18. 46 U.S. (5 How.) 504 (1847).
19. 62 U.S. (21 How.) 506 (1858).
20. *Id*. at 520–21.

> All communities are apt to look to government for too much. Even in our own country, where its powers and duties are so strictly limited, we are prone to do so, especially at periods of sudden embarrassment and distress. But this ought not to be. The framers of our excellent Constitution and the people who approved it with calm and sagacious deliberation acted at the time on a sounder principle. They wisely judged that the less government interferes with private pursuits the better for the general prosperity. It is not its legitimate object to make men rich or to repair by direct grants of money or legislation in favor of particular pursuits losses not incurred in the public service. This would be substantially to use the property of some for the benefit of others. But its real duty—that duty the performance of which makes a good government the most precious of human blessings—is to enact and enforce a system of general laws commensurate with, but not exceeding, the objects of its establishment, and to leave every citizen and every interest to reap under its benign protection the rewards of virtue, industry, and prudence.[21]

But the theory of laissez faire which dominated the thinking of the American Bar Association, founded in 1878, and in due course that of the Supreme Court, was a highly pretentious, highly complex construction which, in effect, presented the American people overnight, as it were, with a new doctrine of natural law—one which thrust the maintenance of economic competition into the status of a preferred constitutional value.[22] Of the distinguishable elements of the theory, the oldest was a benefaction from Adam Smith's *Wealth of Nations*, which assumed a natural "economic order" whose intrinsic principles or "laws" automatically assure realization of the social welfare, provided their operation is not interfered with by judgments which are not based on the self-interest of the author thereof. This famous work appeared the same year as the Declaration of Independence, a coincidence which a president of the Association opined could only have had its origin in the mind of Deity itself. In 1857, John Stuart Mill's *Political Economy* presented the world with a revised version of the *Wealth of Nations*, and was followed two years later by Darwin's world-shattering *Origin of the Species*. As elaborated particularly by Herbert Spencer and his American disciple, John Fiske, the evolutionary conception immensely reinforced the notion of governmental passivity. It was certainly reassuring to know that competition in the economic world was matched by "the struggle for existence" in the biological world, and that those who survived the latter struggle were invariably "the fittest," since that went to show that those who were most successful in economic competition were likewise "the fittest." Nor may mention be omitted of Sir Henry Maine's *Ancient Law*, which appeared two years after the *Origin of the Species*, for here the evolutionary process received, so to speak, a sort of jural sanctification. "The movement of progressive societies," wrote Maine, "has hitherto been a movement from Status to Contract." If hitherto, then why not henceforth? Freedom of contract, too, was a part of the divine plan.

To return to the American Bar Association—its original membership com-

---

21. 3 *Messages and Papers of Martin Van Buren* 344 (Richardson ed. 1897).
22. See Twiss, *Lawyers and the Constitution* 63–200 (1942).

prised avowedly the elite of the American bar. Organized in the wake of the decision in Munn v. Illinois,[23] which one of the members opined was a sign that the country was "gravitating toward barbarism," the association soon became a sort of juristic sewing circle for mutual education in the gospel of laissez faire. Addresses and papers presented at the annual meetings iterated and reiterated the tenets of the new creed: government was essentially of private origin; the police power of the state was intended merely to implement the common law of nuisance; the right to fix prices was no part of any system of free government; "in the progress of society there is a natural tendency to freedom"; the trend of democracy is always away from regulation in the economic field; "the more advanced a nation becomes, the more will the liberty of the individual be developed."

What however, did this signify practically? This question was answered by the president of the association in 1892, in these words: "Can I be mistaken in claiming that constitutional law is the most important branch of American jurisprudence; and that the American bar is and should be in a large degree that priestly tribe to whose hands are confided the support and defense of the Ark of the Covenant of our fathers . . . ?"[24]

The problem remained, nevertheless, of how the tenets of laissez faire were to be translated into the accepted idiom of American constitutional law? This problem was met in part by association papers, in part also by contemporary writings on constitutional law, such as, notably, Cooley's *Constitutional Limitations,* Tiedeman's *Treatise on the Limitations of the Police Power,* James Cooledge Carter's *Law, Its Origin, Growth and Function,* John Forrest Dillon's *The Laws and Jurisprudence of England and America,* among others.

And the final grist of all this grinding for the constitutional law of the period was, first, the doctrine of freedom of contract and, secondly, the doctrine that the regulation of production is exclusively reserved to the states both by the Tenth Amendment and by the principle of federal equilibrium. The doctrine of freedom of contract owes most to Tiedeman, who advanced the proposition that when a court was confronted with a statute restrictive of freedom of contract in the economic field, the principle that statutes are to be presumed constitutional was automatically repealed and the burden of proof was shifted to anyone who pleaded the statute.

The concept of freedom of contract is, of course, post-Marshall, being an offshoot of the substantive doctrine of due process of law, which first received important recognition in the jurisprudence of the Court in Chief Justice Taney's opinion in the Dred Scott case.[25] It reached its culmination in the October term

23. 94 U.S. 113 (1876).

24. See Corwin, *Constitutional Revolution, Ltd.* 87–88 (1941); Twiss, *Lawyers and the Constitution* 174–200.

25. Scott v. Sandford, 60 U.S. (19 How.) 393, 450 (1857). For the antecedents of this dictum, see Corwin, *Liberty against Government* 58–115 (1948).

of 1935 when the Court declared in effect that a minimum wage law was beyond the competence of either the states or the national government.[26] For our purpose we need give this concept no further attention. The other doctrine, however, that of an exclusive state power in the field of production, is immediately pertinent to the purpose of this paper.

The first important case in which this doctrine played a decisive role was the famed Sugar Trust case[27] of 1895, in which the Sherman Anti-Trust Act was put to sleep for twenty years so far as its main purpose, the repression of industrial combinations, was concerned. Early in his opinion, Chief Justice Fuller stated the fundamental rationale of the decision as follows:

> It is vital that the independence of the commercial power and of the police power, and the delimitation between them, however sometimes perplexing, should always be recognized and observed, for while the one furnishes the strongest bond of union, the other is essential to the preservation of the autonomy of the states as required by our dual form of government; and acknowledged evils, however grave and urgent they may appear to be, had better be borne, than the risk be run, in the effort to suppress them, of more serious consequences by resort to expedients of even doubtful constitutionality.[28]

In short, what was needed, the Court felt, was a hard and fast line between the two spheres of power, and in the following series of propositions it endeavored to lay down such a line: (1) production is always local, and under the exclusive domain of the states; (2) commerce among the states does not commence until goods "commence their final movement from their states of origin to that of their destination"; (3) the sale of a product is merely an incident of its production and, while capable of "bringing the operation of commerce into play," affects it only incidentally; (4) such restraint as would reach commerce, as above defined, in consequence of combinations to control production "in all its forms," would be "indirect, however inevitable and whatever its extent," and as such beyond the purview of the statute.[29]

In the Sugar Trust case nullification of the legislation involved assumed, therefore, the guise—or disguise—of statutory construction. A generation later, in the first Child Labor case,[30] the Court invalidated outright an act of Congress which banned from interstate commerce goods from factories in which child labor had been employed. Said Justice Day for a sharply divided Court:

---

26. See Morehead v. New York ex rel. Tipaldo, 298 U.S. 587 (1936). The late Charles Beard charged Marshall with a certain responsibility for the doctrine of freedom of contract on the score of his assigning such a transcendental value to the inviolability of contracts in his dissenting opinion in Ogden v. Saunders, 25 U.S. (12 Wheat.) 212, 331 (1827). This inviolability is derived from the proposition that "the right to contract is the attribute of a free agent. . . ." *Id.* at 350. Ogden v. Saunders is the one and only constitutional case in which Marshall appeared in the minority.

27. United States v. E. C. Knight Co., 156 U.S. 1 (1895).

28. *Id.* at 13.

29. *Id.* at 13–16.

30. Hammer v. Dagenhart, 247 U.S. 251 (1918).

In interpreting the Constitution it must never be forgotten that the nation is made up of states to which are entrusted the powers of local government. And to them and to the people the powers not expressly delegated to the national government are reserved. Lane County v. Oregon, 7 Wall. 71, 76. The power of the states to regulate their purely internal affairs by such laws as seem wise to the local authority is inherent and has never been surrendered to the general government. New York v. Miln, 11 Pet. 102, 139.... To sustain this statute would not be in our judgment a recognition of the lawful exertion of congressional authority over interstate commerce, but would sanction an invasion by the federal power of the control of a matter purely local in its character, and over which no authority has been delegated to Congress in conferring the power to regulate commerce among the states.[31]

In short, the Court bases its decision on the Tenth Amendment, having first taken the precaution to amend the same by inserting the word "expressly" in front of the word "delegated."

And in Carter v. Carter Coal Co.[32] decided in 1935, the Court held void on like grounds an act of Congress intended to regulate hours of labor and wages in the bituminous coal mines of the country. Said Justice Sutherland for the Court:

... [T]he conclusive answer [to defense of the act] is that the evils are all local evils over which the federal government has no legislative control. The relation of employer and employee is a local relation. At common law, it is one of the domestic relations. The wages are paid for the doing of local work. Working conditions are obviously local conditions. The employees are not engaged in or about commerce, but exclusively in producing a commodity. And the controversies and evils, which it is the object of the act to regulate and minimize, are local controversies and evils affecting local work undertaken to accomplish that local result. Such effect as they may have upon commerce, however extensive it may be, is secondary and indirect. An increase in the greatness of the effect adds to its importance. It does not alter its character.[33]

In brief, the distinction between direct and indirect effects is not one of degree but one of kind; and its maintenance is essential to the maintenance of the federal system itself.[34]

Thanks to the Great Depression—André Siegfried has recently pronounced it "probably the most important event in the history of the United States since the War of Independence"—this entire system of constitutional interpretation touching the federal relationship is today in ruins. It began to topple in NLRB

31. *Id.* at 275–76.
32. 298 U.S. 238 (1936).
33. *Id.* at 308–9.
34. See Schechter Poultry Corp. v. United States, 295 U.S. 495, 548 (1935). The spokesman for the Court in Schechter was Chief Justice Hughes, as he was two years later in Jones & Laughlin Steel Corp. In Pusey, *Charles Evans Hughes* (1951), the author endeavors to show that his hero's route from the one position to the other proceeded in a perfectly straight line without any backtracking. The demonstration is far from conclusive. See Corwin, book review, 46 *Am. Pol. Sci. Rev.* 1167, 1171–72 (1952).

v. Jones & Laughlin Steel Corp.,[35] in which the Wagner Labor Act was sustained. This was in 1937, while the "Old Court" was still sitting. In 1941, in United States v. Darby,[36] the "New Court" completed the job of demolition. The act of Congress involved was the Fair Labor Standards Act of 1938, which not only bans interstate commerce in goods produced under substandard conditions, but makes their production a penal offense against the United States if they are "intended" for interstate or foreign commerce. Here Chief Justice Stone, speaking for the unanimous Court, goes straight back to Marshall's definition of Congress' power over interstate commerce in Gibbons v. Ogden and to his construction of the "necessary and proper" clause in McCulloch v. Maryland. The former is held to sustain the power exercised in the Fair Labor Standards Act by way of prohibiting commerce; the latter is held to support the prohibition by the act of the manufacture of goods for interstate commerce except in conformity with the standards imposed by the act as to wages and hours. As to the Tenth Amendment, it was dismissed "as a truism that all is retained which has not been surrendered." Its addition to the Constitution altered the latter in nowise.[37]

Summing up the effects of the Darby case, the late Justice Roberts said in his Holmes Lectures for 1951: "Of course, the effect of sustaining the Act was to place the whole matter of wages and hours of persons employed throughout the United States, with slight exceptions, under a single federal regulatory scheme and in this way completely to supersede state exercise of the police power in this field."[38]

All in all, it is not extravagant to say that the Supreme Court has rarely, if ever, rendered a more revolutionary decision, whether it be judged for its advance over contemporary constitutional doctrine, or for its immediate legislative consequences, or for its implications for future national policy. And in the end it is Marshall's two great opinions which supply its underlying ideology. The great chief justice, embodied, or embalmed, in pronouncements still vital, speaks again, becomes once more the Revolutionist. Can it be supposed that if he had been present in person he would have consented willingly to be thus conscripted in the service of the New Deal? Self-exhumation of the illustrious dead is an accepted literary convention, and I claim the right to invoke it on this occasion. If the right be granted, then the answer to the above question must undoubtedly be "No." For supporting testimony I turn once more to Beveridge, for his account of the strenuous and successful fight which Marshall, with the cooperation of his critic Madison, made in the Virginia constitutional convention of 1829 against manhood suffrage and in support of the oligarchic county court system. As Beveridge phrases the matter:

35. 301 U.S. 1 (1937).
36. 312 U.S. 100 (1941).
37. See *id.* at 113–15, 118, 123–24.
38. Roberts, *The Courts and the Constitution* 56 (1951).

On every issue over which the factions of this convention fought, Marshall was reactionary and employed all his skill to defeat, whenever possible, the plans and purposes of the radicals. In pursuing this course he brought to bear the power of his now immense reputation for wisdom and justice. Perhaps no other phase of his life displays more strikingly his intense conservatism.[39]

"The American Nation," Beveridge adds, "was his dream; and to the realization of it he consecrated his life."[40] At no time, on the other hand, did he contemplate the desirability, or even the feasibility, in a free state, of greatly altering by political action the existing relations of the component elements of society. Liberty, the spacious liberty of an expanding nation, not social equality, was the lode-star of his political philosophy.

39. 4 Beveridge, *The Life of John Marshall* at 488.
40. Id. at 472.

Table of Cases

393

Index

Library of Congress Cataloging-in-Publication Data
(Revised for vol. 2)

Corwin, Edward Samuel, 1878–1963.
    Corwin on the Constitution.

    Includes bibliographical references and index.
    Contents: v. 1. The foundations of American
constitutional and political thought, the powers of
Congress, and the President's power of removal—
v. 2. The judiciary.
      1. United States—Constitutional history—Collected
works. 2. United States—Politics and government—
Collected works. I. Loss, Richard. I. Title.
JA38.C67   1981   342.73   80-69823
ISBN 0-8014-1381-8 (v. 1)